HARVARD HISTORICAL STUDIES

Published under the direction
of the Department of History
from the income of the
Henry Warren Torrey Fund

Volume XCIV

Orthodoxy and Nationality

Andreiu Şaguna and the Rumanians of Transylvania, 1846-1873

Keith Hitchins

Harvard University Press
Cambridge, Massachusetts
and London, England
1977

Copyright © 1977 by the President and Fellows of Harvard College
All rights reserved
Printed in the United States of America
Library of Congress Cataloging in Publication Data
Hitchins, Keith, 1931-
    Orthodoxy and nationality.

    (Harvard historical studies; 94)
    Bibliography: p.
    Includes index.
    1. Romanians in Transylvania—History.   2.   Transyl-
vania—History.   3. Sagune, Andreiu, baron de.
4. Orthodox Eastern Church, Romanian—History.
I. Title.   II. Series.
DR279.9.H57   949.8'4   76-47691
ISBN 0-674-64491-3

To the memory of my parents,
Lillian Turrian Hitchins
and
Arnold Hitchins

Acknowledgments

Many persons have aided me in my work, and I am glad of this opportunity to thank them. His Grace Dr. Nicolae Mladin, Metropolitan of the Rumanian Orthodox Church of Transylvania, allowed me to use the rich archives and library of his archdiocese. My debt to him goes even beyond this, for he offered me the pleasure of stimulating conversations about Şaguna and an insight into the ecclesiastical world in which he lived. Professor Robert Lee Wolff of Harvard University first called my attention to the importance of Şaguna and has unfailingly supported my study of his life and works. From Academician Andrei Oţetea, formerly Director of the Institute of History of the Rumanian Academy in Bucharest and my adviser during my first sojourn in Rumania, I have always received generous encouragement. Academician Ştefan Pascu, Rector of the University of Cluj, has on numerous occasions facilitated my access to valuable materials. Dr. Zsolt Trócsányi, section chief at the Hungarian National Archives in Budapest, went out of his way to help me find relevant materials. Reverend Professor Sofron Vlad, formerly Director of the Rumanian Orthodox Theological Institute in Sibiu, gave me his support when it was badly needed. Dr. István Semlyén, Deputy Director of the Library of the Rumanian Academy in Cluj, has assisted my work in a variety of ways for many years. Mr. Anton Nemeth, section chief at the Austrian State Archives in Vienna, brought numerous important documents to my attention. By her careful editing of the manuscript Mrs. Madeleine R. Gleason has contributed greatly to the clarity and concision of the final text. Above all, I owe a special debt to Protopope Ioan N. Beju, Director of the Library of the Rumanian Orthodox Theological Institute in Sibiu, for his never-failing professional and moral support.

I should also like to thank the librarians and archivists of the following institutions for their generous assistance: Widener Library of Harvard University, Haus-, Hof- und Staatsarchiv in Vienna, Biblioteca Academiei Republicii Socialiste România in Bucharest and Cluj, Biblioteca Universităţii Babeş-Bolyai in Cluj, Biblioteca Institutului Teo-

logic Universitar in Sibiu, and Magyar Országos Levéltár and Országos
Széchényi Könyvtár in Budapest.

Several of my articles listed in the Bibliography—all written before
1969—served as preliminary studies. The material and many of the
ideas they contain have been substantially revised in the present work.

Urbana, Illinois   Keith Hitchins

Contents

Introduction

This study describes the political and cultural development of the Rumanians of Transylvania during the two crucial decades that preceded the Austro-Hungarian Compromise of 1867. During this period they came to a full consciousness of their identity, and for a time it seemed that they must at last take their place among the political nations of the Habsburg monarchy.

The Orthodox Church still stood at the center of national life, as it had done for centuries, but now the paramount role of the clergy was effectively challenged by a dynamic class of lay intellectuals who were eager to set their people on a new, essentially secular, course that should bring them abreast of the advanced nations of Europe in the shortest time possible. In Andreiu Şaguna they found their equal in devotion to the national cause. But he stood for a much older tradition than theirs. As bishop, and later metropolitan, of the Rumanian Orthodox Church in Transylvania, he carried forward the venerable practices of ecclesiastical leadership and upheld the primacy of religion in the life of the nation. The tension he and the intellectuals created provided the motive force of Rumanian national development in the middle decades of the nineteenth century.

The experience of the Rumanians also has significance beyond the boundaries of Transylvania. It elucidates the complex process of national development which all the peoples of the Habsburg monarchy were undergoing and it suggests what the nature of contemporary Austrian policy was with respect to national aspirations in general.

The central problem posed here is the role of the higher clergy and the influence of the church generally in Rumanian society in Transylvania in the decades immediately following the revolution of 1848. For nearly a century and a half the two Rumanian churches—the Orthodox and the Uniate (or Greek Catholic)—had dominated the spiritual and cultural development of the Rumanian people, and the two clergies had stood forth as their political representatives before the ruling estates of Transylvania and the court of Vienna.

This ecclesiastical leadership had its roots in the medieval political and social structure of Transylvania, which since the fifteenth and sixteenth centuries had effectively excluded the Rumanians from the diet and the other high councils of state, because of their plebeian condition and their faith. In a social system dominated by the nobility and the upper bourgeoisie and by Roman Catholic and Protestant churches there was no place among the elect for an Orthodox peasantry. In the seventeenth century social and religious discrimination was compounded by national antagonisms, as the privileged Magyar nobility and the German-Saxon middle classes became increasingly aware of the threat posed to their hegemony by the steadily growing Rumanian population. By this time, however, the Orthodox Church alone survived as a peculiarly Rumanian institution and a defender of Rumanian interests.

In the second half of the seventeenth century the Orthodox Church proved incapable of fulfilling its heavy responsibilities to the nation. It lacked the material resources and the political power necessary to carry out a social mission of its own. Its leaders had been subordinated to a Calvinist superintendent, while the majority of its parish clergy, possessing only a rudimentary training, endured a poverty so abject that they were hardly better off than serfs. Both higher and lower clergy felt keenly the humiliation of their status as "tolerated" schismatics whose continued sojourn in the land was subject solely to the discretion of the prince and the estates.

The incorporation of Transylvania into the Habsburg monarchy in the last decade of the seventeenth century led to far-reaching changes in the status of the Rumanian clergy and, no less important, contributed significantly to the awakening of a Rumanian historical consciousness. The court of Vienna, through its Jesuit emissaries, offered the Orthodox hierarchy and parish clergy all the rights and privileges enjoyed by their Roman Catholic counterparts; in other words, it held out the promise of an end to their tolerated status and reception into the estates in return for the acceptance of the Church Union with Rome.

The Union proved to be a crucial turning-point in the development of the Rumanians, not so much in its strictly religious application as in its long-term cultural and political consequences. In the first place, it laid the foundations of the Rumanian political movement in Transylvania. The court, largely because of unyielding opposition from the Transylvanian estates, found itself unable to carry out its promises of equality to the Uniates. They, in turn, organized themselves during the half-century following the Union and drew up a series of petitions and memoranda which formed the substance of a coherent national program that was to achieve its most forceful expression in the famous Supplex Libellus Valachorum, presented to the Transylvanian diet in 1791.

Intimately involved in this political movement was an intellectual elite within the Uniate clergy, which owed its formation largely to the educational benefits made possible by the Union. The court, thwarted by the Transylvanian estates in its efforts to secure social and economic privileges for the Uniate clergy, nevertheless promoted the training of priests by supporting the construction of Uniate educational institutions and by opening the Roman Catholic schools in Transylvania and the University of Vienna to Rumanian candidates for the priesthood. The highly trained group thus formed, consisting of the bishops, the church bureaucracy, the staffs of several secondary schools, and various members of the secular and monastic clergy, became the chief theorists of Rumanian nationality and the leaders of the movement to achieve practical political goals. This elite remained almost entirely ecclesiastical until the first decades of the nineteenth century. The formulation of higher cultural values, the education of the young, and the representation of national political interests before the civil authority in Transylvania and the court of Vienna was effectively in its hands. The bishops—sometimes in concert, sometimes at odds with the other members of the elite—in the absence of any similar lay authority exercised the functions of national leaders.

The Church Union, despite sanguine claims by Austrian authorities and successive Uniate bishops, had remained far from complete. From the very beginning of the Union there had been pockets of Orthodox resistance; even though no formal hierarchy existed, a network of parishes and a rudimentary administration were preserved throughout the principality, and priests continued to be ordained, for the most part in the neighboring Orthodox Rumanian principalities of Moldavia and Wallachia. In particular, religious life in the villages went on much as it had for centuries. As the decades passed, the Orthodox became increasingly militant. Finally, in 1761, in order to combat a major uprising led by the monk Sofronie, Empress Maria Theresa appointed Dionisie Novacovici, the Serbian Orthodox bishop of Buda, as administrator to oversee Orthodox church affairs in Transylvania. He and his successors, like their Uniate counterparts, performed functions of national leadership, but on a more modest scale. The court and the Transylvanian government only grudgingly acknowledged the right of the Orthodox to freedom of worship and employed every means within their power to hinder the administrative development of the church and to limit its social role. The Orthodox were subject to all manner of restrictions, written and unwritten, on their freedom of action and were denied the material support enjoyed by the Uniates. An intellectual class, similar in composition and preoccupations to the Uniate elite, developed slowly, because of the general absence of opportunities for higher education, and did not attain the same degree of preeminence in national life. Not until Andreiu Şaguna's episcopate did the condition of the Orthodox change significantly.

One of the most obvious and far-reaching results of the Church Union was the division of the Rumanians into two confessions. For most of the century and a half between the beginnings of the Union and the revolution of 1848 the relations between Uniates and Orthodox were strained. The causes of antagonism were legion, but at the center of most disputes lay the competition for converts and the claims of the Uniates to supremacy. As late as the eve of the outbreak of revolution in 1848 many Rumanians sadly acknowledged that they formed not a single nation but two.

Such sentiments were excessively gloomy, for by the end of the eighteenth century a new doctrine had already gained wide currency among Uniate and Orthodox intellectuals and had narrowed their confessional differences: the idea of nationality. As early as the episcopate of the Uniate Bishop Ion Inochentie Micu-Clain, which began in 1729, the designation, "Rumanian nation," had acquired a clear-cut ethnic significance alongside the older, aristocratic meaning of *natio,* a concept still very much alive in the legislation of the Transylvanian diet which excluded the mass of the population from membership in the nation. In his numerous representations to the court on behalf of Uniate rights Clain often made no distinction between clergy and laity or *boier* (a landowner or free man with a patent of nobility, who represented the remnant of the medieval Rumanian nobility in Transylvania) and serf, for in his eyes all were members of the same nation, regardless of social or political status. At the same time other members of the Uniate elite were engaged in elaborating a theory of Rumanian nationality, which had as its basis the Roman origins of the Rumanian people and the Latinity of their language — ideas which were to achieve their fullest expression in the works of a remarkable group of historians and philologists, often called the Transylvanian School, who toward the end of the eighteenth and at the beginning of the nineteenth century produced the first modern grammars of the Rumanian language and the first modern histories of the Rumanian people.

The political ramifications of their theories were first realized in a significant way in the Supplex Libellus Valachorum, which set forth well-documented demands for the recognition of the Rumanian nation (again in an ethnic sense) as a full partner of the Magyars and German-Saxons in governing Transylvania. The Supplex Libellus provides indisputable evidence that the idea of nationality had already bridged the confessional gap between Uniates and Orthodox, since it placed national objectives ahead of partisan religious strivings and represented the common aspirations of Uniate and Orthodox intellectuals, who had joined together to draw it up. There were other signs, too, that this national consciousness represented a serious challenge to the primacy of religion among the educated: serious attempts were made at the turn of the century to bring about a reunion of the two churches, and such narrow religious goals as proselytism were roundly condemned. Nevertheless, episcopal leadership and the church dominance of cultural life prevailed until the very eve of the revolution of 1848.

Rumanian intellectual life in Transylvania did not, of course, develop in isolation; to a great extent it was a reflection of broader currents within the Habsburg monarchy as a whole. The Uniate elite received secondary schooling in Roman Catholic gymnasia in Transylvania and pursued more advanced studies at one of the major university centers, while the Orthodox higher clergy, though generally lacking such opportunities, received its training within the monarchy. Both clergies were affected to a greater or lesser degree by the political and social vicissitudes through which the monarchy passed in the eighteenth and the early part of the nineteenth century, experiencing the hardships of wars and economic crises and, occasionally, even enjoying some of the benefits of periods of prosperity.

This is not to say that the Rumanians of Transylvania had no commerce with Moldavia and Wallachia or that their ties with them were insignificant. Quite the contrary. During the eighteenth century their relations were mainly religious. They were characterized by the steady export of church books of all kinds from the two principalities to Transylvania, books, which, though produced on Orthodox presses, were eagerly sought by Uniates as well as Orthodox; by the continual stream of Orthodox priests to Bucharest and other religious centers for ordination; and by regular material aid to the Orthodox from Moldavian and Wallachian princes and churchmen. After 1800 secular contacts increased. They took various forms, but were largely the result of the quickening of intellectual life on both sides of the frontier. Many young Rumanians from Transylvania went to the principalities in search of careers, while others found stimulation for their intellectual endeavors at home in the literary and cultural life of Bucharest. After the turn of the century the circulation of ideas across the frontier became more intense than before and reached a larger segment of the population, because of advances in communication and publishing and, particularly, the establishment of the first Rumanian newspapers. As a result, Rumanians everywhere were brought closer to one another, and a preoccupation with their national destiny increasingly absorbed the energies of intellectuals. Yet, it would be premature to see in all these activities of the *Vormärz* era a manifestation of irredentism. Even during the revolution of 1848 and for decades afterwards the Rumanians of Transylvania sought a solution to their problems within the monarchy rather than in some new political combination beyond it.

The court of Vienna, however, took a different view of the situation. It always held the Rumanians in some degree suspect. From the very beginning of the Church Union the highest officials in the Austrian bureaucracy had doubts about the sincerity of the Uniate commitment to it, and they gave substantial material support to the new church only when it became evident that failure to do so would place the whole policy of Catholicization in Transylvania in jeopardy. The Orthodox were held in even less esteem. For nearly six decades following the Union, the court, officially at least, regarded the Orthodox Church as having ceased to exist, and hence developed no policy toward its numerous faithful other than one of neglect and repression. Even after the appointment of a bishop the court provided the church with little financial or moral support and, instead, placed the severest limitations on its clergy's activities. During Joseph II's reign (1780-1790) the Orthodox experienced a mild renaissance, largely as a result of the proclamation of religious toleration and the state treasury's modest offerings to the Orthodox clergy and its elementary schools. But the court's policy remained substantially what it had always been and would continue to be until 1848: tight control of Orthodox affairs in the interest of the state. Its intentions are best illustrated by the establishment of the hierarchical link between the Transylvanian church and the Serbian Orthodox metropolis of Carlovitz. Joseph II sealed the new relationship by decrees placing the Rumanian Orthodox under the jurisdiction of Carlovitz in order to discourage contacts with the Orthodox Rumanian principalities and to prevent a foreign hierarchy from exercising control over his subjects.

Needless to say, the court showed even less inclination to recognize the existence of a Rumanian political nation. Leopold II (1790-1792), Joseph's successor, allowed the desiderata expressed in the Supplex Libellus Valachorum to go unanswered. During Francis I's long reign (1792-1835) all overt political activity by the Rumanians ceased, while under Ferdinand I (1835-1848) only modest representations by the Uniate and Orthodox bishops were permitted before the Transylvanian diet. In the Vormärz the Rumanians had no political organization and did not participate as a nation in the diet; only the Uniate bishop, because of his status as a landowner, was allowed a seat. Rumanians could express their rising sense of national consciousness only in various forms of church and cultural activities.

The Rumanian national renaissance was far from monolithic. In the Vormärz latent antagonisms had at last come to the surface in bitter disputes over the future development of Rumanian society. On the one side stood the religious establishment, which strove to preserve the primacy of the church in national life. On the other were ranged the majority of the lay intellectuals who had been deeply affected by the secularization of spiritual values and by the economic and political liberalism that had gained wide currency among the educated classes of all the nations of Transylvania. They raised serious questions about the efficacy of the traditional religious and social bases of Rumanian society and cast doubt on the ability of the clergy to lead.

The outbreak of revolution in the spring of 1848 found Rumanian intellectuals and many of the clergy prepared spiritually to participate in what they—like the Slavs of the monarchy, who had experienced a similar national cultural and political renaissance—regarded as a general movement to free all the peoples of Europe from the "tyrannies of the past." Their enthusiasm for change and their confidence in their ability to achieve it were boundless, but the tradition of ecclesiastical leadership and the social forms and spiritual values propagated for centuries by the church proved more durable than the "Springtime of Peoples."

1 / Apprenticeship

There was little in the Şaguna family tradition to suggest that one of its members would some day become the religious and political leader of the Rumanians of Transylvania. In the early part of the eighteenth century the Şagunas were well-established merchants, who operated out of Moscopole, a thriving economic and cultural center in what is now southern Albania. Like so many of their Macedo-Rumanian compatriots, they were middlemen specializing in the prosperous carrying trade between Venice and various ports throughout the Eastern Mediterranean.[1]

In the second half of the eighteenth century the importance of overland commerce in the southern Balkans and, concomitantly, the function of Moscopole as an emporium were seriously undermined by the decline of Venice and particularly by the continued demoralization of the Turkish administrative apparatus, which encouraged robber bands and local pashas to treat international highways as their own. As a consequence, one Macedo-Rumanian merchant after another transferred his business from Moscopole to the safety and order of Austrian and Hungarian cities, where relatives and associates had often already preceded them. Members of the Şaguna family followed this migration and eventually settled in Miskolc, an important commercial center in northeastern Hungary. There the Şagunas acquired a share of the profitable wine trade of the region and soon occupied a place of rank among the leading families of the Macedo-Rumanian community, which could trace its origins back at least to 1606.[2]

At the turn of the century two Şaguna brothers, Naum and Avreta, inherited the family business from their father. Naum Şaguna had the added good fortune to marry Anastasia Mutsu, the daughter of a wealthy Macedo-Rumanian merchant. The couple had three children, Avreta, Catharina, and Anastasiu, the youngest, who was born on January 1, 1809,* and would, upon becoming a monk many years later, take the name Andreiu. This was far from being a happy household.

*Dates in the text will be given according to the Gregorian calendar unless otherwise noted: dates of GTr and FM according to the Julian calendar.

Naum was sensitive and emotional and appears to have had no head for business. He squandered his wife's dowry and his own inheritance on several worthless enterprises and shortly after the birth of his third child went bankrupt, leaving his family destitute. Anastasia Şaguna left her husband and took her children to live in her father's home in Miskolc.

Little is known of Naum Şaguna's subsequent activities until March 1814, when he was converted from Orthodoxy to Roman Catholicism. His motives are unclear. Without means and in ill health—he died the following year—he may have decided that this was the best way to provide for his children's future, since the Catholic Church regarded the children of male converts as its wards and undertook to educate them at its own expense.[3] Civil law sanctioned this practice, and in October 1814 the court instructed Anastasia Şaguna to place her children in the care of the Roman Catholic archdeacon of Miskolc, who would in turn assume responsibility for their moral and spiritual upbringing in their father's new faith. In October 1815, to avoid carrying out the court's decree, she moved with her children to Pest to the home of her uncle, Anastasie Grabovszky, a wealthy merchant and one of the leaders of the large, socially-conscious Macedo-Rumanian community. There the children attended the Greek school and the Greek-Wallachian church and continued to receive instruction in the Orthodox religion for almost a year.[4]

In the meantime, prolonged legal maneuvers by Anastasia and her father to have the court order rescinded, which led eventually to their petitioning the Royal Lieutenancy of Hungary, were to no avail. The original court decision was upheld, and Anastasia Şaguna had no choice but to return to Miskolc.[5] Her two older children were enrolled in Catholic schools, but little Anastasiu, because of his age, was allowed to attend an Orthodox grammar school until he was old enough to enter the Catholic gymnasium. In 1823, when he was fourteen, he left Miskolc for good and moved to Pest to live with the Grabovszky family. He attended the Catholic gymnasium, from which he graduated in 1826, ranking seventeenth in a class of 103 and winning special commendations for his work in theology and in the Hungarian language. His diploma described him as Hungarian by nationality and Roman Catholic by religion.[6] In reality his devotion to both Orthodoxy and his family's national traditions had remained firm, in spite of his intensive training in Roman Catholic theology and his constant use

of Hungarian. At home, his mother took charge of his religious training and, counteracting the effects of formal instruction in Catholicism,
taught him to revere the moral teachings of Orthodoxy and deepened
his appreciation of its liturgical beauty.

Anastasia Şaguna's concern for religious education was shared by
most Macedo-Rumanians, in whose minds Orthodoxy and nationality
were inextricably linked. The church was not only the center of their
social and cultural life, but,' subject as they were to the pressures of
assimilation by their more numerous neighbors of other faiths and nationalities, it was also a shield behind which they could preserve their
ancient traditions and language. They were convinced that the abandonment of Orthodoxy was merely the first step in the process of denationalization. Such feelings must have impelled Anastasiu Şaguna only
nine days after his eighteenth birthday, when he came of legal age, to
petition the Royal Lieutenancy of Hungary for permission to return to
the Orthodox Church. In a personal appearance before a commission
established to hear his case he declared simply that he wished to live
and die in the faith in which he had been baptized, and insisted that
his own inner convictions rather than the urgings of others had led him
to make this decision. The commission accepted Şaguna's statement,
but required him to take the six-week course in Roman Catholic theology and church history prescribed for all converts from Roman Catholicism to another faith, in spite of the evidence presented that he had
excelled in these subjects at the gymnasium. This mandate failed to
shake his resolve, and after considerable delay the government granted
his petition on September 2, 1828.[7]

The following year he completed his three-year course in philosophy
and law at the University of Pest and had now to decide upon a career.
His intelligence and sophistication, combined with the financial backing of his mother's uncle, opened up to him innumerable possibilities;
a merchant's life was the obvious choice. To the surprise of many
friends he decided to become a priest. In later years, when asked about
his resolution, Şaguna would invariably reply that if he had been born
a hundred times, a hundred times he would have become a priest.[8] A
respect for Orthodoxy and a strong belief in the spiritual mission of the
clergy evidently outweighed the material rewards offered by a successful career in business.

Şaguna's sense of social mission was also highly developed. During
his six years in the Grabovszky home in Pest (1823 to 1829), where he

had eagerly joined the cosmopolitan society, he came into contact with vigorous new social and cultural currents. Of first importance were those ideas that had stirred the national consciousness of Macedo-Rumanian intellectuals and had impelled them to investigate their historical and linguistic heritage.[9] They owed much of their inspiration to the writings of Rumanian historians and philologists from Transylvania, notably Samuil Micu-Clain, Gheorghe Şincai, and Petru Maior, who in the latter part of the eighteenth century and the first two decades of the nineteenth produced the first modern histories of the Rumanians and the first scholarly grammars of their language. These works were especially significant because they made no distinction between the Macedo-Rumanians and their Daco-Rumanian cousins north of the Danube and described them all as the direct descendants of the Roman colonists of the Balkans who had managed to survive the Slavic invasions of the sixth and seventh centuries.[10] All three Transylvanian scholars lived in Buda-Pest at the turn of the century as editors of Rumanian books published by the University of Buda Press. Petru Maior seems to have been the most strongly influenced by contacts with Macedo-Rumanian intellectuals. In his philological writings he drew heavily upon their language for examples of "pure" Rumanian-Latin usage.[11]

Since the closing decade of the eighteenth century the Macedo-Rumanians of the Habsburg monarchy had manifested their growing national self-consciousness particularly in efforts to establish their own identity in the churches and schools they shared with the Greeks. The long, harmonious relationship between the two communities in Buda-Pest was finally disrupted at the turn of the century, when the Macedo-Rumanians (or "Wallachians," as they described themselves in official documents) insisted upon the use of their language in the church services and the common school. They contemplated building a church of their own, after the Greeks refused their demands, and in 1807 petitioned the Serbian metropolitan of Carlovitz, the head of the Orthodox Church in the monarchy and under whose jurisdiction the diocese of Buda lay, to send them a priest who could hold services in their language rather than Greek.[12] In 1811 they decided to build their own school and hire a "Wallachian" teacher.

The scope and maturity of their awakened national consciousness is evident in the historical and philological works of Macedo-Rumanian scholars. Without exception they emphasized the glorious Roman origins of their people and the beauty and distinctiveness of their language. Coupled with this pride was alarm at the general neglect of their historical and linguistic "treasures." Constantine Ucuta, a native of Moscopole and an Orthodox protopope in Posen, then part of Prussia, was deeply distressed by the failure of his countrymen to cultivate their language and make it an instrument of "modern enlightenment." Instead, he complained, they had relegated it to the family circle and in society they preferred to speak Greek or some other language. In *Noua Pedagogie,* a small book of texts in Macedo-Rumanian published in Vienna in 1797, he implored his readers to teach their children to honor their mother tongue and warned that negligence would result in the decay of their national life and eventual assimilation by the overwhelming foreign populations amongst whom they lived.[13]

The same sentiments were expressed in a short treatise dealing with the similarity of the Macedo-Rumanian and Daco-Rumanian languages, entitled *Maestria ghiovăsirii românești cu litere latinești care sînt literele Românilor ceale vechi* ("The Art of Reading Rumanian with Latin Letters, which are the Old Letters of the Rumanians"). It was published in Buda in 1809 by Gheorghe Constantine Roja, a physician at the university hospital.[14] He was not satisfied merely to record proofs of his thesis, but proposed a formula by which a single, "pure" (that is, Latinized) Rumanian language could be created within a short time: words of Latin origin, "gathered" from all the Rumanian dialects, particularly Daco-Rumanian spoken in Transylvania and the principalities of Moldavia and Wallachia, would be used to replace Greek, Slavic, and other "foreign" words; once this process had been completed, the Cyrillic alphabet, in which Daco-Rumanian was written, and the Greek, which the Macedo-Rumanians used, would gradually be replaced by Latin letters. Roja's account of the origins of the Macedo-Rumanians, entitled *Untersuchungen über die Romanen oder sogenannten Wlachen, welche jenseits der Donau wohnen,* published in Pest in 1808, provided the necessary historical basis for the amalgamation of the dialects by showing that the Rumanians both north and south of the Danube were the direct descendants of the Romans and were, therefore, essentially one people.

Perhaps the crowning achievement of these Macedo-Rumanian historian-philologists was the publication in Vienna in 1813 of the first grammar of their language, Mihail G. Boiagi's *Romanische oder Macedonowlachische Sprachlehre.*[15] The author's family also came from Moscopole, and he himself was a teacher of modern Greek at the Greek school in Vienna. He was inspired to compose his grammar, he wrote in the preface, by the hope of raising Macedo-Rumanian from its "existing low state" to a cultural and scholarly level comparable to that of its sister languages, Italian, French, and Spanish, and by the need he felt to instill in his fellow countrymen pride in speaking "[one of] the most harmonious of all the modern languages."

The Macedo-Rumanian merchants of Buda-Pest gave their whole-hearted moral and financial support to this cultural renaissance. None was more generous than Anastasie Grabovszky. He subscribed to all new publications on Rumanian as well as Macedo-Rumanian history and language, notably *Gramatica Daco-Romana sive Valachica* (Buda, 1826) by Ioan Alexi, later Uniate bishop of Gherla in Transylvania, and *Scurtă apendice la Istoria lui Petru Maior* (Buda, 1828) by Teodor Aron. Both Grabovszky and his wife were active in the social life of their community: he as a leader of various endeavors to obtain equality for the Macedo-Rumanians in the management of the joint "Greek-Wallachian" Orthodox Church in Pest; and his wife as president of the Society of Macedo-Rumanian Women of Buda-Pest, which was organized in 1815 primarily to promote education in the native language. Moreover, their own home became a favorite meeting-place for Rumanians from every part of the Habsburg monarchy and from the principalities of Moldavia and Wallachia as well. Among their guests were Petru Maior, Damaschin Bojânca, a historian from the Banat, and members of the Golescu family, who were to have prominent roles in the revolution of 1848 in Wallachia. They made no distinction between Macedo-Rumanians and other Rumanians, but treated all as members of the same nation regardless of political boundaries. For example, Grabovszky gave generously to the Orthodox Church in Transylvania. In 1813 he contributed 100 gulden to the fund for the construction of a bishop's residence in Sibiu, which his own great-nephew, then five years old, would one day occupy.[16]

For nearly a quarter of a century Grabovszky was deeply involved in the controversy between the Greeks and Macedo-Rumanians of Pest over which of them should lead their joint Greek-Wallachian community. For most of the eighteenth century the Greeks had been dominant, but by 1800 the Macedo-Rumanians outnumbered them and had become the more dynamic force in the cultural and business life of the community. Both were reaping the full consequences of a growing national self-consciousness, and, as a result, their disputes were unusually bitter and uncompromising. In 1808 Grabovszky had represented the Macedo-Rumanians in their attempt to have church services performed in their language as well as in Greek. In 1820, as the financial director of the Wallachian school, founded nine years earlier, he again represented his nation in a major dispute with the Greeks, this time over the disposition of the common school. He and his colleagues objected strenuously to the continued pretensions of the Greeks to dominate their joint affairs and pointed out that the Wallachian nation possessed eminent qualities of its own which deserved to be expressed and developed. In 1835 Grabovszky was among those Macedo-Rumanians who attended a joint meeting with the Greeks called by the bishop of Buda, Stefan Stanković, to try to restore peace to the Orthodox community.[17] The effort failed, and the separation became all but complete.

The only precise information about the effect of the Macedo-Rumanian renaissance on Anastasiu Şaguna comes from Nicolae Popea, who relates that Şaguna undertook the systematic study of Daco-Rumanian with his uncle's encouragement.[18] Nonetheless, it is reasonable to assume that a young man of Şaguna's intellectual gifts and religious inclinations could not have ignored a current of ideas that so deeply involved his family and so vitally affected the future of the Orthodox community. If the social consciousness implicit in the new nationalism affected him at all, then his choice of the priesthood as a career was a natural one. The church, it must be remembered, was the only institution which provided the scattered Macedo-Rumanian communities with a semblance of unity and a means by which they could maintain a sense of national identity and, on occasion, even indulge in modest political activity. As a priest, then, Anastasiu Şaguna could satisfy his own strong religious feelings and at the same time meet the urgent responsibilities of public service, a task undoubtedly inspired by Grabovszky's example.

At the urging of Maxim Manuilović, bishop of Vršac and a distant relative of the Grabovszky family, Şaguna began his studies for the priesthood at the theological institute in Vršac in the fall of 1829.[19] A special Rumanian section had been established there in 1822 to train priests for the numerous Rumanian parishes in the Banat and even for the diocese of Transylvania, which lacked adequate facilities of its own. The school's official name was "Serbian-Wallachian Clerical

Institute," and in the first class of 115 students the great majority (84) were Rumanian. It placed great emphasis upon pedagogical training, for among the chief responsibilities of the priest was teaching and the management of the parish school.[20]

Although the three-year course of study lacked sophistication and must have presented few serious challenges to a university graduate, Şaguna was nonetheless initiated into the systematic study of Orthodox theology and the Church Slavonic language. His progress was rapid, and Bishop Manuilović hastened to bring his achievements to the attention of the metropolitan of Carlovitz, Stefan Stratimirović (1790-1836). These were difficult times for the Orthodox of the monarchy, and capable Rumanian priests were too few in number to fulfil the church's myriad responsibilities to its faithful. Stratimirović prevailed upon the young seminarist to take holy orders, an act that would open to him the highest offices in the church. Heeding this advice, in spite of the fact that he found the contemplative life and routine of the cloister a melancholy experience, Şaguna spent nearly a year in the monastery of Hopovo, near Carlovitz, and on October 24, 1833, he was received into the Order of Saint Basil. He chose Andreiu as his monastic name after the Apostle, who, according to tradition, had been the first to preach the gospel in the Rumanian lands.[21]

Stratimirović became his patron, appointing him almost at once as professor of theology at the seminary in Carlovitz and then, in 1835, as his secretary for Rumanian church affairs. During the next decade Şaguna's zeal and efficiency won him the esteem of Stratimirović's two successors as well—Stefan Stanković (1837-1842) and Joseph Rajačić (1842-1861)—who promoted him rapidly, often ahead of men many years his senior.[22] By May 1845, when he was appointed archimandrite of the monastery of Kovil, one of the richest in the archdiocese, he had held every office below that rank in the church hierarchy: deacon (February 2, 1834), protodeacon (Easter, 1835), archdeacon (December 25, 1835), singhel (June 29, 1837), protosinghel (March 25, 1838), superintendent of the monastery of Jazak (October 24, 1839), egumen of the monastery of Bešenova (January 13, 1841), and titular archimandrite of the monastery of Hopovo (October 26, 1842).

During this decade Şaguna gained valuable administrative experience as a member of the archdiocesan consistory in Carlovitz for five years and of the diocesan consistory in Vršac for nearly three years. From his vantage point at the center of a vast religious and national-political organization like that of the metropolis of Carlovitz his appreciation of the church's preeminent role in contemporary society deepened. Under the Carlovitz jurisdiction came not only the traditional Serbian lands of the Habsburg monarchy—the Voivodina—but also the Rumanian parishes of the Banat and the dioceses of Buda, Bukovina, and Dalmatia. By virtue of privileges granted the Serbs (or Illyrian Nation, as they were usually designated) in 1690, the metropolitans of Carlovitz served as both the political and spiritual leaders of their people, and the National Church Congress became the supreme Serbian deliberative and legislative assembly. Politics, constitutional rights, and culture could be said to exist mainly within this ecclesiastical framework. The majority of Serbs accepted it as natural, since the church was the chief repository of their national traditions and culture as well as the propagator of moral and spiritual truths. Consequently the metropolitan, particularly one of the caliber of Stratimirović, enjoyed immense prestige and could on occasion even treat with the ministries in Vienna with almost sovereign authority. This striking example of the church's preponderant role in the temporal affairs of its faithful must have made a strong impression upon Şaguna and undoubtedly served him as a model when he undertook the reorganization of the Orthodox Church in Transylvania.

Şaguna's service in the metropolis of Carlovitz coincided with a period of intense Serbian cultural revival. Stratimirović and his successors launched a major campaign to improve the intellectual and spiritual level of both the secular and the monastic clergy.[23] They established a number of new theological-pedagogical institutes with improved and expanded curricula, and they tried to extend the network of primary schools to every parish in the archdiocese in the hope of making the faithful more receptive to the church's teachings and of providing better qualified candidates for the theological schools. Even more pressing was the need to reform monastic life. Discipline had broken down, funds intended for pious and educational purposes were being put to other uses, and many monks had come to regard their vocation as offering an opportunity for leisure or personal gain.[24] The most effective remedy proved to be the replacement of easy-going or incompetent abbots with vigorous young administrators.

With drastic reform in mind, Metropolitan Stanković appointed Şaguna egumen of the monastery of Bešenova early in 1841 with specific instructions to restore discipline and bring order to its financial affairs. Because of his predecessor's long illness, the monks had become exceedingly lax; they attended church and observed the holy days only occasionally when they felt like it, and they had allowed the monastery buildings to fall into a dangerous state of disrepair.[25] Şaguna had successfully handled a similar situation at the monastery of Jazak the previous year and set to work with characteristic energy to instill in his new charges a deeper awareness of their calling. He used a heavy hand in imposing his will, and within a few months of his arrival the monks were complaining bitterly to the metropolitan about "unjust" punishments and the transformation of their vegetable patch into an "English garden." Şaguna admitted that he had been strict in enforcing the monastic rule, but he denied that he had been unfair; as for the monks' vegetable garden, he had merely removed weeds and accumulated trash from in front of the monastery and had planted shrubs and flowers. He insisted that the monastic clergy be guided by the highest standards of conduct because, in his view, they could accomplish their sacred mission only if they inspired respect and confidence in those they were ordained to serve. A commission appointed to investigate the matter absolved Şaguna of any abuse of his authority, but it recognized the validity of the monks' claim to elect their own abbot, a right which Metropolitan Stanković had ignored. Since Şaguna had been appointed by the metropolitan and since the monks would undoubtedly reject his candidacy, the commission recommended that he be transferred to Hopovo as titular archimandrite, a post that would relieve him of day-to-day administrative chores and allow him to devote full time to his new duties as professor of theology at the seminary in nearby Vršac.[26]

In Vršac Şaguna had an opportunity to observe at first hand the power of national feeling and the variety of its expression, for he found himself in the middle of a serious quarrel between Serbs and Rumanians over their respective rights in the diocese they shared. Both were experiencing a national awakening which was exhilarating but which at the same time exacerbated their legal and economic differences. The situation was the same in the neighboring diocese of Arad, where the Rumanian movement had gained a wide following among both the lay intellectuals and the clergy. The Rumanians claimed that the Serbs monopolized the highest church offices and the headships of monasteries, even in places with overwhelming Rumanian majorities, such as the diocese of Timişoara. The Serbian metropolitans acknowledged the fact, but argued that the reason was not deliberate exclusion but rather the lack of qualified Rumanian personnel.[27] The Rumanians also charged that the Serbian bishops and metropolitans used a disproportionate share of church revenues for specifically Serbian projects, and they demanded greater financial support for Rumanian schools and the establishment of Rumanian gymnasia, theological institutes, and monasteries, where Rumanian priests could be trained for high church office.[28] Language was also an issue. In the 1820s and 1830s the Rumanians had begun to demand that theirs be used in the church service and administration in proportion to their numbers at both the parish and diocesan level. In Arad they demonstrated their opposition to the use of Serbian and emphasized the distinctiveness of their own language (and, by extension, nationality) by using Latin letters in place of Cyrillic in various publications and by introducing the study of Rumanian written in the Latin alphabet in a number of primary schools.[29] The most far-reaching accomplishment of Rumanian nationalists was the election in 1828 of the first Rumanian bishop of Arad in the person of Nestor Ioanovici, after nearly two decades of bitter struggle.[30] It proved to be the first major step toward the separation of the Rumanian hierarchy from the Serbian, a process completed by Şaguna four decades later.

The Serbian hierarchy viewed the mounting national antagonism with genuine alarm as a threat to the very existence of the Orthodox Church in the Habsburg monarchy. In the 1820s and 1830s the Uniate movement, led by Samuil Vulcan, the ardent nationalist bishop of Oradea (1806-1839), won many converts in the Orthodox dioceses of Arad and Timişoara among those Rumanians who preferred a national church to one dominated by foreigners. In Transylvania, during the same period, Uniate Bishop Ioan Bob was conducting an equally successful proselytizing campaign. Stratimirović, using all his influence at court, stoutly defended Orthodoxy.[31] There he had some success, but he made little headway in dealing with his own Rumanian faithful, since many looked upon him as a zealous Serbian nationalist and were, consequently, suspicious of any action he took to heal the breach. His successors, Stanković and Rajačić, recognized better than he the urgent need for concessions to the Rumanians, if the administrative unity of the church was to be saved. To reassure Rumanian leaders of its concern for the progress of their nation, the hierarchy expanded the facilities of the Rumanian section of the Clerical Institute

in Vršac, initiated the practice of conducting the ordination of Rumanian priests at Carlovitz in Rumanian, reserved Rumanian parishes for
Rumanian priests, and observed the principle that bishops in dioceses
with a Rumanian majority should either be Rumanian or should be
able to speak the language fluently. In order to strengthen their ties
with Rumanian communities, both metropolitans appointed Rumanians in increasing numbers to important administrative positions.

Şaguna owed his rapid rise at least in part to the changing nationality emphasis of the Serbian hierarchy. His superiors undoubtedly
counted upon him to play an important role in bringing about a rapprochement between the hierarchy and the Rumanians. He did not
disappoint them. In the early 1840s, using his position as a professor at
the Clerical Institute and as a member of the diocesan consistory in
Vršac, he furthered Rajačić's policy of reconciliation by encouraging
the increased use of Rumanian in the local churches and by improving
the quality of instruction given Rumanian candidates for the priesthood. During this time he composed a grammar of Rumanian, *Gramatica valachica,* which he intended as a means of systematizing his own
knowledge of the language and as a manual for his students.[32]

Şaguna remained barely two years at his teaching post in Vršac, for
Rajačić was grooming him for greater responsibilities. On October 17,
1845, Bishop Vasile Moga, head of the Rumanian Orthodox Church
in Transylvania since 1810, died following a long illness, and Rajačić
enthusiastically recommended the appointment of Şaguna as temporary administrator or general vicar of the diocese until a permanent
successor to Moga could be agreed upon. In a lengthy memorandum
to the Transylvanian Chancellery in Vienna, which had been charged
with finding suitable candidates to propose to the Emperor Ferdinand,
Rajačić, who was well acquainted with conditions in the Transylvanian diocese, complained bitterly about the disorder, simony, and
ignorance which Moga had tolerated in the last years of his episcopate.
There was, he lamented, no one among the Transylvanian clergy
capable of restoring order to the diocese's affairs, and he pleaded that
the duties of vicar be entrusted to one of his own clergy, Andreiu
Şaguna, whose administrative abilities and intellectual attainments he
extolled at great length. He concluded that only Şaguna, who had displayed "exemplary personal conduct and [was] free from any form of
fanaticism," possessed the moral fiber and the drive to further the
spiritual development of the Transylvanian Rumanians and maintain

harmony with the other confessions—objectives which would, he was certain, benefit both the state and the church.[33]

Order and tranquillity—these were the arguments most likely to appeal to the court of Vienna, beset as it was by mounting social and national tensions like those which prevailed in Transylvania in the 1840s. Its uncommon haste to find a suitable successor to Moga, especially in view of the fact that it had required fourteen years (1796-1810) to discover Moga himself, suggests the urgency of the matter. None of the three candidates proposed by the Orthodox consistory in Sibiu was satisfactory: Ioan Popasu, protopope of Braşov, was judged to be too young and inexperienced; Ioan Moga and Moise Fulea, protopopes of Sibiu and nephews of the late bishop, were rejected on the grounds that they were too closely associated with the old regime to be effective reformers. Consequently, and largely on the basis of Rajačić's information, the Transylvanian Chancellery recommended Şaguna's appointment as vicar. In its letter to the emperor it went so far as to express the hope that he would quickly win the loyalty and esteem of his clergy and thereby ensure his election as bishop.[34] Ferdinand responded by sanctioning the recommendation on June 27, 1846.

Şaguna arrived in Sibiu, the center of the Transylvanian Orthodox diocese, on September 2. Those who saw him were struck by his imposing appearance: "He is a handsome man, tall and strong, with a white and handsome face; his forehead is broad and smooth, and he wears a large black beard; he gives the appearance of piety and also of seriousness and authority."[35] Şaguna's own first impressions of his new post were, however, less favorable. He was shocked by the scenes of physical deterioration which confronted him at the bishop's residence. The house, which served as the administrative headquarters of a diocese of some 700,000 faithful, was ramshackle and practically devoid of furniture and in no way distinguishable from the other buildings on the street. At his first meeting with the consistory, the full extent of the church's disorganization revealed itself. The consistory, the highest executive organ of the diocese, had no prescribed agenda, kept haphazard minutes of its meetings, and allowed such vital matters as finance and education to drift from year to year. Moga had not taken the trouble to engage a regular secretary and legal adviser, but rather had developed the habit of entrusting problems as they arose to this or that councillor, as seemed best at the time. As a result, continuity of administration became all but impossible. Especially tangled were diocesan finances, which Moga himself had managed. He had loaned considerable sums to private individuals, most of them Hungarian aristocrats, apparently in the hope of using their influence to obtain modest concessions for his church.[36] Little care had been taken of the diocesan archives and library, and, for the time being, Şaguna could do little more than retrieve books written in Slavonic which had been discarded as "useless."

On September 4, Şaguna left for Cluj to present his credentials to the governor of Transylvania, Joseph Teleki. This trip gave him his first opportunity to observe the widespread material and cultural impoverishment of his parish clergy. This experience, and the knowledge gained during the first few months of his vicarship, convinced him that the very existence of the Orthodox Church was at stake. He concluded that drastic changes in its relationship to both the state and the other churches of Transylvania, and a thorough reform of its own government, would be necessary to save it. The condition of the clergy distressed him particularly, for the well-being of the church and the effectiveness of its mission among the people would, in his view, depend upon their zeal and initiative. He found the average village priest ill equipped intellectually and sometimes morally to meet his responsibilities: he had only the most elementary training, usually from an incumbent priest—often his own father—whom, in accordance with local tradition, he was expected to succeed. A few priests had attended the six-month course at the theological school in Sibiu, which Vasile Moga had established in 1811, but, as Şaguna quickly discovered, farmers, sheepherders, and village notaries, all lacking proper qualifications, were frequently admitted and ordained after the six months had elapsed, upon payment of a fee. He also found that the course of study, which had not been changed in over thirty years, largely duplicated what was taught in the elementary schools and, except for dogmatic and moral theology, provided little specific training for the priesthood.[37] Priests, even on Sundays, sometimes neglected to wear their vestments and frequented taverns and, to use Şaguna's words, were guilty of other acts unbecoming their station. Şaguna had no patience for such slovenliness, and woe to the priest in dirty clothes or an unkempt beard who happened to meet his vicar on the streets of Sibiu or a nearby village.

The physical aspect of the diocese left as much to be desired as its human condition. The church buildings, most of which had been constructed of wood in the seventeenth and eighteenth centuries, were in varying states of disrepair. As a measure of the discrimination which the Orthodox had had to bear for centuries, they were, with but few exceptions, located outside the city and, in some places, outside the village limits. Even in Sibiu there was only a single Orthodox church, a small chapel built by Greek merchants who had obtained a special dispensation from the Sibiu municipality.

The schools operated by the church, all at the elementary level, were also in wretched condition, except for those in the more affluent Rumanian communities of Şchei-Braşov, Răşinari, Săcele, Sălişte, and Năsăud. Only here and in a few other places had teachers received serious pedagogical training; elsewhere, priests acted as the village schoolmasters. The paucity of lay teachers is not hard to explain. The teaching profession offered few inducements to ambitious young men; regular salaries were almost unheard of, and it was up to the teacher himself to try to collect a fee from the parents of each pupil. Instruction was based on church books—a *psaltire* (psalter) and a catechism, or a simple *bucoavna* (ABC reader)—and generally it did not go beyond simple reading and arithmetic, reciting the catechism, and church singing. Parents who wanted to give their sons and, occasionally, daughters more education had to send them to Protestant and Roman Catholic schools. Only a small percentage of the children of school age attended classes; parents were often to blame, because they preferred that their children work in the fields to help the family make ends meet rather than spend time in pursuits which seemed to offer them no future.[38]

Şaguna dealt severely with any deliberate breach of clerical discipline, but he recognized the fact that the individual priest was not alone responsible for his unhappy condition. Poverty as a way of life, for generations unchallenged by a church that was impotent and a state that was indifferent, had consumed his energies and destroyed his self-confidence. The church itself was too poor to provide him with a salary or, as it was called, a canonical portion, usually a small plot of land which offered him life's necessities. The state refused to subsidize his parish because the constitution of the land did not recognize the Orthodox Church as one of the "received" or accredited religions. The parish faithful were generally too poor to support their priest properly. Mostly farmers who lived in poverty or near it, they had little in money or kind to contribute to the church and the school. Many were in fact, if not in law, serfs or were living in some other degree of economic bondage to their landlords. Consequently, the priest had to depend for a living either upon the modest fees he collected for baptisms, weddings, and funerals and the occasional freewill offerings of his flock or upon his own manual labor in fields rented from a landlord or as a simple hired hand. As a result, there was little in his habits of life or appearance to distinguish him from his peasant neighbors, a fact which goes far toward explaining the extraordinary influence the priest exercised over his village.

It was precisely because of this influence and its immense potential for good that Şaguna made the parish clergy the central object of his ambitious program of church reform. He was certain that only with enlightened priests in the villages could he hope to bring his people spiritually and materially into the modern world. But, as he surveyed the meager resources at his disposal, he knew that he must secure the active support of the state.

The main obstacle confronting him was the sometimes hostile and sometimes indifferent attitude of the court of Vienna and the Transylvanian government toward his church. Its origins in Transylvania may be traced back to the fifteenth century, when the Rumanians were excluded from the political union of the three privileged nations (the Magyar nobility, the Saxon patriciate, and the Szekler upper classes).* The Rumanian aristocracy was gradually assimilated by the Magyar nation, a process which left their Orthodox church without political protection. The consequences were evident in the religious settlement between the Roman Catholic and the new Protestant churches in the middle of the sixteenth century; they were "received" into the constitution as the beneficiaries of political and economic privileges, but the Orthodox were barely tolerated by the Transylvanian estates and thereafter became objects of proselytism on the part of zealous Calvinists.[39]

The Habsburgs began to interest themselves in the Rumanians at the end of the seventeenth century, when their armies expelled the Turks from Transylvania and they were faced with the problem of

---

*The Saxons were descendants of German colonists from the Rhine Valley and other parts of Germany who first settled in Transylvania in the twelfth century. The Szeklers were a people closely related to the Magyars who probably settled in Transylvania in the eleventh century. In the eighteenth and nineteenth centuries they differed little from the Magyars in language or political outlook. The term nation is used here in the medieval sense of *natio,* a relatively small group set apart from the mass of men by legally sanctioned privileges.

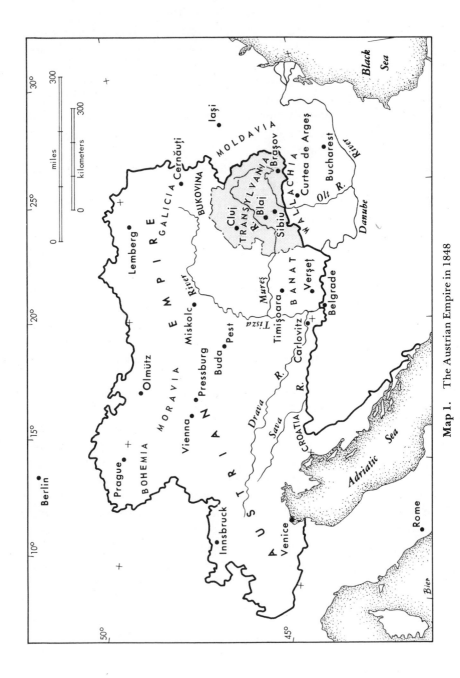

Map 1.   The Austrian Empire in 1848

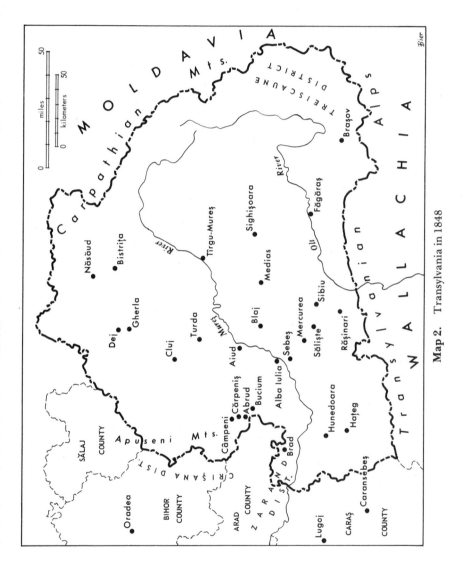

Map 2. Transylvania in 1848

integrating their new possession into the general fabric of their heredi-
tary lands. Their most difficult task was to reduce to obedience the
independent-minded Calvinist Magyars, who had dominated the political life of Transylvania for most of the century. Cut off from Hungary
as a result of the Ottoman conquest following the Battle of Mohács in
1526, the principality, nominally a Turkish vassal state, had in the
course of a century and a half developed institutions and an outlook
that were distinctly its own.[40] Although Emperor Leopold I solemnly
recognized the laws and institutions of the land and confirmed the
privileges of the three nations and their churches in 1691, he was determined to undermine the power of the local estates. One of his instruments was the Roman Catholic Church, and together they saw in the
oppressed and discontented Rumanian Orthodox clergy an extraordinary opportunity to achieve both temporal and religious goals. Its
conversion was entrusted to the Catholic hierarchy of Hungary.

Negotiations with the Orthodox ended in the acceptance, in 1698
and again in 1700, by Metropolitan Atanasie and a number of his
protopopes and parish priests of the so-called Four Points of Union:
recognition of the Pope of Rome as the visible head of the Christian
Church, the use of unleavened bread in the Eucharist, belief in purgatory and in the emanation of the Holy Ghost from the Father and the
Son. In return, Leopold issued two diplomas, one in 1699, the other in
1701, in which he promised all Orthodox priests who would "unite"
the same constitutional status as the Catholic and Protestant clergies.[41]
As time passed, the Hungarian primate-archbishop of Esztergom
assumed a dominant role in the affairs of the new Uniate diocese. The
court confidently assumed that the Orthodox Church had ceased to
exist and that the Uniate clergy would quickly take its assigned place
beside the Catholic estates in their struggles against the Calvinists.

Events proved otherwise. The Uniate clergy was disappointed in its
expectations of equality and, as a result, under the dynamic leadership
of Bishop Ion Inochentie Micu-Clain (1729-1751) it became the chief
representative of Rumanian national interests. Clain and his successors
transformed their see, Blaj, into the most important Rumanian cultural center in Transylvania in the eighteenth and first half of the
nineteenth century.

The Orthodox also showed considerable signs of life. Opposition to
the church union was widespread, and many priests and their faithful
were even unaware that it had in fact taken place. In time, Orthodox

resistance became such a threat to the social and political stability of the principality that in 1761, as we have seen, Empress Maria Theresa reluctantly appointed a "temporary" bishop in the person of Dionisie Novacovici, Serbian bishop of Buda. In 1767 he was succeeded briefly by another Serb and then by vicar-administrators from among the local clergy. The Orthodox obtained their first regular bishop in 1783, when Joseph II appointed Ghedeon Nichitici to the post. At the same time, he subordinated the Transylvanian diocese to the Serbian metropolis of Carlovitz, thereby creating a relationship that was to last until 1864. Joseph had been persuaded to endow the Rumanians with a formal church organization as a means of mobilizing their support for his planned economic and political reforms in Transylvania. His choice of Serbian bishops to head the new diocese, however, betrayed his lack of confidence in the ability of the Rumanians to manage their own affairs and his anxiety to shut out influences from the neighboring Orthodox principalities of Moldavia and Wallachia. Upon Nichitici's death in 1790, Gherasim Adamovici, like him, a Serb, succeeded him almost immediately, but when he died in 1796, the court allowed the see to remain vacant for fourteen years. Finally, in 1810, Emperor Francis II appointed Vasile Moga, the protopope of Sebeş, near Sibiu, as bishop. There was great rejoicing among the Orthodox clergy and lay intellectuals because Moga was the first Rumanian to head the church since Atanasie's conversion to the Union. Even some Uniates, like Petru Maior, saw Moga's appointment as the beginning of a bright new era in the history of the Rumanian nation.

These expectations proved to be largely illusory. The attitude of the court and the Transylvanian government toward the Orthodox Church remained little changed in the course of the century. They continued to treat it as a barely tolerated institution. The clearest expression of their feelings was the so-called Nineteen Points, a humiliating set of conditions which they obliged Moga to accept before his elevation to bishop and which made him little more than a state functionary. They were intended to ensure his obedience to the civil authorities and to discourage any thoughts he may have had about proselytizing among his Uniate compatriots. He was to regard his appointment as bishop as an act of imperial grace, not as a right enjoyed by the Orthodox Church, and he was to keep in mind at all times that his church was merely tolerated; he was not to interfere with the progress of the church union among his own faithful or to allow his clergy to

seek converts among the Uniates; he was to reduce the number of his
own priests and send home any who came to Transylvania from
Moldavia or Wallachia; he was not to communicate with his archbishop, the metropolitan of Carlovitz, on any matter except with the
permission of the Transylvanian government; he was encouraged to
improve the level of training given his priests, but at the same time he
was denied control of modest church endowments which would have
made this possible.[42]

The intolerance perpetuated by the Nineteen Points still weighed
heavily upon the Orthodox Church when Şaguna assumed his duties as
vicar. He was convinced that the attitude of the court and the Transylvanian government was conditioned at least in part by their image of
the Orthodox as passive and easily manipulated, a liability rather than
an asset to the monarchy. He was determined to change their minds,
but the comprehensive reforms he planned found little favor with
either the court or the provincial bureaucracy. His appeals to abstract
principles of national equality and the rights of man, which were
much in favor among Rumanian intellectuals, remained without effect. He therefore decided to base his demands upon law, imperial
decree, and historical precedent, the very sources from which the government drew its own arguments.

He set about the task of asserting the rights of his church in modest
ways at first, and with little success, but he quickly won recognition
among leading intellectuals as an ally in their own struggle for national rebirth. In 1847 he announced the principle that Orthodox students attending the schools of other denominations should receive
regular religious instruction from an Orthodox priest. Although his
statement went largely unnoticed, a few institutions recognized the
validity of his claim; the Roman Catholic gymnasium in Cluj offered a
special room once a week to an Orthodox priest for the purpose, an
extraordinary concession for that period.[43] Rumanian intellectuals,
both Uniate and Orthodox, applauded Şaguna's action, but not out of
concern for religious studies. *Gazeta de Transilvania,* the only Rumanian newspaper then published in Transylvania and the main organ of
the intellectuals, took the occasion to remind its readers that the
church (typically, it did not specify Orthodox or Uniate) had been the
chief refuge of their nationality for seventeen centuries. It pointed out
that children enrolled in the schools of other confessions often ceased
to attend church and warned that once this bond of nationality had

been severed, they would inevitably neglect their own language and adopt the customs and ways of thought of other nations. It concluded that regular catechizing would save these students for their "nation's future."[44]

The Transylvanian government quietly ignored Şaguna's direct appeals for constitutional recognition of the Orthodox. It did not reply to his letter of July 1, 1847, in which he requested equal rights for his clergy and faithful, and protested against the use of such denigrating terms for them as "tolerated" and "schismatic" in official documents and the press.[45] In spite of the modest nature of these demands, the Gubernium,* faced with growing internal unrest, was in no mood to tamper with the centuries-old social and political structure of the principality.

The conservative attitude of the government was not the only obstacle Şaguna encountered as he tried to infuse new life into the church. The lack of material resources appeared to him at times almost insurmountable. The funds available within his own diocese were wholly inadequate, and he could expect little financial aid from the government. His church had no significant holdings in land, and the Transylvanian treasury felt no obligation to render any accounting of its management of the church's other meager endowments. Şaguna found this tutelage utterly humiliating; it was as though the Orthodox were children who could not be trusted to manage their own financial affairs. He himself could not draw on church funds to pay the expenses of an official tour of his diocese or even subscribe to a foreign church publication; in each case he had to petition the treasury for release of the money.[46] Direct appeals to his own faithful for aid were out of the question, since the Nineteen Points prohibited the taking up of collections on the grounds that the faithful should not be subjected to extraordinary burdens.

Şaguna was undeterred. He set about improving the quality of religious life in his diocese with the means at hand. He began to make regular use of pastoral letters to instill in his clergy a sense of their own dignity and a realization of their responsibility to serve the people. He continually stressed the importance of Bible study as the best guide to a true Christian life, and he urged his priests to share this spiritual

---

*The highest executive body in Transylvania, consisting of twelve councillors and a president who bore the title of governor.

treasure by means of regular preaching. To encourage them, he asked
to see copies of their sermons and promised to have the best ones published.[47] His frequent tours of inspection also proved to be effective in
stirring lethargic parishes to life. The imminence of his arrival aroused
a flurry of activity and in some places not a little apprehension, since
word of the punishment inflicted upon the lazy and incompetent had
spread far and wide. The clergy had not seen such scrutiny in nearly
forty years. He inspected the physical condition of the church and
school buildings, verified the registers of vital statistics and the financial ledgers, probed the conduct of priests and parishioners, estimated
the degree to which the community was adequately supporting its
priest, ascertained the qualifications of the schoolmaster, and examined the pupils on church history and a variety of other subjects. If his
visit fell on a Sunday, he invariably preached a sermon that dwelt upon
the importance of education and good moral conduct and emphasized
the obligation of all to obey the law and honor the emperor.[48]

The immediate effect of his labors was slight, as Şaguna himself sadly
acknowledged. Perhaps his most important single contribution to the
welfare of his clergy was the reorganization of the theological school.
Few of those who enrolled had had prior training in a gymnasium, and
some could neither read nor write. Daily instruction and examinations
were conducted in such a loose fashion that students were required
merely to answer yes or no to their teachers' questions.[49] Taking as his
model the Serbian-Wallachian Clerical Institute in Vršac, Şaguna
immediately stiffened entrance requirements by refusing to admit any
student who had not completed the gymnasium or its equivalent; he
improved the quality of instruction by eliminating courses offered at
the secondary school level and introduced in their place advanced
work in, among other subjects, dogmatic and pastoral theology, teaching methodology, Biblical exegesis, and Rumanian grammar; he extended the length of the courses in theology and pedagogy from six
months to a full year; and he scraped together enough money to send
one or two students a year to the University of Vienna to complete their
theological studies. Significant as these changes may have been,
Saguna was under no illusions about what he could accomplish without regular, large-scale financial support from the state. But the
Gubernium showed no inclination to spend additional sums on Orthodox education, and it ignored Şaguna's petition in July 1847 to allocate
money from the church's own Seminary Fund to pay for the training of

forty theological students a year. But others were taking notice of his efforts to improve the education of priests. *Gazeta de Transilvania* praised the performance of the first new class graduating under Şaguna's sponsorship at their public examination in the summer of 1847; it augured well for the future development of the Rumanian nation. The paper gave the credit to Şaguna, "who has perceived the universal truth that only well educated and morally disciplined teachers and priests can raise up and sustain a nation."[50]

Şaguna himself, after nearly a year of uninterrupted effort, was less sanguine than *Gazeta* about the future of his church and less satisfied with what he had accomplished. The intellectual and moral condition of the clergy remained discouragingly low, and education in the villages had made little progress. The legal disabilities under which he was obliged to work and the preferential treatment accorded the Uniate Church were a continual humiliation for him. The Uniate Church, patronized as it was by the court and the Transylvanian government, continued to make converts among the Orthodox, while Şaguna was almost helpless, legally and financially, to counter its proselytizing activities. At the beginning of his vicarship he had thought justice and hard work would triumph, but by the summer of 1847, in moments of dejection, he could foresee only the eventual ruin of the church. The chief cause of these forebodings was his feeling that neither the civil authorities nor, indeed, a substantial party within his own clergy had any particular interest in rejuvenating the church.[51]

Şaguna had more than church problems to contend with. Only a few weeks after his arrival in Sibiu he became deeply involved in the complex social problems confronting Transylvania in the *Vormärz*. Governor Teleki requested him to go to the Apuseni Mountains, a rugged area in western Transylvania, to restore peace among a rebellious peasantry. For decades in this region the independent-minded peasants, who divided their time between farming and mining, had defied their landlords—in this case, the Transylvanian treasury, which demanded labor services as rent for the land they occupied.[52] The peasants, mostly from the communes of Abrudsat, Bucium, and Cărpiniş, claimed that immunities granted them as far back as the period of the native princes of Transylvania (before 1691) had relieved them of any obligations to the treasury. Although their petitions to the emperor and lengthy court cases brought them no relief, they refused to yield. In 1837 the Gubernium, equally determined to have its way,

resorted to force. It dispatched a company of cavalry to the three villages where in the course of several weeks it slaughtered large numbers
of cattle, administered beatings to persons who resisted, and lived off
the inhabitants until a large ransom was paid.[53] The peasants turned
to the courts once again and retained lawyers in nearby Aiud to represent them in anticipation of a long legal test.

At this low point in their fortunes, about 1840, Catharine Varga, a
Magyar peasant woman from Hălmeag, near Braşov, appeared on the
scene. Within a short time she gained immense influence over the
peasants on the strength of promises that she would use her own experience as a petitioner in the courts to aid them. She maintained her
position for many years, in spite of the fact that she accomplished
nothing for those who provided her with food and lodging. Whatever
her motives may have been—personal gain, according to some; altru-
ism, according to others—there can be no doubt that her presence
strengthened the resistance of the peasants and thereby increased the
possibility of renewed violence.[54] By the summer of 1846 a major uprising in the Apuseni Mountains seemed imminent unless the smoldering
unrest could be allayed once and for all.[55]

As a last resort, in order to avoid the expense and bloodshed and
unforeseen consequences of a new military expedition into the mountains, Teleki turned to Şaguna. He did not consider his action in the
least extraordinary because the government had for a century and a
half treated the heads of both the Orthodox and Uniate churches as its
own functionaries and had frequently entrusted them and other members of the higher clergy with special missions.[56] Şaguna accepted the
assignment to restore peace to the area without hesitation; he considered it his duty as a priest to protect his flock from violence and to
do what he could to ensure their well-being; and as a loyal subject he
felt he could do no less than encourage respect for the law.

On September 24, 1846, he travelled to Zlatna, the local administrative center, to discuss the background of the crisis with the district
prefect and other officials before entering the troubled area itself. On
the basis of these conversations he decided to visit each commune in
order to ascertain at first hand the causes of the peasants' grievances
and exert all the prestige of his office to restore peace and ensure
obedience to the law. His initial meetings with the peasants of Abrudsat, Bucium, and Cărpiniş on September 26 and 27 were far from
encouraging; only a few persons turned out to hear him and they lis-

tened sullenly as he pleaded with them to pay their dues to the treasury provisionally until the courts had had time to review their case.[57] After two days of intensive negotiations with village elders, during which the parish clergy served as intermediaries, Șaguna succeeded in extracting grudging declarations from the representatives of the three communes that they would perform the labor services demanded of them until the court had rendered its verdict. But they were careful to specify that their action should in no way prejudice their case as an admission of guilt, and they further stipulated that any obligations to which they might be liable in the future be set down in writing.[58]

Șaguna realized how fragile this agreement was and he urged the local treasury officials, Governor Teleki, and the Transylvanian chancellor, Samuel Jósika, not to presume too long upon the villagers' patience but to effect as rapidly as possible a just settlement of their grievances.[59] He held the Transylvanian government itself largely to blame for the deteriorating situation; by allowing matters to drag on year after year, it had exacerbated the peasants' misery and frustration to such a degree that violence had seemed to them the only way out.

By the end of the year Șaguna's forebodings had proved accurate; the truce he had managed to work out had collapsed. The peasants had grown impatient with the government's failure to act, and Catharine Varga, who had been absent during Șaguna's visit, had returned. On the government side, Teleki, who was now more convinced than ever of the need for drastic action, had decided that Catharine Varga was at the root of the trouble and that her "machinations" must cease once and for all. He turned again to Șaguna to devise some means of accomplishing his design without bloodshed. Since Șaguna shared Teleki's feelings about the inflammatory nature of Catharine Varga's activities, he proposed to make another trip to the mountains to apprehend her and hand her over to local judicial authorities for whatever action they deemed fitting.[60] On January 18, 1847, he arrived in Izbita, a commune near Bucium, to conduct the religious service and deliver a sermon on the virtues of obedience to the law. He had chosen the Feast of the Epiphany for his trip in the belief that his words would have added effect at a time of heightened religious feeling. When he had finished his sermon he asked Catharine Varga, who was in the congregation, to step forward. She did, and after exchanging a few words with her he turned once again to his audience and read an order signed by Governor Teleki that she be returned to her native village

without delay. Thereupon, he and several officials took her to a waiting sleigh outside the church and, without serious resistance from the
peasants, then drove off. Before a tribunal in Aiud she was tried and
found guilty of obstructing justice and was imprisoned in the fortress
of Alba Iulia until May 1851, when she was allowed to return to her
native Hălmeag. After this she disappeared, and the time and place of
her death are unknown.

Teleki was pleased with the outcome of Şaguna's mission. His belief
in Şaguna's adherence to the existing patterns of social and political
life and his confidence in Şaguna's ability to manage the affairs of his
diocese loyally and efficiently were greatly strengthened. The majority
of Rumanian intellectuals also approved of his handling of the matter.
They dreaded the idea of large-scale violence because they could perceive no benefit to their cause from it. *Gazeta de Transilvania,* in com-
menting upon the apprehension of Catharine Varga, accurately
reflected their feelings: "May heaven protect our people from seducers
like her. Not acts of disobedience, but a gradual awakening and cultivation of our people's minds is the way to happiness and the attainment of a place in the world."[61] Şaguna could not have expressed his
own feelings more precisely.

Although the danger of a peasant uprising had been averted for the
time being, the causes of discontent—forced labor services, heavy
taxes, and a hunger for land as strong as ever—remained. As before,
Şaguna held local officials largely responsible for the crisis because of
their indifference to peasant needs, and he urged Teleki to institute
immediate reforms, both educational and economic, as the only
means of dealing effectively with the problem.[62] The Gubernium
thought otherwise; assuming that Catharine Varga had been the chief
cause of all the trouble, it regarded her departure from the scene as an
end to the matter and consigned Şaguna's reports to the archives.
Later, in the fall of 1847, the Gubernium did discuss some of Şaguna's
proposals for improving Rumanian schools in the Apuseni Mountains,[63] but it took no action.

As the first year of his vicarship came to an end, Şaguna became
increasingly anxious over the continued delay in the election of a permanent successor to Moga. He knew the history of the Transylvanian
church well and wished to avoid the baleful consequences of another
lengthy interregnum like the one that had preceded Moga's own
appointment. His guide in all such matters was canon law, and as long

as the office of bishop remained unfilled, he considered orderly church government impossible. One matter in particular—the ordination of priests—caused him special concern. Only the bishop could perform this most sacred of ceremonies, and consequently, since 1845, candidates had been obliged to go to either Arad or Carlovitz. Since such a journey was too costly for most young seminarians, an increasing number of parishes had simply remained without priests when the incumbent died and, to use Şaguna's words, all moral and intellectual training came to a halt.[64] Şaguna was also worried about the effects of a long vacancy on Orthodox-Uniate relations. He was certain that a leaderless Orthodox Church could not hope to combat successfully the proselytizing efforts of the Uniates.[65] Recognizing the troubled mood of the country and persuaded that far-reaching changes in its political and social structure could not be long postponed, he thought it essential that the Orthodox Church have strong leadership to represent it in the highest councils of the state. Otherwise, he was certain that its interests would be ignored, as they had invariably been in the past, when its fate had been decided by others. He considered himself capable of such leadership, but as late as June 1847 he despaired of being elected.[66]

The opposition to his self-professed candidacy was formidable. Within his own church a majority of the forty-two protopopes, who traditionally elected the bishop, refused to support him.[67] Their motives ranged from a concern for the "national interest" to the desire for personal gain. Some protopopes plainly regarded Şaguna as a Serb because of his long service in the metropolis of Carlovitz and were convinced that "foreign domination" of the church would inevitably follow his election. They insisted, therefore, that the norms established by the chancellery in 1809, which required that all candidates for bishop be natives of Transylvania, be strictly enforced.[68] Others professed misgivings about the official favor Şaguna obviously enjoyed and suspected that he had been won over by the Magyar aristocracy, to whom they attributed the saying: "Lemeni* is a clever fellow, but compared to Şaguna he's just a Wallach priest."[69] Some protopopes objected to Şaguna on the grounds that he was the official candidate and that his election would result in increased government interference in church affairs.[70] Still others were less high-minded in their opposi-

---

*1780-1861; bishop of the Rumanian Uniate Church in Transylvania, 1832-1848.

tion to Şaguna's candidacy; some did not like his "innovations" and preferred to keep things as they had been; others, who had enjoyed the favor of the late bishop, were unhappy with Şaguna's ideas about merit as the criterion for advancement. Both groups planned to vote for one of Moga's nephews, Ioan Moga or Moise Fulea, like them, protopopes. Almost all the electors, regardless of party or personal feelings, were jealous of their prerogative of electing the bishop, and they were uneasy about Şaguna's strict adherence to canon law, which stipulated that two parish priests from each district must also have a vote.

From outside the Orthodox Church, opposition to Şaguna came from Bishop Lemeni and other Uniate leaders, who urged the court to postpone the election indefinitely. They preferred a weak Orthodox Church to the vigorous institution planned by Şaguna, whose abilities as an administrator they readily acknowledged.[71]

Criticisms of Şaguna and efforts to impede the election of an Orthodox bishop carried little weight with the chancellery and Gubernium. The maintenance of tranquillity among the Orthodox seemed more important to them than the observance of tradition or even the promotion of the Uniate movement; they had already decided that Şaguna was the candidate who could best fulfil their needs. In June 1847 Chancellor Jósika, citing Şaguna's numerous services to the crown, warmly recommended his election to the emperor.[72] On July 27 Ferdinand convoked an electoral synod for December 2. He specified that the norms followed in the selection of Vasile Moga in 1810 would again apply, but with one notable exception—the candidates need not be native-born Transylvanians nor members of the Transylvanian clergy.[73] There could hardly have been a more forceful endorsement of Şaguna, the only serious candidate from outside the principality. But the patronage of the court could not ensure his election; this decision, at least initially, rested with the protopopes. Each was entitled to vote for three candidates, and, in accordance with a procedure instituted by Joseph II, the names of the three with the highest number of votes were sent to the emperor, who then exercised his prerogative of choosing one among them to be the new bishop.

On December 1, 1847, the day before the election, a group of Moga's and Fulea's supporters called on Şaguna to demand that he withdraw his name from further consideration on the grounds that he was a Serb, and therefore had no right to seek office in a Rumanian diocese. Şaguna angrily retorted that he was as much a Rumanian as they were, and he vowed that he would be their bishop whether they wanted him or not.[74]

Şaguna had his supporters, too. He was the candidate of a forward-looking minority of the protopopes who, like him, wanted to shake the church out of its old ways and place it once again in the vanguard of the spiritual and social life of the nation. He was also the candidate of clerical and lay intellectuals who approved his efforts to give the laity a larger share of responsibility in managing the church's affairs and who wanted to transform the electoral synod into a national congress, similar to the institution enjoyed by the Serbs.[75] Support for him was particularly strong among Uniate and Orthodox lay intellectuals. They welcomed his infusion of new life into the church as a national institution, for they too were planning a vigorous role for it in Rumanian social and political life. They perceived in Şaguna's actions signs that he had a similar goal in mind. For example, they noted that he had complained to the Gubernium against the ill treatment of Rumanians in the Fundus regius* and had bluntly informed Saxon officials of his displeasure. They had also been gratified by his encouragement of their plans for a Rumanian-language newspaper in Sibiu. Pavel Vasici, a young doctor from the Banat, was speaking not only for himself when he referred to Şaguna as "the man of my hopes."[76]

On the opening day of the electoral synod Şaguna made a brief address of welcome, in which he urged the delegates to put aside personal interests and think only of the church's welfare. The synod then proceeded to vote. It gave a plurality to Ioan Moga — thirty-three votes; Moise Fulea obtained thirty-one, and Şaguna twenty-seven; protopopes Iosif Ighian and Ioan Popasu followed with fourteen and eleven votes, respectively. The government seems to have made no overt attempt to influence the outcome.[77] The imperial commissioner certified the results and transmitted the names of Moga, Fulea, and Şaguna to the Gubernium in Cluj.[78] The matter was resolved with great dispatch, for Şaguna received the solid backing of the Gubernium, of the military commander in Transylvania, General Anton von Puchner, and of the chancellery. The Gubernium praised his performance as vicar as "distinguished" and expressed full confidence in his administrative abilities and his devotion to the crown; Puchner described him

---

*The territory inhabited by the Saxons, over which they exercised a large degree of autonomy. It extended roughly between Braşov and Sibiu in southern Transylvania and included the area around Bistriţa in the north.

as the only candidate capable of providing the Rumanian clergy and people with enlightened and unselfish leadership; and the chancellery emphasized the calm that had prevailed among the Orthodox since his coming and ascribed it to his energetic measures to lift the diocese out of the "darkness into which it had sunk."[79] Metropolitan Rajačić's warm and persuasive recommendation was already on record. On January 14, 1848, Chancellor Jósika formally recommended Şaguna, and on February 5 Ferdinand signed the letters of appointment.

Immediately upon receiving word of his confirmation, Şaguna wrote to Rajačić to express his gratitude for his friendship and support and to promise that he would administer his diocese in conformity with canon law and the "spirit of the times."[80] Undoubtedly Rajačić did not grasp the full significance of the latter phrase; if he had, he might have entertained second thoughts about the wisdom of his choice. To Şaguna, the spirit of the times meant the rise of the idea of nationality, and he was determined to further the legitimate aspirations of his faithful. As a result, his path slowly diverged from Rajačić's, since there could be no compromise between the Serbian hierarchy's insistence upon preserving the administrative unity of the church at all costs and Rumanian aspirations for a separate and independent church organization. At his consecration in the cathedral of Carlovitz on April 30, 1848, Saint Thomas's Sunday (*Dumineca Tomii* in Rumanian), Şaguna declared his devotion to his adopted nation and pledged "to awaken the Rumanians of Transylvania from their deep slumber and to lead them along the path to all that is true, beneficial, and good."[81]

As Şaguna spoke, several thousand Rumanian peasants were gathered at Blaj to hear proclamations of Rumanian nationhood and to applaud the abolition of serfdom. The revolution that was soon to engulf all the peoples of Transylvania had begun. When Şaguna returned to Sibiu on May 6, little more than a week remained before a great assembly of the Rumanians was to take place, an event that suddenly thrust upon him all the responsibilities of national leadership.

2 / Revolution

The travail of the old regime in France which began with the over-throw of King Louis Philippe in Paris in the last days of February 1848 quickly became a general European phenomenon. Within a few weeks disorders had spread to the Austrian Empire. Prince Metternich, the great symbol of the age of conservatism, departed Vienna for a life of exile in England, and those who succeeded him were challenged by forces with which neither training nor inclination had equipped them to contend. The problem of Hungary, where liberalism and national-ism took extreme forms, proved to be their most severe test.

The most striking display of Magyar liberalism, and that which had the most telling effect upon the other peoples of historic Hungary, was the proclamation of a democratic government in Pest on March 15 by a group of young radicals and idealists led by the poet Sándor Petőfi. By democratic they meant a ministry responsible to the electorate, uni-versal suffrage, equal treatment before the law, freedom of association and of expression, and taxation based upon the ability to pay, and they established a Committee of Public Order with full powers to make abstract principle a reality. Although the committee was soon super-seded by a more moderate government sanctioned by the imperial court and headed by Count Lajos Batthyány as prime minister, its pro-gram lost none of its attractive force. The Batthyány ministry itself solemnly pledged to be responsive to the "national will" and to protect the constitutional rights of all the citizens of Hungary regardless of nationality or religion.

But liberal political ideas represented only one facet of Magyar aspirations; even stronger, because of their irresistible emotional ap-peal, were the claims of nationality. Since the last decades of the eigh-teenth century Magyar intellectuals had been cultivating the idea of nationality, and after nearly half a century their consciousness of themselves as the heirs of a great cultural and historical tradition had reached its height. Like their counterparts elsewhere in Europe during the "springtime of peoples," they too sought fulfillment in the creation of a national state. When, therefore, the Committee of Public Order proclaimed Hungary's full constitutional autonomy vis-à-vis German

Austria it was carrying out an unwritten but none the less imperative mandate. The Batthyány ministry went further; it asserted its intention of reconstituting the boundaries of medieval Hungary through the incorporation of Transylvania, Croatia, and other territories it claimed as dependencies of the Crown of Saint Stephen into a new Magyar state. The leading exponent of these policies was Lajos Kossuth, the minister of finance, who had won a large popular following in the Vormärz because of his liberal political views and his opposition to Habsburg rule. His attempts to carry out Magyar national goals ran counter to the aspirations of the other peoples of Hungary to achieve their own national ambitions and led to what has aptly been called "the central tragedy of 1848."

The attitude of Rumanian intellectuals toward the Magyar program must be judged against the background of their own political and cultural development of the preceding half-century. They were intent upon protecting their nationality, but at the same time they looked forward to building a new Transylvania in accordance with the most enlightened principles of the age. Since they shared the liberal aspirations of many Magyar intellectuals and political leaders, a solid basis existed for understanding and cooperation between the two nationalities.

The generation of 1848 were the heirs of the great Rumanian *Aufklärer* of the late eighteenth and early nineteenth centuries, who in their native Transylvania and in Vienna and Rome had been deeply influenced by the general European movement of ideas. Not only the rationalism of the Enlightenment but also the currents of Romanticism —both mainly through an Austrian filter—provided the framework for their vigorous investigation of national origins. Their research and writing on Rumanian history and language contributed immeasurably to the awakening of national consciousness. The major figures were Samuil Micu-Clain, the author of a monumental four-volume *Istoria, lucrurile şi întâmplările Românilor* and numerous other works on history, language, and theology; Gheorghe Şincai, whose main historical work was *Chronica Românilor şi a mai multor neamuri* in three volumes and who collaborated with Clain on *Elementa linguae daco-romanae sive valachicae* (Vienna, 1780), the first published Rumanian grammar; and Petru Maior, whose compact, polemical *Istoria pentru începutul Românilor în Dacia* (Buda, 1812) exercised an immense influence on his own and later generations and who propounded the theory of the derivation of Rumanian from vulgar rather than classical Latin, as his contemporaries believed.[1]

These men bequeathed a rich heritage to the forty-eighters. In the first place, they elaborated and refined the theory of the Roman origins of the Rumanians and the Latinity of their language and their uninterrupted occupation of the territory of ancient Dacia ever since the Roman conquest in the second century. These ideas formed the substance of Rumanian national consciousness and lay at the heart of political programs drawn up in the 1840s. The Aufklärer also left behind a belief in the reasonableness of man, a respect for law, and a sense of mission to lead the common people toward a better life. Conscious of their noble origins and their inherent worth as a nation, the forty-eighters could no longer tolerate their second-class status.

In March and the beginning of April 1848 most Rumanian intellectuals enthusiastically greeted the liberal pronouncements of the Committee of Public Order and the Batthyány ministry as the opening of a new era in the history of Transylvania. The editors of the two Rumanian newspapers—George Barițiu of *Gazeta de Transilvania* and Timotei Cipariu of *Organul Luminării*—were confident that the political and economic organization of Transylvania would henceforth be based upon the principles of liberty, equality, and fraternity and that, consequently, all nationalities would have full freedom to develop in an atmosphere of mutual trust and understanding.[2] Barițiu, the most consistent voice of liberalism among the Rumanians and an ardent admirer of the English constitutional system, confessed to being overcome with emotion upon reading the reports of the new liberties proclaimed in Western Europe, Vienna, and Buda-Pest.[3] He warmly applauded the program of the Magyar liberals, for civil and religious equality seemed to him the prerequisites for social progress, and freedom of speech as natural to man as eating and drinking. He was convinced that universal suffrage, an annual parliament, and a ministry responsible to the electorate would protect the peoples of Transylvania from the reimposition of arbitrary government and would guarantee their right to develop as separate nationalities within common political boundaries.[4]

Barițiu, Cipariu, and the majority of intellectuals recognized the importance of the proposed union of Transylvania with Hungary—Barițiu called it the "reform of reforms"[5]—but they did not consider it a serious threat to their own national development. Rather, they

looked upon the union as a means of solving long-standing social problems and of eliminating centuries-old inequality among the nationalities; they were preoccupied especially with serfdom and were eager to
abolish what they characterized as an "accursed spoliation."[6]

They were, of course, fully aware of the Magyars' efforts to achieve
their own political ambitions. The controversy over the so-called Magyar language law, introduced in the diet in 1842, which provided for
the gradual introduction of Magyar into all branches of government
from the Gubernium to the village council and its obligatory use in cultural institutions like the Orthodox and Uniate churches and their
schools, had evoked an emotional wave of protest from Rumanian intellectuals. On that occasion Simion Bărnuţiu, a professor of philosophy at the Uniate lyceum in Blaj, wrote a passionate defense of language as "man's most precious possession":

The more cultivated the language the more cultivated the people; language is the
measure and the medium of culture. A people's mode of thought and feeling, its desires and aspirations are reflected in its language; the character and nationality of a
people are based upon it. If a people should lose its language, it would at the same
time lose its character and nationality. It would no longer be honored by other peoples,
but would be an object of mockery before all.[7]

Cipariu, on behalf of the Uniate consistory, condemned the law because of its tampering with language in the schools and its consequent
threat to "our moral and spiritual life and — what is no less grievous for
us — our nationality."[8] Bariţiu characterized the law as a "death sentence for the Rumanian nation."[9]

These anxieties faded into the background under the heady impress
of the March days. Rumanian intellectuals were caught up in the general tide of enthusiasm; they felt themselves to be a part of the general
European awakening of peoples, and they saw before them an opportunity to fulfil their historical destiny as a nation and to achieve freedom as a universal human principle. They could not, therefore, conceive of the Magyars, who had declared these principles to be their
own, as capable of violating them.

In the midst of this general chorus of praise for Magyar liberalism,
only Simion Bărnuţiu, among Rumanian leaders of the first rank,
struck a note of alarm at the general trend of events. He was the first to
warn of the fateful consequences of an easy acceptance of the union of
Transylvania with Hungary. In a letter composed on March 24 and

circulated among friends and colleagues in Sibiu and other cities he urged them to make the preservation of Rumanian nationality their chief concern. The union, he admonished them, might well result in the strengthening of Magyar rule in Transylvania and thereby lead to the eventual extinction of their own nationality. He pleaded with them to ensure the full legal equality of the Rumanian nation and to ascertain its will at a representative general congress before making a decision about the union.[10]

During the next several weeks, independent of Bărnuţiu's admonitions, Rumanian intellectuals and clergy throughout Transylvania gathered in small groups to assess the situation and decide upon a course of action. The most important of these meetings took place in Blaj on March 25, at which the canons of the cathedral, the teachers at the lyceum, and a number of young seminarists voted to convoke a national congress. A week later another meeting was held at Blaj, at which Avram Iancu and a number of other young lawyers from Tîrgu-Mureş reached an agreement with Cipariu that the congress should meet at Blaj on April 30.[11]

By the beginning of April expectations of momentous change had spread to all ranks of society. In every city and town where there were Rumanian intellectuals discussions of the great issues of the day took place in an atmosphere of keen anticipation. In the villages, too, the words "liberty" and "freedom" had filtered down to the peasants. Without waiting for learned explanations, they simply assumed that these principles, once expressed, had acquired the force of law and they interpreted them as meaning that their dues and services to landlords had ceased. In many parts of the country the peasants refused to perform labor services and demanded the return of pasture and forest lands, which, they claimed, had been taken from them illegally.[12]

Governor Teleki watched this burst of activity by the Rumanians with alarm, for he saw in it the antithesis of the old order of estates and of Magyar domination in Transylvania. In an effort to stem the tide, on April 17 he forbade the holding of the proposed Rumanian congress on the grounds that it had been organized by "irresponsible persons" and would, by bringing together great masses of peasants, increase the general unrest and inevitably lead to violence. Resorting to a time-honored device employed by other Transylvanian governors at such times, he made the Orthodox and Uniate bishops responsible for the actions of their people. He informed Bishop Lemeni and the Orthodox consistory (Şaguna was already on his way to Carlovitz) that he had prohibited the congress and instructed them to keep their priests at home. But he expressed a willingness to allow the protopopes and a few intellectuals of each church to hold "private conferences" at some future date and invited Lemeni to suggest a time.[13] It was Teleki's intention to weaken the force of the national movement by dividing the Rumanians along religious lines, and he therefore gave his approval only for separate Orthodox and Uniate meetings. The intellectuals objected to Teleki's interference in their national affairs, but they grudgingly accepted a postponement of the general congress until May 15, the date set by Lemeni. Nonetheless, they went ahead with plans to hold a more limited meeting on April 30, for they were more determined than ever to assert their leadership over their own people and to make it clear that religious divisions were a thing of the past.

The meeting took place as scheduled with some six thousand persons, mostly peasants, in attendance. Bărnuţiu, whose influence had grown steadily since the circulation of his manifesto, was the principal speaker. He began his address with a flat declaration that the time had come at last for the Rumanian nation to recover its ancient rights and privileges, and for serfdom, which had held them in bondage for centuries, to be swept away. His audience responded enthusiastically, but what he said next quickly sobered them. He admonished them not to behave like revolutionaries who tried to achieve their ends by violence and thereby showed themselves unworthy of liberty, but rather to respect the law and give the landlords their due until matters could be set right by constitutional means.[14] Bărnuţiu's attitude was shared by most of the forty-eighters. In spite of a romantic belief in the inevitability of progress and a solemn acceptance of their responsibilities toward the common people, they had preserved their faith in reason. Considering themselves the most reasonable of men, they thought it their prerogative to dictate the means of achieving social justice and national equality. They had an equally strong faith in the efficacy of "just" laws and "good" institutions, and once they had secured both, they had no doubt that the grievances of the masses could be quickly settled. For these reasons Bărnuţiu and his colleagues urged the peasants to be patient and not to upset the "normal" process of change by acts of violence. The peasants at Blaj heeded this advice and returned peacefully to their villages. Bărnuţiu and his colleagues judged the meeting a success and hastened their preparations for the great assembly scheduled for May 15.

As a result of the wide-ranging political discussions of the preceding month most Rumanian leaders had come over to Bărnuţiu's position that priority be given to the defense of Rumanian nationality. Of those who still remained publicly uncommitted, Şaguna was considered the most important, and it was with some anxiety that the intellectuals awaited his return from Carlovitz. He had been gone from Sibiu since early April, on yet another mission entrusted to him by Governor Teleki. Between April 5 and 12 he visited over fifty villages in Hunedoara County in southwestern Transylvania, the Apuseni Mountains, and the adjoining Hungarian counties of Arad and Krassó in an attempt to calm the restless peasants, apparently with only modest success. As he had done in the Apuseni Mountains the previous year, at each stop he gathered the peasants together at the village church and urged them to be patient and to trust their monarch and "those placed above them" to lighten their burdens. He also used the occasion to hear peasant grievances. They complained to him mainly about heavy labor services imposed by landlords and county officials and their own inability to rectify abuses. Şaguna reported what he had heard to Teleki and warned him that the peasants would simply resort to violence unless something were done immediately to end the "harsh treatment of the poor" by local authorities.[15] On April 13 Şaguna proceeded to Carlovitz for his consecration as bishop. He remained there longer, on account of illness, than he had planned and he found it impossible to honor Teleki's request that he return to Transylvania at once because of the growing unrest.[16] On the thirtieth, just after the ceremony had been concluded, a delegation of Rumanians from Transylvania presented itself. They informed him of the dramatic events that had taken place in his absence and urged him, on behalf of the intellectuals, to return home as quickly as possible.[17]

The intellectuals still regarded Şaguna with reserve, for, in spite of his energetic church reforms, they had lingering doubts about the strength of his commitment to the national cause. To some, he was still an outsider, who could hardly be expected to show much sympathy for a cause he barely knew; to others, he seemed to be a man of the regime, always willing to place himself in its service. But the majority simply had no precise information about his political views, a situation for which Şaguna himself was partly responsible.

Şaguna later admitted that during his first two years in Transylvania he had concerned himself almost exclusively with church affairs.[18] Nonetheless, experience had taught him to appreciate the dynamism of national feeling, and he recognized both its destructive and its creative potential. In Pest in the 1820s he had witnessed the break-up of the Greek-Wallachian community, and in Carlovitz and Vršac in the 1830s and 1840s he himself had become involved in the strife between Serbs and Rumanians. Consequently, the problems of nationality in Transylvania were hardly foreign to him. He sympathized with the aspirations of Rumanian intellectuals for some form of autonomy as a means of improving the material and cultural existence of their people. But he could never become one of them because he could never make the idea of nationality his master, as they had done. He viewed the national movement both in 1848 and later on as only one aspect of the complex process of social change. Although he recognized the idea of nationality as the dominant motive force in contemporary Europe, he consistently measured its aspirations and accomplishments against what were for him "eternal values" — the teachings of Christianity and those worldly ideas that had already proved their validity in the long course of human development. Consequently, he believed that whatever progress the Rumanian nation might make would depend upon the welfare of the Orthodox Church and loyalty to the Habsburg dynasty.

Șaguna arrived back in Sibiu on May 6, and in the days that followed, intensive discussions took place about the future course of the national movement. On the eighth, Bărnuțiu and other leaders agreed upon the essential points of their program: rejection of the unconditional union of Transylvania with Hungary and the creation of an autonomous Rumanian nation as a constituent part of Transylvania.[19] Negotiations then ensued between Bărnuțiu and Șaguna, whose adherence the intellectuals considered indispensable to their cause since he, as bishop, would find himself in the traditional role of intermediary between his people and the Transylvanian government. Șaguna accepted the Bărnuțian principles of Rumanian nationhood, but he insisted upon adding to them an oath of loyalty to the imperial house. On the evening of May 11 their agreement was publicly celebrated by a torchlight procession of Orthodox and Uniates through the streets of Sibiu to Șaguna's residence. When he came outside to welcome them, Bărnuțiu stepped forward and on behalf of his colleagues declared that Șaguna alone was capable of leading the Rumanian nation in the crucial months that lay ahead.[20]

On the day before the great assembly — after special Sunday services in the Uniate cathedral of Blaj, at which both Orthodox and Uniates were present in a show of solidarity—Rumanian leaders met to draft the final text of a national program. The initiative still lay with Bărnuţiu. In a forceful speech, which epitomized the thinking of his generation, he again warned his colleagues against the acceptance of the union of Transylvania with Hungary, characterizing it as an instrument to maintain Magyar hegemony and stifle the development of the Rumanian nation. He urged them not to be misled by Magyar promises of universal suffrage, a responsible ministry, and other freedoms, for the price would be their nationality; these benefits were offered to the Rumanians only as individual citizens of Greater Hungary, not as a corporate entity, a nation, with its own destiny to fulfil. Hence, he concluded, liberty had no meaning unless it was national, and only in an autonomous Transylvania, where they constituted a majority of the population, could the Rumanians hope to preserve their most precious possession—their nationality.[21]

In the lengthy discussions that followed three issues were paramount: political autonomy, religious discord, and the status of the peasantry. On the first Bărnuţiu was obliged to modify his stand on the primacy of nationality and to accept limitations on the right of the Rumanians to self-determination. Moderates, led by Şaguna, Lemeni, and Bariţiu, among others, persuaded the conference to couple the proclamation of Rumanian nationhood with an oath of loyalty to the House of Habsburg and to place the protest against the union at the end rather than the beginning of its program. Şaguna and his associates were guided by what seemed to them the practical realities of their situation. On the one hand, they considered their nation too weak to pursue a wholly independent policy, and hence they looked to the court of Vienna for the protection they needed. On the other hand, experience had taught them that Austria might eventually come to terms with the Magyars and that, as a result, they would have nowhere at all to turn. For the time being, therefore, they urged a middle course that would maintain "correct" relations with both Vienna and Buda-Pest.

Bărnuţiu and the younger intellectuals, who were his most ardent followers, also had to yield to the moderates on the issue of a reunion of the Orthodox and Uniate churches. They condemned the internal religious division as anti-national and eagerly sought some formula for ending the strife between Orthodox and Uniates. But it was clear from both Şaguna's and Lemeni's attitude that a forced reconciliation would lead to an even wider split and hence seriously impair national unity at a moment all recognized to be crucial. The matter was dropped, and the article in the national program dealing with the religious question merely expressed the general desire for religious harmony and the independence of the "Rumanian church."

The peasant question was also discussed at some length. There was unanimous agreement that serfdom, which encompassed the great majority of the peasantry, was an inhuman institution and should be abolished without delay. But no one—neither Bărnuţiu and his supporters nor Şaguna and the moderates—considered it desirable for the peasants to carry out their own liberation. Instead, they recommended that emancipation be accomplished through legislation and be accompanied by expanded opportunities for technical and humanistic education. A majority argued against giving the landlords any indemnity for services lost, and everyone agreed that the peasants should not be made to pay for their own emancipation. But no one seems to have thought very much about how the new freeholder was going to remain economically independent on an inadequate plot of land.

The national congress opened on the morning of May 15 in a meadow, later designated the Field of Liberty, outside Blaj where some thirty thousand peasants had gathered during the preceding week. A remarkable calm and order prevailed during the next three days, as the vast assembly, conscious of an almost divine mission it was fulfilling, carried out its tasks with fitting solemnity. The first day's business consisted of a welcoming address by Bărnuţiu, an oath of loyalty to the Rumanian nation and the Habsburg dynasty, and the election of officers. The assembly chose Şaguna and Lemeni as presidents, in keeping with the tradition that the bishops were the official representatives of the nation, and Bărnuţiu and Bariţiu as vice-presidents.

On the following day the national program was read and explained to the assembly article by article:

1. The Rumanian nation, basing itself on the principle of liberty, equality and fraternity, declares its national political independence, so that it may have, as the *Rumanian* nation, its own representatives in the diet of the land in proportion to its members, and its own officials in all administrative, judicial, and military branches of government in the same proportion, and that it may use its own language in all matters which concern it, both legislative and administrative. It also demands the right to hold a general national assembly every year.

2. The Rumanian nation declares that the Rumanian church, regardless of denomination, is and shall remain free and independent of any other church and shall enjoy the same rights and benefits as the other churches of Transylvania. It demands the restoration of the Rumanian metropolis and the annual general synod, in accordance with its ancient rights. In this synod there shall be lay and ecclesiastical deputies, and here Rumanian bishops shall be freely elected by a majority of votes.

3. The Rumanian nation, conscious of individual human rights, demands the immediate abolition of serfdom without payment of compensation by the peasants in the [Magyar] counties or the [Saxon] districts or the [Szekler] regions or the military frontier. It also demands the abolition of the tithes as . . . harmful to the economy.

4. The Rumanian nation desires industrial and commercial freedom with the dissolution of the guilds and of privileges and all other impediments to commerce in neighboring countries including the abolition of customs duties at the frontier.

5. The Rumanian nation urges that the tax levied for some time upon animals which, because of limited grazing lands, are kept in neighboring countries at great expense, unspeakable hardship, and even danger to life, be completely abolished as a clear hindrance to industry and trade, and that the treaties concluded between the ruling house of Austria, the Ottoman Porte, and the Rumanian Principalities dealing with animal husbandry be maintained in all respects.

6. The Rumanian nation demands the abolition of the tithe on metals mined in this country as . . . a true impediment to the development of mining. It asks further that all the owners of mines, large and small, be treated alike when the boundaries of their mines are determined.

7. The Rumanian nation demands the freedom to speak, to write, and to print without any form of censorship, that is, it seeks liberty of the press for any kind of . . . publication, without either journalists or printers being required to pay the heavy surety bond.

8. The Rumanian nation demands the assurance of personal liberty, so that no one may be arrested for political reasons. It also demands freedom of assembly, so that men shall not be suspect if they gather merely to discuss and settle their affairs peacefully.

9. The Rumanian nation demands courts with juries, where the proceedings shall be open and public.

10. The Rumanian nation demands the arming of the people or a national guard in order to defend the country from its enemies within and without. The Rumanian Militia shall have its own Rumanian officers.

11. The Rumanian nation demands the establishment of a mixed commission composed of Rumanians and the other nations of Transylvania to investigate cases involving the delimitation of farm and forest property lines, the occupation of common lands and serf holdings, and other matters of this sort.

12. The Rumanian nation demands the endowment of the entire Rumanian clergy by the state treasury on the same basis as the clergies of the other nations.

13. The Rumanian nation demands the creation of Rumanian schools in all villages and towns, and of gymnasia, military and technical institutes, and seminaries for priests, as well as a Rumanian university endowed by the state treasury—all in proportion to the number of taxpayers. All these institutions shall have the right to choose their own directors and teachers and to organize their curricula and to have the liberty to hold classes.

14. The Rumanian nation seeks the sharing of public burdens by each person in accordance with his status and wealth, and the abolition of privileges.
15. The Rumanian nation desires a new constitution for Transylvania to be drawn up by a constituent assembly of all the nations of the land, . . . based upon the principles of justice, liberty, equality, and fraternity. It also desires that new civil, penal, and commercial codes be drawn up in accordance with the same principles.
16. The Rumanian nation demands of its fellow nations that they in no way debate the question of the union with Hungary until the Rumanian nation has become a constituent and organized nation with full powers to deliberate and vote in the legislative chamber. If, however, the diet of Transylvania should decide to take up the matter of the union in our absence, then the Rumanian nation solemnly protests. [22]

In its concern for human liberties and the progress of nationality the Sixteen Points was a characteristic manifesto of the intellectuals of 1848 in Central Europe. It represented the most comprehensive and forceful statement of Rumanian aspirations made up to that time, and in its essentials it provided the national movement with its program for the next half-century. Bărnuţiu and his supporters, who were mainly responsible for its final form, no longer justified their demands on the basis of historical right or imperial patent but rather upon a principle they believed to be universally valid: the natural rights of man. They now extended these rights, subsumed under the slogan "liberty, equality, and fraternity," from individuals to entire nations. Their preoccupation with the "nation" is nowhere more evident than in the Sixteen Points themselves.

They proclaimed the independence of the Rumanian nation and its full equality with the other nations of Transylvania and declared their intention of maintaining its rights by creating a new political system based upon liberal principles. For the first time in such a public document they stressed the connection between economic development and the progress of nationality; hence, their forceful statement on serfdom and their demand for equality of opportunity in commerce and the trades, which reflected particularly their belief in the importance of a native middle class. They also recognized the need for a well-informed, literate citizenry, if liberal political institutions were to prosper and, therefore, they made provision for a modern school system. Unlike their more cosmopolitan forebears of the Age of Enlightenment, who fostered the spread of knowledge for its own sake, they insisted that education was a task that could be performed successfully only in national schools and in the national language. Religion, too, was subordinated to nationality, and Christianity as such appears largely irrelevant. The intellectuals gave expression to a widespread desire of Orthodox and Uniates to be rid of Serbian Orthodox and Hungarian Roman Catholic interference, respectively, in their affairs, but their main objective was rather political and cultural than canonical—to enable the churches to serve the national cause effectively.

When the reading and explanation of the Sixteen Points had been completed, the assembly roared its approval. Later in the day two delegations were chosen to represent the assembly before the court of Vienna and the Transylvanian diet in Cluj. Şaguna headed the first, Lemeni the second. In order not to lose the momentum they had generated and to assure continuity to the national movement the leaders of the assembly established a permanent committee, consisting of twenty-five members with Şaguna as president and Bărnuţiu as vice-president. The committee was the first standing political organization the Rumanians had ever had, and, chosen as it was by a representative assembly, it could justly claim to speak in the name of the entire nation.

The assembly concluded its business on May 17 with a brief ceremony. The great throngs of peasants returned peacefully to their villages; the members of the two delegations made ready to leave at once for their respective destinations; Bărnuţiu, who, because of Şaguna's mission to the court, assumed direction of the permanent committee's activities, went to Sibiu with the other members to find permanent quarters and make plans for a second national congress; and Şaguna, postponing his departure to Vienna, travelled to Cluj to discuss the general political situation with Governor Teleki and take the oath of loyalty to the constitution required of all newly-installed bishops.

Two figures dominated the congress—Bărnuţiu and Şaguna. Bărnuţiu was without equal as the popular hero; it was he who gave the clearest expression to the enthusiasm and aspirations of the intellectuals. Had it not been for him and his supporters, the national program adopted on the Field of Liberty would probably have been limited to an expression of loyalty to the ruling house and a few generalities about the desirability of reform. Bărnuţiu's role as the spirit of the national movement was similar to that of Joseph Mazzini in Italy.

Şaguna, to extend the comparison, was not unlike Cavour; both men distinguished themselves in their respective national movements as organizers and diplomatists who were little swayed by the enthusiasms of the moment. Şaguna pondered a given situation to determine what was both right—that is, consistent with the "spirit of the times," the spiritual principles of Orthodoxy, and the prerogatives of the civil authority—and feasible, in that order. Only then did he act. Caution and deliberation were qualities that rarely produced a popular hero, but Şaguna's directness elicited the respect of friends and opponents alike among the intellectuals, and he wielded great influence over the peasantry by virtue of his ecclesiastical office. It was, indeed, to his "commanding presence" that the two royal commissioners and other observers at the assembly attributed the order and dignity with which the participants conducted themselves.[23]

To a number of intellectuals Şaguna seemed too conciliatory to the old regime and not nationalistic enough. They found fault with his public pronouncements to his faithful, especially his pastoral letter of May 16,[24] in which he emphasized obedience to the law, respect for the rights of landlords, and faith in God and the emperor. It seemed strange to them that as president of a national assembly he should have addressed himself only to the Orthodox; that he did not once mention the words "Rumanian nation"; and that he tried to persuade the peasants that their Magyar landlords were sincerely interested in their welfare.[25] These critics overlooked the fact that Şaguna was carrying out his duties as the spiritual leader of the Orthodox, which he regarded as his chief responsibility, and that, consequently, he was using language that seemed to him appropriate for his audience, given the extreme tension that prevailed across the land. He was making no attempt to cover up the iniquities of a system that he himself had sworn to change. He was well informed about the measures taken by the Transylvanian government to terrorize a recalcitrant peasantry, and at the first session of the national congress he had joined his colleagues in protesting against the erection of gallows in numerous villages and the arrest of Rumanian intellectuals and priests as wholly contrary to the spirit of liberty, equality, and fraternity.[26]

Şaguna arrived in Cluj on May 19 and spent almost a week conferring with various government officials. He had high hopes that a peaceful and just solution to the nationality and other problems could be found by men of good will who, whatever their specific disagreements might be, had respect for the law and human rights. Now and throughout the summer he clung to the belief that the Hungarian government would keep the promises of March. If his hopes were fulfilled, then he foresaw a bright new era for the Rumanian nation and the Orthodox Church. His own policy was to foster understanding and confidence among all the peoples of Transylvania, so that they might settle their differences through reason rather than violence.

In Cluj, therefore, he continued to play the role of conciliator. On the one hand, he agreed to chair the Rumanian delegation to the so-called Commission on the Union, which was charged with working out the details of the union of Transylvania with Hungary, and he issued another pastoral letter urging the peasantry to remain calm and respect the property rights of their landlords;[27] on the other hand, he stoutly defended the right of the Rumanian nation to organize itself politically and to take part in public affairs as the equals of the Magyars and Saxons. In particular, he gave the lie to charges by Governor Teleki and other officials that the permanent committee was an illegal organization engaged in "subversion." He insisted that the committee was operating in strict conformity with the law and the spirit of the times and pointed out that in concerning itself with the welfare of the Rumanian nation it was simply carrying out the stated intentions of the government itself. It was, after all, he concluded, merely exercising a right that had been granted to all the peoples of Transylvania and its actions had no subversive intent.[28]

The Transylvanian government took such outspoken criticism from an Orthodox bishop because in this time of troubles it appreciated the usefulness of a moderate. Governor Teleki and the Transylvanian Chancellery agreed that Şaguna should be given a seat and a vote in the forthcoming diet as a means of placating the Rumanians, but, because of the confused situation in Vienna, the emperor's sanction, which was necessary for such unprecedented action, could not be secured in time. Nonetheless, an official of the chancellery urged Teleki to ensure Şaguna's presence in Cluj at the opening of the diet and to keep him fully informed of its deliberations as they affected his people.[29]

Şaguna decided instead to return to Sibiu to prepare for his trip to Vienna. On June 1 he met with the consistory to ensure the continuity of administration during his absence, and on the following morning he set out to join his delegation. During a stopover in Buda-Pest he had a fruitful meeting with Archduke Stephen, the Palatine of Hungary, which encouraged him in the belief that the Rumanian program would receive a sympathetic hearing at the court.[30] But upon his arrival in Vienna on June 13 he was dismayed to find his colleagues demoralized and on the verge of returning home. He discovered that part of the delegation had gone to Innsbruck, where the court had taken refuge from the Viennese revolutionaries, and on May 30 had presented the Sixteen Points to Emperor Ferdinand in the form of a petition. Their haste had been dictated by anxiety to forestall imperial sanction of the union, but their mission had been an utter failure. Prime Minister Batthyány had also come to Innsbruck and on June 10 had obtained Ferdinand's sanction of the union as it had been enacted by the Magyar-dominated diet of Transylvania on May 30. On the following day Ferdinand had communicated his decision to the Rumanian delegation and had suggested that as a result of the union their demands had now largely been satisfied. In effect, he had rejected the fundamental premise underlying their whole program, that of national self-determination.

Şaguna refused to accept the emperor's statement as final. He quickly assembled his delegation and persuaded them to submit a new petition which he himself drafted in large part. Because Şaguna realized that the court could not make specific commitments to the non-Magyar peoples of Hungary so long as it felt obliged to appease Magyar nationalism, the new document was couched in rather general terms, but it was no less forceful than the first in its defense of Rumanian nationality. It reaffirmed the Rumanians' conviction that language and nationality were their most precious possessions, and it protested once again that the union of Transylvania with Hungary would eventually lead to the destruction of both: "Have the Rumanians waited four centuries for the day of liberty, equality, and fraternity in so much want and adversity . . . simply to be humiliated at the dawn of the holy day? Are they to be the only ones not legally recognized in a land where they constitute the overwhelming majority? . . . The Rumanians desire to preserve their nationality for all time; they desire to speak their own language and to be heard in it." Justice, they concluded, demanded fulfillment of the Sixteen Points.[31]

A small, select group led by Şaguna returned to Innsbruck and on June 23 were granted an audience. Ferdinand received their petition graciously enough, but simply repeated his earlier statement that the laws enacted by the Hungarian diet—equality of all citizens before the law, freedom of the press, jury trials, proportional taxation, state support of both Rumanian churches and their schools—had already satis-

fied the major points they had raised. He recommended that they negotiate directly with the Hungarian government on matters of detail.[32]

Beset by similar petitions from all sides, the court with some relief
shifted responsibility for the Rumanians onto the Magyars. The Rumanians had traditionally counted for little in the calculations of
Austrian policy makers, who viewed them as a raw mass of peasants incapable of contributing anything of substance to the governance of the
empire. But in the spring of 1848, threatened with the collapse of the
world they knew, these officials discovered uses to which even these
outcasts could be put. At the beginning of June the council of ministers
discussed ways of mobilizing the Rumanians and Slavs to combat the
"aggressive" policies of the Magyars. The minister of finance, Karl von
Krauss, feared that they might, if unchecked, become the dominant
element in the empire. The minister of war, Count Theodor von Latour, broached the possibility of an alliance between the German provinces and those peoples of Hungary who saw their own advantage in
the maintenance of a unitary empire. He suggested that the Rumanians might well serve as the core of this alliance, which might ultimately even enable Austria to extend her influence into the Danubian
principalities.[33] Most of Latour's colleagues approved such a policy in
principle, but because of the dangerous situation in which the empire
found itself, they recommended caution and concessions to the Magyars.

Neither Şaguna nor other Rumanian leaders could perceive the full
extent of the court's duplicity. Şaguna himself took Ferdinand's statement of June 23 as the official inauguration of a new policy toward the
nationalities and tied his own actions to it until the spring of 1849.
Even the permanent committee, which was far more wary than Şaguna
of cooperation with the Austrians, accepted the emperor's declaration
as evidence of good faith and sympathy for the Rumanian cause, and
Gazeta de Transilvania solemnly declared: "His Majesty now guarantees the Rumanians their nationality and all concomitant political
rights."[34]

At the end of June Şaguna together with several members of his delegation travelled to Buda-Pest to participate in the work of the commission on the union. There he had encouraging talks with his friend
from university days, Joseph Eötvös, now minister of education, and
with Count István Széchenyi, whose liberal views on political and nationality questions were widely known and respected by Rumanian

leaders. Their pledges of support convinced Şaguna that the Hungarian government was ready to make substantial concessions to Rumanian national feeling. He made a special effort to establish a friendly rapport with Hungarian leaders, particularly Széchenyi, with whom he had several private meetings and who invited him to the ceremony celebrating the completion of the famous Chain Bridge across the Danube.[35]

The commission on the union held its first meeting on July 16, but, charged as it was with all the problems relating to the amalgamation of Transylvania with Hungary, it got to the nationality question only three weeks later. On August 7 the Magyar majority moved that no additional legislation be proposed to satisfy Rumanian demands, since the new Hungarian constitution of April 25 and the union itself had abolished the old regime in Transylvania and had guaranteed equal civil rights to all citizens. In reply, Şaguna declared such a solution wholly unacceptable to the Rumanians and certain to increase rather than diminish tension in Transylvania. What the Rumanians wanted, he insisted, was specific legislation guaranteeing their nationality, the independence of their two churches, and the use of their language in political and cultural life. Partly because of his forceful statement and partly because of pressure from influential members of the Batthyány ministry, notably Eötvös and Bertalan Szemere, the minister of the interior, the commission decided to go into the matter further.

During this period, in spite of ominous reports from home about government harassment of intellectuals and clashes between peasants and troops, Şaguna appears to have believed that the court and the Hungarian government intended to implement fully the liberal principles proclaimed in March and April and that the function of the commission was simply to work out the details of their application. Impressed by the swiftness with which the old order had yielded to the forces of change from one end of the Continent to the other, he could not conceive of a return to the pre-March status. He revealed his faith in the permanence of the new order by pressing ahead with his plans to restore constitutional government to the Orthodox Church. As a first step he scheduled a general diocesan synod for October 1, to be composed, in accordance with canon law, one-third of clergy and two-thirds of laymen, chosen by electors from each parish.[36] Furthermore, Şaguna was impressed by the Hungarian government's determination

to ensure the complete equality of all Christian churches, as demonstrated by the enactment of appropriate legislation in April, by its apparent intention to provide the Orthodox clergy with a regular subvention as a means of raising its standard of living, and by the frequency
with which Eötvös consulted him on the content of pertinent bills to be
submitted to the diet. In his letters home, both private and pastoral,
he expressed his approval of the new Hungarian constitution and the
legislation proposed to implement it, and he recited the benefits which
had accrued to the Rumanians. Once, he reminded an elderly priest,
the Rumanians, because they were peasants and Orthodox, had had no
rights, but now, as a result of the new "wave of liberty" that had swept
across Europe, they enjoyed the same civil and political rights as their
neighbors and would soon choose their own representatives to the diet.
He also pointed out that they were now members of a free church that
would soon be able to govern itself; that henceforth they would have to
bear only their fair share of taxation and other public burdens; and
that they would enjoy greater opportunities in education, commerce,
and the artisan trades.[37] These confident pronouncements frequently
had an effect opposite to the one Şaguna had intended. Instead of
calming the peasant, they increased his impatience with labor services
and dues. For example, in Sebeş-săsesc, near Sibiu, the Orthodox interpreted one of his pastoral letters as announcing the end of the tithe
paid to the local Lutheran pastor and the Transylvanian treasury,
whereupon they immediately ceased to pay both.[38]

Şaguna's pastoral letters during this period should be read within
the context of his overall policy of conciliation. Convinced that a "period of adjustment" for all the nations of Transylvania would be necessary before they could begin to enjoy the "full fruits of the new liberties," he tried to foster a climate of peace and understanding through
appeals to "higher principles": faith in God, loyalty to the emperor,
obedience to local officials, and Christian charity toward all.[39] In the
face of growing unrest, he warned his faithful to beware of "secret
meetings," popular demonstrations that disturbed public order, and
other "unlawful" acts, which only "brought dishonor to those who
committed them."[40] When he learned that he himself had been impli-
cated in a widespread (though ill-organized) protest movement in
southern Transylvania—that meetings were being convoked in his
name and that instructions, attributed to him, were being circulated

among the people — he thought the matter serious enough to make his
disavowal public. His statement, which was published in *Gazeta de
Transilvania,* offers additional insight into his political philosophy:

I have in the past given my counsel to the people entrusted to my care through pastoral
letters, and I shall continue to do so; I have brought my plans and desires for the happiness of the Rumanian nation before the highest authorities in the land, that is, before those from whom we may expect satisfaction, and I shall continue to do so.

   I therefore desire nothing more fervently than that our whole people shall be at
peace and calm, with confidence that its wishes shall be fulfilled by just and legal
means, which alone can enable us to achieve our goals. But if someone should try to
use force to achieve this goal, not only will he fail, he will bring us total destruction.[41]

In Şaguna's view, then, there was a higher morality operating in politics that rewarded good deeds and honest endeavor and punished violence and evil.

   Events in Transylvania during the late spring and summer of 1848
followed the very pattern Şaguna had hoped could be avoided. Public
order and the brief interlude of harmony among the nationalities collapsed under the weight of the old regime. The pace of change, as
measured by the liberal legislation enacted in Buda-Pest and in Cluj,
was far more rapid than men's ability (or willingness) to adapt to the
new principles of public behavior. The Transylvanian government
persisted in its refusal to recognize the existence of a separate Rumanian nation. In so doing, it represented the attitude of the overwhelming majority of Transylvanian Magyar leaders. Political conservatives
and liberals closed ranks on the question of the union. Even a staunch
conservative like Governor Teleki, who found the union of Transylvania with liberal Hungary extremely distasteful, accepted it as the only
practical means of preserving Magyar supremacy. Not surprisingly, his
government accused the permanent committee in Sibiu of subversion
because of its opposition to the union. There was some basis for the
charge, since neither Bărnuţiu nor the committee as a whole had made
any secret of their true feelings in the matter. But Bărnuţiu (and Şaguna from Pest) argued that the committee was operating well within
the limits of the law, which granted all citizens the right to organize
and participate in public affairs, and, on that basis, they emphatically
rejected Teleki's order to disband.

   The government also suspected the committee of promoting a pan-
Rumanian movement, the alleged goal of which was the creation of a

Daco-Rumanian state extending from the Black Sea to the western boundaries of Transylvania. To be sure, the identity of language, culture, and religion of Rumanians on both sides of the Carpathians had been reinforced in the preceding two decades by increasingly frequent direct contacts: private visits, the emigration of intellectuals from Transylvania to Moldavia and Wallachia, and, especially, the collaboration of Moldavians and Wallachians on *Gazeta de Transilvania* and its literary supplement, *Foaia pentru minte, inimă și literatură*. As a result, there was sympathy and understanding in abundance, and the idea of a united Rumania was certainly present. In a period of rapid and far-reaching political and social change, it was natural for Rumanian intellectuals to speculate on the possibility of their union into a single state, but the government's fears of irredentism on the part of the Transylvanian Rumanians were largely groundless.

The initiative for some sort of pan-Rumanian action seems to have come mainly from the Wallachians. Representatives of the liberal provisional government that had come to power in Bucharest following the overthrow of the Russian-supported regime of Prince George Bibescu in June made various proposals to the Transylvanians. A.G. Golescu and Ioan Maiorescu, representatives of the new Wallachian provisional government, both of whom passed through Transylvania on diplomatic missions to the West, suggested a united Rumania under either Austrian or Russian auspices.[42] In more lyrical terms, Alecu Russo, an exile from the abortive revolution in Moldavia in April, spoke of "one powerful nation, with the sea and two rivers as barricades and with Roman blood in our veins, . . . no longer Moldavia, nor Transylvania, nor the Banat, but only Rumania, with its capital to be named Rome."[43]

In Transylvania such ideas were expressed in strictest confidence, for the members of the permanent committee were anxious to avoid the taint of disloyalty towards Austria, which might irreparably damage their own cause. They showed little enthusiasm for political union as an attainable goal in the foreseeable future, as their practicality—a trait historians do not often associate with the forty-eighters—clearly shone through the haze of idealism. They recognized, in the first place, that the two Rumanian principalities did not give the appearance of strength and stability: the liberal opposition in Moldavia had been quickly squelched, and the existence of the provisional govern-

ment in Wallachia was at best precarious. In the second place, the
members of the permanent committee were conscious of their own
weakness—lack of money and organization, primarily—and were
coming to realize that Austrian aid would be necessary if they were to
surmount the challenge of Magyar nationalism.

In the meantime, the prospects for a peaceful solution of Transylvania's manifold political and social problems became increasingly dim.
By early summer, unrest among the Rumanian peasantry had become
widespread, and in a number of places their frustration gave way to
acts of violence against government officials and landowners. The
main cause was the discrepancy between lofty principles, which raised
the hopes of ordinary men for a better life, and reality, which showed
no slackening of harshness or injustice. The Gubernium announced
that labor services and the tithe would be abolished as of June 18, but
landlords continued to exact dues and services from their peasants
until all the details of emancipation, including indemnification, had
been worked out. Unrest spread rapidly throughout the country.[44] In
political life, too, the ruling classes clung stubbornly to their ancient
privileges. The Rumanians of Sighişoara were shocked to discover that
liberty, equality, and fraternity could not be translated by proportional representation and universal suffrage. It seemed to them that all
their sacrifices had gone for nought when the Saxons took both seats
alloted to Sighişoara in the elections to the Hungarian diet and most
Rumanians were kept from voting by high property or tax qualifications.[45]

Local officials added to the tension by treating any demonstration
or protest as a criminal act, and hence subject to the most severe penalties. The Rumanian parish clergy, both Orthodox and Uniate, became the special object of exasperation on the grounds that they were
fomenting peasant opposition to the government.[46] In general, both
the civil and military authorities mistook the whole movement in the
countryside, particularly the peasants' hunger for land, as "commu-
nism," and arguments to the contrary—that the peasants were inspired
by the "most ardent sense of property," to use Bariţiu's phrase[47]—fell
on deaf ears. When peasants tried to impose their will by force, bloodshed almost invariably resulted, as in the village of Mihalţ, on June 2,
when troops killed twenty-one peasants who had refused to give up
some pastureland to a local landlord.

At this critical time the leadership of the national movement was badly divided. Fundamental disagreements over immediate tasks and long-range policy, which had never been far from the surface ever since the national assembly at Blaj, finally broke into the open over Şaguna's protracted negotiations with the Magyars concerning the union. What especially rankled some members of the permanent committee was the apparently easy acquiescence of the Orthodox higher clergy in the union, and they singled out the consistory in Sibiu as a prime culprit because of the readiness with which it disseminated the decrees of the Hungarian government.[48] In reality the consistory's action implied neither acquiescence in nor support for the union; it was simply carrying out the traditional role of the clergy as the intermediary between the people and the civil authority. Nonetheless, national solidarity inevitably suffered because much of the official material the consistory was obliged to handle stood in direct contradiction to the pronouncements of the intellectuals.

The permanent committee held Şaguna responsible for the consistory's "anti-national" conduct. But it was his own participation in the work of the commission on the union that brought matters to a head. A majority of the committee accused Şaguna, their nominal chairman, of having exceeded his authority by going to Buda-Pest, since his mandate from the national assembly had expired with the presentation of the Sixteen Points to the emperor. They also objected strenuously to the manner in which he had made his decision. He had not bothered to consult the committee beforehand on the question of negotiating with the Magyars — action which to Bariţiu and others signified recognition of the union or, at the very least, a major deviation from the decisions reached at Blaj. Şaguna's "high-handedness" seemed to presage a reversion to the one-man direction of national affairs characteristic of the pre-March era when the bishops did the bidding of the government and ignored the intellectuals. At the end of July Bariţiu and several other committee members, thoroughly exasperated by Şaguna's conduct, drafted a letter of censure and demanded his immediate return home.[49]

Şaguna never saw the letter, since it was never sent, but he was, nonetheless, fully aware of the committee's state of mind. He defended his activities in Buda-Pest by reminding his colleagues of the oath they had all taken on the Field of Liberty to defend their cause by every available means and to remain loyal to the emperor. He considered his participation on the commission on the union both an obligation to the Rumanian nation, because it was good political sense to be present when one's own fate was being decided, and a duty to the emperor, because it was his expressed will. Not only did Şaguna continue to chair the Rumanian delegation on the commission, he also took his seat in the House of Magnates of the Hungarian diet, to which the emperor had appointed him, and served on its committees dealing with the union and the abolition of serfdom.[50]

Şaguna's persistence was not without effect. As the recognized spokesman of Rumanian interests he obtained government intervention in a number of cases involving either his clergy or the peasantry. At his urging, the minister of finance instructed the Transylvanian treasury to end its collection of the tithe, and the minister of justice, Ferenc Deák, agreed to investigate the complaints of three small communes near Turda against their landlord.[51] Such matters were minor, but Şaguna interpreted the government's responsiveness to his requests for action as a sign that the Orthodox (and the Rumanian nation) had already begun to enjoy the fruits of liberty and equality.

Şaguna also thought that he and his colleagues on the commission on the union were making progress towards an understanding with the Magyars. But during its sessions in August he continued to insist that the general law enacted by the Hungarian diet covering civil rights, religious freedom, and related matters, however liberal, was unsatisfactory to the Rumanians. He pointed out that similar legislation in the past, like Law LX of 1791 of the Transylvanian diet, which had guaranteed the Orthodox the free exercise of their religion, had been stillborn, and he demonstrated how the recent Law of Union had failed to bring about genuine equality among the nations of Transylvania, but had instead merely perpetuated the supremacy of the Magyars and Saxons. He insisted that only a specific guarantee of their nationality could satisfy the Rumanians.[52] Outside the commission, Şaguna and his colleagues enlisted the support of Hungarian leaders like Prime Minister Batthyány, who expressed sympathy for the Rumanian cause,[53] and Şaguna himself called on Kossuth to explain the Rumanian position.[54]

On September 27 — after hard bargaining among its own members, and bowing to the urgings of Batthyány and Szemere — the commission approved a bill which recognized the Rumanian nationality and the autonomy of the Orthodox and Uniate churches, allowed the free use of the Rumanian language in village affairs, the church, and elementary and secondary schools, and provided for the appointment of Rumanians to public office in proportion to their numbers.[55]

Owing to the deteriorating situation in Transylvania and the increasingly strained relations between the court and the Hungarian government, a peaceful solution of the nationality problem became daily more remote. In Transylvania the conflict between the government and the permanent committee finally reached the breaking-point in the middle of August, when Miklós Vay, the Hungarian government's special commissioner for Transylvanian affairs, dissolved the committee and ordered the arrest of all its members on the grounds that they were obstructing the lawful union of Transylvania and Hungary. Vay also contemplated the arrest of Şaguna as the titular head of the committee, but finally decided that the case against him was not strong enough. Only two members of the committee were apprehended, and they were soon released when it became apparent to the authorities that their continued detention would lead to large-scale violence.[56] Nonetheless, the government had succeeded in dispersing the committee, which ceased to function until its reconstitution under another form at the end of September.

Even if these events had not intruded upon the work of the commission on the union, it is by no means certain that its bill would have restored peace to the principality. Rumanian intellectuals had gone far beyond language rights and church autonomy in their thinking and would not be satisfied with anything less than *national* autonomy, a matter about which the bill said nothing. The Rumanian members of the commission were aware of its inadequacies and seemed to regard it as merely a first (though important) step towards a resolution of the nationality problem. While accepting it, they declared their intention of seeking the fulfillment of all sixteen articles of their national program.[57]

Further negotiations between the Hungarian government and the Rumanian representatives were halted by the conflict between Buda-Pest and Vienna and the growing enmity between the Magyars and the other nationalities of Hungary. By the beginning of September the general mood had become such that the exhilaration and brotherhood of spring seemed to belong to another century. The battle lines between the two principal antagonists — the Austrian court and the Magyar liberals and nationalists led by Kossuth, who, as a member and, from October 8, chairman of the Committee of National Defense, became the dominant political figure in Hungary — were sharply drawn. Successes against the revolutionaries in Bohemia and in northern Italy between June and August had convinced the court of the efficacy of a similar armed intervention against the Magyar national movement. It found willing allies among the non-Magyar peoples of Hungary, who had come to see their own existence jeopardized by Magyar aspirations. Austrian officials now began seriously for the first time to court the Rumanians along with the Croats, Serbs, and Slovaks. Their interest was mainly military, as a support for the regular army in Transylvania, which was small and inadequate for the tasks it would inevitably have to perform if war broke out. In spite of these limited aims, Austrian commanders unwittingly provided additional stimulus to the national movement in the course of negotiations with Rumanian intellectuals.

In order to rally as wide support as possible for the imperial cause the commanding general in Transylvania, Anton von Puchner, gave his blessing to a second national congress at Blaj at the end of September. Organized by Simion Bărnuțiu and other members of the defunct permanent committee and attended by some six thousand persons, it reaffirmed the Rumanians' total opposition to the union, repudiated the authority of the Hungarian government in Transylvania, and pledged anew their loyalty to the imperial house. But the true significance of the congress lies in its demonstration of growing political self-confidence; Rumanian intellectuals now proposed that the permanent committee be reconstituted as a provisional executive authority, endowed with powers to create an independent civil administration and to convoke a popularly elected, constituent assembly. Once recognized, the new "National Committee" might then establish an autonomous Rumanian duchy in Transylvania.[58] After the congress, on September 30, Bărnuțiu and several colleagues met with Puchner to work out the general principles that should henceforth govern their relations. They agreed to give one another all possible aid in the coming struggle with the Magyars for the control of Tranyslvania, and the Rumanians came away from the meeting convinced that their reward for services rendered would be full political autonomy.[59] But Puchner carefully avoided any reference to a Rumanian nation and refrained from any commitment to support its political aspirations.[60]

Two weeks later, on October 18, Puchner, publicly repudiating the authority of the Hungarian government in Transylvania and its special commissioner, Miklós Vay, proclaimed himself civil governor of the principality and issued an appeal to all its inhabitants to defend the rights of the Habsburg dynasty and their own "liberties" against what he termed a "regime of terror." Rumanian intellectuals responded at once with a call to arms and proceeded, with Puchner's authorization, to recruit a national guard. Far more significant for the development of a tradition of self-government than these military preparations was the organization of a Rumanian civil administration in predominantly Rumanian areas, notably in Hunedoara. Under the chairmanship of Bărnuţiu the national committee took on the attributes of a provisional government and expected Austrian officials to treat it as the sole legal representative of the Rumanian nation. The Rumanians within its jurisdiction did so with alacrity, turning to the *gobern românesc,* as they called it, for the satisfaction of all their needs.

The formation of the national committee was a milestone in the development of the Rumanian national movement. For the first time lay intellectuals took firm control of the movement and in the fall of 1848 seemed well on their way toward giving it an orientation that was secular and Western, and hence at considerable variance with its ecclesiastical traditions. The intellectuals did not regard their alliance with Austria as inconsistent with their principles. In the face of Magyar nationalism, Austrian aid seemed to them the sole means by which they could achieve their national goals, and they still clung to the idea that the Habsburg monarchy would somehow be transformed into a liberal constitutional monarchy.

From Buda-Pest Şaguna had watched with deep misgivings as the crisis developed in Transylvania. Convinced by the end of September that further negotiation would be fruitless, he left for home. In the fall of 1848 his position remained what it had been at Blaj: loyalty to the imperial house. His work on the commission on the union and in the Hungarian diet did not signify an abandonment of this principle. He considered his actions those of a loyal subject of the emperor rather than of a citizen of Hungary, and his pastoral letters from Buda-Pest, as we have seen, were filled with exhortations of loyalty to the throne, but made no similar pleas for the Batthyány ministry. Shortly after his return to Sibiu he offered his full support to Puchner. Miklós Vay appealed to him to use his influence to prevent a complete rupture between their two peoples, but Şaguna refused on the grounds that anything he might do or say would be futile, since the Rumanians would now be satisfied only with complete political equality. A week later, in a pastoral letter dated October 19, he urged his faithful once again to defend the prerogatives of the emperor and to support Puchner's military regime as the only legal government of Transylvania.[61] Vay thereupon suspended him as bishop.

A similar fate befell Lemeni, but at the hands of Puchner. Almost alone among Rumanian leaders he remained sympathetic to the union because of the benefits he thought inclusion in a liberal Hungary would bring to his people. He therefore instructed his clergy and faithful to ignore Puchner's "illegal" seizure of power and to obey only those decrees which came from Commissioner Vay. The Rumanian national committee immediately denounced him, and on November 9 Puchner suspended him as bishop. Lemeni played no further role in the national movement, and after the revolution he was interned in a monastery in Vienna, where he died in 1861.

By the first week of November Puchner appeared to have achieved his immediate goals; his own army and its Rumanian auxiliaries had brought most of Transylvania at least nominally under imperial control. Having no further use for his Rumanian peasant soldiers, whom he had always regarded with suspicion as a potential threat to the existing political and social order, he proceeded at once to disarm them. His subordinates shared his views, and, consequently, relations between the two allies were strained. The national committee repeatedly complained to Puchner about the lack of material support given its army and objected strenuously to the interference of Austrian "advisers" in its own military and civil affairs. All its protests were to no avail, since Puchner had no intention of dealing with the committee as a legal entity.

But Puchner's military position soon deteriorated, and his disdain for the Rumanians proved to be supremely embarrassing. Hungarian forces, quickly regrouping, had taken the offensive, and by the middle of December they had recovered large areas in the central Transylvanian plateau and were threatening the Saxon strongholds of Sibiu and Braşov along the Wallachian border. Puchner was forced again to appeal to the Rumanians for aid, but even in adversity he refused to recognize them as a distinct political entity. He completely by-passed the national committee and turned instead to the Orthodox and Uniate hierarchies. He proposed separate meetings for each for the sole purpose of increasing the Rumanian contribution to the war effort.

But it soon became evident that such a maneuver was impractical, since Lemeni's deposition had deprived the Uniate Church of effective leadership and most Rumanian leaders were determined to separate the national movement from its ecclesiastical connections. Puchner thereupon requested Şaguna to convoke a limited conference of intellectuals and his own protopopes.[62]

Under Şaguna's chairmanship a national conference, the third of the year, met in Sibiu on December 28 with some 250 persons in attendance, including members of the national committee and officers from Puchner's staff. They solemnly reaffirmed their allegiance to the Habsburg dynasty and took an oath of loyalty to the new emperor, Francis Joseph, who had replaced Ferdinand on December 2 in the wake of a quiet court revolution. But they were mainly concerned with their own nation's development, and they used the occasion to restate their attachment to liberalism and the idea of nationality. Şaguna's own opening remarks were in this vein and served as the keynote for the subsequent deliberations. In spite of the critical situation in which they found themselves, he urged them not to lose heart but to preserve their faith in the two "enduring principles" of the age—liberalism and nationalism. The former he defined as a striving toward free political development, and the latter as a unique feeling which bound together all those who belonged to the same ethnic group and spoke the same language. He recognized that these principles had created an "indomitable will" to self-fulfillment in all the peoples of Central Europe, but at the same time he urged his listeners not to treat liberalism and nationalism as "mere abstractions," but to be guided by a higher morality, which he defined as faith in God and obedience to the legal temporal authority.[63]

The delegates then turned to what in their minds was the main business at hand—the drafting of a national program to enlighten the new emperor and his advisers about their political maturity and aspirations. The new document, consisting of thirteen articles, reiterated earlier protests against the union and demanded the dissolution of the Magyar-controlled government in Cluj and its replacement by an interim military administration until peace could be restored and permanent institutions created. Behind these specific demands, which did not differ markedly from the Blaj resolution of May, lay the assumption that an autonomous Rumanian duchy, albeit without fixed boundaries, had already come into being. The conference proposed that the emperor formally recognize its existence by designating the national committee as a provisional government until such time as the Rumanians could organize themselves as a fully constituent part of the empire, and the delegates did not hesitate to order 50,000 rifles for the national guard "on the credit of the Rumanian nation."[64] They obviously assumed that a new monarchy, transformed by the principles of political liberty and national equality, would arise out of the ruins of the old regime and enable all its diverse peoples to develop as they wished. Any other solution to the monarchy's problems seemed to them an absurdity.[65]

Şaguna was chosen to convey these sentiments to the court of Vienna, but before he could leave he was entrusted with a hazardous mission south of the Carpathians. The advance of Hungarian armies under the command of General Joseph Bem had been so precipitous and his victories so overwhelming that it seemed only a matter of time before they would encompass all of Transylvania. Puchner considered his position desperate, and on December 28 he informed Field Marshal Alfred Windischgrätz, commander of all imperial armies facing Hungary, that he wished to call in Russian forces deployed across the Carpathians in Wallachia. Windischgrätz himself had been contemplating similar action ever since Russian armies had occupied Bucharest and dispersed the revolutionary government in September, but he was eager to avoid the embarrassment of having to admit publicly that Austria could not keep order in its own house. Nevertheless, he was not averse to some informal arrangement whereby Russian troops could be used if needed.[66]

Puchner's anxiety was shared by Şaguna and Franz Salmen, the Saxon count, who urged him to seek Russian aid against Bem. Puchner, who was already sending courier after courier to Russian military headquarters in Bucharest, used the ploy suggested by Windischgrätz. Declaring that he had no authority to summon foreign aid, he informed Şaguna and Salmen that they might do so on their own on behalf of their respective nations, but he warned that if the Russians actually crossed the frontier, he would, for the sake of form, be obliged to protest.[67]

Later that same day Şaguna called a meeting of Rumanian and Saxon leaders to discuss the situation. Some members of the national committee were adamantly opposed to the idea of Russian intervention. Their spokesman, Bărnuţiu, argued that the Rumanians on both sides of the Carpathians would ultimately have to pay for the whole operation, since Austria would undoubtedly give Russia a free hand in Moldavia and Wallachia in return for services rendered.[68] Nor did he think that the Rumanians of Transylvania would gain any particular merit in the eyes of the court, since the onus of having called in foreigners would simply be shifted onto them. Bărnuţiu also resented the fact that the Austrians were using the Rumanian nation merely as a tool and had not even seen fit to consult its legal representatives (the national committee), but had, as in the past, engaged in private negotiations with the bishop. Only Şaguna's dramatic intervention saved the plan from defeat. He warned that unless Russian aid was sought at once he would no longer be responsible for the safety of his people and would immediately resign as bishop. Shaken by this unexpected turn of events and, at the same time, somewhat reassured by a hasty note from Puchner that he would not protest the entry of Russian forces into Transylvania and would assume the burden of provisioning them, Bărnuţiu and his colleagues reluctantly gave way.[69] The conference then chose Şaguna and Gottfried Müller, a professor at the Saxon Law Academy in Sibiu, as its representatives to negotiate with General Alexander Lüders, the Russian military commander in Bucharest.

Guided across the mountains to Curtea de Argeş by shepherds from nearby Răşinari and Sălişte, Şaguna reached Bucharest on January 5, 1849. The next day he had a lengthy meeting with Lüders, who expressed sympathy for the Rumanians' plight, but declined to act without specific instructions from St. Petersburg.[70] Şaguna found the atmosphere in Bucharest oppressive; because of his role at the national assembly in Blaj, the Wallachian hierarchy and the members of the new provisional government considered him the leader of the Transylvanian liberals and avoided contact with him in order not to compromise themselves in the eyes of their Russian masters. He rested for a few days and then resumed his travels, this time to Olmütz, in Moravia, where the court had established itself after a new revolutionary outbreak in Vienna. He reached his destination on February 4 after a roundabout journey through Moldavia, Bukovina, and Galicia, to avoid arrest by Hungarian authorities.

Şaguna's arrival in Olmütz set in motion the second, and ultimately tragic, phase of the Rumanian revolution of 1848. During the remaining weeks of February he and a delegation from the recent conference in Sibiu worked ceaselessly to draft an entirely new national program.

The original document they had expected to present to the emperor had been made obsolete by changes in their own political objectives. At Şaguna's urging, Rumanians from Bukovina and the Banat had joined them, and together they had constituted themselves a single delegation representing all the Rumanians of the Habsburg monarchy. The main issue to which they now addressed themselves with a remarkable singleness of purpose was Rumanian political unity and autonomy. There was strong sentiment in favor of both among intellectuals in all three provinces. Şaguna had sounded out opinion in Bukovina during his trip from Bucharest to Olmütz. In Cernăuți he had conferred with the Hurmuzachi brothers, members of a leading Rumanian family, and had obtained their enthusiastic support for the inclusion of their province in a Rumanian duchy. Some members of the delegation had taken the route to Vienna through the Banat expressly to meet with Rumanian leaders there, especially the influential Mocioni family. The result of their discussions was a resolution drawn up in Timişoara on January 16, 1849, demanding the immediate union of all the Rumanians of the Habsburg monarchy.[71]

By the last week of February the new program was ready for presentation at court. It consisted of just eight articles, all of which dealt with a single theme — the establishment of an autonomous duchy encompassing all the Rumanians of the Habsburg monarchy. It reiterated the Rumanians' desire to hold a national congress immediately after the cessation of hostilities in order to set up separate political and ecclesiastical institutions and to elect a chief executive (*Nationaloberhaupt*) and an archbishop, to whom all Rumanian bishops would be subordinate. It also provided for an annual national assembly where all matters affecting the general welfare were to be considered; the introduction of Rumanian as the official language; proportional representation for the Rumanian nation in the imperial parliament; a special commission to advise the court and the council of ministers on Rumanian affairs; and the assumption by the emperor of the title "Grand Duke of the Rumanians."[72] There was one important omission. Şaguna and his colleagues spoke only of a national *administration* and made no mention of a national *territory*. They thereby tacitly acknowledged the impossibility of drawing political boundaries that would separate all Rumanians from the rest of the inhabitants of Transylvania. Instead, they followed the example of the Saxons, who lived commingled with Rumanians and Magyars on the Fundus regius, but who had, nonetheless, preserved their administrative unity through the office of the count and the *Universität,* or central council, which represented all Saxon districts and towns. Although the Rumanians did not press the issue of territory at this time, there can be little doubt that they expected such overwhelmingly Rumanian areas as Hunedoara County to form the nucleus of their new duchy.

No other document before it had expressed so clearly the ideal of Rumanian unity within the Habsburg monarchy. A sense of national solidarity pervades each article and reduces all other issues to secondary importance. On the religious question, for example, its authors drew no distinction between Orthodox and Uniate, nor did they refer to separate ecclesiastical jurisdictions like those of the Orthodox in Transylvania and Bukovina. Instead, their intention was to free the "Rumanian Church," as they called it, from dependence upon both the Serbian Orthodox metropolis of Carlovitz and the Hungarian Roman Catholic archbishopric of Esztergom. The new program also represented an implicit acceptance by the Rumanians of the idea of federalism as the only solution to the monarchy's nationality problems that would allow them sufficient latitude for self-determination. Şaguna's specific contribution to the final text of the document is unknown. The vagueness with which the future organization of the Orthodox Church was treated cannot have pleased him and must, as at Blaj, be ascribed to the pressure exerted by the intellectuals. But the idea of national unity and the plan for a federalized monarchy, as will be seen later, seemed to him consistent with the general course of contemporary historical development.

On February 25 Şaguna and his small delegation presented their petition to Francis Joseph in the name of the "Rumanian Nation of the Grand Principality of Transylvania, the Banat, the adjoining districts of Hungary, and Bukovina." The emperor thanked them for their renewed expressions of loyalty and, as was customary on such occasions, promised to give their desiderata careful consideration. Their views on self-determination and a federalized monarchy had already gained wide support among Croat, Slovak, and Serb leaders, who were busy pressing their own causes on an increasingly hostile court and bureaucracy.

Şaguna and his colleagues left the audience in a sanguine mood, not suspecting that the major decisions affecting their future had already been made in the highest councils of state. A week later, on March 4, a new imperial constitution embodying current official thinking on the nationality problem was promulgated. At first glance, it seemed to satisfy the main Rumanian postulates: article 5 granted all the peoples of the monarchy equality before the law and the right to cultivate their language and nationality without outside interference, and article 71 specifically brought Hungary and Transylvania within the scope of these guarantees. But its omissions were a shattering disappointment to the Rumanians. It contained no mention of a Rumanian duchy or even an allusion to the existence of a Rumanian nation. Instead, it provided for the reestablishment of the historical crownlands like Transylvania, a clear indication that the court did not intend to recognize any new political entities. This neglect was all the more unbearable for the Rumanians because the constitution granted the Serbs of the Voivodina a large measure of autonomy and retained the privileges of the Saxons in the Fundus regius.

Şaguna tried at once to remedy the situation. On the day following the promulgation of the constitution he submitted a detailed memorandum to the council of ministers explaining precisely what the Rumanians had meant by autonomy and how its realization would further both the internal and the foreign policies of the court. The union of all the Rumanians of the monarchy, he argued, was the logical extension of the principle of national equality. To achieve this "primordial right" in Transylvania he proposed that old political boundaries and even national territories be abolished, since under the old regime these had been the means by which one people had kept another in subjection, and recommended that each people, in order to maintain its separate national existence, might then group itself around a central administrative body, like the Saxon *Universität*. Şaguna was at some pains to point out that this was how the Rumanians intended to bring their own duchy into being without infringing upon the rights of the other peoples of Transylvania. He pointed out that such a duchy, once constituted, would be of inestimable value to the monarchy as a counterweight to the other nationalities, particularly the Magyars, and as a link between Austria and the neighboring Rumanian principalities.[73]

Had Şaguna's proposals concerning autonomy been adopted, the centralized monarchy would have been on its way toward some sort of federation of national duchies bound to one another by allegiance to the dynasty and to common imperial institutions. But his explanations were in vain; Austrian officials showed little inclination to satisfy national aspirations. They regarded nationalism—with good reason—primarily as a menace to the territorial integrity and "good order" of the monarchy. If in the constitution of March 4 they had recognized Croatia, the Voivodina, and Transylvania as crownlands, they had done so not to satisfy the desires of their respective peoples for autonomy, but rather to punish Hungary by dismemberment. They had no intention of experimenting with new constitutional forms. Since these new crownlands had had "historical pasts," they could be safely reestablished; a Rumanian duchy, however, had never existed and hence it was presumably not entitled to a "historical present."

At its meeting on March 10 the council of ministers perfunctorily dismissed the whole idea of a Rumanian duchy. It concluded that the foundation of a separate Rumanian territory would violate the new constitution, which had recognized those areas inhabited by the Rumanians—Hungary, Transylvania, and Bukovina—as historical crownlands whose boundaries could be altered only by special legislation. It declared an autonomous administration for civil and church affairs likewise unconstitutional, since the powers sought by the Rumanians had already been granted to the imperial and provincial diets, and recommended that the petitioners turn to these bodies for the settlement of their grievances. Under no circumstances, it concluded, would it treat with Şaguna and his delegation as the plenipotentiaries of the Rumanian nation.[74] Because of the need for continued Rumanian support against the Hungarian armies in Transylvania, the ministers decided to withhold their decision from Şaguna for the time being.

The Rumanians in Olmütz could take little comfort in the military situation or in their relations with the Saxons at home. By the middle of March Bem had captured Sibiu and Braşov and had driven Puchner's army across the Carpathians into Wallachia. The Rumanian national committee had fled Sibiu on March 11, many of its members also taking refuge in Wallachia. The only important resistance to Hungarian armies that remained was confined to the Apuseni Mountains, a great natural fortress in western Transylvania, which Avram Iancu, the chief Rumanian military hero of the revolution, and his peasant militia were to defend successfully until the very end of the war.

Under the impress of defeat and the widespread destruction of lives and property Rumanians and Saxons, nominal allies, indulged in mutual charges and counter-charges. In numerous reports to the court and various ministries in Vienna Franz Salmen, the Saxon count, lamented the annihilation of the Germans of Transylvania, "the bearers of civilization," in the struggle between the "Wallachs" and the Magyars. As fearful now of Rumanian nationalism as he had been earlier of Magyar nationalism, he went so far as to warn that the creation of a Daco-Rumanian empire encompassing the Rumanians on both sides of the Carpathians was close at hand.

Şaguna took the lead in defending the Rumanians at court and used the opportunity to point out the obvious discrepancies between what the imperial constitution had to say about national equality and the actual status of the Rumanians in the Fundus regius. His memoranda to the emperor on March 12 and to the council of ministers on March 23 were buttressed by the traditional arguments of historical right and by the newer devices of population statistics. The Saxons, he declared, were comparative newcomers to Transylvania, for the Fundus regius had already been inhabited by the Rumanians for a thousand years by the time they had settled there in the twelfth century. For this very reason, he continued, the kings of Hungary had decreed that there be complete equality of rights between the original population and the new settlers, but "by force of circumstances" the Saxons eventually secured a privileged status for themselves, which had lasted until 1848. Şaguna warned that the Saxons were determined to maintain their dominant position, in spite of their protestations about national equality and in spite of the fact that, according to their own statistics, they formed only a minority in the Fundus regius — 163,896, to 297,783 Rumanians. Recognition of Saxon jurisdiction over the region, he concluded, would merely perpetuate a life of hardship and injustice for the Rumanians and make lasting peace and prosperity in southern Transylvania unattainable.[75] At the personal level, Şaguna also tried to win the support of Windischgrätz and Puchner for his cause by demonstrating how much greater the Rumanian contribution to the war effort was than that of the Saxons.[76]

All Şaguna's efforts proved futile. His arguments had not the slightest effect on the policies of the court or on the conduct of its representatives. The council of ministers did not deign to acknowledge his memoranda or communicate officially with the Rumanian delegation. Instead, on April 8, the minister of the interior, Franz Stadion, informed Şaguna confidentially of the decisions taken in March and warned of the council of ministers' growing displeasure at the Rumanians' "refractoriness." Stadion was aware of the impact that the rejection of their petition of February 25 would have on the Rumanians, and he tried to soften the blow by pointing out that the constitution had granted "rights, freedoms, and institutions" which offered the Rumanians the "necessary opportunities" to develop their nationality. He suggested that any grievance left unresolved could be dealt with later through established constitutional procedures. Although he seemed to hold out some hope that further negotiations on autonomy might be possible, Stadion made it clear that the initiative was henceforth to come from official quarters, not from the Rumanians themselves, and he advised Şaguna that the best course of action for the Rumanians to follow was loyalty and obedience to the emperor.[77]

Şaguna could make no reply. He was at a loss to explain how the Rumanians could demonstrate their attachment to the dynasty more ardently than they had already done. He was at last convinced that further petitions and memoranda would be to no avail and that the most urgent task that lay before the Rumanians was to establish some sort of "constitutional base" within the monarchy, from which they might continue to develop their unique cultural and spiritual qualities. He thought that the church, as in the past, could best serve this purpose, and consequently, in the following decade, he directed all his energies towards its regeneration. Believing that his mission in Austria was over and had been a failure, he resolved to return home at the earliest opportunity.[78]

His last public effort on behalf of Rumanian autonomy during the revolution came on April 26, when he joined the Croat and Slovak leaders, among them Ivan Mažuranić and Ludovit Štur, respectively, to present a joint petition to the emperor urging the federalization of the monarchy. They argued that the establishment of separate crownlands for each nationality was necessary to achieve the national equality proclaimed in the March constitution, and they expressed dismay at the omission of such a provision from the fundamental law of the land. It seemed to them axiomatic that the foundation of a strong and united Austria must be a federation of equal and autonomous nationalities rather than continued partnership—long-standing but narrow—with the Magyar aristocracy or excessive centralization.[79] As we have seen, the court had already made its decision in the matter, and this newest intrusion of the nationalities into high policy-making went unanswered.

The fighting in Transylvania had taken a dreadful toll on all sides and had made the combatants receptive to peace initiatives. Between April and July several major efforts were made to bring about a cease-fire between Iancu and the Hungarian armies that faced him, but they all came to nought because of the refusal of Kossuth, who now, as governor, headed an independent Hungary, to grant the Rumanians political autonomy. He offered amnesty to all Rumanians except Şaguna, whom he accused of treason, and promised full rights of citizenship and the use of their language in churches and schools, the courts, and local government, but he obstinately refused to "compromise" the political unity of Hungary.[80] He was now prepared to go the limit in achieving Magyar national aims, since the Hungarian parliament, at his urging, had proclaimed the deposition of the Habsburgs on April 14.

It was only on July 29, in the last days of liberal Hungary, that the diet finally enacted into law the bill proposed by the commission on the union the previous September. It was an act of desperation, for Austrian and Russian armies, which had finally intervened on a large scale in May, were closing in on the few remaining Hungarian strongholds and had rendered their opponents' military position utterly hopeless. Iancu in a letter to Kossuth on August 3 acknowledged the gesture, but sadly pointed out that it had come too late:

We keenly regret that present circumstances make negotiations for the restoration of peace with our Hungarian brothers impossible. Our position is too difficult: Hungarian forces are far away, and Russian armies are steadily advancing. Moreover, much time and effort would be needed to reawaken friendly feelings toward you in our people. Nevertheless, in the coming struggle, to prove the genuineness of our esteem for the Hungarian nation, we have decided to remain neutral. We shall not attack Hungarian troops unless they attack us.[81]

What is striking is Iancu's use of the term "brothers" in addressing the Magyars, after almost nine months of bitter warfare. Like most of his colleagues, he had preserved his respect for Magyar liberalism and had not allowed his opposition to the nationality policies of the Hungarian government to turn itself into hatred for the Magyar people.

Ten days later, on August 13, the main Hungarian field army surrendered at Világos, and by the end of the month all organized resistance had ceased. In Transylvania a host of Austrian officials, led by the new governor, General Ludwig Wohlgemuth, descended upon the principality with orders to restore it to the status of an imperial province as quickly as possible. Their activities inaugurated the so-called "Decade of Absolutism," which was to last until 1859 and was temporarily to alter the direction of the Rumanian national movement.

3 / Absolutism

Şaguna returned to Transylvania at the end of August 1849. As he traversed the principality on his way to Sibiu unimaginable scenes of destruction confronted him in village after village. It seemed to him that his church had been a special object of the war's fury. Many parish churches had been demolished or badly damaged—later he calculated the number at nearly three hundred; books, icons, and other religious objects had been destroyed or carried off; at least twelve priests had been killed and uncounted numbers forced to flee their parishes.[1] In Sibiu his own residence lay in ruins, having been used by Bem's troops as a barracks. Şaguna's library of some three thousand volumes, his personal papers, and almost the entire archive of the Orthodox Church had been reduced to ashes. This assault on the church, as he characterized the war, had not only disrupted normal religious life throughout the diocese but had also caused the suspension of all educational activities, since the church was responsible for maintaining the village school and providing its teacher. To Şaguna, therefore, the revolution had been nothing less than a catastrophe; it had swept away the modest reforms he had introduced as vicar and obliged him now to begin all over again with greater handicaps than before. The physical effects of the war continued to be felt for many years; as late as the fall of 1851, for example, scores of churches remained closed for want of ritual books and priests.[2]

Şaguna was eager to begin the work of rebuilding, and he looked forward to a new era of cooperation between his church and the imperial government, based upon the principle of national equality enunciated in the March 4 constitution. Although he had given up hope of achieving the specific political goals he and his colleagues had sought during the revolution, notably national autonomy, he expected the court and especially the new government of Transylvania to treat the Rumanian nation and the Orthodox Church as full partners in the Transylvanian community. But the regime that installed itself under Governor Wohlgemuth in the fall of 1849 showed little inclination to accept any of the lessons of the revolution.

The actions of the military government in Transylvania corresponded to the general aims of Alexander Bach, the Austrian minister of the interior, who had assumed primary responsibility for the formulation of domestic policy. Initially, he seems to have felt a genuine obligation to satisfy the aspirations of the Rumanians to national equality and progress. His report to the emperor in early September on the future status of the Rumanians proposed that ways be found to enable them to enjoy in equal measure the constitutional rights guaranteed to all the peoples of the monarchy. He even went so far as to acknowledge a moral debt to them because of their services to the imperial cause during the revolution, but his motivation was practical: they had awakened to a "consciousness of their numerical superiority" and, if not handled properly, they might become a serious impediment to the restoration of order in Transylvania.[3]

In spite of a desire to satisfy the requests of the Rumanians at least partially, neither Bach nor any of his colleagues thought of inviting them to take part in determining their own future. Instead, the ministers empowered Wohlgemuth and his staff and the new imperial commissioner for Transylvania, Eduard Bach, to gather information about the status and needs of the Rumanians and to make recommendations for action. Bach justified this procedure on the grounds that the Rumanians were still essentially a *Bauernvolk,* who were so little developed intellectually and politically and who possessed so few men fit for public office that they could under no circumstances be expected to manage their own affairs. He and his associates considered the mass of the peasantry a highly volatile force requiring the strictest control and supervision—tasks formerly entrusted to the Orthodox and Uniate clergies. However, because of their leading role in the revolution and the obvious social and economic interests that bound them to the great mass of the population, they, too, particularly the parish clergy, were highly suspect. Yet they fared better than the intellectuals, against whom Austrian officials—who regarded them as the chief carriers of nationalism—allowed the police apparatus to exercise its full powers.

Bach's modest proposals concerning the Rumanians begot modest results. The Rumanians (and the Slavs, too) counted for little in the minds of Viennese policy-makers, and in the press of restoring the old regime their interests were largely ignored. In Austrian domestic affairs officials concerned themselves mainly with the creation of an efficient administration that would preserve the essential features of the monarchy which had prevailed as far back as the reign of Joseph II. In foreign affairs their main objectives were to restore the monarchy's position as a major power and, particularly, to reassert its supremacy in Germany. Inevitably perhaps, such a regime underestimated the importance of the nationality concept. It had, in fact, no nationality policy at all except the subjugation of Hungary and the thwarting of Magyar (and other) national aspirations. Even these aims were pursued haphazardly and with little thought for the future, and no attempt was made to fashion the Rumanians and Slavs into permanent counterweights to the Magyars. Not surprisingly, therefore, the hallmarks of the system that came into being in the fall of 1849 and the spring of 1850 were centralism, absolutism, and Germanization.[4]

The restoration in Transylvania exhibited all these characteristics. Wohlgemuth was energetic and even well intentioned, but he had little understanding of the complex nature of Transylvanian society, and within a short time he had succeeded in alienating Magyars, Saxons, and Rumanians alike. He seems to have been aware that a nationality problem existed — he described it as "national rivalry" — but he had no plan for dealing with it except to reduce everyone to the same level of obedience. As governor, his will was law. The state of siege, which had been proclaimed in September 1848 and was not to be lifted until December 1854, gave him almost unlimited powers. He was not responsible to the local population, nor was he bound to respect their laws and customs, and there was no appeal from his decisions except to the various ministries in Vienna or to the emperor himself.[5] Even after 1854, the governor's authority remained undiminished, since the government of the principality was provisional until 1860. No diet was summoned during the decade, nor did any other form of consultation with the public, however limited, take place.

The governor relied, rather, upon a host of subordinates to carry out his orders, including an executive council composed of the heads of various departments, a large bureaucracy, the regular army, and the gendarmerie. The most important positions were held by Austrians: a Glanz was in charge of finance, a Weiss of justice, a Häufter of education. Other posts, including those at the *Kreis* (district) level, were also filled by imperial functionaries imported for the most part from Bohemia, Moravia, Bukovina, and Galicia.[6] They had been chosen for their experience and knowledge of German, but they were generally ignorant of the languages and customs of the people they

were supposed to govern, and their appearance in Magyar, Rumanian, and even Saxon villages caused consternation and confusion.[7]
Administratively, Transylvania was divided into ten counties, which
were subdivided into seventy-nine Kreise and six urban departments.
Their boundaries had been drawn by the new bureaucracy, which took
little formal note of nationality; the Magyars and Saxons, nonetheless,
fared better than the Rumanians and succeeded in preserving some
semblance of their pre-1848 administrative and territorial unity. The
core of provincial administration was the Kreis, headed by a prefect
whose powers extended to the smallest details of everyday life and who
was directly responsible to the governor.[8] His chief function was to
maintain order and discipline, and he permitted no activity, especially
one with nationalist overtones, which might excite passions or disturb
the tranquility of his district.

Rumanian intellectuals found the new order unbearable. It dashed
their hopes for national autonomy and liberal political institutions and
seemed to be a reversion to the former system of three privileged nations. They found many reasons to be discontented with their lot. The
Magyars, Saxons, and Szeklers had preserved something of their old
territories, while numerous Rumanian communities, denied a unity of
their own, were incorporated into the new entities. The Saxons seemed
to them especially fortunate. The boundaries of the Fundus regius survived largely intact, and the Sibiu Kreis was even expanded to include
a number of Rumanian villages, which now came for the first time
under Saxon jurisdiction.[9] The organization of the judiciary also
seemed to perpetuate the subservience of the Rumanians to their
neighbors. In August 1849 senates, or supreme courts, were established for the Magyars and Saxons which gave every indication of
carrying on their respective legal traditions. When Rumanian intellectuals suggested that such partiality violated the principle of national
equality enunciated in the constitution, the government excused itself
on the grounds that a separate senate for each nationality would be too
heavy a burden for the state treasury. Access to public office also
seemed easier for Magyars and Saxons. In the whole central bureaucracy of the principality at the beginning of the decade there were only
three Rumanians: an Orthodox and a Uniate school inspector and a
translator for the official gazette. At the district level few Rumanians
held positions of responsibility, even where the population was largely
Rumanian. In Zarand County, for example, all new appointments

were given to Germans from Bukovina or to Saxons, and in Blaj Kreis, the center of the Rumanian national renaissance for over a century, no Rumanian could hope to be appointed prefect. Everywhere German was a prerequisite for high public office.[10]

The intellectuals refused to accept anything less than national autonomy. Even as the fighting drew to a close in the summer of 1849 and the victory of the imperial idea over liberalism and nationalism could no longer be in doubt, they clung to the hope that the court meant what it had said about national equality and would recognize their right to self-determination.[11] As the true state of things gradually became apparent, their mood changed. They were at first shocked and then angered at what they regarded as Austria's ingratitude and perfidy, and in the fall of 1849 they organized a protest movement of considerable proportions. Its leaders were those who had distinguished themselves during the revolution: Bărnuţiu, Bariţiu, August Treboniu Laurian, a native Transylvanian who had taught for a number of years in Bucharest, Iancu, and Papiu-Ilarian among the laymen, and Simion Balint, a Uniate priest from the Apuseni Mountains, and Ioan Popasu, Orthodox protopope of Braşov, among the clergy. They and their supporters organized meetings of protest from one end of Transylvania to the other at which petitions to the emperor and the council of ministers were drawn up and proxies circulated recognizing Şaguna, Bărnuţiu, Laurian, Popasu and others as official representatives of the Rumanian nation. The wide distribution of these documents owed much to the diligence of Orthodox and Uniate priests whose respective networks of protopopates and parishes provided an efficient means of communication. In some areas protests bid fair to erupt into violence, as peasants hoarded weapons in anticipation of clashes with the army.[12]

The intellectuals were also busy on other fronts. They made good use of *Gazeta de Transilvania* and *Foaia pentru minte, inimă şi literatură* to inform their people of their rights and to arouse them to action.[13] Bariţiu was eager to prove the importance of the Rumanian contribution to the Austrian victory in Transylvania and proposed to publish in full the final reports of Avram Iancu and other Rumanian military commanders to the emperor. Many intellectuals established themselves in Vienna, where they repeatedly made the rounds of the various ministries in an attempt to change the course of events in Transylvania. The Minister-President Felix Schwarzenberg, Alexander

Bach, and others listened to them politely, but to the intellectuals' chagrin they knew nothing of the national program drawn up on the Field of Liberty in 1848 and had not read the reports of Iancu and his comrades. All the Rumanians' efforts were to no avail, for, as Laurian remarked: "They have promised to do their best for us; they ask only that we have faith in the government. The same old story."[14]

Austrian authorities were in no mood for disobedience. In Transylvania Wohlgemuth reacted to the protest movement with characteristic forcefulness. Orthodox and Uniate priests, whom he accused of being the "ringleaders" of "secret meetings" and "political conspiracies,"[15] became the special object of his displeasure. Large numbers were taken into custody for interrogation about their political activities and opinions, and some were imprisoned for as long as a year until they could demonstrate their innocence of any crime, usually by producing a "certificate of good conduct" from a church superior, a village elder, or a responsible civil official.[16] There was some truth in Wohlgemuth's accusations—the Rumanian clergy were, in fact, extremely active in the fall of 1849—but involvement in politics, far from having a subversive intent, was an exercise of their age-old authority as the leaders of their villages. Now, as during the revolution, they worked closely with the lay intellectuals and performed valuable services for the national cause. For example, they were chiefly responsible for collecting signatures on petitions and proxies[17]—the only way the Rumanians could choose their representatives and make known their desires, since they lacked political institutions of their own and had been forbidden to hold a national congress.

The intellectuals were more suspect than the clergy because of their uncompromising national sentiments and their relations with Moldavian and Wallachian liberals. In Transylvania they were kept under constant surveillance by the gendarmerie—even Şaguna was no exception[18]—and some, like Avram Iancu, were arrested and interrogated a number of times about their activities during the revolution and their political aims.[19] The police carried out frequent searches of private homes for incriminating letters and books, and as late as the fall of 1850 a country-wide search was instituted for brochures printed in Vienna by Rumanian students containing Bărnuţiu's address at Blaj in May 1848.[20] In Vienna, which for a few months in the fall of 1849 became the headquarters of the national movement, the intellectuals fared no better. Bărnuţiu, Laurian, and a number of their colleagues were interrogated by the police and ordered to leave the city when their temporary residence permits expired. When Bariţiu condemned these "abuses of authority" in print, Wohlgemuth ordered *Gazeta de Transilvania* to cease publication on March 9, 1850.[21]

By the fall of 1850 the intellectuals had finally accepted defeat. Their failure to achieve self-determination was all the more bitter, since they had already experienced it briefly under the national committee and had come to expect it as both a natural right consonant with the new principles of the age and a just reward for their defense of the dynasty. Papiu-Ilarian gave eloquent testimony to their feelings in a letter to George Bariţiu: "We shed our blood for the emperor and our nation, not for medals or money. Forty thousand Rumanians died and three hundred villages were burned to save the throne, but in return we groan under the same tyranny as before. Indeed, our position is more unbearable than before 1848; at least then we had not yet tasted liberty. But now we have and we have sacrificed for it and still it is denied us."[22]

In spite of their momentary discouragement and recognition of failure, the intellectuals' national feeling had in no way been diminished. On the contrary, the idea of nationality had emerged out of the recent conflict as the dominant spiritual force among Rumanian intellectuals, a place it was to have until the union of Transylvania with the kingdom of Rumania in 1918. It gave meaning to their lives and endowed them with a sense of mission every bit as strong as that felt by the devout Christian.

The revolution for them must not be judged a "turning-point at which modern history failed to turn"; their own social and political thought had matured quickly under the impress of rapid and dramatic change. They were no longer the same men they had been in the Vormärz. Their experience had helped to clarify their thinking about the direction their movement should take. The idea of autonomy, both political and cultural, had been firmly implanted in their consciousness, for the events through which they had lived had accustomed them to think in terms of self-determination. Their attitude toward Austria and the Habsburg dynasty, consequently, was never the same as it had been before 1848. Subsequent national programs would speak insistently about national equality, liberal political institutions, and federalism — all expressions of a political awareness that could no longer be satisfied with a passive role in public affairs. Paradoxically,

Rumanian intellectuals came out of the revolution with an enhanced confidence in their ability to manage their own affairs; the *gobern românesc* had demonstrated, at least to their satisfaction, their capabilities of self-government. Matters had gone well enough during those few months to convince them that their nation could achieve genuine progress only if it were free to determine its own future under its own leaders. To achieve their goals they turned from a preoccupation with abstract principle to practical questions of political organization and economic development, matters which increasingly absorbed their energies down to 1918.

Under the prevailing conditions of absolutism any attempt at political organization was certain to bring swift reprisals. Consequently, the forty-eighters turned to cultural and intellectual pursuits as the best means of fortifying the national spirit. But writing and publishing in that spirit, however moderate, proved difficult, as the editors of Bărnuţiu's speech at Blaj in May 1848 and Alexandru Papiu-Ilarian, who wrote a two-volume history of the Rumanians, discovered.[23] Both works were confiscated by Austrian officials in Transylvania on the grounds that they would rekindle national passions. The Transylvanian government also showed little favor toward new institutions, which, to its way of thinking, might produce similar results. Hence, neither a Rumanian literary society nor a law academy, both ardently desired by the intellectuals, could gain official sanction.[24]

It is indicative of the nature of the Rumanian national movement in Transylvania that the intellectuals in their frustration turned not to revolution to achieve their ends but rather to the law. The young forty-eighters, like Papiu-Ilarian and Ioan Raţiu, the future president of the Rumanian National Party, took up the study of law, while a few of the older generation, notably Bărnuţiu, returned to it. Their studies must not be thought of as an extension of the Enlightenment into the middle of the nineteenth century. They indeed respected learning for its own sake, but they no longer shared the naive faith of their fathers in it as the ultimate key to human happiness. Their preoccupation with knowledge was more pragmatic: they envisioned a large body of men trained in the law who would occupy important positions in the imperial bureaucracy, serve as the new, "modern" leaders of the national movement, and, when the time came, provide the personnel for a self-governing Rumanian province. Creating such a force was to have been the task of a Rumanian law academy, but until it came into being, they

looked to universities elsewhere in the monarchy — chiefly in Vienna
and Padua — and the Saxon Law Academy in Sibiu to serve their purposes. Even in these endeavors, it was the idea of nationality that sustained them and infused their routine studies with a sense of mission.
Bărnuţiu stated their feelings precisely when he wrote to Papiu-Ilarian
from Padua in 1852: "We did not come to Italy simply to study the
Corpus juris and the Austrian code, but rather to see with our own eyes
and bring back little chips from the family tree to our hearths in Dacia
in order to keep the embers of our nationality burning."[25]

In a sense, the intellectuals also turned to the church. They had no
interest in theology or, as one of them put it, "the hairsplitting of scho-
lastics about purgatory," but they were deeply concerned about the
Orthodox and Uniate churches as social institutions. As the only truly
national institutions they possessed, they were eager to expand the
churches' role in the national movement. They were disgusted with
Orthodox-Uniate strife and demanded that the two clergies set aside
their "petty" differences and work together to promote the national interest; as an article in *Foaia pentru minte* put it: "We are fully convinced that neither the union with Rome nor the lack of union, but
rather the national and patriotic spirit will save the Rumanians from
their enemies."[26]

Throughout this turbulent first year of absolutism Şaguna had to
adjust to an entirely new role. The revolution had thrust him into the
forefront of Rumanian political life, a position he was to have for
nearly two decades. In the absence of any sort of political organization
and with the Uniate Church still leaderless because of Lemeni's deposition, the intellectuals appealed to him, as chairman of the Rumanian
delegation in Olmütz and Vienna, to take the lead again in pressing
their cause at court. That he was willing to carry out the duties demanded of a national leader cannot be doubted, but he had first of all
to reconcile the aims of the conflicting forces around him with his own
conceptions about the church, the nation, and the monarchy.

To the immediate question of whether to carry on the protest movement he gave a negative answer. His observations of the political scene
in Vienna in the spring and summer of 1849 had convinced him that
further delegations and petitions would not change the course of
events; he could see no benefit from keeping the people in a state of
constant agitation by promises of things that could not be.[27] But his
refusal to accept the political role the intellectuals offered him did not

signify his abandonment of politics or of the national cause. On the contrary, the goals he had set for himself required his many-sided involvement in temporal affairs. He had already conceived the broad principles of a social and political philosophy that was to guide him for the rest of his life. It was, as he himself described it, an activist philosophy that demanded of the church and its clergy participation in every phase of public life as the means of creating the proper conditions for a true Christian life. He also had great respect for historical continuity and felt keenly the responsibilities he had inherited from his predecessors to defend the Rumanian nation and make it prosper. His own extroverted nature seems to have found a certain fulfillment in politics, and his reputation as a master of the art was well deserved. He was never satisfied with the role of a mere bystander, but felt compelled to be an actor in his own times.

An analysis of Şaguna's role in public life — cultural and political — must begin with the fact that he was a Christian, for whom the teachings of the church had never lost their validity, and that he was, before all else, a man of the church, who viewed his own role in society primarily as one of fulfilling his responsibilities as bishop. He never wavered in the belief that the church through its moral and spiritual teachings was the decisive influence on the development both of the individual and of society as a whole. But he was equally convinced that the Rumanian Orthodox Church in the Habsburg monarchy had never succeeded in doing for the Christian and the Rumanian what the Creator had meant it to do. He attributed this failure largely to the unsettled legal status of the church and its lack of autonomy. As a result, over the centuries it had drifted first one way and then another, subject always to the dictates of changing political conditions and the prejudices of other churches. The supreme task to which he dedicated his episcopate was, therefore, the establishment of Orthodoxy on a strong constitutional foundation, an achievement, he was certain, that would eliminate all the ambiguities in its relationship to the state, the other churches of Transylvania, and the Serbian metropolis of Carlovitz.

His efforts centered on the restoration of the Orthodox metropolis of Alba Iulia as it had existed before the Union with Rome, but he made the establishment of a proper relationship with the state a prerequisite for any substantial constitutional or cultural reform within the church. In his view, the state was bound to recognize the "right" of the church to manage its own purely religious affairs and to administer its charitable and educational institutions without interference from the civil authority or the officers of another church.[28] But he rejected the idea of the separation of church and state; separation was an impossibility, since, in his words, "the church [is] in the state, and the state [is] in the church, and the Christian [is] a citizen and the citizen [is] a Christian." The ideal relationship between state and church was, then, one of harmony and cooperation in the building of a vigorous and enlightened Christian community. Under this arrangement the state furthered the aims of the church by providing material support for its clergy and its schools, while the church urged upon its faithful due obedience to the legally established temporal authority, payment of taxes, and defense against the enemies of the state.[29]

In church-state relations as well as in all other social and political questions Şaguna's guide was the law as established by imperial decree or parliamentary legislation. He insisted upon respect for the law as the only means by which a true constitutional system could be created and maintained. Moreover, as the leader of a numerous body of Christians and as the chief executive of an important social institution in a Christian state, he considered it both his sacred and his legal duty to work within the existing political framework. As a political realist confronted by the new absolutism, he counselled against open defiance as merely an invitation to Wohlgemuth and his gendarmerie to indulge in further acts of repression. His pastoral letters during this period exhorted his faithful to refrain from acts of violence and to await the satisfaction of their grievances by legal means, and in private he tried to dissuade the intellectuals from drawing up petitions and manifestoes, which, in his view, could not achieve their purpose and would merely antagonize the authorities at home and, more seriously, damage their cause at court.[30]

Şaguna had an even more compelling reason for his attempts to reconcile the intellectuals to the monarchy, however justified he considered their protests against the absolutist form it had assumed. From his readings in the history of Transylvania and his knowledge of its institutions he had become convinced that the destiny of the Rumanians had been inextricably linked to the Habsburg dynasty ever since the establishment of its rule over Transylvania at the end of the seventeenth century and that the dynasty held the key to the successful development of the Rumanian nation and of Orthodoxy. In his view, it alone was capable of bringing about a satisfactory solution of the nationality problem in all its ramifications. He reasoned that the emperor stood above local partisan struggles, like the nationality conflict in Transylvania, and had the general welfare of the monarchy always in view. At the same time, he was so thoroughly convinced of the justice of the Rumanians' and the other nationalities' claims to self-determination that he had no doubt that the dynasty would eventually recognize its own self-interest in satisfying them.

Şaguna proposed to fulfil the aspirations of the nationalities through constitutional means. During the revolution he had come to see in the federalization of the monarchy the most effective way of harmonizing the interests of the dynasty and the nationalities, and he must, therefore, be counted among the earliest Rumanian advocates of "Greater Austria," an idea which was to gain wide currency among Rumanian (and many Slav) political leaders at the turn of the century. His conception of "united Austria," to use his words, combined elements of both centralism and federalism. He was, for example, eager to extend a uniform Austrian law code or constitution to the whole monarchy as a means of eliminating local privileges which, in his mind, had lost all validity in the modern age and were merely obstacles to social progress. At the same time, he wished to preserve a sufficient degree of provincial autonomy to allow the several nationalities to pursue their own development in accordance with their distinctive character and within the general historical and geographical framework that had become an integral part of their existence. This was the main reason for his advocacy of Transylvanian autonomy and his efforts to instill a "Transylvanian consciousness" in all the inhabitants of the principality. But he had to postpone any serious attempt to realize these ends until the 1860s, when liberal political activity was once again tolerated.

Şaguna's loyalty to the dynasty and his support of the idea of Greater Austria did not imply acquiescence in the type of regime that had installed itself in Transylvania. At first, he regarded absolutism as an aberration or, at worst, a temporary ill occasioned by the complete breakdown of public order during the final months of the revolution. But after a year's experience of it, he judged that Wohlgemuth had little intention of respecting either the spirit or the letter of the March 4 constitution. In a comprehensive memorandum to one of the ministries in Vienna in July 1850[31] he condemned the absolutist tendencies of the regime in the strongest terms as the antithesis of national equality and as deliberately discriminatory against the Rumanians. He pointed out

that—the revolution, the constitution, and the will of the emperor
himself notwithstanding—the three nations had managed to preserve
their hegemony in Transylvania by means of separate territories, their
own law codes, and, to a great extent, their own local officials and languages of administration. The Rumanians, on the other hand, whom
he classified as the most numerous of all the nations of Transylvania
and the most loyal to the dynasty, had been completely ignored and
were in danger of falling permanently under the tutelage of their former masters, divided up as they were among so many "foreign" jurisdictions. He suggested that if genuine peace and order were the ultimate goals of the new regime, then the quickest way to achieve them
was through the introduction of genuine national equality. There was
no reply.

Perhaps Şaguna did not expect one. In any case, by the summer of
1850 he had decided to wage a campaign of his own against Wohlgemuth, whom he held responsible for abuses of authority that amounted
in his mind to a deliberate policy of terror designed to stifle any expression of ideas critical of the new regime. He had been shocked by the repeated spectacle of soldiers leading intellectuals and priests through
the streets of Sibiu on their way to interrogation or prison on the flim-
siest of charges, and he was dismayed by the suspicion which sur-
rounded his own activities. The abuses of which he had first-hand
knowledge were legion. First of all, there was the general antipathy
displayed by local officials, of whatever nationality, toward the Rumanians and, in particular, their priests, which expressed itself in a refusal to conduct business in any language except German or Magyar
and in the application of complicated procedures for settling even the
simplest cases. Then, there were frequent acts of physical brutality in
the conduct of investigations, a practice which drew repeated demands
from Şaguna that Wohlgemuth punish those responsible.[32]

Relations between Şaguna and Wohlgemuth finally reached the
breaking-point over the latter's continuous meddling in internal
church affairs. Şaguna objected strenuously to the imprisonment of his
priests without trial and the dispersal of parish meetings because of alleged anti-government activities. He pointed out that it was customary
in his church for priests and their faithful to meet regularly to discuss
the whole range of church problems from finance to education; if they
touched upon the issues of the day, which he admitted was more than
likely, they were simply exercising the right of association guaranteed

by the constitution. He warned that Wohlgemuth's strong-arm tactics were undermining the confidence of his clergy and the great mass of the peasantry in the government and diminishing their respect for the law. He confessed that he himself had come to doubt the integrity of local administrative bodies because their actions reminded him of earlier times when the whole apparatus of government had been used to oppress the Rumanian nation.[33] Wohlgemuth, in turn, accused the Orthodox clergy of subversion and, suggesting that Şaguna's behavior was encouraging "political machinations," took it upon himself to tell Şaguna what his duties as bishop were. This was the last straw. In a face-to-face meeting Şaguna bluntly told Wohlgemuth that his accusations were lies and that he, Şaguna, was the bishop of his church and would tolerate no usurpation of his authority.[34] When Şaguna went to Vienna in October 1850 to attend a conference of Orthodox bishops he complained personally to several ministers about Wohlgemuth's behavior. Finally, in February 1851, the accumulated mass of evidence persuaded the court that Wohlgemuth's heavy-handedness had outlived its usefulness, and he was recalled.

Şaguna was not satisfied merely to protest. Within a few months after his return home in August 1849 he had begun to put into effect a plan designed to enable the Rumanians to take what he considered their rightful place in the public life of Transylvania and, eventually, in the monarchy as a whole. He thought it essential, first of all, that the court's attitude toward the Rumanians be changed. In order to demonstrate that they were an element of order and stability and were steadfast in their loyalty to the throne, he proposed that Rumanian "advisers" be appointed in all the ministries to keep officials informed about what the Rumanians were thinking and thereby eliminate the long-standing dependence of Austrian officials upon the "misinformation" of those "foreigners" (presumably Magyars and Saxons) who wished the Rumanians only ill.

Şaguna realized that the improvement of one's image depended mainly on externals; his primary concern was, rather, to improve the actual quality of Rumanian life. He attempted to instill in the ordinary citizen a sense of civic responsibility and an appreciation of his worth and accomplishments as a member of the Rumanian nation. To bring about this substantial change in the popular mentality he tried to create a feeling of belonging and contributing to some larger social framework beyond the narrow (in his view) limits of the nation. He therefore advocated the broadest possible participation of the people in the political life of Transylvania and the monarchy generally. As a beginning, he urged a reduction in the property qualifications for voting which would enable large numbers of Rumanian peasants at last to have a voice in matters that vitally affected their welfare. He considered such experience the foundation of self-government, which he thought could not be long delayed.

It was axiomatic to Şaguna that if a people aspired to greatness it must possess a consciousness of its own worth, a quality he thought lacking among the Rumanians. He admitted that such a consciousness could be cultivated among the well-educated by historians, but again he was concerned about the broader masses of the population and tried to offer them some tangible sign of national accomplishment. Such thoughts were behind his efforts to memorialize the heroism of Avram Iancu and his peasant soldiers during the revolution by erecting a suitable monument to them in the Apuseni Mountains. Wohlgemuth approved a public subscription to raise money,[35] but the project could not be realized in Şaguna's lifetime because funds for it were lacking.

For similar reasons of national pride he fought against the dissolution of the Rumanian border regiments. They had been established in 1763 along the frontier between Transylvania and the Rumanian principalities, and during the revolution of 1848 they had adhered to the national program drawn up at Blaj; but they had also been steadfast in their loyalty to the crown.[36] In a memorandum of July 22, 1850, Şaguna defended them against charges that they had been responsible for the disasters suffered by Puchner in the winter of 1848.[37] He admitted his own lack of expertise in questions of miliary strategy, but he suggested that the real causes of the defeat of imperial armies were their inadequate soldiers and supplies and the failure of their commanders to judge the strength of the enemy accurately and carry on the war with enough vigor and imagination. He insisted that the Rumanian border regiments had fought as well as could have been expected under these conditions and had remained true to their oath of loyalty to the emperor, in spite of all inducements by the Hungarian government to join its cause. Şaguna suspected that they had been singled out for blame simply because they were Rumanian, and he asked why they were being held responsible for the shortcomings of others. His memorandum was never answered in writing, but on January 22,

1851, the court made its point by abolishing the military frontier in Transylvania and by replacing the border regiments with regular infantry and cavalry.

While acknowledging the importance of self-respect, Şaguna put his hopes for the progress of the Rumanian nation in more tangible accomplishments: the improvement of their material conditions of life and the strengthening of their spiritual and intellectual culture. To accomplish the first, as a beginning, he did his utmost to protect the peasant from the cupidity of his landlord and the prejudices of the bureaucracy. In December 1849 he urged Wohlgemuth to revive the old institution of the *pauperum advocatus,* under which a peasant too poor to hire a lawyer could obtain legal advice in drawing up petitions and other official papers. He proposed that a Rumanian with a knowledge of Magyar and German be appointed to head this office, since the great majority of the peasantry were Rumanian, and that he have an adequate staff to assist him. Wohlgemuth was unmoved; he considered such an official superfluous in view of the fact that his own chancellery had made "adequate provision" for aiding petitioners.[38] Şaguna also wished to make certain that the peasant knew exactly what his rights were, and to this end he would sponsor the publication of a commentary on the imperial patent of 1854 regulating landlord-peasant relations and instructed his clergy to inform their faithful of its contents.[39]

Şaguna shared the almost messianic faith of Rumanian intellectuals that the middle class was the creator of modern Europe, that it was mainly responsible for the rapid economic growth and the no less astonishing political liberalization of the West. Like them he felt keenly the absence of a Rumanian middle class, for, in his own words, it deprived the Rumanians of the possibility of "meeting the makers of policy on their own level."[40] But he was certain that in time a native middle class could be created. He was reconciled to a slow development, since the Rumanians had several centuries to make up, but he saw no better way to begin than by encouraging the peasants to take up trades and assert their newly-won right to join Saxon craft and commercial guilds.

Şaguna had little success in achieving his social and political goals under the conditions of absolutism, and after 1850 he largely abandoned politics. His greatest accomplishments during the decade were, rather, in the areas of church reform and education, which will be discussed in later chapters.[41]

The decade of absolutism, in spite of the contrast it presented to the "springtime of peoples" of 1848, was by no means a merely negative influence on the development of the Rumanians. Once the restoration of Austrian rule had been completed under Wohlgemuth and the regime had convinced itself that the revolutionary spirit had been quelled, the government of Transylvania settled into a routine that offered an efficient administration of public affairs and a reasonably impartial judicial system. The order it brought was welcomed by the majority of the population, which had suffered not only severe material hardship but an exhausting depression of the spirit as well.[42]

The Rumanians benefitted from the new order in various ways. The imperial patent of 1854, which implemented the decree abolishing serfdom in 1848, gave promise of a better life for the Rumanian peasantry,[43] and the end of the *de jure* rule of the three nations offered qualified Rumanians enhanced opportunities in economic life and the civil service. But the Rumanians were also being affected by the general economic and social transformation of the monarchy. After 1848, and in part because of the revolution, Austria's development from a largely semi-feudal, agricultural country into a modern state with a capitalist social and economic structure was accelerated. These changes were also felt in Transylvania, though on a more modest scale than in other parts of the monarchy. Increasing amounts of Austrian and foreign capital began to be invested in mining and metallurgical enterprises, and transportation facilities were expanded and railroad construction begun in the 1860s.[44] New employment opportunities opened up for Rumanians at the clerical level in business and in the regulatory agencies of government and, generally, in the expanding bureaucracy. One of the consequences was the strengthening of the middle class. As its numbers and influence grew, it supplanted the clergy as the leading element in Rumanian society, and, as a result, the character and objectives of the national movement became more exclusively political and economic than during the pre-March era of ecclesiastical leadership.

In spite of almost continuous aggravation and countless disappointments, Şaguna had found it possible to work within the absolutist framework. His loyalty to the dynasty, because of what it represented to him, had never flagged. When war between Austria and France and Sardinia broke out in April 1859 he called upon his clergy and faithful to defend the emperor's "prerogatives" with all their spiritual and material resources, and he used the occasion to remind them of the benefits they had received from the House of Habsburg.[45] Şaguna's support was most welcome; officials in Transylvania, who had never ceased to suspect the Rumanian clergy and lay intellectuals of secret irredentist or, as they put it, Daco-Rumanian aspirations, looked to him to keep such tendencies in check.[46] Their anxiety was hardly justified. Although the gendarmerie was extremely diligent in ferreting out bits of information — mostly hearsay — about the alleged desires of Rumanian intellectuals for a political union with Moldavia and Wallachia,[47] there is no evidence of any formal plan to bring it about. To be sure, the election in January 1859 of Alexandru Cuza as prince of both Moldavia and Wallachia and the consequent *de facto* union of the two principalities were treated at length in the Rumanian press in Transylvania and elicited widespread approval from Rumanian intellectuals.[48] But, as in 1848, those who were most deeply concerned about the future of the Rumanian nation in Transylvania did not view the political union of all the Rumanians as an attainable goal in the near future.

The deference with which officials treated Şaguna during the international crisis was only in small measure owing to their concern about the security of Transylvania. It was, rather, his dominance of the Orthodox clergy and, through them, his hold over a large segment of the peasantry, his skill as an administrator, his accomplishments in education and other cultural endeavors, and, not least of all, his willingness to work within the existing political framework that had impressed the court and successive governors of Transylvania with his value to the monarchy. He had proved himself to be that rare type of national leader who could harmonize the policies of a centralized monarchy with the centrifugal tendencies of his own people, and it was in that capacity that the court chose to deal with him during the ensuing period of imperial reorganization.

4 / A Change of System

Defeat in the war against France and Sardinia, financial instability, and continued discontent among the Magyars and other nationalities had convinced Francis Joseph and his advisers that some new formula must be devised to restore the international position of the monarchy as a great power and enhance the authority and prestige of the dynasty at home. Even before the final Peace of Zurich on November 10, 1859, had been concluded, by which Austria ceded Lombardy, Tuscany, and Modena, Alexander Bach had resigned and had been succeeded as minister of the interior and head of the cabinet by the Polish aristocrat Agenor Goluchowski. Goluchowski's charge from the emperor was to construct a new political system that would grant modest concessions to liberalism and nationalism where absolutely necessary, but without seriously altering the social or political structure of the monarchy. The court was clearly not prepared for any drastic change of course; it intended, rather, to preserve in as unadulterated a form as possible the centralist regime of the preceding decade, and it continued to rely upon its traditional sources of support—the conservative aristocracy, the Roman Catholic Church, the military, and the German bureaucracy.

Innovation was also lacking in the court's approach to the nationality problem. A few concessions to the Magyars were contemplated, such as the transferral of Hungarian affairs from the jurisdiction of the imperial ministries to a reconstituted Hungarian Chancellery. Presumably Francis Joseph considered these measures sufficient to retain the loyalty of the Magyar aristocracy, one of the few classes he thought qualified to exercise political power. He seemed willing even to recognize Hungary as a "historico-political individuality" so long as its government remained in the hands of the aristocracy and the other possessing classes and no concessions were made to Magyar liberalism or nationalism.

The other nationalities of the monarchy were accorded less attention. Francis Joseph's thinking about Slavs and Rumanians was aristocratic and absolutist; he could not conceive of their peasant masses managing their own affairs, let alone possessed of some natural right to form autonomous provinces. In his mind, the demands of the non-Magyar nationalities of Hungary for self-determination represented nothing less than a threat to the established social order. Neither he nor the Viennese bureaucracy understood the nature of the burgeoning national movements. Nor could they appreciate the depth of feeling that spurred the non-Magyar intellectuals to seek a reorganization of Hungary based upon separate national territories. Consequently, in the eight years between Bach's resignation and the Austro-Hungarian Compromise of 1867 the court devised no comprehensive or consistent nationality policy, nor did it seem fully to grasp the fact that the aspirations of the Rumanians and Slavs coincided with its own central objective of thwarting Magyar national ambitions. The resultant compromises between centralism and federalism, the reliance upon the person of the emperor to solve difficult political problems, the use of Magyar aristocrats to reconcile the court with Magyar nationalism—all those operations that solidified ancient practice at the expense of modern principle—were nowhere more clearly manifest than in Transylvania.

In 1860 and 1861 the court, engaged in a bitter constitutional struggle with the Magyars, relaxed somewhat the restrictions on civil liberties in force for nearly a decade. The resumption of public debate on Transylvania's future and on such previously forbidden subjects as national rights aroused intense political activity among the Rumanians.

In the spring of 1860 Rumanian leaders thought that political developments in the monarchy might well follow a pattern resembling their own ideal. The convocation of a large consultative assembly of notables, the so-called *Verstärkter Reichsrat,* on March 5, 1860, appeared to be the beginning of representative government. The court's goal was indeed to obtain a sampling of opinion on the planned reorganization of imperial institutions, and, to this end, leading figures from all parts of the monarchy and from among all the nationalities were summoned to Vienna. Şaguna was selected to represent the Rumanians of Transylvania and thereby received official recognition of his position as their national leader. The Rumanians of Bukovina were represented by Nicolae Petrino, a landowner, and those in the Banat and Hungary proper by Andrei Mocioni, a wealthy and prominent figure in Banat political life. The Verstärkter Reichsrat was empowered to consider "all important matters of general legislation," but it had no right to propose laws itself or to discuss questions not specifically laid before it.

Its members were to serve six-year terms and could be called into session whenever the emperor thought it necessary. By and large, they
came from the possessing classes and had been carefully chosen on the
basis of their past support of the dynasty and the idea of a unified monarchy.

The Reichsrat opened on May 31, 1860. After only a few meetings
the majority of the delegates had adhered to one of the two main currents of opinion on the future reorganization of the monarchy. They
were for the most part conservative aristocrats from Hungary and
Bohemia, who favored recognition of the "autonomous historico-political individualities," that is, of the historical crown lands, with their
own administrative and legislative organs exercising almost sovereign
authority within their respective jurisdictions. They urged adoption of
the principle of federalism, under which, as they conceived of it, the
powers of the central government would be limited largely to the common affairs of the whole monarchy and control of the respective crown
lands would once again be in the hands of the traditional ruling classes.
A minority of the delegates, the so-called "centralists," favored greater
uniformity of laws and practices throughout the monarchy. They advocated the concentration of legislative power in a representative central parliament and the gradual reduction of provincial autonomy to
purely administrative functions.

Neither plan was acceptable to Şaguna, who occupied a middle
position. He objected because there was no specific guarantee of the
free development of the Rumanian nation or the Orthodox Church,
nor was there even any general statement recognizing the validity of
the national idea. In his view neither federalism nor centralism, as
they had been presented, offered a lasting solution to the fundamental problem confronting the monarchy—nationalism—the search for
which, he thought, was the main reason for their assembling. He
pointed out to his fellow senators that for several decades all the
peoples of the monarchy—the least as well as the most advanced—had
engaged in an "arduous struggle" to achieve recognition of their nationhood. No one, he thought, had to be reminded of what had happened in 1848, the experiences of which had made it evident that no
nation would willingly renounce its own political existence or sacrifice
its language or acquiesce in anonymity or assimilation by another nation; such notions were a thing of the past. Failure to respect the "natural" aspirations of all the peoples of the monarchy for a life of their

own, he concluded, would merely perpetuate rivalries and conflict, and Austria — the framework within which they were all destined to seek their self-fulfillment — would be weakened and the several nationalities themselves exhausted by vain struggle.

As the first step towards a solution of the nationality problem Şaguna proposed the formal enactment into law of the principle of national equality. He was certain that such a law would create an atmosphere of peace and brotherhood, which could not but advance both the common good and the interests of each individual nation.[1] He reminded his colleagues that recognition of the principle of national equality meant an end to the old order in Transylvania with its discriminatory legislation and territorial divisions. He argued that any attempt to restore government by the three nations would be an anachronism in an age that was experiencing the full force of liberalism and the idea of nationality. To back up his assertion, he pointed out that the old regime had consistently ignored the Rumanians, in spite of the fact that they were the oldest and most numerous inhabitants of the land and had willingly sacrificed their lives and goods for the general welfare. He tried to show that the old order had not even served the needs of the great mass of the Magyars and Saxons, whose oppressive existence was not unlike the Rumanians'; it had benefitted only a small aristocracy and middle class.[2] He therefore appealed to the Reichsrat to renounce the past with its "injustices and barren rivalries" and in its place build a new Transylvania where all its nations might find peace and self-fulfillment.

At the final working session of the Reichsrat on September 26, 1860, Şaguna offered as an alternative to federalism and centralism his plan to attain the elusive goals of cooperation and self-determination. It provided for a new structure of the monarchy that would combine recognition of Austria's oneness and the maintenance of the emperor's prerogatives with respect for local custom and the principle of national equality. Accordingly, the autonomy of existing crown lands would be maintained, but new constitutions for each would be drawn up incorporating these general principles, and the new provincial diets would adapt them to local conditions and ensure their extension to all the branches of government. Under his plan, the primary tasks of the provincial legislatures and administrative bodies were to ensure freedom of the press and assembly, to further education and industry, and to guarantee the use of all languages at all levels of public administration; the chief responsibility of the central government in Vienna was to see to it that each constituent part of the monarchy respected the broad principles upon which the whole was founded.[3]

During the ensuing decade Şaguna did not substantially change the position he had taken at the Reichsrat on the reorganization of the monarchy and the future of Transylvania. His commitment to the idea of a unitary monarchy under the House of Habsburg remained firm, and he invariably looked to the court to provide the necessary political initiative. But he was just as firmly committed to the idea of an autonomous Transylvania as the best way of preserving the individuality of all the peoples of the principality and, particularly, of ensuring the well-being and progress of the Rumanian nation and the Orthodox Church. He revealed his true feelings in the matter in a private letter written a few months after the Reichsrat: "We shall not allow Transylvania to be turned into a Magyar country; we shall try to keep Transylvania as Transylvania. Just as Transylvania could not be Germanized, so shall it not be Magyarized. It must exist as Transylvania, that is, all its nations must live as nations of Transylvania equal in all things."[4]

This belief in the efficacy of Transylvania lay behind Şaguna's efforts to reconcile conflicting national aspirations at the Reichsrat and, later on, at the Conference of Alba Iulia in February 1861 and the Transylvanian Diet of Sibiu in 1863. On all these occasions he pointed out that "destiny" had brought the Rumanians, the Magyars, and the Saxons together in one place and that in the course of time their existences had become intertwined and dependent upon one another; he therefore urged his "fellow Transylvanians" to look for ways of promoting the common good rather than perpetuate their vain contest for hegemony over their neighbors. To prove that cooperation among them was possible he cited the political alliance effected in the tenth century between the Rumanian Duke Gelu and Tuhutum, the leader of the first Magyar settlers in Transylvania, which, according to Rumanian historical tradition, had created a condominium of equals over the land they would henceforth share; and he never tired of repeating the dictum of King Saint Stephen of Hungary in the eleventh century that "*Regnum unius linguae est imbecile et fragile.*"[5] He generally did not dwell upon what had actually taken place between the eleventh and nineteenth centuries when the Rumanians had fallen under the domination of their neighbors, but rather tried to reassure the Magyars and Saxons that the Rumanians in their turn did not aspire to replace the three nations. He conceded that in an era dominated by liberal and national ideas account would have to be taken of the Rumanians' large numbers and the size of their contributions to the general welfare in taxes and conscripts for the army, but he always returned to his favorite theme — national equality; it was this principle alone, he insisted, that would protect all Transylvanians from the arbitrary rule of one nation over the rest and allow the fullest opportunity for self-development.

Şaguna preferred, therefore, to maintain the territorial framework of existing crown lands in the belief that peoples who had shared a common historical past were better equipped than outsiders to solve the delicate problems that confronted them in the present. In a sense, he had abandoned plans for a Rumanian duchy to be carved out of various Magyar counties and Saxon districts, but the idea of a union of the Rumanians of the monarchy remained fresh in his mind. He considered a political-territorial union both impractical, because of the great intermingling of nationalities, and unnecessary, if his conception of Transylvania prevailed, and he turned his attention to what might best be described as a spiritual union.[6]

Şaguna won little support for his plan among his fellow senators at the Reichsrat. A majority of thirty-four voted in favor of maintaining the historico-political crown lands, sixteen favored a modified centralism, and six, including Şaguna, abstained. In spite of this failure, Şaguna's performance at the Reichsrat had been a personal triumph. His spirited defense of Rumanian nationality and his bold initiative in proposing an alternative to both federalism and centralism that would permit its unfettered development had been widely discussed by the intellectuals and reported in detail in the Rumanian press. Addresses of support poured into Vienna from every part of Transylvania and from Uniates as well as Orthodox; many were accompanied by petitions detailing long-standing grievances and urging Şaguna to persevere in his struggle for national autonomy.[7]

Amidst the general chorus of praise, a few dissonances could also be heard. A number of intellectuals, among them George Bariţiu and his younger friends and supporters like Ioan Raţiu, could not accept the fundamental premises behind Şaguna's proposals. They were unwilling, for example, to leave the political initiative in the hands of the court; they wanted instead to create their own political institutions and assume responsibility for their own affairs. They were equally unhappy with his emphasis upon "Transylvania" and the apparent ease with which he had renounced the idea of a separate Rumanian territory. Like him, they believed in liberal, constitutional government and readily accepted the principle of national equality, but at the same time they insisted that since Transylvania was the "ancestral home of the Rumanians" and they themselves formed a majority of the population, they should henceforth have the leading (if not the dominant) role in its affairs.

On September 29, 1860, Francis Joseph personally prorogued the Reichsrat, and, thanking the delegates for their labors, he promised to weigh their opinions carefully. In fact, the most important decisions about the future organization of the monarchy (and Transylvania) had already been made and were embodied in the so-called October Diploma. Promulgated barely three weeks after the close of the Reichsrat, on October 20, 1860, the Diploma was an attempt at a compromise between the court and Hungary with the Magyar aristocracy as the intermediaries. On the whole, it represented a victory for the proponents of historical right. While it left almost untouched the ruler's control of military and foreign affairs and created a central parliament, thereby ensuring the continued unity of the monarchy, it reserved extensive powers to provincial diets and administrations where the traditional possessing classes would hold sway.

The authors of the Diploma, foremost among them Count Antal Szécsen, a leader of the Magyar court aristocracy, had as their main objective the restoration of the historical constitution of Hungary and the consequent end of the Viennese bureaucracy's control of Hungarian affairs.[8] They found the court's reliance upon the privileged classes congenial and hoped eventually in return for their support to limit Hungary's political dependence upon Austria to a recognition of the historical rights of the Habsburg dynasty. Such a plan left little room for liberal reforms or concessions to national feeling. On the question of Transylvania, which the Diploma recognized as a separate province, but whose final disposition was the key to any lasting settlement between the court and Hungary, Szécsen and his group deviated sharply from their own theory of historico-political individualities, for they envisioned the eventual incorporation of the principality into Hungary. It must have been evident to them that if any of the Austrian crown lands had a claim to recognition as a historico-political entity it was Transylvania. But like Kossuth during the revolution and Ferenc

Deák, the leader of the Magyar gentry, afterwards, they insisted that the union of Transylvania with Hungary in 1848 was legal and binding and, like the liberals and nationalists, they regarded it both as an inevitable stage in the reconstitution of an independent Hungary and as a practical necessity for the maintenance of Magyar dominance in Transylvania.[9] Their stand demonstrated the futility of the court's attempts to settle the question of Transylvania — and the nationality problem in general — by relying upon the Magyar aristocracy.

Although the October Diploma offered few specific guarantees of nationality, Rumanian leaders interpreted it as a commitment by the court to establish constitutional government and preserve Transylvania's status as a separate principality. It therefore proved to be a great stimulus to political activity; once again, after a full decade, public meetings and the drafting of programs and petitions took place on a broad scale in the chief centers of Rumanian intellectual life. Two main groups emerged — one in Braşov, where George Bariţiu was the guiding spirit, and one in Sibiu, where Şaguna's influence was paramount. The Braşov group, composed of intellectuals, merchants, and a few priests, was avowedly liberal and nationalist. It demanded the formal recognition of Rumanian political autonomy and the redrawing of the county boundaries in Transylvania according to nationality; the recognition of the Rumanian language as one of the official state languages, and local option regarding which language would be used at the county and village level; moderate property qualifications for voting; guarantees of personal liberty and freedom of the press and association; and the immediate convocation of a national congress to enable the Rumanian nation to organize itself formally.[10]

The Sibiu group was primarily Orthodox and somewhat more conservative than the Braşov group. Its members had come together informally in the middle of November 1860 after the conclusion of the Orthodox diocesan synod. Şaguna had forbidden use of the synod itself as a political forum, since he wished to avoid compromising what little autonomy his church had by an "unwarranted mixing" of religion and politics. But before returning to their homes some fifty prominent Orthodox laymen and clergy met in private to discuss the future of their nation and decide what principles should govern their own political conduct. They came to no final conclusions except to reiterate their opposition to a union of Transylvania with Hungary.[11] They seemed to be following Şaguna's lead of waiting for the court's next move, but it is evident that they shared his irritation at the Viennese bureaucracy's failure to consult the Rumanians before disposing of Transylvania's future in the October Diploma.

Neither the Braşov "liberals" nor the Sibiu "conservatives," as it turned out, went as far as other Rumanians in accepting the full implications of the idea of nationality. It was left to the hardy intellectuals of the Apuseni Mountains, many of whom had fought with Avram Iancu in 1848 or had studied law in the 1850s and had returned home to serve the peasantry from whom they had sprung, to proclaim an unequivocal faith in "unity, liberty, and national independence." Theirs was the most radical of all the Rumanian programs enunciated on the eve of the constitutional experiment. They were deeply conscious of the sacrifices that the forty-eighters had made on behalf of national unity, and they admonished the Rumanians of 1860 not to settle for something less. They insisted that a separate Rumanian principality be created and that its boundaries coincide roughly with those of historical Transylvania together with the Banat and the Partium.* They made no provision for dividing Transylvania up into separate Rumanian, Magyar, and Saxon national territories, for they regarded the principality as the ancestral home of the Rumanians, which they were not at liberty to alienate. At the same time they were committed to the principle of national equality, and they promised the Magyars and Saxons proportional representation in the new diet and the extensive use of their languages in public affairs. They also wanted government by the people, and they promised all citizens the full enjoyment of fundamental human rights, including the right to choose their own representatives and officials, regardless of nationality. The formula by which they proposed to bring their own duchy into being was democratic; they specified that a general congress be held on the Field of Liberty at Blaj.[12]

Whatever their particular program, all Rumanian leaders agreed that their common task should be the immediate restoration of national solidarity, which had been sorely tried during the preceding decade. Accordingly, on October 4, immediately after his return home from the Reichsrat, Şaguna had publicly urged an end to the rivalry

---

*An area of eastern Hungary, including Zarand, Közép-Szolnok, and Kraszna counties and Kővár district, which for longer or shorter periods between the sixteenth and the second half of the nineteenth century were attached to Transylvania.

between Orthodox and Uniates, which, he admitted, would impede
the quest for national rights. Without understanding and cooperation
among the Rumanians themselves, he could foresee little success in
their achieving any of their goals. The lay intellectuals and most of the
clergy of both churches needed no additional urging and applied pressure of their own to bring about a speedy rapprochement between the
two hierarchies. Although the laity was little disposed to prolong the
political leadership of the bishops and would have preferred some kind
of broad-based political party as an alternative, the tradition of episcopal preeminence in national affairs was not easily broken, and it was
also evident that for the time being at least the court would recognize
no other national representatives.

The Uniate Archbishop,* Alexandru Sterca Şuluţiu, readily ac-
ceded to Şaguna's appeal of October 4, and during the following
month he and Şaguna met almost continuously with various groups
and individuals in order to reconcile conflicting opinions and find
some common ground for the Rumanians' formal reentry into the
political life of the monarchy. The general outlines of a national program were at last agreed upon and a delegation chosen to convey it to
the emperor in Vienna. As the supreme act of reconciliation Şaguna
invited Şuluţiu to head the delegation. In his letter of November 16 he
characterized the question of the future organization of Transylvania
as one of life or death for the Rumanian nation and warned that powerful elements at court — by which he meant the Magyar aristocrats —
were ceaselessly at work to nullify the October Diploma and thereby
destroy Transylvania's autonomy once and for all and bring about its
incorporation into Hungary. The political situation seemed to him to
be in a state of flux. He considered the Diploma a fragile piece that
was unlikely to accomplish all that the court had hoped, because of
intense Magyar resistance to anything short of a complete restoration
of the Hungarian constitution. Speaking in his own name and that of
the "Orthodox intellectuals," he urged Şuluţiu not to refuse the chairmanship of the delegation and pressed him to leave at once for Vienna,
since the Rumanians could ill afford to remain inactive at such a critical moment. Şaguna suggested that the delegation use his own proposals at the Verstärkter Reichsrat as an instrument for negotiation,
and he urged, in particular, that they try to obtain the emperor's

---

*The Uniate bishopric had been elevated to an archbishopric in 1853.

unequivocal sanction of Transylvania's autonomy.[13] He excused himself from returning to Vienna so soon after the protracted sessions of
the Reichsrat on the grounds that his own diocese had suffered from
his prolonged absence and that, consequently, he had much work to
do at home. Undoubtedly the main reason he invited Şuluţiu to head
the delegation was to demonstrate to the court and the Magyars that in
matters of grave national importance the Rumanians stood united,
regardless of their religious differences.

Şuluţiu, although in poor health, was eager to serve the national
cause and agreed to meet with the emperor. The delegation consisted
of some twenty persons, including Ioan Popasu, who served as Şaguna's
personal representative, but not George Bariţiu, whose influence was
great among the intellectuals but who preferred to give his advice by
letter from Braşov. Immediately after their arrival in Vienna in November, the members began to make the rounds of the various ministries, seeking support for their program. On the whole, they were disappointed, since none of the officials they interviewed was willing to
make a commitment on specific issues. Count Rechberg, the minister-
president, could promise them little more than "suitable" representation in the Transylvanian diet and administration, and Joseph Lasser,
the minister of justice, while expressing his pleasure at the continued
loyalty of the Rumanians to the dynasty, spoke only in general terms
about assisting them to improve their position. Apparently no official
call was made on Anton von Schmerling, who was to become minister
of state on December 13, but the delegation was heartened by reports
that he favored a coalition of Croats, Serbs, and Rumanians to oppose
the Magyars.[14]

On December 10 Şuluţiu and Popasu (but not the whole delegation)
were received by Francis Joseph. They presented a petition on behalf
of their nation which in general restated the points Şaguna had raised
at the Reichsrat. In the brief conversation that followed they requested
permission to hold a national congress or, if not that, then a "consultation" between the Transylvanian chancellor and a small number of
Rumanian leaders (to be selected by Şaguna and Şuluţiu) on the drafting of a new electoral law and other important issues concerning the
reorganization of the principality. Francis Joseph spoke reassuringly of
his concern for national equality, but made no commitments. Nonetheless, Şuluţiu came away from the audience convinced that it was
only a matter of time before the Rumanians "gained all the liberties to
which they [were] entitled."[15]

Other members of the delegation were less sanguine. They had been struck by the fact that the Magyar aristocracy had had the decisive voice whenever the future of Transylvania came up, and they harbored no illusions about its attitude toward their cause. Their fears were confirmed by a conversation between Ioan Axente, one of Iancu's comrades-in-arms in 1848 and a member of the delegation, and Baron Ferenc Kemény, the new provisional Transylvanian chancellor. Kemény professed to see no reason why the Rumanians should not enjoy the same rights as the other nations of Transylvania, and he was even willing to allow a new diet to determine the validity of the laws of 1848. But he had little sympathy for democratic or national aspirations (other than Magyar), and he made it clear that he had no intention of allowing the Rumanians to have a majority in the forthcoming diet. He was also reluctant to appoint Rumanians to high administrative or advisory positions and made no secret of his resentment against the members of the national committee of 1848.[16]

Neither the Rumanians nor the Magyars appear to have made a serious attempt to settle their differences. On the Magyar side Joseph Eötvös, the liberal minister of religions and education in the Batthyány ministry in 1848, suggested a meeting to discuss the matters at issue. He sent word to the Rumanian delegation through Emmanuel Gojdu, a leading Rumanian political figure in Hungary and a close friend of Şaguna, that he was ready to meet with them at their convenience.[17] But no meeting seems to have taken place, and, as events were to show, a rare opportunity for an exchange of views was allowed to slip by.

Şuluţiu left Vienna on December 23 and, at the insistence of his delegation, he went directly to Sibiu to report personally to Şaguna. Şaguna was disappointed by the refusal of any of the ministers to state their opinions on specific points raised in the petition, and he was troubled by the fact that the entire delegation had not been admitted to the audience with the emperor and had not taken an official part in subsequent negotiations. It all reminded him of the treatment accorded the national committee and the various delegations in 1848, when Austrian officials had refused to deal with them as the legal representatives of the Rumanian nation but had preferred instead to negotiate with individuals (mainly himself). He realized that they wished to avoid binding commitments, but he had had his fill of soothing words and vague promises about a better life.[18] The appointment of Kemény as provisional Transylvanian chancellor and of Count Imre Mikó, a leader of the Transylvanian Magyar aristocracy, as provisional governor, merely confirmed his suspicions about the decisive influence of the Magyars at court and the fragility of the newly-inaugurated constitutionalism.

Nonetheless, at the beginning of the new year Rumanian leaders had reason to be optimistic. The court had finally given its consent for their national congress, and although it was to be limited to persons appointed by the two bishops, most Rumanians took it as a sign that they were henceforth to be treated as partners — junior, to be sure — in settling the future of Transylvania. This conviction was strengthened by the announcement that a conference of Magyar, Saxon, and Rumanian representatives would be held in Alba Iulia in February — after the Rumanian national congress — to discuss the general principles that would shape the new Transylvanian constitution. Rumanian leaders were particularly impressed by the fact that this meeting would be the first at which they would negotiate with the former privileged nations as equals. But they did not understand that the Court and Schmerling, who had become the dominant figure in the cabinet, had no interest in encouraging Rumanian nationalism; the Austrians' main concern was to prepare Transylvania to take its proper place in the *Gesamtmonarchie*. Schmerling, though he had given his consent to the conference, wanted to limit it to twenty or thirty persons and to avoid giving it an official character. He had approved the conference as the lesser of two evils; it would preclude the holding of a large number of private or secret meetings that would arouse more excitement and be more difficult to control than a public assembly.[19]

An air of expectation was clearly discernible among the delegates to the Rumanian national congress when it opened in Sibiu on January 13, 1861.[20] Although some were dissatisfied because they had been nominated by the two church leaders rather than elected by their constituents — a procedure which seemed contrary to the democratic principles they themselves were demanding be incorporated into the new Transylvanian constitution — few could find fault with the representative character of the congress; the 150 delegates were evenly divided between Orthodox and Uniate, and all segments of what may be loosely described as the Rumanian middle class — priests, teachers, public officials, businessmen, and lawyers — were present. Solidarity was the order of the day, and the deliberations, both public and private, proceeded harmoniously, as befitted a body that felt itself to be on the threshold of a new era.

Şaguna, cochairman with Şuluţiu but by all accounts the dominant figure at the congress, set the tone by appealing to the delegates for unity and steadfastness in overcoming the obstacles they were certain to encounter in the months ahead. He also reminded them that the Rumanians were not alone in Transylvania and warned that if they hoped to achieve an enduring solution to the political and social problems that afflicted their land, they must practice as well as preach the principles of national equality and fraternity; they, the Magyars, and the Saxons must consider themselves "sons of the same fatherland" and must learn to work together in a spirit of genuine constitutionalism for the common good; otherwise, the quest for national fulfillment would be vain and illusory.[21]

Şuluţiu echoed these sentiments. In fact, he went out of his way to assure the Magyars and Saxons that the Rumanians had no ulterior designs, and he discounted as "totally unfounded" rumors that they wanted to establish a "Daco-Rumanian empire" by uniting Transylvania with the Danubian principalities. But he made no effort to hide the deep attachment the Transylvanian Rumanians felt toward their brothers beyond the Carpathians, and he expressed the hope of all those present that they would prosper.[22]

The delegates went about their work with uncommon zeal in the conviction that they were laying the foundations of genuine constitutional government. There were no serious divisions about matters of broad principle. Everyone agreed that the Sixteen Points of 1848 and, most recently, the petition which Şuluţiu had presented to the emperor on December 10, 1860, should guide their deliberations. The achievement of national equality for the Rumanian nation was uppermost in their minds. Basing their position on the October Diploma, which they interpreted as having given the Rumanians equal status with the other peoples of Transylvania, they insisted that the Transylvanian diet take up first the detailed regulation of the constitutional position of the Rumanian nation and its two churches; that the incorporation of Transylvania into Hungary be rejected for all time; that all legislation discriminating against the Rumanians be annulled; and that an "adequate" number of Rumanians be appointed to responsible positions in the Transylvanian Chancellery.[23]

Their demands were embodied in two petitions to the emperor drafted by Şaguna[24] and approved by the intellectuals. The first presented their national program; the second dealt with a practical mat-

ter of nationality: the composition of the forthcoming conference at
Alba Iulia. The Rumanians characterized the proportions devised by
Chancellor Kemény as "unnatural" and wholly contrary to the principle of national equality, since there were to be twenty-four Magyars
representing 500,000, eight Saxons representing 200,000, but only
eight Rumanians representing 1,400,000.[25] Yet, as in equally important questions of organization, they offered no specific suggestions on
how the principle of national equality could be better served. They
seemed willing, at least for the time being, to leave the initiative to the
court.

At the final session, on January 16, the delegates chose a new permanent committee, with Şaguna and Şuluţiu as cochairmen, to coordinate future political activity. The intellectuals, notably Bariţiu and
Ioan Raţiu, thought its main task should be to create a regular political party based upon Western European models, for they were eager to
press forward with their own program and needed a suitable instrument. But Şaguna was hesitant about taking a course too independent
of the court, lest the Rumanians cut themselves off from what, in his
view, would be the determining force in their future development. The
intellectuals could not reconcile themselves to his "inactivity," and the
mounting friction between them ultimately provoked a lengthy and,
for a time, debilitating crisis within the national movement. Some
among them, particularly members of the Braşov group, even went so
far as to ask themselves what they would do if the court rejected their
program. In private meetings between sessions of the congress they expressed keen disappointment at how slowly the court had responded to
their previous proposals and how little inclined it seemed to further
national equality. If worse came to worse, they considered resorting to
passive resistance, by which they meant an abstention from elections to
the imperial and provincial legislatures and a boycott of county government. Such a policy was widely discussed in the press,[26] but any
application of it was considered premature, since the reorganization of
Transylvanian affairs had just begun. During the next few years the
matter receded into the background, but in this fleeting suggestion of
passive resistance lay the first overt sign of opposition by Rumanian
intellectuals to the court's tutelage. None of these mental reservations
were evident at the banquet that brought the congress to a close. In the
presence of the retiring governor, Friedrich Lichtenstein, and other

high officials, the delegates drank toasts to the emperor, the governor, the Rumanian nation, and brotherhood among the peoples of Transylvania.[27]

The solidarity that had made the national congress a success was carried over to the Conference of Alba Iulia, which met a few weeks later on February 11 and 12. The purpose in bringing Magyar, Saxon, and Rumanian representatives together for the first time was to give them an opportunity to exchange views on the future organization of Transylvania and, specifically, to make proposals for a new electoral law. In this sense, the conference represented a further, if highly tentative, step in the direction of constitutional government, even though Chancellor Kemény, who served as its chairman, restricted the discussions to matters he specifically placed before the delegates as the emperor's personal representative. The court, and Schmerling in particular, were anxious to incorporate Transylvania into the new imperial system as smoothly as possible, but in spite of the appointment of a few additional Rumanian civil servants, they were not prepared to rely upon the support of the Rumanian peasant masses. The court therefore went about the business of organizing the government of Transylvania in an exceedingly strange way: it relied upon the Magyar aristocracy, to whom it had granted a safe majority at Alba Iulia, to renounce the principle of historical right and the continuity of Hungarian law, to which they were so firmly committed, and to yield ultimate authority to the Austrian central bureaucracy—thereby undermining Magyar dominance of Transylvanian public life. As in 1848, the court tried to deal with nationalism by ignoring the nationalities.

The conference accomplished little except to demonstrate once again how difficult it would be to gain Magyar support for anything less than the full recognition of Hungary's historical claims.[28] The forty delegates inevitably divided into three separate parties according to nationality. They displayed no acrimony as they went about their work, but neither did they show any inclination to compromise positions that had long since become fixed. The Magyars had an eloquent spokesman in Lajos Haynald, Roman Catholic Bishop of Transylvania, who sustained the validity of the Law of Union of 1848 and insisted that the only proper business of the conference was to decide how Transylvania should elect its representatives to the Hungarian diet in Pest, which, in his view, had sole jurisdiction over the affairs of Transylvania. His Magyar colleagues to a man, along with three Saxons, supported him. The other Saxons held views similar to those of the Rumanians, but their first concern was to maintain their own autonomy.[29]

Şaguna and Şuluţiu, who headed the eight-man Rumanian delegation, could speak with authority as their nation's recognized leaders. Their theme was the same as it had been at the national congress: national equality in all matters and an electoral law based upon the principle of universal suffrage. It probably escaped no one, least of all the Magyars, that equality among the nationalities and democracy were not necessarily compatible. Clearly, if there were no property qualifications limiting the right to vote, the Rumanians with their superior numbers would, in effect, become the dominant nation, whether that was their intention or not. Claims by their leaders that Transylvania was the ancestral home of the Rumanians lent weight to Magyar and Saxon charges that they would be satisfied with nothing less than a monopoly of political power. Yet there was abundant evidence that Rumanian leaders were, in fact, firmly committed to the principles of national equality and constitutional government and that they believed in the ability of reasonable men to work out their problems by free discussion and respect for law. Even some of the Magyar delegates at Alba Iulia were agreeably surprised and impressed by the Rumanians' attachment to constitutionalism; they had thought the Rumanians wedded to absolutism because they had supported the dynasty in 1848.[30]

Şaguna made a special effort to dispel any suspicions and misunderstandings about the Rumanian position. He tried to persuade his fellow delegates not to despair because of the differences among them, since they were simply the expressions of strong convictions about how the well-being of their country could best be secured, not manifestations of hostility.[31] He pointed out that the Rumanians had come to the conference not to impose their will upon others, but rather to seek liberty and enlightenment for their neighbors as well as themselves. By the term liberty, Şaguna explained, they meant a "normal constitutional life" that would assure them honor as a nation and the opportunity to achieve their noblest ambitions, and by enlightenment they referred to the means they would use to attain their goals—language, nationality, and religion. In small gatherings outside the conference room, too, he tried to assuage the bitterness that still lingered from the revolution of 1848. In the hope that in private some common ground for negotiation might be found he accepted the invitation to stay at Bishop Haynald's residence in Alba Iulia, where, moreover, most of the Magyar aristocrats attending the conference were lodged. Although Şaguna won the personal admiration of many of his Magyar colleagues, he could not persuade them to modify their stand on the Law of Union and all that it represented. He remained hopeful that the idea of national equality would prevail, but he was taken aback by the intransigence displayed by the Magyars, and now more than ever he looked to the court to sustain the Rumanian cause.

By the end of the second day it was obvious that the delegates could not resolve their differences and that further debate was pointless. The leaders of the three parties decided, therefore, to submit separate recommendations to the chancellor and return home. Kemény found none of the reports entirely to his liking, but he objected most strongly to the Rumanian proposal for universal suffrage, which he condemned as incompatible with the monarchical principle and likely to bring about its "complete subversion."[32] He favored instead a tax qualification of eight florins forty kreutzers for voting in elections to the Transylvanian diet — a sum, he calculated, that would ensure a Magyar majority, and hence a vote in favor of the union of Transylvania with Hungary.

As it turned out, the discussions at Alba Iulia, like the deliberations of the Verstärkter Reichsrat, had little influence on court policy. Important changes in the October Diploma were already being contemplated before the Alba Iulia conference convened, and barely two weeks after its close, on February 26, the emperor issued a patent which purported to be merely a "supplement" to the Diploma, but which in fact was a wholly new constitution. The February Patent, as it came to be known, corresponded more closely than the Diploma to the views of Schmerling and his circle. They had been disturbed by the centrifugal tendencies they discerned in the Diploma. German centralism of a mildly bourgeois stamp was the core of Schmerling's own political philosophy, and the February Patent, consequently, signalled a retreat from the old conservative idea of historico-political entities toward a middle-class, slightly liberal centralism. Power was concentrated in the central organs of government in Vienna at the expense of provincial administrations and diets, and the emperor's exclusive control of foreign and military affairs remained untouched. The Reichsrat, which under the Diploma had been envisaged as an enlarged crown council, now took on the attributes of a true imperial parliament, and the powers of the provincial diets were correspondingly reduced. In Schmerling's view, the most important function of the diets was to elect the provincial delegations to the central parliament. But this concern with parliaments did not imply a general liberalization of political life. Schmerling continued to rely upon the possessing classes, now expanded slightly to include the upper ranks of the middle class, and he intended to supervise closely the activities of elected bodies.

Şaguna found the Patent closer to his own idea of a united Austria than the Diploma, and he was encouraged to think that it was a major step toward the attainment of that harmony between the imperial authority and the strivings of the nationalities for self-determination he had outlined at the Verstärkter Reichsrat. At the same time he noted the "unhappy fact" that the Patent contained nothing in the way of a comprehensive nationality policy. This omission is indeed curious in view of the fact that reconciliation with (or subjection of) Hungary had been the key issue in the constitutional shuffling that had been going on for more than a year. Schmerling now intended to treat Hungary like a province — albeit privileged — of the monarchy and refused to honor earlier promises by his predecessors and by the emperor himself about a restoration of its historical rights. He recognized the value of support from the non-Magyar nationalities in his efforts to neutralize both Szécsen's aristocrats and Deák's liberal nationalists, but he dallied too long with the Slavs and Rumanians to make them effective partners. He seems to have counted upon their "natural" historical animosity toward the Magyars to serve as an adequate substitute for a formal policy of his own.

5 / National Fulfillment

The era of constitutional experiment in the Habsburg monarchy ushered in by the October Diploma and the February Patent was to last nearly five years, until the spring of 1865. For a time the court and the Rumanians discovered a mutual convenience in supporting one another's aims, and, as a consequence, the Rumanians were able, briefly, to attain that equality of status they had sought ever since the beginning of the eighteenth century. But this "alliance," like the one in 1848, struck no deep roots of principle: the court pursued the welfare of the Gesamtmonarchie and shunned a coherent nationality policy, while the Rumanians sought fulfillment in the idea of nationality. Their cooperation was founded upon a fleeting coincidence of interest—the need both felt to contain Magyar ambitions for a restoration of Hungary's ancient constitution and administrative autonomy. In a sense, then, it was the Magyars who brought them together and, in the final analysis, it was they who also forced them apart. When the court came to the realization that a compromise with the Magyars was the only acceptable way out of the severe constitutional crisis that afflicted the monarchy, it lightly abandoned its brief experiment with Rumanian self-determination.

During this period the Rumanians engaged in the most intense political activity they had ever known. Their enthusiasm rarely flagged; they had convinced themselves that what they said and did mattered, and their faith in the ultimate triumph of nationality assumed the proportions of a law of nature. They held a second national congress and innumerable smaller conferences; they drew up projects and programs that touched upon every aspect of political and social life; they sent three delegations to Vienna to argue their cause before Francis Joseph and his ministers; and—to them most exhilarating of all—they legislated their own emancipation.

Of all those who made a significant contribution to the achievement of national goals during these eventful years, Şaguna has the strongest claim to leadership. From the spring of 1861 to the spring of 1864 there was no important political event, whether it was a national congress, a parley of leaders, representations to Vienna, or strategy in the

Transylvanian diet, in which he did not have a preeminent or decisive role. Moreover, because of his unceasing labors to restore the Orthodox metropolis of Transylvania, to improve the legal and economic status of his clergy, and to raise the general level of Orthodox education and Rumanian culture, he benefitted from an enormous prestige among his own faithful and many Uniates as well. Besides an astonishing capacity for work and political acumen born of his diverse experiences in Carlovitz and Vienna, not to mention Transylvania, he possessed a temperament that made politics a satisfying occupation. He enjoyed the exercise of power and willingly bore the heavy responsibilities it imposed. All in all, the position of national leadership he attained in these years rivalled that of Bishop Inochentie Micu more than a century before him, and was never again to be held by an ecclesiastic, Orthodox or Uniate.

There were, of course, other Rumanians who could claim a wide following and who rendered outstanding service to the national cause. Foremost among them, perhaps, was George Barițiu. His long-standing commitment to liberalism and the ideal of national self-determination made him the dominant influence among the younger lay intellectuals. During the period of constitutional experiment his ideas, which he presented to a broader public in *Gazeta de Transilvania,* evoked lively discussion and, in many circles, aroused strong enthusiasm.[1] But Barițiu was a cautious man who shunned political responsibility. Among others who were widely respected was Archbishop Șuluțiu. He participated in almost all important policy decisions, but he owed his position in the national movement mainly to his church office rather than to outstanding qualities of leadership or political sagacity. Account must also be taken of the younger lay intellectuals, like Ioan Rațiu, who were playing an increasingly important role in political life. Since they were little attached to the tradition represented by Șaguna of ecclesiastical direction of the national movement, which they conceived of in purely secular terms, their time for leadership still lay in the future.

Șaguna's main political goal during this period was to reconcile Rumanian national aspirations with the demands of a united Austria, as he conceived of it. It struck him as unfortunate that neither his own colleagues nor the court fully realized how necessary they were to each other. It seemed to him, on the one hand, that the Rumanians were too weak to bring about by themselves the changes they desired, and,

on the other hand, he predicted failure for the newly inaugurated constitutionalism unless the previously disenfranchised nationalities rallied to its support. The crux of the problem for both the court and the
nationalities, as he saw it, was Magyar nationalism; they had a common interest in checking the more extreme demands of Magyar nationalists and at the same time in seeking a *modus vivendi* with more
moderate elements. He concluded that the success of the October
Diploma and the February Patent and, concomitantly, the fruition of
Rumanian hopes would depend chiefly upon how skilfully the court
and the Rumanians together met the Magyar challenge.

Şaguna's immediate objective was to secure for the Rumanians a
fixed legal position within the new monarchy. He preferred that it be
accomplished through constitutional procedures rather than by some
deus ex machina like an imperial decree. This goal largely determined
the strategy he employed. His respect for law and his commitment to
orderly change made all forms of coercion and subterfuge abhorrent
to him. In his view, the essence of the political process lay in a respect
for high moral principle and a willingness to negotiate. If these were
the qualities that were to characterize the new monarchy—and he took
the October Diploma and the February Patent as tangible signs that
they were[2]—then he thought that the Rumanians could easily find
their places in it, since they had always been at heart an orderly, law-
abiding people, who had been roused to acts of violence only by extreme provocation. Their contribution, then, would be as an element
of stability and reasoned change—primary aspects, in his view, of
modern constitutionalism. But their potential services to the monarchy
did not end here. Şaguna also saw the Rumanians as the bearers of the
two dominant ideas among all the peoples of Eastern Europe: self-
determination and political liberty, neither of which had as yet been
recognized in the legislation of the monarchy as a whole or of Transylvania. He concluded that the Rumanians could contribute to the well-
being of both empire and principality by helping to bring their institutions into conformity with the "spirit of the times."

Şaguna had great faith in the power of ideas; he regarded them as
the chief determinants of social development. This conviction had led
him to reevaluate the importance of the revolution of 1848. At first,
because of its destructiveness, he had judged it to be an enormous
aberration in human behavior, but as time passed and he observed the
effects of the ideas of the revolution on his contemporaries, he was cer-

tain that 1848 had ushered in a new era in European history and that it would be impossible to return to the Vormärz. From this experience he concluded that laws and institutions were determined by the evolution of men's thoughts and that this process constituted the true motive force of history. Not surprisingly, therefore, he judged the strength of the Rumanian cause to lie in its adherence to the ideas of justice and equality.

But he was also a political realist. The power of ideas notwithstanding, he had no illusions about the essential weakness of the Rumanians; they had neither the resources nor the influence to bring about, unaided, the changes they desired. In keeping with his belief that the Rumanians and the dynasty were natural allies, he urged reliance upon Vienna as the cornerstone of Rumanian policy. But his support of the Schmerling government was less than wholehearted. While impressed by the Diploma and the Patent as steps in the right direction, he was dubious about the court's true intentions. The Patent raised many questions in his mind, mainly because its tendencies toward a rigid centralism accorded little scope for local self-government, an institution he considered essential if the Rumanians were to acquire political maturity and if they and their neighbors were to settle their problems and live together in peace. He could not escape the feeling that they were living in a time of great uncertainty, when everything was in a state of flux, and, at the beginning of the constitutional period, he refused to pledge his nation to a particular course of action until the court had clarified its future.[3]

Şaguna thought that the historical principality of Transylvania offered the Rumanians the most suitable framework within which to develop their national life. He chose, therefore, to treat the Banat and the Partium as separate entities. This course of action was dictated partly by his own attachment to existing constitutional forms and partly by his belief that the court would be more easily moved to make concessions if the Rumanians proceeded along a fixed legal path rather than appealing to abstract principles like the rights of nationality. He did not for a moment doubt the justice of their claims to equality and self-determination, nor did he fail to perceive the enormous creative potential inherent in national consciousness, but in his experience neither of these ideas had proved effective in compelling bureaucrats to take action; only precedent and law seemed capable of moving them. He was, consequently, reluctant to give up a strong constitutional position in Transylvania, however little it seemed to offer for the time being, in exchange for a new division of provinces that might destroy any possibility of a corporate national existence. This concern for constitutional precedent helps to explain why Şaguna and most other Rumanian leaders clung so tenaciously to the idea of "nation" long after it had lost its original significance and had indeed become something of an anachronism; and why, hence, they insisted that only through formal proclamation of them as a fourth nation could equal status be achieved. It also helps to explain why Şaguna made no effort to cooperate with the other non-Magyar nationalities of Hungary, as he had done fleetingly in the spring of 1849; he could now see nothing to be gained (and much to be lost) by linking the Rumanian cause to totally different legal and historical problems in the other provinces of the monarchy.

In limiting his activities to Transylvania, Şaguna in effect abandoned the idea of a political unification of all the Rumanians of the monarchy, a goal he had strongly advocated in the spring of 1849. He continued, nonetheless, to pursue the ideal of national unity, but now under a different form. In the intervening decade he had turned from a political to what might be called a spiritual union, and his instrument was to be the church, under whose protection he hoped to unite all the Rumanian Orthodox of the monarchy—of the Banat, the Partium, and Bukovina as well as Transylvania—into a single metropolis. Here, too, he based his position upon law and precedent—the canons of the Eastern church and the historical evolution of Rumanian Orthodoxy in Transylvania—not upon the idea of nationality. Since his plan made no provision for the Uniates, it found little favor as a substitute for political unity among the lay intellectuals, who considered the end result merely "half a union."

Şaguna favored the maintenance of the traditional role of the bishops as the leaders of the national movement. The historical evolution of the Rumanian nation had made them the natural leaders of their people, to whom they had always turned in times of crisis.[4] He also justified the role of the bishops by citing the church's preeminence in cultural and spiritual life. It had been the most vital force in the whole history of the Rumanians, and he was determined not to relinquish any of his own responsibilities in an age of growing materialism and religious indifference. But he was also aware of the dangers inherent in the church's deep involvement in purely secular affairs and, paradoxically, he tried to keep the church out of politics and to maintain a clear distinction between his roles as bishop and as political leader.

Confident of his right to lead, Şaguna decided to impose "discipline" upon the independent-minded individuals and the loosely organized groups who made up the national movement. Their cause had always suffered from a lack of coordination and, as a result, its loyal supporters had frequently wasted their energies on trifles. He warned his colleagues that if the Rumanians were ever to be taken seriously by the court and the Magyars, they must stop the tendency to go in all directions at the same time and, instead, submit to some kind of central direction.

Şaguna's main goal in the two years that followed the Alba Iulia conference of February 1861 was the passage of legislation recognizing the legal existence of the Rumanian nation and its two churches and guaranteeing them full equality with the other nations and churches of Transylvania;[5] such a law would give the Rumanians precisely that solid constitutional position he considered necessary if they were to escape the tutelage of others. It was essential that the Rumanians themselves have a role in this "noble undertaking," and he urged adoption by the court of three measures that would make their participation worthwhile: first, the holding of a new national congress where the various opinions on the future of the nation could be fused into a common plan of action; second, the convocation of the Transylvanian diet to carry out the long-overdue reform of the principality's laws and institutions; and finally, the promulgation of an electoral law liberal enough to give the Rumanians adequate proportional representation in the diet.[6]

These were also the goals of most Rumanian intellectuals. Like Şaguna, they advocated constitutional and democratic methods — a national congress and a freely elected diet with proportional representation for each nation — and they looked to Vienna to tip the scales in their favor against the Magyars and Saxons. But for them, unlike Şaguna, the idea of nationality was paramount. They acted as if it were a law unto itself and knew no limits except its own fruition. The link with the dynasty was for them not an organic one, as it was for Şaguna, but was, rather, a means to an end. Their advocacy of federalism, for example, was intended primarily to promote national development, not to reform the monarchy. They were eager to bring about the union of all the Rumanians of the monarchy into a single political entity as quickly as possible. Regarding union as an act of national fulfillment, they were not overly concerned about the legal and constitutional questions that weighed so heavily in Şaguna's thinking.

As the opportunities for political debate and the expression of national feeling increased, the intellectuals found it ever more difficult to reconcile their own eagerness for immediate results with Şaguna's cautious approach to politics. They came to resent his dominant role in political affairs because it seemed to them that he (and, to a lesser extent, Şuluţiu) lacked sufficient independence in dealing with the court and sometimes put sectarian interests ahead of the national welfare. They were also irritated by his and Şuluţiu's assumption that they spoke for the nation, and they suspected that the two bishops encouraged the emperor and his ministers to treat directly with them rather than with the elected representatives of the Rumanian people. But in the interests of national unity everyone was careful to avoid an open break, and when, in the spring of 1863, it appeared that at last the Rumanians would gain constitutional recognition, animosities dissolved in a new spirit of cooperation. Şaguna's policy seemed vindicated.

The year 1861 saw feverish activity by Rumanian intellectuals. Convinced that they could seriously influence the course of events, they joined enthusiastically (if not always effectively) in the reorganization of county government and in preparations for the convocation of the diet. Their chief political instrument was the permanent committee set up at the national conference in January. Presided over by Şaguna and Şuluţiu and representing a broad cross-section of opinion, it met frequently in the spring and summer to plan strategy and draw up memoranda for the edification of the emperor and various ministries.

In spite of the high hopes and hard work of its eighteen members, the permanent committee failed to function effectively. The causes must be sought in the general weaknesses of the national movement rather than in any particular defects of the committee itself. It was, in fact, two committees: one in Sibiu and Orthodox, and the other in Blaj and Uniate; and before any major decisions could be taken, several journeys between the two places by parties of negotiators were often necessary to avoid offending one side or the other. Şaguna and Şuluţiu did not get along. In spite of their public displays of harmony and genuine efforts at cooperation, they could not avoid friction, as each, conscious of his ecclesiastical responsibilities, worked to protect the interests of his respective church. Moreover, the committee lacked a sufficient number of qualified leaders at all levels to perform those myriad tasks essential for the development and continuity of a large-scale political movement. Finally, there was a chronic lack of money, which severely restricted the committee's activities and once drove an exasperated Barițiu to complain that he could not even afford postage stamps to invite members to meetings. To make up deficits the committee usually had to resort to public subscriptions among intellectuals and the clergy.

In spite of these difficulties, the committee could have done more to create a strong central organization and set up a permanent network of local branches in the cities and larger district towns. Șaguna must bear the chief responsibility for this lack of initiative, since he was the acknowledged leader of the national movement. He preferred to conduct political affairs in the traditional manner through direct, *ad hoc* negotiations with the court. Well aware of the reluctance of Francis Joseph and his ministers to entrust too much authority to the "peasant nations," Șaguna was anxious to avoid any political action—like the organization of a broadly-based political party—that might be interpreted as anti-dynastic. He was apprehensive lest a general clamor for national rights jeopardize favorable action on the step-by-step constitutional plan he and some of his colleagues had devised or even persuade the court that its own best interest lay not in cooperation with the nationalities but in an accommodation with the Magyars. He shared the fears of most Rumanian leaders that the Magyar aristocrats, for whose continued influence at court they all had the deepest respect, might succeed in mediating the differences between the dynasty and Hungary and thereby reestablish Magyar hegemony over Transylvania as it had existed before 1848.[7] His sanguine public pronouncements notwithstanding, he had serious doubts about how deeply the Austrians were committed to satisfying national aspirations. Consequently, he thought it all the more necessary for the Rumanians to prove their worth to the court by using every opportunity to demonstrate their loyalty and their respect for law and order; in this way, they might put to rest suspicions about their irredentism and doubts about their capacity for self-government.

Șaguna was also concerned about the growing differences between Rumanian intellectuals and Magyar leaders in both Hungary and

Transylvania. Like his colleagues on the permanent committee, he realized that if the Magyar conservatives succeeded in maintaining their control of county government and the court system in Transylvania, there would be no justice for the Rumanians and, hence, no peace between the two nationalities. Şuluţiu summed up their feelings when he remarked that the Magyars were strict constitutionalists in all questions except Rumanian rights in Transylvania. Most Rumanian leaders expected little else even from Magyar liberals. Promises by Ferenc Deák to give Rumanian proposals a sympathetic hearing, and urgings by Bishop Haynald that the Rumanians negotiate with "Hungarians from Hungary" on the grounds that they viewed Transylvanian problems from a broader perspective than the Transylvanians evoked no serious response.[8] Rumanian leaders, including Şaguna, were wary of such assurances; they were reminded of promises they had heard in the spring and summer of 1848, particularly at the Committee on the Union, which were followed by the total disregard of their national rights later in the year. Yet Şaguna, for one, was anxious to avoid a break with the Magyars, for he could not conceive of a prosperous Transylvania without their full participation in its affairs. Thinking always as a Transylvanian, he regarded cooperation between Rumanians and Magyars as foreordained; they had lived side-by-side for a thousand years, and the Magyars were as much a part of Transylvania as the Rumanians.

The year 1861 also saw a hardening of attitudes by the three parties most concerned with the future of Transylvania — the court, the Magyars, and the Rumanians. Their positions had remained remarkably close to what they had been in 1848, and hence the prospects of compromise and a settlement acceptable to all seemed remote. At all events, the decisive contest was again to be between Vienna and the Magyars.

In the spring and summer the Magyars mounted an effective campaign against the February Patent and Austrian designs for Hungary in both Pest and Transylvania. They were determined not to yield on the question of the validity of Transylvania's union with Hungary in 1848. At the Hungarian diet in May Deák argued that the union had been carried out in a legal, constitutional manner, since it had been approved by both diets and sanctioned by the emperor. He admitted that the great majority of Rumanians had had no say in the matter, but he pointed out that their lack of representation in the Transylvanian diet was owing chiefly to the aristocratic social and political institutions of the time rather than to deliberate national discrimination; he demonstrated that the Rumanian and Saxon noble had the same voting rights as the Magyar, while the Magyar peasant suffered from the same legal disabilities as his Rumanian counterpart. He argued that the union had actually benefitted the great mass of the population by abolishing the privileged status of the Magyar, Szekler, and Saxon nations and by extending civil and political rights to all classes and nationalities, and he professed to see no reason why the Rumanians should fear it.[9] Joseph Eötvös echoed Deák's sentiments. Other deputies also assured the Rumanians that they would have ample opportunity to develop their cultural life and use their language in local affairs, the schools, and the courts. But they all made any concessions dependent upon the maintenance of Hungary's territorial integrity. However sincere their desire for an agreement with the nationalities, they would not tolerate political movements that tended to create "states within a state."

The Magyars made any settlement of the nationality problem in Transylvania conditional upon the recognition by Austria of Hungary's own right of self-determination within the monarchy. Ignoring the Diploma and the Patent, Deák and his supporters demanded the recognition of Hungary's political and territorial integrity and the appointment of a responsible Hungarian ministry—desiderata they incorporated into the diet's address to the throne in May. The reply from Vienna on July 21, reiterating the provisions of the Diploma and the Patent, rejected Magyar pretensions. As for Transylvania, the court denied that the union had become law in 1848 and opposed it now on the grounds that it provided insufficient guarantees for the maintenance of the Gesamtmonarchie and ignored the interests of the non-Magyar nationalities. The diet was quick to respond in kind. On August 10, in a second address, it repeated everything that had been said in the first. Neither side showed any inclination to compromise, whereupon Francis Joseph dissolved the diet on August 21, and the Schmerling ministry undertook to organize the provincial and local governments of Hungary.

The restoration of county government in Transylvania found the court and the Magyars equally at odds. Shortly after the promulgation of the February Patent Francis Joseph had instructed the Transylvanian Chancellery to complete the organization of local administration by April 1861, so that elections to the diet and the dispatch of its representatives to the imperial parliament could take place as soon as possible. Again demonstrating its reluctance to drop its aristocratic partners and seek new leadership, it entrusted these tasks to Chancellor Kemény and Governor Mikó; both men had shown little sympathy for the principles enunciated in the Patent and were intent upon achieving the only objective that really mattered to them — the maintenance of Magyar supremacy through the union of Transylvania with Hungary. Furthermore, the court made no serious attempt to redefine the juridical relationships between the various nationalities, but instead allowed the chancellery to be guided by the political system in force before 1848. As a result, the very elements which opposed the court's policies gained ascendancy; Magyars dominated most of the county assemblies, which showed no hesitation in proclaiming their approval of the Law of Union of 1848.

The Rumanians were by no means idle, and in largely traditional ways they tried to bring their own views to bear on the struggle between the court and the Magyars. The permanent committee, under Şaguna's direction, decided to concentrate its efforts in Vienna as a more likely source of concessions than Pest. In May and the beginning of June the committee and independent groups of intellectuals met almost continuously in Sibiu and Blaj to plan strategy. They agreed that, initially, their most effective course of action would be to inform the emperor and his new ministers at first hand about their proposals (especially a new national congress) and, by way of contrast, to point out the "true nature" of Magyar aims in Transylvania. Accordingly, in the middle of June the committee dispatched a delegation to Vienna consisting of Ioan Raţiu, Elie Măcelariu, and Iacob Bologa, the latter two councillors at state tribunals in Sibiu and, unlike Raţiu who was a Uniate, prominent Orthodox laymen. The composition of the delegation was meant to symbolize the unity of the Rumanian nation even in its religious diversity. Its true significance lay in the fact that it was the first official Rumanian delegation to the emperor not headed by a member of the clergy and that it afforded the lay intellectuals their first opportunity to deal directly with the court.

The delegation decided to travel by way of Timişoara and Pest in order to sound out the Rumanian leaders in the Banat and Hungary on possible joint action. They found the Banaters, led by the Mocionis, eager to hold a general congress of all the Rumanians of the monarchy

rather than one restricted to Transylvania. Like most Rumanians in
the adjoining counties of Bihor and Zarand, they were anxious to be
included in Transylvania should any redrawing of provincial boundaries occur, for otherwise they faced incorporation into Greater Hungary, an event they thought would reduce them to the level of an insignificant minority. Consequently, they urged the Transylvanians to
work for the creation of a large autonomous duchy that would accommodate all the Rumanian-inhabited territories of the monarchy.[10]

In Pest Raţiu and his colleagues found Rumanian deputies in the
Hungarian diet, which had opened on April 6, 1861, equally determined to defend the national cause, but more inclined than the
Banaters and Transylvanians to consider a compromise with the Magyars. The Rumanians, led by Emmanuel Gojdu and Alois Vlad, a lawyer, thought that the Magyar deputies would finally come around to
the idea that each nationality, like the Magyars, should have the right
to develop along its own lines. But Raţiu remained skeptical. In conversations with Bishop Haynald, Domokos Teleki, a prominent member of the Upper House of the diet, and other Magyar leaders he
greeted their promises of full rights for the Rumanians with the obser-
vation that only the "recognition of their nationality" could satisfy
them.[11]

The delegation arrived in Vienna on June 22. The weeks that followed were largely taken up with official visits. Although Bariţiu had
not made the trip, his influence was strongly felt, for he and Raţiu
were in continuous correspondence. On the whole, the Austrians were
very encouraging and displayed a more than perfunctory interest in
the plight of the Rumanians. Raţiu and his companions were wary
about committing their people to unlimited cooperation with the
court, suspecting that the Austrians might try to use them merely to
force the Magyars into some kind of agreement. Once they had served
this purpose, promises about national rights would be forgotten, as in
1848.[12] They preferred, therefore, to maintain their freedom of action
and to leave the door open (however slightly) for an understanding
with the Magyars.

On July 1, Francis Joseph received the delegation at a private audience. Raţiu presented the petition he had brought from Sibiu requesting the convocation of the Transylvanian diet and a national congress
for the Rumanians (of Tranyslvania only), and Bologa recited at
length how the three nations had mistreated the Rumanians in the

past and how the reorganization of county government then underway was perpetuating this injustice. Francis Joseph replied that he knew what the status of the Rumanians before 1848 had been and assured them that the discrimination would cease. Raţiu quoted him as saying that he understood why the Rumanians opposed the union of Transylvania with Hungary and that he would never approve it.[13]

Schmerling was equally reassuring. He seemed better informed than other Austrian ministers about Rumanian problems, probably because his secretary, who read *Gazeta de Transilvania,* reported to him regularly on the situation in Transylvania. He asked Raţiu for a detailed memorandum on existing voting requirements and the changes which would benefit the Rumanians. He seemed genuinely surprised when Bologa explained how the 1,000 Magyar inhabitants of the village of Olahfalu elected the same number of deputies to the diet—two—as the 200,000 Rumanians of the whole Haţeg district and declared that "such absurdities" could no longer be tolerated, since the Rumanians formed a majority of the population in Transylvania and owned more land than the Magyars. Schmerling promised that the property qualifications for voting would be reduced and that the Rumanians would be "well represented" in the diet.[14] He also asked for a list of prominent Rumanians who could serve as regalists (appointees of the emperor) in the forthcoming diet. When Bologa warned that the Transylvanian Chancellery and Gubernium would probably choose only the two bishops and "loyal" civil servants rather than true representatives of Rumanian public opinion, Schmerling assured them that the emperor himself would make the appointments.

Discussions with the Transylvanian chancellor were less satisfactory and offered little hope that Magyar-Rumanian differences could be resolved amicably. Kemény, eager to strengthen the bonds between Transylvania and Hungary, would consider the future status of the Rumanians only in that context. He opposed the convocation of the Transylvanian diet on the grounds that the fate of the principality had been definitively settled in 1848, and he was unwilling to grant to the Rumanians or the Saxons any boon other than those rights enjoyed by all individual citizens of Hungary. If, in spite of everything, the diet were held, then he intended to assure the same kind of upper-class Magyar majority as had characterized the diets before 1848. As an aristocrat himself, he expressed a horror of the *rohe Volksmasse* and proposed to maintain the high property qualifications applied in electing the diet of 1791, thereby restricting the franchise to the larger land-owners and "intellectuals."[15] It followed that he was utterly opposed to the formation of a Rumanian national territory and could see no need for a national congress.

From Sibiu Şaguna kept track of the delegation's activities with mounting irritation. He accused its members of exceeding their authority by negotiating with Schmerling and other officials, since their mission had been precisely defined: deliver the petition, make verbal representations to the emperor and the ministers in support of it, and return home. In Şaguna's view, their subsequent activities made it appear as though the Rumanian movement had no central direction and that individuals could pursue their own aims without consulting the permanent committee.[16] He was particularly upset by the delegation's efforts to obtain approval for a general national congress, in view of the official position that only a limited, Transylvanian congress should be held. As head of the national movement, he should at least be consulted about changes of policy. In a brusque letter to the delegation he pronounced their mission terminated and declared that he would not communicate with them again. Bologa and Măceleriu left Vienna in the latter part of July, partly, it seems, because of the lack of money, but Raţiu stayed on (at Bariţiu's urging) in order to advise Schmerling and other officials on Rumanian opinion and at the same time keep his friends in Transylvania abreast of events at court. This bitter incident was the first open breach between Şaguna and the intellectuals. Symptomatic of deep divisions within the leadership of the national movement, it reinforced the intellectuals' conviction that ecclesiastical control had become an intolerable burden.

While the court was attempting to force its new order upon the Magyars and was fumbling about in search of a nationality policy, the Rumanians provided the chief opposition to the Magyars' reorganization of Transylvania, with an intensive, if poorly coordinated, political campaign which extended from one end of Transylvania to the other —to the surprise of both the court and the Magyars. The occasion was the reestablishment of a regular county administration after nearly twelve years of "provisional" government. Except in a few counties where the Rumanians were in the overwhelming majority the Magyars succeeded in dominating the county commissions, bodies of one hundred members responsible for drafting county statutes and appointing officials. Their objective was to restore the old system and ratify the union of Transylvania with Hungary as quickly as possible. As a result, they lightly passed over Rumanian demands for proportional representation and the use of Rumanian as an official language, and they ignored protests that the procedures followed by the majority were contrary to the provisions of the October Diploma and other imperial decrees guaranteeing national rights. By the middle of May 1861 it had become apparent to Rumanian leaders that further protests at the local level would be to no avail. It was at this point that the permanent committee had decided to send Raţiu and his colleagues to Vienna.

At the same time, a widespread Rumanian opposition movement developed. Organized mainly by lay intellectuals working outside the permanent committee, it took the form of passive resistance, that is, a refusal to obey the new county officials.[17] Orthodox and Uniate priests were extremely active, too, and in many villages they personally directed the protest movement. The lay intellectuals counted heavily upon clerical support, and they urged protopopes and priests to participate fully in the county assemblies and other political activities. The chancellery and the Gubernium gave credence to numerous reports from local Magyar officials, accusing priests of "encouraging civil disobedience" among their faithful and warning of the danger of open violence. They blamed Şaguna for much of the unrest because of his alleged failure to curb the political activities of his clergy.[18]

Şaguna had observed the growing tension with deep misgivings. It seemed to him that the Magyars and Saxons were trying to reestablish their old privileged status at the expense of the Rumanians. He was especially critical of the Saxons for their disregard of Rumanian claims to equality in the Fundus regius. Convinced that the Rumanians had a legitimate right to defend their own interests, he was incensed at the accusations of illegal activity made by Chancellor Kemény and the Saxon count, Franz Salmen, against his clergy. He pointed out to both in blunt terms that in a constitutional state Rumanian priests were, after all, citizens and had as much right as anyone else to take part in public affairs. He denied that they were guilty of any unlawful acts; on the contrary, the meetings they had organized and the petitions they had signed were intended to accomplish the full restoration of legality by bringing Transylvanian institutions into harmony with the principle of national equality. They had good reason to take the initiative themselves, especially in the Fundus regius, because no one in authority had seen fit to consult the Rumanians.[19]

In the fall of 1861 the court attempted to break the political stalemate in Transylvania and, at the same time, to apply pressure on Magyar leaders in Pest. On September 19, ignoring the great confusion in Transylvania, Francis Joseph instructed Governor Mikó to make all necessary preparations for the convocation of the diet on November 4. Mikó refused. Using arguments advanced earlier by Deák in the Hungarian diet, he insisted that the Law of Union was still in force, and hence no diet was necessary.[20] The constitutional crisis deepened, and the status of Transylvania became more uncertain.

Under the impress of these events, and apprehensive lest the indecisiveness of the court presage a compromise with the Magyars, Rumanian leaders met at the end of September to plan new strategy. At a series of meetings of the permanent committee the effect of Magyar intransigence in the counties on Rumanian leaders was manifest. Reserve toward Vienna had all but disappeared, as in 1848 when Rumanian intellectuals had been impelled by events over which they had had little control to seek an alliance with the court. Now, as then, the result was to frustrate any hopes they may still have had of an understanding with Magyar liberals. They perceived the incongruity of cooperation with conservative Austria, and they blamed the Magyar aristocracy both at Vienna and in Transylvania for keeping their two peoples apart. But Şaguna and other members of the permanent committee were pragmatists who were painfully aware of the precarious situation in which they found themselves, and they decided to stay with tradition. A new delegation was dispatched to Vienna under the leadership of Şuluţiu. Şaguna pleaded ill health as the reason for not accompanying him.

The delegation, which arrived on October 8, met with a sympathetic reception. The only disturbing notes were inquiries by Austrian officials about the loyalty of *all* Rumanians to the dynasty and about internal political differences that had allegedly divided them into several contending parties.[21] Şuluţiu urged Şaguna to come to Vienna without delay in order to give the lie to rumors of disunity and to lend his considerable influence to the delegation's efforts to extract something more than vague promises from the bureaucracy. Şaguna would not budge. Poor health, about which he now began to complain regularly, undoubtedly discouraged long-distance travel, but he was also clearly reluctant to compromise the dignity of his church by being cast in a subordinate role to the Uniate metropolitan.[22]

The delegation settled down in Vienna and showed signs of becoming a permanent embassy — an institution, moreover, that a number of its members, notably Raţiu and the Rumanians from the Banat, were eager to create. They viewed it as a means of counteracting allegedly false and misleading information about Rumanian aspirations and events generally in Transylvania. But the chronic lack of money cut short their stay. The permanent committee had to take up a collection in order to pay their expenses home.[23] Nonetheless, on November 5, before leaving Vienna, they decided to offer the *Österreichische Zeitung* a monthly subsidy to print articles favorable to the Rumanian cause as a means of exerting at least some influence on official and public opinion. Vincenţiu Babeş, a member of the Hungarian diet from the Banat, was to supply the necessary material, and the sum of two hundred florins a month was to be raised for his compensation by a private subscription among Rumanian leaders,[24] but the venture seems to have gone no further.

In spite of numerous disappointments, the delegation did succeed in accomplishing its main task. At a private audience with Francis Joseph on October 26, Şuluţiu delivered a strong protest on behalf of the permanent committee against the Gubernium's obstruction of the diet and tried to enlighten him on the general attitude of the Magyar aristocracy in Transylvania. As usual, Francis Joseph's reply was encouraging; he insisted that the diet would be held, that organs of government would be established to foster the well-being of all the peoples of Transylvania, that the union of Transylvania with Hungary would not be approved, and, finally, that the Rumanians would have full equality with the other nations.[25] Şuluţiu came away convinced that at last the Austrians had begun to understand the role of the non-Magyar nationalities in the monarchy. He detected in the emperor's little speech an awareness of Magyar separatist tendencies and an intention to proceed with the consolidation of the monarchy by relying upon the Rumanians and Slavs to support the dynasty. In spite of his optimism, Şuluţiu had already become aware that such promises could only be fulfilled if the court was willing to make national equality the cornerstone of its policy; otherwise, relations between Austria and the nationalities would again be compromised, this time, perhaps, irrevocably.[26]

While the delegation was still in Vienna important changes took place in the composition of the Transylvanian government which tended to confirm Şuluţiu's optimistic assessment of the situation. On

November 7, Count Ferenc Nadásdy, a Magyar whose family had long
served the imperial cause and who was himself minister of justice from
1857 to 1860, was appointed Transylvanian chancellor to succeed Kemény, who had been forced to resign, and a few days later Count
Ludwig Folliot de Crenneville replaced Mikó as governor. On the
ninth, the Rumanians had their first meeting with the new chancellor,
who assured them of his determination to carry out the principle of
national equality as set forth in the October Diploma and the February
Patent. He outlined the procedures he intended to follow: the immediate convocation of the Transylvanian diet, the selection of its representatives to the imperial parliament, and the enactment of legislation granting full equality to all nationalities. He also went into
detail about the changes he planned to make in local government, the
most notable being to appoint additional Rumanian officials in areas
with Rumanian majorities. The delegation came away from the meeting certain that the time of national fulfillment was close at hand. A
few days later, at Nadásdy's request, Şuluţiu and Raţiu submitted a
memorandum with statistics on the Rumanian population in Transylvania, to serve as a guide in determining the proportion of Rumanian
representation in the diet, and a list of Rumanians recommended for
appointment to the diet as regalists.[27]

Nadásdy's statements about national equality were undoubtedly sincere, yet he did not feel comfortable in his new partnership with the
Rumanians. Like his colleagues, he seriously doubted the political maturity of the intellectuals, and he feared the peasantry as an unstable
element easily moved to excesses. These feelings may account for his
repeated exhortations to Şaguna and Şuluţiu to maintain peace and
order among their faithful.[28] During his tenure as chancellor Nadásdy
strove to keep control of Rumanian political developments in his own
hands and to discourage Rumanian leaders from embarking upon any
truly innovative course of action such as the formation of an independent political party. His overriding concern was to see that the
Rumanians served the interests of Vienna, a strategy that was never
more forcefully applied than during the two sessions of the Transylvanian diet in 1863 and 1864.

The delegation finally left for home on November 30. As was
customary, Şuluţiu travelled directly to Sibiu to report to Şaguna on
the results of his mission. Şaguna thought that his colleague had accomplished as much as could have been expected, but he displayed a

marked skepticism toward Austrian intentions. He was not yet convinced that the court would go so far as Francis Joseph and Nadásdy had said it would. Consequently, he chose not to endorse Nadásdy's plan for the convocation of the diet until, as he confided to Şuluţiu, the precise "needs of the future" could be ascertained.[29]

Most Rumanian leaders were more confident than Şaguna; they judged their first full year of renewed political activity to have been a promising beginning. The future looked bright as they contemplated their nation's development over the centuries. They were heartened by the knowledge that they had survived nearly two millennia of foreign domination, and they discerned in the "moral fiber" of the Rumanians, as one of them put it, their strongest guarantee against assimilation.[30] A new sophistication and self-confidence were also discernible. They were no longer satisfied merely to bask in the reflected glory of Rome or to congratulate themselves that they had not perished; now they were asking one another whether the Rumanian nation did not in fact have some higher calling to contribute to the general progress of Europe, of which they felt themselves to be so intimately a part.

Their immediate preoccupations, however, centered about the composition of the diet, which they viewed as the instrument through which they could shape their own destiny, and the demarcation of a national territory. Because they were anxious to secure a majority in the diet, they pushed for the adoption of a liberal franchise. At the same time they conceived of representation in terms of nation, that is, on the basis of the total amount of land possessed by the members of each nationality and the total contribution of each to the general welfare in taxes and recruits for the army.[31] Acutely aware of their own lack of organization, they did not dare risk everything in an open election campaign, but preferred that the court assign them a fixed number of seats according to these criteria, which they were certain would assure them of the majority they needed. For these reasons they insisted upon the preservation of the constitutional device of the nation long after it had ceased to have any legal significance.

While there was general agreement on the diet, Rumanian leaders differed on the need for a separate territory. At one extreme were the disciples of Simion Bărnuţiu, who demanded immediate federalization of the monarchy. They were prepared to do away with "medieval" provincial boundaries and to divide the various peoples into separate and autonomous national "duchies." They promised full equality to minorities but showed less interest in such "subsidiary questions" than in the fulfillment of their own idea of nationality.[32]

In the center was George Barițiu. He was willing to keep existing provincial boundaries for the sake of convenience, but he proposed that county and district boundaries be redrawn so as to include only one "homogeneous genetic nation." In places where such clearcut divisions were impossible, he insisted upon the free development of each nationality. A single language for the provincial administration would be a convenience that all could accept, but he proposed that each person be allowed to use his mother tongue in the parliament, any branch of the administration, and the courts. He saw no danger that a state with so many nationalities and languages would disintegrate; liberal that he was, he was convinced that a "noble rivalry" among the nations of Transylvania could bring only good to all.[33] His model was Switzerland, whose cantonal system he had advocated as a solution to the nationality problem since the 1840s.

The third group, led by Șaguna, consisted of those who wished to maintain the historical, autonomous Transylvanian principality. They were no less federalist in their thinking than Barițiu, but they were more reluctant than he or Bărnuțiu's followers to tamper with long-established constitutional forms. Șaguna's arguments in favor of preserving Transylvania as a separate entity within the monarchy were many: tradition and law had sanctified it; the national interest and the welfare of the Orthodox Church made experimentation with new political forms extremely hazardous; and to abandon the autonomy of Transylvania for various new territorial subdivisions would be to remove the strongest legal barrier to the incorporation of the Rumanians into Greater Hungary and — given the mixed nature of the population in many areas — to risk subjecting large numbers of them (and of Orthodox) to Magyar or Saxon jurisdiction. In the back of Șaguna's mind was always the thought that Austria and the Magyars might reconcile their differences before federalism became a reality and that the Rumanians, without the protection of a Transylvania, would be left in a sort of constitutional limbo — a position that would invite others to decide their fate. Of no less importance to him was the hope for a Magyar-Rumanian rapprochement, which might be effectively obstructed by the creation of separate territories.[34]

Rumanian expectations of an immediate settlement of Transylvania's future proved premature, as Magyar opposition on all fronts in-

creased in intensity. In Transylvania large numbers of officials resigned, and a campaign of passive resistance to Austrian authorities
spread rapidly from county to county. The orderly processes of
government were so far undone that preparations for the diet had to
be postponed indefinitely. Yet Schmerling still hesitated to turn his
back on the Magyars and rely upon the Rumanians to carry out the
political reorganization of Transylvania. He evidently hoped to apply
enough pressure in Vienna and Pest to bring the Magyars into line
and, in any case, he took little comfort in the prospects of an alliance
with the Rumanians, who had done nothing to persuade him that they
were fit for great political responsibilities. As a result, 1862 was a year
of uneasy stalemate. The Rumanians watched and waited, and their
intense activity of the previous year was not repeated. The Magyars,
who showed no signs of weakening, were now joined in their passive resistance by the Czechs and Croats. The constitutional crisis deepened,
as the imperial senate (*Reichsrat*) and other institutions provided for
in the February Patent functioned fitfully. Schmerling needed a forceful demonstration in support of his policies, and the most likely place
for it seemed to be Transylvania. In order to set the constitutional machinery in motion he proceeded with uncommon haste to satisfy the
long-standing demands of the Rumanians for a national congress and
an extended franchise.

His first step was to recommend the convocation of a national
congress. Accordingly, on October 18, 1862, Francis Joseph instructed
the Transylvanian Chancellery to "propose ways of enabling" the Rumanians to "consult with one another" and participate in framing the
principality's new constitution. On February 17, 1863, acting on the
advice of the council of ministers, he granted the Rumanians permission to hold a national conference of up to 150 delegates and allowed
Şaguna and Şuluţiu to decide upon the method of selecting them and
the date. The council of ministers' action had been far from unanimous. Folliot de Crenneville objected to any kind of general meeting
on the grounds that it would cause the Magyars and Saxons to demand
the same, thereby creating even greater disorder than already existed;
Count Rechberg warned against providing any stimulus that might
lead the Rumanians of the monarchy into a "closer communion" with
their brothers beyond the Carpathians.[35] Even Nadásdy, who favored
the congress, opposed any sort of electoral campaign out of fear that
widespread demonstrations would result and a majority be chosen that

would be difficult to manage. He and a number of his colleagues still harbored strong doubts about the genuineness of the Rumanian intellectuals' loyalty to Austria and were prepared for some act of defiance.[36]

Through Rumanian employees of the chancellery Şaguna kept himself well informed of these official misgivings and, to avoid what he considered unnecessary complications, he appointed the seventy-five Orthodox delegates himself. In selecting them he took into account geographical distribution and diversity of opinion, and he respected the traditional proportion of two laymen for every priest maintained in his church on such occasions. Nearly all the protopopes—twenty-one—and the most important laymen were present. Although this was a highly representative group, many intellectuals, both Uniate and Orthodox, resented the fact that Şaguna had not allowed an election but had merely perpetuated ecclesiastical control of national affairs.[37] Şuluţiu, pressed by Bariţiu, Raţiu, and others, allowed the Uniate clergy and intellectuals to choose their own representatives at small local gatherings.

The conference opened in Sibiu on April 20, and, as he had done on the last occasion, Şaguna dominated the proceedings. Although he shared the president's chair with Şuluţiu, it was he who provided the agenda and led the discussions and, in the end, won the delegates over to his point of view.[38] He used the occasion to press for the adoption of a national program that would combine the maintenance of Transylvania's autonomy with the creation of new federalist ties between all the provinces and Vienna. Once again he pleaded for a "common Transylvanian spirit" that would enable the inhabitants of the principality to settle their differences and contribute their talents to the general good.[39] He was, however, quick to point out that Transylvania could not stand by itself; it possessed neither the political strength nor the economic resources to maintain a separate existence. They had no choice but to join a federalized system with strong central institutions that would manage the common affairs of all its parts such as defense, foreign relations, and finances and at the same time impose respect in each province for the "enlightened principles" that would guide the constitutional development of the whole monarchy. To demonstrate their allegiance to the new Austria he urged the delegates to accept the October Diploma and the February Patent as the foundations of their new constitution.[40]

There was little opposition to anything Şaguna said. All the speeches and debates displayed the same loyalty to Austria and the same willingness to incorporate the Diploma and Patent into the fundamental law of Transylvania. But there was some reluctance on the part of Bariţiu, Raţiu, and other intellectuals to accept everything the court wanted, including the sending of deputies to the imperial parliament, until it had fulfilled its promises about Transylvanian autonomy and national equality. They reminded their fellow delegates that they had all seen too many drastic political changes in the last fifteen years to commit their nation irrevocably to some course of action before they had first obtained firm guarantees of its right to exist.[41] Bariţiu was disturbed about the unconditional acceptance of the Diploma and Patent because neither contained a "Bill of Rights" or said anything about personal liberty, the inviolability of one's home, freedom of speech and of the press, and religious liberty, and he demanded that these fundamental human rights be specifically mentioned in any representations the conference might make to the throne.[42] But he got no further than the enunciation of his principles. Dimitrie Moldovan, a councillor of the Transylvanian Chancellery, assured his colleagues that all these matters would be satisfactorily resolved in the forthcoming diet, whereupon the conference proceeded to draft an address of gratitude to the emperor.

At its final session on April 23 the conference approved the declaration of national policy it intended to submit to Francis Joseph. It repeated earlier statements about the autonomy of Transylvania, constitutional recognition of the Rumanian nation and its two churches, and proportional representation in the diet and public office, and now for the first time in detail its authors formulated specific educational and social recommendations. They requested a share of the income derived from common lands in the Fundus regius for use by Rumanian schools and churches and proposed the creation throughout Transylvania of permanent endowments by the provincial treasury, similar to those it had established for Roman Catholic and Protestant schools and churches. These proposals reflected Şaguna's continuous (and hitherto unsuccessful) efforts to obtain regular state support for the Orthodox Church. The delegates also urged the immediate establishment of a provincial university and an agricultural credit bank, likewise with state funds. The final act of the conference was the election of a delegation to convey its program to the emperor. Şaguna agreed to lead it, since Şuluţiu was too ill to make the long journey.

The Rumanians received a warm welcome in Vienna. On May 4 an audience was quickly arranged, at which Şaguna repeated his nation's vows of loyalty to the ruling house, and Francis Joseph expressed his pleasure at Rumanian support of the Gesamtmonarchie in the "present difficult circumstances." In the days that followed the Rumanians were the guests of honor at several banquets, where they were the object of unstinting praise by Schmerling and other officials for their "Austrian patriotism." These occasions seem also to have been personal triumphs for Şaguna. Both his imposing appearance and his conviviality were carefully noted in the Viennese press, as were his toasts on behalf of a united Austria.[43]

But national conferences were merely occasions for debate, and delegations were little more than ceremonial in function; decisions, as the Rumanians had already learned, were the prerogative of the court. These truisms manifested themselves in the final preparations for the convocation of the Transylvanian diet. On April 21 an imperial rescript convoking the diet for July 1 set forth the principal topics for its deliberations: the legal recognition of the Rumanian nation and its churches, the settlement of the language question in public affairs, the drafting of a new electoral law, the election of Transylvanian deputies to the imperial parliament, a new political division of the country, the reorganization of the administration and court system, the modification of the agrarian patent of 1854, and the establishment of a credit bank. On the same day the emperor also promulgated a new electoral law which greatly increased the number of Rumanians eligible to vote. Although the tax qualification for voting remained eight florins in direct taxes as in 1848, it now included the capitation as well as the land tax. In addition, priests, doctors, lawyers, notaries, teachers, and certain other social categories were automatically enfranchised. For the first time, nobles as well as non-nobles were required to meet the tax qualification, a provision which eliminated many lesser Magyar nobles who had long since lost their wealth and social position. As a result of the new law, the total number of voters increased from about 15,000 to over 160,000.[44]

These two imperial acts suggest that the court had finally decided that the interests of the Rumanians coincided in some measure with its own. Their provisions were clearly intended to strengthen the Rumanians' position in the forthcoming diet and, at the same time, to neutralize much of the opposition that could be expected from the Magyars. Political equality was by no means intended; the idea of universal suffrage was still utterly foreign to the court, and gerrymandered electoral districts and representation weighted in favor of cities and towns, where Magyars and Saxons generally predominated, were preserved. As a result, the Magyars with a population of 500,000 would elect forty-four deputies, the 200,000 Saxons thirty-three, and the Rumanians, who were nearly twice as numerous as the other two nations, would elect only forty-eight deputies.

All these defects notwithstanding, Rumanian leaders, even the most skeptical, were now convinced that Schmerling and Nádasdy had meant what they said about national equality, and in May and June they entered enthusiastically into what was to be the most open electoral campaign in Transylvania up to that time. At first, their élan far exceeded their organizational abilities; they frequently divided their support among two or more Rumanian candidates, while their Magyar and Saxon opponents acted like seasoned professionals. There were also difficulties of another sort: many county and district electoral boards were dominated by Magyars and Saxons, who attempted to pad the voting rolls with unqualified or non-existent electors of their own choosing and to exclude as many Rumanians as possible. As Ioan Axente noted, everyone wanted to be a candidate, but no one took easily to discipline.[45]

The church once again came to the rescue. The network of Orthodox and Uniate protopopates and parishes compensated for the lack of political organization, and the authority of the two bishops did much to instill a sense of discipline among their clergy and faithful. Şaguna spared no effort to make the elections a success. He filled the columns of his newspaper, *Telegraful Român,* with editorials urging his protopopes and priests to place themselves in the forefront of the electoral campaign. He urged them particularly to see that in their districts and parishes Rumanian electors did not divide up into small cliques but rather supported a single candidate. He also sent out numerous pastoral letters of advice and encouragement, warning in particular against subterfuge by local officials designed to prevent a large turnout of Rumanian voters.[46] In many areas the clergy followed his advice to the letter; they led Rumanian voters to the polling places with church banners flying.[47]

Şaguna's personal intervention helped to decide a number of contests. In the county of Cetatea de Baltă, for example, Augustin Ladai, the prefect, a Rumanian, reported to Şaguna on the zeal with which

Orthodox priests and laymen were working for the election of their candidate. He requested Şaguna's intervention in two electoral districts where the same Rumanian candidate, a George Roman, was running. In the one, where Roman stood little chance of winning, owing to the large number of Magyar voters, Ladai asked Şaguna to instruct the local clergy to support the one Magyar candidate who favored Schmerling's program. In the other, Ladai himself was running against Roman and asked Şaguna's advice on which of them should withdraw in order to avoid splitting Rumanian votes and thereby enabling the Saxon candidate to win. Ladai thought that a word from Şaguna would be enough to settle these matters. Şaguna replied that he would instruct his protopope to have all Rumanian electors support the progovernment Magyar candidate in the one race; he suggested that in the other Ladai himself withdraw, since by virtue of his office he would undoubtedly be appointed to the diet as a regalist.[48]

Şaguna himself was certain to receive an imperial appointment, but at the request of the inhabitants of Sălişte, a large and prosperous Rumanian commune near Sibiu, he stood for election as their deputy. He won a nearly unanimous victory—483 to 1—and when, as expected, the emperor appointed him to the diet as a regalist, he asked permission to decline the honor. He explained to Nadásdy that the Sălişteni were mostly shepherds who had put off their traditional spring trek to the lower Danube in order to vote for him, and he could not therefore bring himself to renounce his mandate and, in a sense, betray their trust.[49] Nadásdy concurred.

The diet opened on July 15, 1863, in Sibiu.[50] The Rumanians had a slight plurality, fifty-seven deputies, including regalists, to fifty-four for the Magyars and forty-three for the Saxons. They were deeply conscious of the historical significance of what was taking place, for by their very presence in the diet they had achieved *de facto* recognition as a constituent nation of Transylvania. But before they could get down to work, the court once again attempted to overcome Magyar opposition. Led by Bishop Haynald, forty-four elected Magyar deputies and eight regalists announced on July 22 that they would boycott the diet on the grounds that it was both illegal and superfluous, since the diet of 1848 had already settled the fate of Transylvania.[51] The Transylvanian government held new elections at once, but the results were almost the same. Hence the Rumanians and Saxons had to carry on alone.

The first session was, nonetheless, fruitful. The chief demands of the Rumanians — the equality of their nation and two churches with the other three nations and the Roman Catholic and Protestant churches, and the recognition of Rumanian as one of the official languages of the country along with Magyar and German[52] — were enacted into law and sanctioned by the emperor. Before they could have the force of law, both bills would require a second reading in the diet and resubmission to the emperor for final approval; these seemed to be mere formalities. The diet also took steps to improve the lot of the Transylvanian peasant. The initiative belonged to the Rumanians and, in particular, to Ioan Raţiu, who was already widely known for his tenacious court defenses of Rumanian and Szekler peasants. At the end of September, a few weeks before the diet adjourned, Raţiu proposed that certain classes of peasants be given full legal possession of the land for which they had rendered labor services and dues before the abolition of serfdom in 1848, and full access to common pasturelands and forests.[53] All the Rumanian delegates warmly supported these bills. Since they were themselves at most only one generation removed from the village, they understood the peasant and sympathized with his hard and unrewarded existence. They also saw in him the free proprietor of his own farm, who would be the foundation of that large and prosperous middle class in which they placed such high hopes. But the first session of the diet disappointed them; it adjourned before any of Raţiu's proposals could be seriously considered.

Although the diet had some major accomplishments to its credit, it failed to live up to its sponsors' expectations. It went about its work in a slow and cumbersome fashion. The use of the three languages inevitably took time, and the debates in both committee and plenary sessions were often long-winded and far removed from the subject at hand. The fine points of constitutional law and procedure and historical right were especially popular topics. Though the Rumanians must bear a major responsibility for such a plodding course, it can be ascribed only in part to their lack of parliamentary experience. Their respect, even reverence, for law and the constitutional process, which had characterized the national movement from its beginnings in the eighteenth century, combined with their long exclusion from public affairs, made them savor every minute of their parliamentary labors. The diet seemed to them the climax of their own struggles and an inevitable step in the general progress of human society toward still greater freedom. They did not concern themselves with time, for they were certain that it was on their side.

As it turned out, such was not the case. The Austrians had made a bargain and they expected it to be kept. They had offered the Rumanians equality and other benefits; in return they expected unconditional support of a unitary monarchy. But they were enormously unhappy with the way the Rumanians had conducted themselves in the diet. Nadásdy echoed the feelings of his colleagues when he complained that, instead of proceeding immediately with the enactment of the government's program, the Rumanians had decided that true parliamentarism consisted in criticizing everything and trying to improve everything down to the smallest detail. He reiterated the government's sympathy for the Rumanians, but warned that "everything had its limits" and prophesied that such an opportunity to accomplish so much might never come again. He pointed out that the ultimate decisions regarding the future of Transylvania would not be made by his chancellery but by the *Staatsrat* and the *Ministerconferenz,* that is, by men whose main concern was the well-being of the monarchy as a whole and who would judge the Rumanians' performance accordingly.[54] The diet of Sibiu, then, was in some measure a testing ground to enable the court to judge how effective the Rumanians would be in managing the affairs of Transylvania and how well they could follow orders. They had evidently failed the test.

Şaguna was one of the few Rumanians at the diet who grasped the seriousness of Austrian aims and who viewed the problems of Transylvania from the same broad perspective of the Gesamtmonarchie. His work in the diet followed the same general pattern that had characterized his political activity since 1848. The government's program, which promised the Rumanians so much, and the diet itself were for him the "natural emanations" of the October Diploma and the February Patent, and he urged their immediate and unconditional incorporation into the constitution of Transylvania. He was also anxious to enact the government's draft laws concerning national equality essentially as they were written in order to avoid lengthy and fruitless debate on minor points, but he insisted nonetheless upon the use of precise language in defining rights and obligations so that local authorities would no longer be able to interpret the law to suit themselves.[55] He also supported most of the democratic and social reforms advocated by the lay intellectuals and was himself sometimes responsible for extending the debate on certain measures to the very limits of official patience.[56]

Later, after 1867, when the compromise between the court and the Magyars had become a reality, Şaguna was severely criticized for his haste in accepting Austrian terms. Bariţiu, who spoke for many, complained that he should have obtained a special imperial diploma recognizing the existence of the Rumanian nation before approving the Diploma and the Patent and sending the Transylvanian contingent to the Reichsrat. Şaguna indeed had had strong doubts about the willingness and ability of the Schmerling government to keep its promises, yet he had pressed for the speedy enactment of its program in order to assure Transylvania's autonomy and through it provide the Rumanians with a constitutional shield against "unforeseen events." He much preferred this "solid" constitutional approach to some contrivance like an imperial writ.

An assessment of Şaguna's role at the diet must also take into account his desire to promote a "Transylvanian patriotism." He reiterated his belief that all the inhabitants of the principality were "sons of one and the same fatherland," and, as he had done at the Alba Iulia conference, he went out of his way to assure the Magyars and Saxons that the Rumanians did not seek to replace the rule of the former three nations with a hegemony of their own. Nor, he emphasized, was his own object to abolish all the previous legislation of Transylvania and start again with a *tabula rasa;* he wanted instead to "repair and expand" the constitution of the country so that all its peoples might find a place in it. As for the sensitive question of language, whose importance in stimulating national feeling and creating a sense of community he recognized, he urged that the study of Rumanian, Magyar, and German be obligatory for all students and public officials.[57] He thought that if ideas like these could find a permanent place in the consciousness of each nation, then suspicion and antagonism must inevitably give way to trust and cooperation—the only basis upon which they could hope to solve their common social and economic problems.

The first session of the diet came to an end on October 13, 1863. Its members were generally satisfied that they had set Transylvania on a new course. Twenty-four of them were elected to represent Transylvania in the lower house of the Reichsrat; Şaguna and Şuluţiu, among others, were appointed to the *Herrenhaus.* At a banquet in their honor in Vienna Schmerling toasted the Rumanians for their "rare acts of devotion and patriotism" and promised that they would soon see what it meant to be a part of the empire.[58]

The second session of the diet opened on May 23, 1864. The Magyars continued their boycott and were now joined, strangely enough, by a number of Rumanian leaders. Şuluţiu was absent for long periods, and Bariţiu came only towards the end. Şaguna stayed away entirely, pleading illness and the need for rest and medical treatment.[59] The state of his health, however poor, did not prevent him from attending to his endless duties as bishop. It appears that his illness was more political than physical. He had made no secret of his disgust with the efforts of certain officials, especially Transylvanian Vice-Chancellor Franz Reichenstein, to cajole and pressure deputies into voting as the government wanted them to. Şaguna looked on helplessly as the deputies' freedom of action and integrity, which he considered indispensable to the law-making process, were undermined and as, in such an atmosphere, honest differences of opinion among Rumanian leaders grew into irreconcilable conflicts. He saw his plans for a truly autonomous Transylvania, where all its inhabitants would be able to work out their own destinies, gradually replaced by a form of centralism which threatened to bring back all the harsh realities of the decade of absolutism. When asked to return to the diet, he refused because (he is alleged to have said) he did not wish to be a party to the death sentence of his nation. He seemed, in fact, already to have sensed a shift in Austrian policy away from cooperation with the nationalities and towards an accommodation with the Magyars. In August he confided his premonitions of disaster to Bariţiu and urged him to do everything in his power to save the cultural association* which the two of them had worked so hard to establish in 1861; if, as he now feared, the Rumanians lost the political position they had gained at the diet of Sibiu, they would still have this "forum of culture and language" to protect their nationality. Bariţiu, writing many years later, admitted that he had grasped the full meaning of the warning only after the changes Şaguna had foreseen had begun to take place.[60]

Although the diet gave the laws on the national equality of the Rumanians and the official use of the three languages a second read-

---

*Asociaţia transilvană pentru literatura română şi cultura poporului român (The Transylvanian Association for Rumanian Literature and the Culture of the Rumanian People). It was generally referred to by its abbreviation, ASTRA.

ing and took up a variety of administrative and economic questions, its second session had little to show for five months' work. The laws remained unsanctioned and never took effect, and bills dealing with such vital questions as the organization of public administration and justice and a permanent electoral law remained bogged down in committee. A modest agrarian law offered by the government was passed after long and acrimonious debate, but consideration of Raţiu's far-reaching amendments was put off to some later date.[61] The diet adjourned on October 29, 1864, in order to allow its representatives to attend the Reichsrat. When it met again, nearly a year later, its sole task would be to proclaim the union of Transylvania with Hungary.

6 / The Great Compromise

During the new session of the Reichsrat, which lasted from November 14, 1864, to July 27, 1865, Şaguna's perception of far-reaching changes in the court's policy toward Hungary was sharpened. He recognized that the intransigence of the Magyars, combined with the mounting resistance of the Czechs and Croats to the regime instituted by the February Patent, had severely undermined the raison d'être of Schmerling's constitutional experiment. Entrusted by the emperor with devising and maintaining a system that would strengthen the position of the dynasty and ensure peace and prosperity at home while enhancing the power and influence of the monarchy in international affairs, Schmerling by the spring of 1865 was instead presiding over a breakdown of normal governmental operations and a rising tide of opposition from the very elements he had depended upon for support. Not only had the nationalities proved to be unmanageable—even the "loyal Rumanians" had displayed a surprising and disagreeable independence at the diet of Sibiu. The German liberals, who in 1860 had acclaimed the new regime as the beginning of a new and forward-looking era in imperial politics, had also become disenchanted with what had become for them merely a sham and had even gone so far as to propose an agreement with their Magyar counterparts. Faced with the possibility of genuine parliamentary government, which would limit the emperor's control of foreign affairs and the army and would oblige him to work with politicians, whom he detested, and troubled by strained relations with Prussia over the affairs of Germany, Francis Joseph now made the settlement of domestic political problems his first priority. No serious politician could doubt that success ultimately depended upon a compromise on outstanding constitutional issues between the court and the Magyars. Preliminary discussions with Magyar leaders in Vienna and Pest led in June 1865 to the resignation of Schmerling and those ministers who had supported his policies, including Nadásdy, and then to Francis Joseph's visit to Buda-Pest—events which suggested progress toward a rapprochement.

At first, most Rumanian leaders simply refused to believe that the replacement of Schmerling and Nadásdy, whom they had regarded as their chief patrons in the government, signalled any drastic changes in the relationship between Transylvania and Hungary or in their own newly-won constitutional status. A union of Transylvania and Hungary on Magyar terms would, they thought, negate so many rescripts and diplomas and annul so much prior legislation as to cause the complete alienation of the non-Magyar nationalities. It threatened also to arouse such uncertainty about the future that still greater discord and confusion would inevitably result. They were certain that the court wanted to avoid both of these "calamities." Barițiu took the occasion to remind his colleagues that it was customary for the Germans and Magyars to fight and then make up and "leave the Rumanians on the outside looking in," and asked ironically whether they were ready to resume the role they had had before 1863 or even 1848. The significance of what was taking place was clear to Șaguna also: the Rumanians had again been caught up in a constitutional experiment like those of 1850 and 1861 and would have little to say about the outcome.[1]

Șaguna's prognosis proved correct. In August the council of ministers made final decisions about the future of Transylvania without bothering to consult the Rumanians or the other nationalities. In effect they abandoned the October Diploma and the guarantees of national equality that had been so solemnly proclaimed just a few years before. On the nineteenth Count Franz Haller, the new Transylvanian chancellor, formally proposed the sacrifice of Transylvania's autonomy in return for a *modus vivendi* with the Magyars. The diet of Sibiu would be dissolved and a new one convoked, with the sole object of "revising" Article I of the Transylvanian diet of 1848, that is, approving the union of the principality with Hungary.[2] To ensure a Magyar majority, voting rights would be restricted to those persons who qualified under the laws of 1791 or who paid eight florins in direct taxes, not including the capitation tax. In addition, there would be a *restitutio in integrum* of the Magyar county and Szekler district governments: they would resume functioning with the same personnel they had had in 1861 before the removal of Kemény and Mikó from office and would be entrusted with the holding of elections to the diet. These proposals were given their definitive form at a meeting of the council of ministers on August 27. Francis Joseph and a few others raised some objections to the sweeping nature of these concessions to

Magyar nationalism and expressed the hope that some way could be found to satisfy the "just demands" of the Rumanians and Saxons. But these objections sound a little hollow, since the emperor had brought in a new government for the express purpose of reaching a settlement with the Magyars and he was himself perfectly aware of their feelings about Transylvania.

The manner in which the court chose to communicate its decisions to the Rumanians was evidence enough of how little the aspirations of the non-Magyar nationalities counted. It decided not to recognize the permanent committee or any other body of elected representatives as the official spokesmen of the Rumanian nation and thereby assume some obligation to admit them to the bargaining table; rather, it summoned Şaguna to Vienna to inform him privately of what had taken place. At an audience at the end of August, Francis Joseph sketched the reasons why the vital interests of the monarchy had necessitated an abandonment of the October Diploma and the adoption of a new policy toward Hungary. He expressed regret that he would be unable to keep all the promises he had made to the Rumanians, but assured Şaguna that he could rely upon his special protection and asked for his support. In a brief reply Şaguna promised that the Rumanians would not falter in their traditional loyalty to the throne. He could not conceal his anxiety at the complete turnabout in the court's policy, and was heard to remark upon leaving the audience chamber that the Rumanians had been "handed over to the Hungarians."[3]

Events now moved rapidly toward the denouement the Rumanians had opposed for two decades. On September 1 an imperial rescript summoned the Transylvanian diet back into session at Cluj on November 19 for the purpose of "reconsidering" the union of Transylvania with Hungary; on September 7 Ferenc Kemény, the former Transylvanian chancellor, was appointed president of the diet; on September 20 the October Diploma and the February Patent were formally suspended; and almost everywhere in Transylvania outside the Fundus regius the old, Magyar-dominated county committees quickly reconstituted themselves and took charge of organizing the election of the new diet.

The enthusiasm and determination of the Magyars contrasted sharply with the disillusionment and general disarray of the Rumanians. The immediate reaction of most intellectuals to the Austrian about-face was anger and a sense of having been betrayed. Ioan Raţiu demanded to know what crime the diet of Sibiu had committed to justify the "destruction" of the Rumanian nation in "such a brutal fashion"; he told Bariţiu in disgust that the rescript of September 1 turned his stomach.[4] He and his colleagues were also incensed by what they considered the emperor's snub of the Rumanian nation by communicating his decisions to a single person rather than to its chosen representatives, and they suspected Şaguna — unjustly — of having sold them all out to the Austrians. Their shock was to have the profoundest effect upon the future development of the national movement. Şaguna's actions, real and imagined, finally brought their long-smoldering resentment of episcopal leadership to an open break, and this latest "Austrian infidelity" convinced them that the Rumanian nation must henceforth think first of its own best interests and make its policy accordingly.

The immediate objective of the intellectuals was to convoke a new congress, where they intended to ascertain the national will and draw up specific political and social demands. An overriding sense of urgency pervaded their discussions; such drastic changes had occurred in such a short period of time that they feared the union of Transylvania with Hungary would be proclaimed before they themselves had a chance to be heard. The congress became their chief hope of thwarting Magyar ambitions. It offered them the opportunity to rally the entire Rumanian nation to their cause and thereby repair the damage done to national unity by the disintegration of their pro-Austrian policy. So strong had their belief in the sovereignty of the nation become that they were confident they could make it a force to be reckoned with in any future dealings with the court. Not the least of their objectives was to oblige the court to deal with a representative body that truly reflected public opinion rather than with the two bishops, who, in their view, spoke for no one but themselves.[5]

The issue of the congress and national unity soon became entangled in an increasingly bitter controversy among the Rumanians themselves over the extent of their participation in the forthcoming diet. Everyone agreed on the need for concerted action, but all attempts to achieve it were frustrated by a widening split between the majority of the intellectuals, on the one hand, and Şaguna and his supporters, on the other: at issue were the significance of the new diet of Cluj and the precise role the Rumanians ought to play in it. Bariţiu, Raţiu, and many, but not all, of their followers strenuously promoted a boycott of elections to the diet. To act otherwise, they contended, would constitute recognition of the new order of things, especially the incorporation of Transylvania into Hungary, and would signify the abandonment of every principle they had held sacred.[6] As a practical matter, they also pointed out that Magyar unionists were in charge of the whole election and would undoubtedly use all the powers at their command to prevent the choice of candidates favoring Transylvanian autonomy; that gerrymandered electoral districts and the unfair electoral law, which reduced the number of Rumanian voters, had made the results in most constituencies a foregone conclusion; and, finally, that the prohibition against a national congress and the lack of a political organization and a common program would leave large numbers of Rumanian voters at the mercy of the threats and blandishments of unionists. Taking all these things into account, they could foresee only disaster for themselves at the polls, while the government would gain the inestimable advantage of being able to argue that the Rumanians, by virtue of having participated in the election, had in effect been consulted and must, therefore, submit to whatever decisions the diet might make.[7]

Barițiu and Rațiu travelled the length and breadth of Transylvania to drum up support for their plan, but innumerable meetings with prominent laymen in the most important cities and towns failed to create the unanimity or arouse the sense of urgency that the crisis seemed to demand. Communications were difficult, and the lack of organization hindered their attempts to coordinate what was at best an amorphous movement. They resorted to the press to educate public opinion on the issues of the day and rally support for their cause, but Iacob Mureşanu, the editor of the one newspaper available to them, *Gazeta de Transilvania,* refused to take their side against Şaguna. Since its establishment by Barițiu in 1838 *Gazeta* had always been unequivocal in its support of the national movement, but now—as further evidence of the divisions which rent the Rumanian cause— Mureşanu found that he could no longer discern what the true course of the national movement should be. Rather than lead, as Barițiu had done, he preferred simply to present all sides of the question and hope that some common ground for action could be found. Consequently, Barițiu and Rațiu toyed for a while with the idea of forming a joint-stock company to finance a newspaper of their own with Barițiu as editor, but they finally abandoned such plans because of the lack of money. The press had such a commanding role in national affairs that now, deprived of it, they thought their cause was nearly hopeless.[8]

They still clung to the idea that a national congress could somehow revitalize the nation's forces and impress its adversaries with its solidarity and determination. Encouragement came from an influential and respected source, Archbishop Şuluţiu. Disturbed as much by being ignored as by the dissension in the ranks of the intellectuals, he sponsored a meeting of clergy and professors at Blaj at the end of September. Yielding to strong pressure from the supporters of Bariţiu and Raţiu, and indulging in a rare act of defiance, the group decided to hold a national conference on October 20, the fifth anniversary of the October Diploma, with or without the permission of the government. They also contemplated a direct appeal to the emperor setting forth all their grievances and asking his intervention in the interest of justice and national equality. Such a procedure recommended itself particularly because it would allow the Rumanians to bypass the diet and, Raţiu and his colleagues thought, thus avoid compromising the autonomy of Transylvania and their own moral position.

Largely because of Şaguna's unrelenting opposition and the stern countermeasures threatened by the government, none of these plans came to fruition. Both Chancellor Haller and Governor Folliot de Crenneville had become increasingly apprehensive as unrest spread among the Rumanians. By late fall they were prepared for some sort of armed uprising, as "Daco-Rumanian" activity along the border with Wallachia was reported and as handwritten proclamations turned up in various parts of the country summoning all "Rumanians and Brothers" to a mass meeting at Blaj to renew the oaths taken there in 1848. Under these circumstances, Crenneville flatly rejected all requests to hold a national congress. He reminded Rumanian leaders that the Austrian government did not recognize the existence of a Rumanian nation "possessing well established rights in law like the Saxons." Hence they could hold a general assembly only with the permission of higher authority, which judged each case on its own merits. Haller was even more emphatic. He forbade any kind of political gathering or demonstration and threatened severe punishments for those who persisted in their disobedience.[9]

The disintegration of national unity had added greatly to Şaguna's feelings of depression. The private efforts of Bariţiu and Raţiu, and even of Şuluţiu, to cope with the complexities of imperial politics would, he was certain, lead to disaster; they were simply confirming the ingrained prejudices of both Magyars and Austrians that the Rumanians were not a nation at all and could, therefore, be ignored with impunity. Personally, Şaguna resented the way he himself had been shunted aside and he was angered by charges, widely disseminated in spite of the lack of any evidence, that he had sold out the national cause to curry favor with the court and the Magyars on behalf of his church. But he did not descend to the level of personal vindictiveness. His position remained what it had been since 1848—one of strict conformity to the law and respect for constitutional procedures. He argued that the nation's business ought to be conducted on the highest moral level, by the permanent committee, and decisions taken and public pronouncements made only after due deliberation by its members rather than by individuals "running in all directions" and indulging in "reckless appeals to emotion." He warned his colleagues that they could ill afford any action that might compromise their honor or the justice of their cause, for honor and justice were the only weapons that remained to them. He therefore rejected out of hand Şuluţiu's invitation to cosponsor the projected meeting at Blaj, warning that to hold an "illegal assembly" would merely destroy what little bargaining power they still had.[10] He reiterated his opposition to the union of Transylvania with Hungary and the manner in which it was being carried out, though he was fully aware that the court was determined to reach a settlement with the Magyars and would, consequently, brook no opposition from the Rumanians or anyone else. He concluded that it was in the best interests of the Rumanians to accept these facts and to use all the legal means available to influence the final Austro-Magyar settlement in their favor. To boycott the upcoming elections or to ignore the diet seemed to Şaguna a signal to their adversaries that they had lost the will to resist.

To many contemporaries the quarrel between Şaguna and the passivists was inexplicable. Both sides were deeply concerned about the future of their people: they insisted upon the validity of the laws passed by the diet of Sibiu; they defended the autonomy of Transylvania; and they demanded a voice in all matters affecting their nation. Their differences, then, seemed to lie mainly in tactics rather than in final goals. In fact, quite divergent social and political philosophies underlay their respective positions.[11] So strongly did they manifest themselves that for the first time a polarization of Rumanian intellectuals into two irreconcilable camps occurred, and the near unanimity and willingness to compromise that had characterized the national movement until this time disintegrated.

In addition to its obvious effects, the bitter rivalry between the two factions precluded a rapprochement with the Magyars. Şaguna and his followers refrained from making contact with Magyar leaders for fear they would be accused of betraying the national cause and thereby risk the loss of what support they had for their activist policy. As a result, the rigid position taken by Bariţiu and Raţiu on the union prevailed. Even though the Magyars seemed willing to make serious concessions in return for Rumanian support of the union, no effort was made to negotiate with them.[12] In view of what was to follow, the Rumanians might better have maintained some sort of continuing dialogue with Magyar leaders in both Transylvania and Pest. There is good reason to believe that they could have gained a more favorable settlement in 1865 than they eventually got in the Law of Nationalities of 1868; the Austrians had not yet formally conceded either the union or the other Magyar demands, and all parties foresaw much hard bargaining ahead. It was precisely for this reason that the Rumanians took no action. They desperately hoped that negotiations between the court and the Magyars would eventually break down and that the emperor would then be obliged to turn again to the Rumanians and the other non-Magyar nationalities for support. Resistance to the Magyars, so this line of reasoning went, would put the court in their debt.[13]

As it was, Rumanian political activity, of whatever intensity, proved to be ineffectual. The attempted boycott of the elections failed, partly because its proponents lacked organization and partly because Şaguna and his supporters worked feverishly to get out the vote. Moreover, many Rumanians could not bring themselves to stand on the sidelines and permit the election of Magyars or Magyarophiles in largely Rumanian districts,[14] and many civil servants feared the loss of their jobs if they stayed home on election day. On the other side, local Magyar officials used every means at their disposal to secure a large Rumanian vote for unionist candidates. They alternately wooed Rumanian electors with outright cash payments or promises of lower taxes if they voted "correctly," and threatened them with fines and other unpleasantness if they abstained or voted for national candidates. At Turda, for example, peasants coming in from the outlying villages were met by militiamen at the city's gates and were escorted directly to the polling places in order to prevent any meetings with Rumanian intellectuals, who were leading the boycott.[15] The results of the election clearly revealed the baneful effects of Rumanian disorganization, official intimidation, and the discriminatory nature of the new franchise. Only 14 Rumanians won seats in the new diet, as compared to 46 in its predecessor. The subsequent appointment of 34 regalists raised their representation to 48, but even this number could do little more than register a protest againt the decisions imposed by the overwhelming Magyar and Szekler majority of 195.

From the opening day of the diet on November 19, 1865, it was evident that the Magyars would not budge from the position they had held in 1848 and in 1860. They insisted once again that the union of Transylvania with Hungary had been legally accomplished in 1848 and that, as a result, only the Hungarian diet in Pest could exercise jurisdiction over the affairs of Transylvania. Rumanian deputies, after long and heated discussions, succeeded in restoring a semblance of national solidarity before they entered the diet. Raţiu, who had in the end stood for election from the overwhelmingly Rumanian district of Haţeg, decided to take his seat, and Şaguna was appointed a regalist. They were able to agree on a memorandum they intended to read at the start of the first session and then transmit to the emperor. It declared the existing diet illegal and demanded the convocation of a new one based upon the liberal electoral law passed (but not sanctioned) by the diet of Sibiu in 1864. Only such a body, they contended, by providing fair, proportional representation to all the peoples of Transylvania, could legitimately claim to act on their behalf. Raţiu drafted the final text, and Şaguna agreed to lead the floor fight for its adoption. But their agreement was a fragile thing. Raţiu and his supporters still clung to the idea that the Rumanian cause would be compromised if any of their deputies took part in the actual work of the diet; the whole delegation must therefore withdraw as soon as the memorandum had been read and its transmission to the emperor assured. Şaguna firmly rejected such an idea, protesting that their traditional loyalty to the emperor and their own nation's best interest made their presence mandatory. The majority agreed with him.[16]

The battle between the Rumanians and Magyars over the fate of

Transylvania was joined on December 2, during the debate on an address to the throne. Şaguna took the lead in denouncing the whole proceeding as unconstitutional and the diet itself as a remnant of a bygone age, when only the Magyar, Szekler, and Saxon political nations existed and when the Rumanians were denied rights to which history and natural justice entitled them. He pointed to the inequities of the electoral system which had prevented a genuine expression of Rumanian public opinion and he urged approval of the points contained in the Rumanian memorandum as the best means of restoring constitutional government to Transylvania.[17] Raţiu seconded his motion, observing that in a true constitutional state legislation reflected the wishes of the majority of its citizens. But their logic and eloquence were to no avail; the Magyars listened in stony silence. On December 18 the diet adopted the text of an address to the throne which the Magyars had drawn up, and it inserted the Rumanian memorandum in the minutes as a simple minority report rather than as an official declaration of the Rumanian nation.

On December 25 Francis Joseph replied. He accepted the idea of the union, but made it conditional upon a satisfactory settlement of outstanding constitutional issues between the imperial government and the Magyars and upon guarantees of the continued existence of the Rumanian and Saxon nations and their respective churches. He said nothing about how these conditions would be enforced, and the remainder of his statement coincided largely with the Magyar point of view. It designated the diet of Pest as the most appropriate place to resolve the constitutional questions between the various lands of the Hungarian crown (including the union) and "invited" Transylvania to send its representatives there without delay.[18] Since the Hungarian diet had already opened on December 14, the emperor instructed the Transylvanian government to hold elections as soon as possible. On January 6, 1866, he prorogued the diet of Transylvania *sine die*. Since he never reconvened it, this act marked the end of the period of Transylvania's legal history which had begun with the Diploma Leopoldinum in 1691; it had ceased *de facto* to exist as an autonomous principality.

Under the impress of these events the tenuous understanding between Şaguna and Raţiu at the diet came apart completely, and the two political currents within the national movement—"passivism" and "activism"—now emerged as separate political parties. To some extent the division occurred along religious lines. The so-called passivists were mostly lay intellectuals and some clergy—largely, but not exclusively, Uniate—whose sympathies lay with Barițiu and Rațiu. They adhered to two principles which distinguished them from the activists: that the Rumanian nation must henceforth rely primarily upon its own resources and develop a policy independent of Austrian direction, and that it must do nothing that might be construed as acceptance of the new regime in Transylvania. They were embittered by the official attitude that the Rumanians could be discarded whenever they were no longer needed, and they found it impossible to accept Austrian tutelage as previous generations had done, even though the circumstances in which they now found themselves obliged them to seek the emperor's grace. In some ways passivism is a misnomer; as a political weapon, it was applied only to those acts which might compromise the autonomy of Transylvania or signify recognition of the Austrian-Magyar agreement. The passivists continued to press for a boycott of elections to the Hungarian diet, but their energetic measures at the local level belied their name. Paradoxically, they were no less active than the activists; the initiative in political organization lay with them rather than with their opponents, and theirs were the more dramatic acts, like the memorandum of Barițiu and Rațiu to the emperor in December 1866 or the *Pronunciament* of Blaj of May 1868. They were not afraid to operate on the very limits of legality.

The distinguishing mark of the activists, on the other hand, was their willingness to work within the prevailing system. They accepted Şaguna's dictum that the most effective way to defend the accomplishments of the diet of Sibiu, and hence the autonomy of Transylvania, was to participate fully in the political life of the state. Consequently, while no less critical than the passivists of the evolving Austrian-Magyar compact and the way in which it had come about, the activists urged their compatriots to wage a vigorous electoral campaign and, afterwards, to participate fully in every phase of parliamentary activity. Şaguna was their undisputed leader. It was his powerful influence over the Orthodox clergy and faithful that held the most diverse elements together and gave their movement a certain ideological coherence. But his activities produced other results that were not beneficial to the national cause. As the head of the Orthodox Church, his strenuous support of activism tended to associate that doctrine with his church and once again to force the religious issue to the surface of the national consciousness. The same could be said of Şuluţiu's support of passivism, although the real direction of it lay firmly in the hands of the intellectuals. This division along religious lines, which neither side desired, offered more evidence to the laity of both churches that some authority other than episcopal prerogative was needed to provide national leadership in the true sense of the term.

During the electoral campaign in January and February 1866 to choose Transylvania's representatives to the Hungarian diet the old arguments for and against participation were again aired, but now with even greater vociferousness and even less willingness to compromise than in the previous fall. Since the passivists had little central direction, their boycott took the most diverse forms: some, like the well-to-do peasant electors of the village of Sălişte, near Sibiu, declared a total boycott in order to demonstrate their disgust with the union and the "feudal" electoral law; many others, including the electors of Braşov, the district of Nasăud in the northeast, and the Apuseni Mountains, were willing to send deputies to Pest but only to attend the emperor's coronation, out of a sense of duty and loyalty to the throne, and they made it plain that such action should not constitute recognition of the union. Raţiu decided to run in a largely Rumanian district in order to prevent a Magyar from winning, but he had already decided not to take his seat, if elected.[19]

The activists waged just as vigorous a campaign to get out the vote. Şaguna argued the case for activity with great effectiveness in the columns of his newspaper, *Telegraful Român*. Although he had entrusted the editorship to Nicolae Cristea in 1865, he personally approved all the lead articles and editorials, which consequently reflected his opinions on the major issues of the day. It was his way of entering controversial political debate without compromising the independence of his church. He pointed out that abstention from voting could not possibly yield the desired results, since the Rumanians did not control Transylvania as the Croats, for example, controlled their country. Only in a few areas like Făgăraş, Năsăud, and Haţeg, where the Rumanians formed an overwhelming majority of the population, did he think a boycott could have any chance of success; even if the Rumanians achieved a 100 percent abstention, Transylvania would still send its representatives to Pest, and the diet would still decide its fate and the fate of the Rumanians along with it.[20] Şaguna hoped that they might yet salvage something from the catastrophe that had overtaken them, since a great deal of hard bargaining lay ahead of the Austrians and Magyars. He thought there was a chance that the Rumanians could have their say, too, but not if they sat on the sidelines. The Magyars would not simply yield to their demands; they would have to fight for their rights and bargain for them, and the proper place to do that was the diet.[21]

As he had already done at the Alba Iulia conference, the diet of Sibiu, and most recently at the diet of Cluj, Şaguna directed his powers of persuasion to the three questions he considered the most vital for the future of the Rumanian nation: loyalty to the ruling house, liberal constitutional government, and understanding among the peoples of Transylvania. Not only tradition but now self-interest as well, he argued, obliged the Rumanians to do the emperor's bidding, for he had become their main hope of salvation.[22] He also thought it essential that they demonstrate their commitment to the principle of constitutional government not merely by respecting the laws of the state but by strengthening its legal institutions. He pointed out that they could accomplish both goals and serve themselves at the same time by participating fully in the political process; only in this way could they hope to be fairly represented in all the branches of government and thus be in a position to promote the general welfare against the special interests of one class (the Magyar aristocracy).[23] In the final analysis, it seemed to him, peace and prosperity in Transylvania depended upon mutual respect and understanding. He could see no other course, since "fate" had decreed that Rumanians and Magyars should inhabit the same land.

There were other activist voices besides Şaguna's. A number of laymen supported him and looked to the Orthodox and Uniate clergy for leadership. They urged village priests to impress upon their faithful the importance of supporting Rumanian candidates and to make certain that all eligible voters registered and went to the polls. Şaguna tacitly but wholeheartedly approved of the involvement of his clergy in this political struggle. Many activists were afraid that the Magyars would appeal to class prejudice to woo the Rumanian gentry (*boieraşi*) and officeholders away from the national cause. Although these groups were small in numbers, their potential for leadership was great and their defection could, consequently, be a serious blow. The activists warned their compatriots to resist all temptations to personal gain and to remember that in the not too distant future their status would depend upon nationality rather than social class.[24]

The Rumanians succeeded in electing only fourteen deputies, as in the diet of Cluj, all of whom, except Raţiu, took their seats in March 1866. They cooperated with Rumanian deputies from the Banat and Hungary proper and even formed a Rumanian parliamentary club, but they clearly preferred to pursue their own special objectives. The preservation of Transylvania's autonomy continued to be the heart of the political program which they drew up. Together with the laws passed by the diet of Sibiu it formed the legal bedrock upon which Şaguna and his followers (and the passivists as well) had decided to build a new national movement. Because of their respect for constitutional and historical continuity and their reluctance to abandon what appeared to be a strong position, they shied away from associating themselves too closely with the policies and programs of their brothers in the Banat and Hungary. This concern also accounts in large measure for their reluctance to enter into any binding commitments with the Serbs and Slovaks, in spite of their common interest in preventing the establishment of a unitary Magyar nation-state.

The Rumanians continued to demand proportional representation in a reconstituted Transylvanian diet and bureaucracy, and a formal guarantee of equality to their Rumanian nation and its churches. But they also concerned themselves with social and economic problems. They pressed for an improvement in the condition of the Rumanian peasantry, as class differences, such as they were, proved once again to be of little importance when the national welfare was at stake. Consequently, as at the diet of Sibiu, Rumanian deputies lent their support to all projects for an agricultural credit bank, an agricultural chamber of commerce, and a new provincial university with special faculties of agronomy and commerce, and they demanded the creation of special commissions to adjudicate disputes between peasants and landlords.[25] But little action was taken before the diet adjourned on June 26, 1866, owing to the outbreak of war with Prussia.

During the brief struggle Rumanian soldiers fought bravely in defense of the empire, as they had done in previous wars, and from civilians there were offers of special contributions, including the promise by Rumanian intellectuals in Năsăud to set aside 5 percent of their salaries for the purchase of military equipment.[26] Bariţiu and Raţiu

and a few of their colleagues tried to demonstrate the loyalty and usefulness of the Rumanians by proposing the establishment of three or
four battalions of volunteers to keep order in Transylvania.[27] Although
they did not say it in so many words, they intended this force to be used
to suppress possible armed uprisings by anti-Habsburg Magyars. Austrian officials took a dim view of their zeal. Chancellor Haller rejected
their offer on the grounds that Transylvania, because of its critical
nationality problem, was no place to experiment with private armies;
battalions of the sort recommended by Barițiu and Rațiu, he said,
would merely promote "national tendencies," which were "contrary to
the best interests of the state."[28]

The war lasted barely seven weeks, and a definitive peace was speed-
ily concluded at Prague on August 23. As a result of Austria's overwhelming defeat by Prussia, the court's bargaining position vis-à-vis
the Magyars had been seriously undermined. But Rumanian passivists
misread the situation and thought that the whole matter of the rapprochement was once again in doubt. Consequently, they made a
strenuous effort to derive some benefit for themselves from Austria's
military debacle. They decided to draw up a memorandum detailing
the attitude of the Rumanians toward the impending reorganization of
the monarchy and reaffirming their devotion to the throne, and they
declared their intention of delivering it to the emperor in person. Once
again Barițiu and Rațiu took the lead. To ensure the success of their
undertaking, they sought to patch up their quarrel with Șaguna and
the activists, for they were certain that their memorandum would have
the desired effect if it were to emanate from the whole Rumanian nation.

The annual meeting of ASTRA, scheduled for August 28-29 at Alba
Iulia, offered them a convenient opportunity to seek Șaguna's endorsement. About ninety persons attended, but, as usual, political matters
were not discussed in the public sessions, since such action would have
violated the association's statutes and provided grounds for its dissolution by the government. In his opening remarks Șaguna confined himself to the literary and cultural activities of the association during the
preceding year.[29] The other speakers followed his example. But in
small private gatherings outside the hall the proposed memorandum
was hotly debated. Activists and passivists reiterated their respective
points of view on the political situation, but no one was inclined to
change his mind. Șaguna led the opposition to the Barițiu-Rațiu plan,

for he was certain that the emperor would not receive an official delegation; the only result would be to diminish still further the standing of the Rumanians at court. He was convinced of the court's determination to proceed with its policy of rapprochement with the Magyars and to make substantial concessions to achieve it; the best course for the Rumanians would be to maintain an unequivocal constitutional position. After lengthy discussions he finally yielded to appeals to his sense of national duty and to his own anxiety to forestall the sending of a delegation of private persons, which the passivists threatened to do if he refused to go. He agreed to take the memorandum to Vienna, but he stipulated that its contents must be acceptable to him and that he go alone.[30]

What took place subsequently is unclear. Ratiu claimed that the meeting with Şaguna broke up without any agreement on either the contents of the memorandum or the means of conveying it to Vienna.[31] Şaguna insisted just as firmly that all present had unanimously agreed to incorporate into the memorandum the program set forth by Rumanian deputies at the diet of Cluj in December 1865, to submit it to both church leaders for final approval, and to entrust its delivery to him alone.[32] Both sides recognized the gravity of the situation and saw in a direct appeal to the emperor their last hope of altering the course of events, but it was evident at Alba Iulia that the majority of lay intellectuals who supported Bariţiu's and Ratiu's various endeavors also shared their impatience with Şaguna's cautious approach to the political crisis. They could no longer accept his stewardship of the nation's affairs because they were convinced that he was too fully committed to the court to be able to pursue an independent national policy. They interpreted his stand at Alba Iulia as conclusive evidence that he would not deviate from the course of strict constitutionalism he had set the previous year, and they decided to proceed without him.[33]

In the first weeks of September Bariţiu and Ratiu sought moral and financial support for a mission of their own to Vienna to replace Şaguna's. The memorandum they intended to present was to be more forceful and explicit in describing their grievances than one that Şaguna would have approved. The initial response of the intellectuals and the Uniate clergy greatly encouraged them.[34] Şuluţiu offered his personal support and acquiesced in the establishment of a committee of clergy and professors at Blaj to coordinate the whole enterprise. This committee took charge of circulating proxies (*plenipotenţe*) to be

signed by all Rumanian "patriots" giving Barițiu and Rațiu the authority to represent them.[35] In this way they hoped to prove that the
contents of the memorandum represented the will of the entire Rumanian nation, not of just a few individuals. The committee also appealed for donations to pay the delegation's expenses to Vienna.[36]

Until the middle of October Barițiu and Rațiu ignored Șaguna completely, apparently hoping that their own success would destroy his
influence in national affairs. But as proxies and money trickled in
slowly and the Orthodox clergy, obeying Șaguna's injunctions, remained aloof,[37] they began to have second thoughts. Because of the
respect which both the court and the Transylvanian government had
for him and because of his authority over his faithful, they reluctantly
concluded that even his token support was essential for the success of
their mission. Șuluțiu agreed to serve as their intermediary. On October 23 he wrote to Șaguna urging him to put aside the differences that
had come between them and to join him in leading a delegation to
Vienna with the memorandum. He then suggested that, if, after all,
Șaguna found it impossible to go, he might nonetheless help by sending a proxy to Barițiu in the name of his church and by taking up a
collection to help defray the expenses of the journey.[38]

Șaguna had watched the development of the Barițiu-Rațiu enterprise with a mixture of anxiety and exasperation, but he had kept his
feelings largely to himself. Now, Șuluțiu's letter stung him with its con-
descending tone and its offhand dismissal of the principles he had defended at such great cost to his own prestige and the cause of national
unity. In his curt reply, which marked the final break between the two
men, he denounced the Barițiu-Rațiu mission as a "private adven-
ture," which its supporters had "imposed upon the whole nation by
arbitrary and illegal means." These men, he contended, had abandoned the traditional paths followed by the national movement and
had ignored its recognized leaders and institutions; they had chose instead to improvise, and in the process they had succeeded only in de-
stroying the constitutional position which they had all labored so hard
to establish in the preceding six years. He concluded by stating that he
would not associate himself in any way with the activities of Barițiu
and Rațiu and their friends.[39]

Rațiu was furious at Șaguna, but for the moment he could do little
except carry on without him. Nonetheless, as a result of the exchange

between Şaguna and Şuluţiu, the split between passivists and activists widened. Şaguna's enemies now undertook a systematic campaign to discredit him in the eyes of the nation on the grounds that he had betrayed the national cause,[40] and they went so far as to accuse him— falsely—of having taken bribes from the Hungarian government.[41] Even more ominous for the future of national solidarity was the bitter polemic carried on in the newspapers. For the first time the Rumanian press, which had traditionally been one of the promoters of unity, was deeply divided on fundamental questions of policy and contributed no little to an unedifying and generally destructive war of words. The controversy frequently descended to personal invective between the editor of *Telegraful Român* and George Bariţiu, who helped to turn *Gazeta de Transilvania* into the chief organ of passivism.[42]

Many Rumanians also vented their frustration in public meetings. One of these, which was large enough to attract the attention of Chancellor Haller, was held in Haţeg on October 26 to protest the abrogation of the October Diploma and the annulment of the laws of the diet of Sibiu. Elsewhere, local officials reported that "tribunes" were roaming the countryside calling upon the people to support a "Danubian Confederation" as a means of bringing about full national equality. There were also rumors of "Daco-Rumanian activity" by a number of younger intellectuals and priests in the Apuseni Mountains who were allegedly "fraternizing" openly with Rumanians from Bucharest and who were making no secret of their hostility to Austria.[43]

The chancellery and the Transylvanian government, lumping these activities together with the preparations for the mission to Vienna, saw it all as an organized campaign against established authority. They held the Uniate clergy and intellectuals chiefly responsible, and Governor Folliot de Crenneville sternly rebuked Şuluţiu for having permitted the "Blaj intellectuals" to engage in "illegal acts." Crenneville, like his predecessors, regarded the Uniate bishop as a civil servant duty-bound to carry out instructions from Vienna and Cluj. He expected the same services from Şaguna also, but his tone was more courteous. Both the governor and Haller preserved the Austrian bureaucracy's suspicion of any Rumanian political manifestation. Haller, who was evidently upset by criticisms of the government that had been appearing regularly in *Gazeta de Transilvania,* was uncompromising in his attitude toward dissent. He urged Crenneville to enforce the press laws to the letter and to make certain that persons who held public office — he referred specifically to Iacob Mureşanu, the editor of *Gazeta,* who was also a school principal — knew the penalties for "agitation."[44]

By the end of December, in spite of ceaseless and exhausting controversy and official hostility, Bariţiu and Raţiu had collected enough money for the trip and thirty-seven proxies bearing 1,493 signatures. Bariţiu, because of illness, stayed at home. Raţiu arrived in Vienna on December 28 with no assurance that the emperor would receive him. But three days later a brief audience was arranged for him as a private citizen, "whose views might be of value to the state," not, as he had wished, as the authorized spokesman of the Rumanian nation. Francis Joseph was "affable" and "in good spirits," but he granted Raţiu only a few minutes to present his case and offered little more in reply than the usual assurances that he would "carefully consider" the matters that had been laid before him.[45]

Raţiu postponed his departure from Vienna for ten days, hoping for some sign of favorable action on the memorandum. In the government offices he visited he could sense the displeasure he had caused just when the rapprochement with the Magyars had been all but sealed; by the time he left he was certain that the Rumanians would again be the "victims of their loyalty to the throne." His earlier contention that the Rumanians would ultimately have to rely upon their own resources being thus confirmed, he decided to make a new attempt to restore national unity. He proposed, reluctantly, that an effort be made to heal the breach with Şaguna, but in the same breath he complained that it was an unfortunate fact of their political life that the Rumanian people could still not get along without their bishops.[46] At the beginning of February 1867 the Transylvanian Chancellery confirmed this opinion. It recommended that his petition be rejected because neither he nor any of the signatories was authorized to represent the Rumanian nation; only the two archbishops had the right to come before the throne as the "organs of the Rumanian nation."[47] Francis Joseph concurred, and the memorandum went unanswered.

All that the Rumanians could do was to look on in frustration as the terms of the Austrian-Magyar rapprochement were systematically carried out. On February 17, 1867, the restoration of the Hungarian constitution was officially proclaimed, and the nomination of a responsible ministry immediately followed. On the twenty-seventh the new Hungarian ministry informed Haller that it would begin at once to fuse the administrative apparatus of Transylvania with the government organs of the rest of Hungary and that, as a result, the Transylvanian Chancellery would soon cease to exist. In May, Count Imre Péchy, royal commissioner for Transylvania, assumed what remained of executive functions from Governor Crenneville. Upon his arrival in Cluj, Péchy declared his main objective to be the reestablishment of harmony and cooperation between Rumanians and Magyars. To this end he embarked upon an extensive study-tour of the country. The mood which he found among the Rumanians everywhere — whether in Turda, one of the centers of passivism, or in Sibiu, the headquarters of the activists — was one of defiance toward the new political system.[48] Péchy, ill-prepared for such an unfriendly reception, finally dropped his conciliatory tone and bluntly reminded Rumanian leaders that the union was an accomplished fact; if they expected to get on in the new Hungary they had best learn to obey its laws.[49]

Rumanian deputies in the Hungarian diet, which had reconvened on November 19, 1866, found a similar attitude animating the majority of their Magyar colleagues. They again organized themselves into a political club, but their small numbers and the unpopularity of their cause hindered them from altering the decisions of the majority. Despairing of any success in winning concessions through parliamentary procedures and plagued by disagreements among themselves,[50] they decided to appeal directly to Ferenc Deák. On June 3, 1867, they had a friendly and relaxed meeting with him in his apartment. He advised them to drop their opposition to the union, since there was no possibility of repeal; instead, they should seek the greatest benefit for their people from the extensive civil rights the Hungarian constitution guaranteed to all citizens regardless of nationality and religion. He also tried to reassure them that the forthcoming nationalities law would respect their linguistic and cultural autonomy, at least at the local level.[51] The Rumanians appreciated Deák's sympathy and forthrightness, but his assurances about individual civil rights and cultural autonomy could not satisfy them any more now than in 1849; all parties, whether activist or passivist, demanded a separate political existence, which, they had come to believe, would alone provide the conditions necessary for full national development.

Francis Joseph's coronation as King of Hungary, the ceremonial ratification of dualism, took place in Buda on June 8. On the twelfth he sanctioned a series of fundamental laws, including Article XII, the dualist pact, which had been concluded in the name of all the lands of the Hungarian crown, in spite of the fact that knotty constitutional questions — particularly, the status of the non-Magyar peoples — were still unresolved. On the same day he also dissolved the prorogued diets of Sibiu and Cluj and declared the legislation of the former null and void.

Under the shadow of dualism, now a fait accompli, Rumanian intellectuals gathered in Cluj in August for the annual meeting of ASTRA. The passivists, out of sheer frustration, were determined to punish Şaguna for his refusal to support the Raţiu mission and for his imputed complicity in the union of Transylvania with Hungary. Because they were eager to have ASTRA play a more important role in political affairs, they were unhappy with Şaguna's strict adherence to its statutes, which forbade such activity. Long before their arrival in Cluj they had decided to remove him from the presidency, a post he had held since the association's founding in 1861. In his place they elected Vasile L. Pop, a distinguished jurist who had briefly served as president of the supreme court of Transylvania in 1865 and who shared their political philosophy.[52] Their support of Pop was also intended as a vote against the new political order in Transylvania. At the banquet following his election many toasts were drunk, but the retirement of Şaguna, who had remained in Sibiu, and his immense services to the association were passed over in silence.[53]

The following year, 1868, brought little comfort. In their helplessness the majority of Rumanian leaders considered passivism their only effective weapon, since they were determined to do nothing that would help the new regime to consolidate.[54] They desperately hoped that if they bided their time, dualism, like the other constitutional experiments of the past quarter-century, would eventually prove barren. But they were not inactive. They attempted to place both the Uniate Church and ASTRA fully at their disposal, and they had frequent recourse to the courts to defend Rumanian peasants against the efforts of Magyar landlords and local officials to restrict their use of pasture and other common lands or impose new labor services and dues.

They were also anxious to hold a national conference for the purpose of reorganizing themselves politically, now that they had, so they thought, largely divested themselves of ecclesiastical leadership. But the Hungarian government, fearful of giving added impetus to nationalist "agitation," would not hear of it. The Rumanians responded by holding a number of local protest meetings, the most famous of which took place at Blaj on May 15, 1868, to mark the twentieth anniversary of the great assembly on the Field of Liberty.[55] Ioan Raţiu was the organizer. At the beginning of May he had persuaded the clergy and intellectuals of Blaj to hold a demonstration appropriate to the occasion and, as they had done twenty years before, to draw up a declaration of Rumanian rights and grievances.[56] The resulting *Pronunciament* repeated earlier demands for the recognition of Transylvania's autonomy and the restoration of the legislation of the diet of Sibiu and protested against a system of government that forced them to resort to public manifestoes as their sole means of participating in the political process. Iacob Mureşanu published it in full in *Gazeta de Transilvania*.

The significance of the Pronunciament does not lie in the originality of its contents, but rather in the government's reaction to it. It became the first of a long series of *causes célèbres* over the nationality question in Hungary, as the government initiated criminal action against its authors and Mureşanu on the grounds that they were guilty of agitating against the unity and security of the state. Such procedures were to become a regular feature of Hungarian political life until the dissolution of the monarchy itself in 1918 and may have contributed more than anything else to alienate the non-Magyar nationalities from Greater Hungary. In Parliament Elie Măcelariu, a deputy from Mercurea, near Sibiu, objected strenuously to what he described as the government's total disregard for the fundamental rights of its citizens. He contended that the authors of the Pronunciament had used legal means to air their grievances and that to criticize a "hasty and arbitrary act" like the union, which had ignored the vital interests of two million people, was no crime.[57] The ministry of the interior, which had initiated the proceedings, thought otherwise and continued its investigation. Raţiu became chief counsel for the defense. He was determined to pursue the case to the bitter end in order to publicize the national cause and expose the abuses of power to which the Hungarian government had subjected the Rumanians. He was delighted when several foreign newspapers rallied to their cause and he even hoped that Napoleon III of France, whom he and his colleagues regarded as the chief patron of subject nationalities, might be persuaded to intervene on their behalf.[58] But on December 16, 1868, before the case came to trial, Francis Joseph, with the approval of the Hungarian government, ordered the indictments quashed.

The government's decision not to pursue the case may have been intended as a gesture of conciliation following the recent passage of a comprehensive nationalities law. If so, its magnanimity was ill placed, for the law failed to satisfy the demands of the Rumanians and was, consequently, universally unpopular among the intellectuals. The efforts of a handful of deputies in the parliament to modify the text, giving the non-Magyar nationalities greater cultural and political autonomy, were to no avail. After less than two weeks' debate — very little time for a measure which was to determine the future of the majority of Hungary's inhabitants for the next half-century — Article of Law XLIV, or, as it came to be known, the Law of Nationalities, was passed by an overwhelming majority of the diet on December 6.[59]

The Law of Nationalities appeared to most Rumanians, passivists and activists alike, as the final calamity in a series that had begun with the convocation of the diet of Cluj in 1865. Their petitions against the union and their protestations of loyalty to the dynasty had proved to be utterly fruitless. Not only had they been unable to influence the course of events, but, because of deep divisions among themselves, a malaise had settled over the national movement that bade fair to paralyze effective political action for some time to come. Alarmed at their impotence, activists and passivists agreed that the restoration of unity must take precedence over all other questions, and they saw in a broadly representative national conference the remedy for their ills.

The passivists again took the initiative. Towards the end of 1868 a small group headed by Barițiu began to make plans for a general conference of Rumanian electors. The immediate issue before them was the new elections to the Hungarian parliament scheduled to take place in March 1869, but they gave equal attention to the problems of political organization and leadership and long-range national policy. They were anxious to end the strife with Șaguna's supporters, but on their terms and without direct negotiations with the bishop. Although they had not announced it publicly, they were determined to exclude the Orthodox and Uniate hierarchies from any part in the conference and, in so doing, make good their own claims to national leadership.[60]

Barițiu entrusted the actual organization of the conference to Visarion Roman, an energetic journalist who had edited *Telegraful*

Român for a time and who was later (1871) to found the first Rumanian bank in Transylvania. He and his colleagues worked in secret,
fearing both the intervention of the government and what they supposed would be Şaguna's unrelenting opposition. They spared no effort to win the support of all Rumanian intellectuals, Orthodox as well
as Uniate, passivist and activist. At the beginning of the new year they
achieved their first public successes. On January 9 the Rumanian electoral committee of Sibiu overwhelmingly endorsed passivism as a national policy and voted down every attempt by Şaguna's supporters to
nominate a candidate for the upcoming parliamentary elections. Similar manifestations followed in the county assemblies of Solnoc-Interior
on the eleventh and twelfth, in Hunedoara on the fourteenth, and in
Făgăraş on the twenty-first, where Rumanian members vigorously protested against the union. In February and the beginning of March
Rumanian electors in Dej, Cluj, Gherla, and Abrud followed the same
course, proclaiming a total abstention from the elections.[61]

For the first time in over three years the efforts of the passivists
achieved truly national proportions. Many Orthodox, including
clergymen, gave them unqualified support; they worked closely with
their Uniate colleagues to promote the national conference and create
a united front against the new political system. One of the most striking examples of Orthodox-Uniate cooperation occurred in the Braşov-
Făgăraş region, where Ioan Meţianu, Orthodox protopope of Zârneşti,
near Braşov, and a protégé of Şaguna, joined with Ioan Antonelli,
Uniate episcopal vicar in Făgăraş, to win over their respective faithful
to a policy of strict passivity and to persuade them to put aside religious differences in the interest of national unity.[62]

On February 21, 1869, Roman, Măcelariu, and several colleagues
approved the contents of a carefully worded invitation to all intellectuals to meet at Mercurea on March 7 for the purpose of formulating a
common policy toward the upcoming elections. Măcelariu, under
whose signature the conference was officially convoked, satisfied the
requirements of the law by informing Commissioner Péchy of the action they had taken. Péchy hastily assumed that the object of the conference was to nominate candidates and otherwise prepare for full participation in the elections, and he immediately approved the idea.

The conference was well attended; 291 delegates from all over Transylvania were officially registered. The great majority came from the
educated classes—lawyers, teachers, priests, and civil servants—and

they dominated the conference.[63] They were all determined to stay within the bounds of legality. The first order of business was a declaration of loyalty to the Habsburg dynasty, which, moreover, expressed the true feelings of the delegates, and a pledge to obey all the laws of the land. In the same breath they declared their intention to seek the repeal of all those laws which "had left the Rumanians without rights in their own country."[64] The delegates then proceeded to debate once more the relative merits of passivism and activism. Although they said little that had not already been said, they succeeded in defining their goals more precisely and, in so doing, established their lineal descent from the generation of 1848. Visarion Roman put the case eloquently for passivism. He argued that the time had come for them to put Rumanian interests first, since both Austrians and Magyars had amply demonstrated indifference to their plight. If they were to achieve their goals, he continued, they must have their own instrument — a political party — that would give them the direction and discipline they so desperately needed. To objections from the floor that they needed a program before a party he replied that they already had one — the Sixteen Points adopted at Blaj in 1848. Their situation now, he contended, was in fundamentals no different than it had been twenty years before, for the Magyars were again offering civil liberties as the price of nationality. To emphasize the point he read a quotation from the famous speech of Simion Bărnuţiu on the eve of the assembly on the Field of Liberty: "We have no need of laws that destroy our national character; the true liberty of any people can only be national." In the wake of the enthusiastic applause his reading had evoked, he made a final appeal for complete abstention from the elections.

The activists were present in force and vigorously defended their position. Iosif Hossu, a lawyer from Cluj and a member of the Transylvanian diet in 1865, and Ion Cavaler de Puşcariu, one of Şaguna's confidants, were their chief spokesmen. Hossu argued that passivity was nothing less than an abdication by the intellectuals of their responsibilities to the peasantry. He was convinced that without proper leadership they would fall victim to the "machinations" of their enemies. He urged the delegates to campaign with all their hearts in order to make the parliament an instrument for social improvement and a forum from which they could attract the notice of all Europe to their cause. In his turn, Puşcariu had to admit that Rumanian deputies in the diets of Cluj and Pest had accomplished little, but he argued that at least they had been heard. He contended that passivism, however complete, would fail because the Rumanians were not the sole inhabitants of Transylvania; the Magyars and Saxons would choose their deputies, and the diet would legislate no matter what they did.[65]

In spite of all arguments to the contrary, the motion to adopt passivism as a national policy won overwhelming approval. Only four votes were recorded as opposed. The conference then proceeded to elect an executive committee of twenty-four members to draw up statutes for a national political party. Once again the opposition was negligible. Much to the surprise of the passivists, the conference had succeeded in restoring a sense of national solidarity, which had been one of their primary objectives. But, if they had taken the trouble to see beyond the polemics in *Telegraful Român,* the main organ of the activists, they would have discovered that its editorial policy did not differ substantially from the views they themselves espoused. Under Şaguna's direction it openly attacked dualism as an "unnatural alliance" between the Germans and Magyars to dominate the empire; it condemned the union of Transylvania with Hungary and the Law of Nationalities for ignoring the "inalienable right" of the Rumanians to a separate existence; it castigated the Magyars for their total renunciation of the principles of liberalism and national equality; and it summoned the Rumanians to defend themselves by all legal means, including the establishment of a single political party that would bring all their resources to bear on the great issues of the day. *Telegraful Român* still espoused activism, but not at the expense of national unity, and its advocacy of such a policy was more moderate than during the previous year.[66] For all these reasons Şaguna's supporters at Mercurea refrained from taking any action that might have exacerbated ill-feeling and prolonged disunity. A few days after the close of the conference Măcelariu went to Sibiu to report personally to Şaguna and was warmly received. Şaguna expressed his pleasure at the decisions reached by the majority,[67] which he interpreted — mistakenly — as an important step toward the resumption of full political activity.

The immediate result of the conference was a widespread boycott of the elections to the parliament. Only a few Rumanians were chosen, and, of these, two — Măcelariu and Ioan Antonelli — declined to accept their mandates. But the passivists' successes were costly. Now, for the first time, as punishment for their support of the boycott, numerous Rumanian civil servants were dismissed. When Commissioner Péchy realized, somewhat belatedly, what Măcelariu and his friends had really been up to, he ordered the newly formed national committee to cease all activity at once. Consequently, the meeting it had scheduled for April 8 for the purpose of implementing the decisions taken at Mercurea had to be postponed indefinitely.[68]

Nonetheless, the Conference of Mercurea was a landmark in the history of the Rumanian national movement. It signalled the formal end of the bishops' domination of the national movement, which had begun with Ion Inochentie Micu-Clain in the first half of the eighteenth century, and the rise to power of the lay intellectuals, a process that had first manifested itself in the 1830s. Thus, the traditional patterns of Rumanian political behavior were considerably altered, as men of the middle class took charge of national affairs. A concentration upon political and economic problems replaced the earlier preoccupation with educational and general cultural advancement, although these continued to occupy an important place in the national consciousness. The new leaders organized their own banks, agricultural cooperatives, workingmen's associations, literary societies, and political organizations as a means of preserving their national identity in the face of the increasingly intolerant nationality policies of successive Hungarian governments. The church, too, participated in the defense of nationality, but none of its leaders, either Uniate or Orthodox, ever enjoyed the preeminent position in national affairs that Șaguna had held between 1848 and 1865.

Throughout his episcopate Şaguna pursued two careers: he was at once the head of a large and increasingly self-sufficient body of Christians and the chief spokesman of his nation. In the one position he was the promoter of sectarian interests; in the other he was obliged to transcend them. This dual role was complicated by the division of the nation into two separate churches, Orthodox and Uniate, each with its own long-established traditions and ambitions. As Şaguna discovered, the best interests of Orthodoxy did not always correspond to the aspirations of those who put nation before church. Indeed, the idea of nationality bade fair to replace religious belief itself as the dominant influence on men's minds. During his episcopate there was also discord within the greater Orthodox family in the Habsburg monarchy—it, too, caused in large measure by the rise of national feeling. Şaguna therefore found himself almost continuously at odds with his own coreligionists in Carlovitz over the separation of the Rumanian hierarchy from the Serbian. It became his task in the 1850s and 1860s to reconcile the conflicting aims of religion and nationality, an endeavor in which he was only partially successful.

The pervasiveness of the idea of nationality among educated Rumanians in the middle of the nineteenth century produced a crisis within both the Orthodox and Uniate churches. It had been in the making ever since the rise of national consciousness in the final decades of the eighteenth century, and it had manifested itself forcefully for the first time in the bitter controversy between Bishop Lemeni and the young lay teachers and some of the clergy at Blaj in the 1830s and 1840s. The causes of the conflict were manifold,[1] but the underlying issue was the adaptability or, as the intellectuals saw it, the inadaptability of the church to the new liberal and national spirit of the times. The educated laity had not only grown steadily in numbers since the latter part of the eighteenth century when Joseph II's enlightened absolutism had expanded opportunities for employment in state service and education, but had by the decade preceding 1848 also become markedly secular in outlook. They did not reject the church or religious faith, but they did demand that the church and its clergy be more responsive to the worldly needs of the faithful and, in particular, that they promote the "national welfare."

Şaguna saw no necessary contradiction between the spiritual and social missions of the church or between religious belief and national sentiment, but, confronted by the effervescence of ideas set in motion by the revolution of 1848, he recognized the urgent need to delineate the "proper" boundaries of each and, at the same time, find some means of coordinating the whole. He was particularly sensitive to manifestations of the "national spirit," which he judged to be the most compelling social force in contemporary Europe, and accepted the fact that the institutions of the church must come to terms with it. Such a course of action seemed to him a natural one, since the Orthodox Church was by its very essence a national church. Both its canons, as he was to demonstrate over and over again in his long struggle to restore the Rumanian Orthodox metropolis, and its unique role in the political struggles and cultural development of the Rumanians rendered it peculiarly adaptable to the demands of modern national consciousness.

Even if no such strong historical or canonical links had existed between the church and the nation, the church's role, in Şaguna's view, would have been the same in an age of nationalism. The church, he contended, had a dual mission, the one spiritual and transcendental, the other primarily social. In carrying out the first, which, moreover, he always regarded as the more important, the church concerned itself with the propagation of universal Christian truths and the salvation of souls for the eternal life after death; by their very nature these preoccupations were timeless and unchanging, and thus not subject to the vicissitudes of politics or economic crises. But, Şaguna insisted, the church was of this world, too; it was a social institution and, as such, it had manifold responsibilities towards its faithful to promote their moral and material well-being. It carried on its social mission through a variety of institutions—an enlightened, vigorous clergy, modern schools, and various associations devoted to cultural development. Şaguna believed that the church had a special duty to take the lead in those secular matters that vitally affected the faithful precisely because it was the repository of eternal spiritual and moral truths. During his long episcopate the Orthodox Church became a far more active social force than it had been at any time in the preceding century and a half.

Şaguna regarded his own involvement in the national movement as a duty. Nationalism was for him a social phenomenon that could be neither ignored nor suppressed; it was a problem, or rather a series of problems, which demanded the attention and understanding of everyone, the clergy as well as the laity, who believed in the efficacy of peaceful social change. He accepted the overwhelming evidence he encountered on all sides that both his own people and all the other peoples of the Habsburg monarchy had awakened to full consciousness of themselves, and he did not hesitate to characterize the period since 1848 as the age of nationalism. His own association with the aspirations of the Rumanians for self-determination was deep and abiding, but his national feeling was of a broadly humanist character that had as its primary goals the achievement of collective moral and spiritual fulfillment and the guarantee of individual integrity, rather than specific political goals. His main concern was not politics at all; he was not an original political theorist or even a skilled political organizer, despite his reputation as a diplomat and negotiator at court. Nor was his nationalism of the emotional variety that made the nation or *Volk* the be-all and end-all of human endeavors and set it up as a law unto itself; he was too cosmopolitan and too rational to indulge in such fantasies. His training and culture were, after all, Hungarian and Serbian and general Orthodox as well as Rumanian, and he regarded the traditional framework of church and empire, rather than the nation-state, as the most suitable one for the development of nationality.

This is not to minimize Şaguna's services to the movement for political self-determination; they were, as we have seen in 1848 and the early 1860s, ample and, in a certain sense, decisive. But it is equally true that he did not initiate great political undertakings, since his primary frame of reference was always the church. Rather, his political action was a response to the obligations he thought incumbent upon him as bishop both to the existing civil authority and to his own faithful. He engaged in politics because he thought it part of his mission to preach a social gospel and to foster the material well-being of his flock; at the same time he also tried to keep the church from becoming entangled in partisan political strife. It was, then, primarily as a churchman that he chose to deal with the problems of nationalism.

Ever since his consecration as bishop in 1848 he had made the restoration of the Rumanian Orthodox metropolis of Alba Iulia, which had ceased to function with the conversion of Bishop Atanasie to the Union with Rome, the principal goal of his episcopate. He claimed that his purpose was to bring the government of his church into harmony with the canon law of the ecumenical eastern church and, in so doing, to place it on a solid constitutional foundation vis-à-vis the state and the other denominations of the Habsburg monarchy. Yet he made it abundantly clear that he considered the Orthodox Church a national institution and he marshalled an impressive amount of evidence from learned theological treatises and the decisions and opinions of the ecumenical councils to support his demand that all the Rumanian Orthodox of the monarchy be united in a single metropolis. He was convinced that success would depend mainly upon a formal separation of the Rumanian church from the Serbian metropolis of Carlovitz, under whose jurisdiction Joseph II had placed it in 1783, and on the inclusion in the restored metropolis of the Orthodox diocese of Bukovina, which was also subordinate to Carlovitz but had never had any hierarchical connection with Transylvania.

Şaguna did not base his position solely upon legal briefs, and in his efforts to achieve his objectives he revealed the full extent of his national sympathies. His insistence upon a Rumanian metropolis, a Rumanian clergy to serve predominantly Rumanian parishes, and a proportional Rumanian share of common church funds, especially in the Banat, eloquently attest to his awareness of the strength of national feeling among his own people and the Serbs as well. When asked by the Serbian bishops why the Rumanians could not worship God just as well under a Serbian metropolitan as under a Rumanian one, Şaguna replied that the church was also of this world. He argued that the hierarchy must recognize the immense power of nationalism and try to adapt the outward forms of church organization to it. Only in this way could the church harness the vast creative energy which nationalism generated and channel it toward constructive ends. He was certain that the church would cease to be a vital force in the life of its people, if it acted otherwise and divorced itself from their most deeply rooted aspirations. In his view, then, the moral and intellectual growth of the Rumanian Orthodox in the Banat, and in Bukovina as well, depended upon their achieving independence from Carlovitz and joining with their brothers in Transylvania.

The Uniate movement presented Şaguna with a special problem and necessarily made his role in national affairs more complex. As the heir to a long tradition, he considered himself the national leader of the Orthodox in both secular and religious affairs, but in times of political crisis, as in 1848, he found himself acting as the spokesman for both Uniates and Orthodox. He never made a distinction between them on national grounds, nor did he regard the Orthodox as somehow better Rumanians than the Uniates. But his ecclesiastical position brought him into frequent conflict with his Uniate counterpart, since both of them felt compelled to further the interests of their respective churches. Sometimes, as during the decade of absolutism, the rivalry between the two churches became exceedingly bitter, and national solidarity was badly shaken. Most of the time Şaguna felt himself to be on the defensive and was, consequently, doubly zealous in asserting the autonomy of his church and its institutions. But confessional strife, induced largely by a competition for converts, appears to have been a surface manifestation of long-established rivalries on the local level and never seriously interfered with the pursuit of national goals in periods of great crisis.

The solution Şaguna found for the problem of Orthodox-Uniate relations accorded fully with his respect for the law as the proper means of regulating human affairs. He seems never to have seriously contemplated a union of the two churches or the absorption of one by the other; he opposed amalgamation in 1848, and a few years later he summarily rejected a suggestion that he could bring about religious peace by becoming head of the Uniate metropolis, which was about to be created. Instead, he urged observance of the principle of religious equality and respect for the right of each church to manage its own affairs without interference from the other. To these ends he proposed a number of agreements to Şuluţiu covering such diverse matters as proselytism and mixed marriages. During the constitutional period of the early 1860s accords were finally reached, which in later decades substantially reduced conflict between Orthodox and Uniates. Şaguna regarded the restoration of the Orthodox metropolis as the keystone of any permanent *modus vivendi* with the Uniates, for he thought it necessary to assert the full constitutional autonomy of the Orthodox before they could expect to be treated as equals.

The connection between his diocese and the Serbian metropolis of Carlovitz presented Şaguna, as a national church leader, with a somewhat different problem. His early, and largely unsuccessful, efforts to bring about a separation of the Serbian and Rumanian churches had brought him into conflict with his former patron and friend, the Patriarch Joseph Rajačić. At his consecration in Carlovitz in April 1848, at which Rajačić was the chief celebrant, he had taken upon himself a "sacred mission" to revivify "our Transylvanian diocese" in accordance with canon law, the needs of the people, and the spirit of the times.[2] Although none of those present understood it as such, his vow constituted a declaration of independence from the Serbian church, since adherence to canon law would, in his mind, require the reestablishment of a separate Rumanian metropolis, and respect for the spirit of the times would necessitate substantial concessions to national feeling. Inexorably, Rajačić's and Şaguna's paths diverged, as each identified himself more and more with the aspirations to self-determination of his respective people.

The revolution of 1848 greatly accelerated the process by placing both men in positions of national political leadership—Rajačić as patriarch of the Serbian nation, a title bestowed upon him by the court of Vienna in 1848, and Şaguna as the chairman of the Rumanian national assembly at Blaj and, subsequently, as his people's chief representative at court. During his service in the Serbian church in the Banat and then as vicar in Transylvania Şaguna had often felt the tension caused by the subordination of the Rumanians to the Serbian hierarchy and had early come to appreciate the indomitable force of nationalism. Only a few weeks after his consecration he took his first important steps toward a resolution of the problem. In discussions with other Rumanian leaders concerning the contents of the national program to be presented to the Assembly of Blaj he succeeded in inserting an article demanding the independence of the Rumanian church and the reestablishment of a Rumanian metropolis. In order to avoid disrupting national solidarity at a critical time, he made no specific reference to either a Uniate or an Orthodox organization, but he showed not the slightest indecision as to what he himself intended.

During the revolutionary events of the next year and a half he relentlessly pursued what was to be the primary objective of his episcopate — the restoration of the Rumanian Orthodox metropolis as it had existed before the church Union with Rome. His campaign manifested itself in various ways: in the general petition of all the Rumanians of the Habsburg monarchy presented to Francis Joseph at Olmütz on February 25, 1849, which demanded an independent Rumanian church; in a memorandum of similar content addressed to the imperial Council of Ministers on March 5; in a personal appeal to Rajačić on March 28 proposing, for the first time directly, a separation of the Rumanian from the Serbian hierarchy; and in a petition of July 20 to the Cultus-ministerium requesting permission for all the Rumanian Orthodox of the monarchy to hold a church congress and elect a metropolitan of their own.[3] His most systematic and carefully documented argument on behalf of the metropolis was a brochure published in Vienna in the spring of 1849 in which he attempted to prove the historical existence of an Orthodox metropolis of Alba Iulia by lengthy citations from the works of Rumanian and foreign scholars.[4] None of his writings elicited the least response from those to whom they were addressed. By the end of 1849, however, the main issues between him and Rajačić had been clarified, and for the next decade his campaign to restore the Ruma-nian Orthodox metropolis would determine the nature of their rela-tions.[5]

After the revolution Şaguna was eager to settle the problem of the metropolis as quickly as possible so that he could proceed with his ambitious program of church reform. He repeatedly urged Rajačić to convoke a synod of bishops at which the major questions of church organizatioń could be discussed and recommendations forwarded to the Cultusministerium. Three postponements by Rajačić, who wished to avoid any official debate on the metropolis, brought forth an angry warning from Şaguna that such action was endangering the welfare of the whole church.[6] This disagreement was only a foretaste of the bitter disputes of the next two years which destroyed the possibility of genu-ine cooperation between the two men.

At the synod of bishops, which finally met in Vienna on October 15, 1850, after the Cultusministerium had exerted pressure of its own on Rajačić, no compromise was possible between Şaguna's insistence upon a separate Rumanian metropolis and Rajačić's determination to maintain and, if possible, tighten the administrative unity of the church. Şaguna had the enthusiastic support not only of his own dio-cese, where a synod held in March 1850 had petitioned the Cultusmin-isterium to approve the restoration of the metropolis, but also of lead-ing laymen and clergy in the Banat, Crişana, and Bukovina,[7] and he attempted to bring the matter before his episcopal colleagues without delay. Accordingly, in early November he proposed that all the Ruma-nian Orthodox of the monarchy be united in a new metropolis co-equal with that of Carlovitz. Such action, he observed, would be in

strict conformity with canon law and would in no way weaken the
church, since the two hierarchies would continue to be united by the
strongest bonds of all: a common dogma and the tradition of a century
and a half of succor from Carlovitz to the Orthodox of Transylvania.

Rajačić, as chairman of the synod, continually obstructed any serious discussion of the metropolis. When Bishop Eugen Hacman of
Bukovina finally raised the question at the session of March 23, 1851,
Rajačić ruled him out of order, and the synod proceeded to other business.[8] Disgusted by such behavior, Şaguna decided to take his case
directly to the Cultusministerium, and on April 20 he submitted a long
memorandum in which he appealed once again to canon law and history to prove the rightness of his cause. In particular, he cited the decisions of the early ecumenical church councils which had granted to the
bishops of every people the right to have their own metropolitan and to
be free from the interference of other metropolitans in their affairs. It
was perfectly true, he admitted, that canon law also obligated a metropolitan to take under his protection the people of a neighboring metropolis which, because of oppression and persecution, was unable to
function properly, as had happened in Transylvania after the church
Union with Rome. But now, he argued, the situation of the Orthodox
of Transylvania had changed for the better, and the tutelage of Carlovitz was no longer necessary; it had, rather, become the cause of deep
unrest. Only the reestablishment of their ancient metropolis, he concluded, could ensure the welfare and progress of the Rumanians.[9] This
appeal of Şaguna's to the ministry incensed Rajačić, and he tried to
discredit his adversary by publishing anonymously a brochure which
ascribed Şaguna's whole campaign to restore the metropolis to over-
weening personal ambition.[10] The appearance of the brochure led to
an angry confrontation, at which Şaguna declared Rajačić unworthy
of his high office. In these melancholy circumstances the conference of
bishops came to an end on July 3, 1851, with little to show for its nearly
ten months of deliberations. Its failure confirmed Şaguna's doubts
about the ability of the Serbian hierarchy to govern the church effectively and strengthened his determination to establish a separate
Rumanian church organization.[11]

In the months following the conference Şaguna zealously guarded
the autonomy of his diocese against what he regarded as encroachments by the Serbian hierarchy. In the fall of 1851, the consistory of
Carlovitz passed along to Şaguna instructions it had received from the

government of the Voivodina and the Banat concerning the proper method for the clergy of Transylvania to observe the emperor's birth and name days. Şaguna wrote back at once to Rajačić, as president of the consistory, to complain about the supercilious tone of the letter and the "false notion" it contained that the Orthodox of Transylvania were under the jurisdiction of Carlovitz and subordinate to it. There was, he insisted, no basis in canon law for such a presumption; "aberrations" like this, he warned, merely caused "confusion" in church government and served as invitations to the civil authorities to intervene in church affairs.[12] A similar exchange took place at the beginning of 1852, when the consistory of the diocese of Timişoara requested the consistory of Transylvania to investigate a divorce case and make a report as soon as possible. Şaguna decided to reply personally and gave the consistory of Timişoara a lecture on "courtesy" and the "proper relations between eparchies." As he had done earlier in his letter to Rajačić, he pointed out that his diocese was not subject to the jurisdiction of Timişoara and suggested that henceforth they allow their relations to be governed by canon law.[13]

These two cases seem minor, but to Şaguna they were serious infringements of principle. He had built his whole concept of church government on the rule of law, and he could allow no deviation from it lest the restoration of the metropolis be jeopardized. At the same time, he was trying to establish the relations between church and state on the same solid foundation of law, and he was convinced that this goal could never be achieved until church leaders themselves had learned the meaning of constitutional government.

The next serious clash between Şaguna and Rajačić occurred on the eve of the electoral synod of Carlovitz on November 8-10, 1852. For almost two years Şaguna had been urging both the Cultusministerium and Rajačić to convoke such a synod so that the vacant sees of Arad, Timişoara, and Vršac could be filled, and he eagerly accepted his invitation from the ministry to participate. He intended to use the occasion to press for the recognition of Rumanian rights. But Rajačić sent no invitation, and when Şaguna presented himself in Carlovitz at the beginning of November, he was informed that he had no right to attend the synod. Rajačić argued that, while the bishop of Transylvania might take part in the general business of the synod, the election of bishops was the sole prerogative of the Serbian nation, and hence Şaguna, as an outsider, must acquiesce in his exclusion. Şaguna protested

at once to the emperor's representative in Carlovitz and, failing to receive a satisfactory reply, he returned to Sibiu. On November 24, he
appealed directly to the emperor to annul the proceedings of the synod
(on November 10 the Serbian hierarchy had filled the three vacancies)
on the grounds that Rajačić had not only misinterpreted the documents he had used to support his contentions but had also blatantly
ignored the will of the emperor himself. In the long run, far more serious for the development of Rumanian-Serbian relations was Şaguna's
accusation, now expressed openly for the first time, that the Serbian
hierarchy was using its jurisdiction over the Rumanians not to enhance
the welfare of the church but rather to promote Serbian national interests. He concluded that the Rumanians could obtain justice and assure
their progress only if they were permitted to have a metropolis of their
own.[14] The emperor recognized the fact that Rajačić had acted im-
properly and on March 9, 1853, admonished him to refrain from such
behavior in the future. But he allowed the elections of the three bishops
to stand.

After this episode Şaguna decided that further negotiations with
Rajačić over the establishment of a separate Rumanian metropolis
would be fruitless, and henceforth he dealt directly with the court. He
justified his seeking the emperor's intervention in ecclesiastical affairs
by pointing out that the connection between Carlovitz and the Orthodox of Transylvania had no basis at all in church law, but rather had
come about when Joseph II by his decrees of 1783 and 1786 had subordinated the Transylvanian diocese to the Serbian hierarchy. These
edicts were, in Şaguna's opinion, political acts which could be annulled
simply by a new exercise of the imperial will.

Although Şaguna did not approach Rajačić again on the matter of
the metropolis and their relations were understandably cool, contacts
between them were frequent. The initiative was largely Şaguna's. He
still considered his diocese a part of the metropolis of Carlovitz and
recognized the authority which canon law conferred upon Rajačić as
its head. Outside this formal framework, too, Şaguna continued to
seek the advice of his former patron and on occasion confided to him
his innermost feelings. He was convinced that the welfare, perhaps the
very existence, of Orthodoxy in the Habsburg monarchy, especially
during the 1850s when a strong Catholic resurgence was underway,
depended upon the cooperation of its leaders and their respect for its
laws and traditions. But he also recognized that the vitality of the

church did not depend solely upon the hierarchs. He reminded Ra-jačić that the church was a living organism and had constantly to adapt itself to the changing needs of the faithful, and he urged him to find ways of strengthening the bonds between the hierarchy and the mass of believers.

Although the question of the Rumanian metropolis was never very far from the surface, Şaguna and Rajačić avoided overt clashes. Per-haps the closest they came to controversy was their exchange over the convocation of a new synod of bishops. Şaguna repeatedly urged, even pleaded with Rajačić to allow him and his fellow bishops to consult together on the needs of the church.[15] If the hierarchs were to fulfil their mission, he contended, then they must be constantly in touch with the living church. Their degree of success and the consequent health of the church would depend upon how well they used the synod at all levels—parish, protopopate, eparchy, and metropolis—for it alone offered the faithful an opportunity to make known their needs and desires and to convince themselves about the probity and effi-ciency of their bishops and priests. Rajačić agreed that a general synod was necessary, but continually postponed it.[16] He may, as before, have been reluctant to provide an occasion for public debate on the Ruma-nian metropolis. Whatever his reasons, no such synod was held during his lifetime.

Besides the metropolis the most important problem to intrude upon the relations between Şaguna and the Serbian hierarchy was the Uni-ate movement. Şaguna made no bones about his hostility to the Union; he regarded its main purpose to be the undermining and eventual destruction of Orthodoxy in Transylvania and the Banat. He was par-ticularly chagrined by the establishment in 1853 of a Uniate metrop-olis for Transylvania "on the ruins of the old Metropolis of Alba Iulia," while his own efforts on behalf of an Orthodox metropolis had been totally ignored by the court. Moreover, it seemed to him that Şuluţiu, the new metropolitan, had arrogated to himself the role of national leader of the Rumanians, since he had taken to addressing the Orthodox along with his own faithful in some of his official pro-nouncements.[17] During this period Şaguna characterized the Uniate clergy as proselytizers who habitually treated the Orthodox as inferi-ors. As a case in point, he cited their aggressive behavior in the matter of mixed marriages; in village after village they ignored the traditional practice of having the betrothal in the bride's parish and the wedding

ceremony in the groom's, and insisted upon performing both themselves. Sometimes, Şaguna complained, the Uniate clergy simply used
force and official influence to achieve its ends, as it did in a small village near Cluj where the Uniate protopope, with the acquiescence of
local authorities, installed a defrocked Orthodox priest in his former
parish.[18] Şaguna suspected that the new Concordat between the court
of Vienna and the Vatican, signed in 1855, had something to do with
such high-handed behavior, but, he lamented, it was mainly the favor-
itism that the court had consistently shown Uniate priests, together
with their own thorough training as missionaries, that made the ordinary Orthodox priest, with his poor education and inferior social
status, ill prepared to meet the challenge.

Şaguna regarded the situation in the Banat as especially critical.
Here, he thought, the Uniates were trying to take advantage of national antagonisms between Serbian and Rumanian Orthodox. The
establishment at Lugoj of a suffragan bishopric of the new Uniate
metropolis was, in his mind, a deliberate attempt to draw the Rumanians away from a Serbian-dominated church into a purely Rumanian
one. He regarded *Gazeta de Transilvania* as a major instrument of
Uniate proselytism because of its articles about the alleged denationalization of the Rumanians of the Banat.[19] Such activity, he complained,
was all the more disturbing because *Gazeta* claimed to be a national
organ and had served the national cause well in the past and, as a result, had been widely respected by both Orthodox and Uniates. He
finally became so incensed at its "supercilious" and "hostile" attitude
toward his church that he forbade his clergy and faithful to read it.[20]

Perhaps to combat the Uniate movement more than for any other
reason Şaguna strove to maintain his link to Carlovitz. In so doing, he
was carrying on one of the traditions of Transylvanian Rumanian Orthodoxy that went back to the beginning of the eighteenth century,
when, after the church union with Rome, the Rumanian Orthodox
had been left to shift for themselves. Possessing no bishop of their own
and regarded by the court as having ceased to exist, they gradually
came under the protection of the Serbian hierarchy—informally in
1761 with the appointment of the bishop of Buda, Dionisie Novacovici, as administrator of the diocese and then officially, two decades
later, as a result of Joseph II's decrees.[21]

Şaguna was convinced that the most effective defense against the

Uniate movement would be the reestablishment of the Rumanian Orthodox metropolis encompassing the Rumanians of the Banat, Cri-
șana, and Bukovina as well as Transylvania; it would go far toward
settling the nationality problem within the church and would, consequently, be the very salvation of Orthodoxy in the Banat. But Șaguna
realized the uselessness of bringing up the matter again with Rajačić.
The closest he came to broaching the subject in writing was his suggestion in 1857 that a solution to the Uniate problem in the Banat be
found in keeping with the "spirit of the times," a phrase he generally
used to describe national aspirations. On several occasions he urged
Rajačić to convoke a synod of bishops to discuss the Uniate problem
and draw up a memorandum to the emperor, but Rajačić never replied.[22]

The decade of absolutism was hardly an auspicious time to seek
either a settlement of the Rumanian-Serbian controversy or the means
of combatting the Union with Rome; the Cultusministerium under
Count Leo Thun was chiefly interested in promoting the Uniate movement and had no particular desire to pressure Rajačić into negotiating
with the Rumanians. But with the collapse of the Bach ministry and
the court's renewed interest in the Rumanians as junior partners in
reshaping the political life of Transylvania, official rigidity toward a
separate Rumanian metropolis gradually softened.

The Verstärkter Reichsrat in 1860 offered Șaguna a favorable setting in which to raise the question again with Rajačić. As before, none
of his arguments could budge the aging patriarch. At two meetings
with a Rumanian delegation representing Transylvania, the Banat,
and Bukovina on June 28 and 30 he refused to discuss even the idea of
a Rumanian metropolis. Instead, he went into great detail about his
own plans for a further centralization of church government. Rajačić's
ideas were completely unacceptable to Șaguna and his colleagues, for
they would have strengthened Serbian control of Rumanian dioceses
by requiring the election of all bishops by the synod of Carlovitz and by
making them administratively and financially subordinate to the patriarch.[23] His stand confirmed the Rumanians' fears that he was
mainly interested in promoting Serbian national interests at their expense, in spite of the fact that in the Banat as a whole they were far
more numerous than the Serbs. His demand that the Cultusministerium create a special department for Orthodox affairs and staff it with

Serbs and that the ministry of war change the name of the Rumanian-Banat border regiment to "Serbian-Banat"[24] brought the discussions abruptly to an end.

Rajačić's death in December 1861 removed a major obstacle to the creation of the metropolis, but nearly three years were to pass before the Serbian hierarchy could bring itself to return to the conference table. By this time Francis Joseph had made it clear to all concerned that he favored the restoration of the Rumanian metropolis and would not tolerate further procrastination by the Serbs.

The convocation of the Serbian National Congress at the beginning of August 1864 to elect a successor to Rajačić provided the occasion for the resumption of negotiations between the Rumanians and the Serbs. No Rumanian delegates attended the congress, for they considered it strictly a Serbian affair. But on August 15 a synod of bishops met in Carlovitz, at which Şaguna, supported by a numerous delegation of clergy and laity from the Banat, once again set forth the arguments on behalf of a separate metropolis, and the new patriarch, Samuil Maši-rević, defended the principle of hierarchical unity, as he called it. In lengthy speeches and written memoranda each side appealed to canon law and history to buttress its position. Şaguna took a conciliatory tone. He acknowledged the importance of Orthodox unity, even though the Roman Catholic and Uniate dangers had subsided as a result of the new constitutionalism, for, in his opinion, the Orthodox had not yet achieved full equality with the Roman Catholic and Protestant churches of the monarchy. He therefore proposed that a permanent synod of bishops be created and that it meet periodically under the chairmanship of the two metropolitans alternately, in Carlovitz and Sibiu, to discuss matters of common interest to all the Orthodox of the monarchy. The Serbian bishops were adamant in their insistence that Carlovitz was the true center of the church and that the Serbian patriarch enjoyed precedence over the other bishops, and they went so far as to demand recognition of Slavonic as the official common language of church administration. Şaguna replied simply that his people were too deeply concerned with their own national development ever to accept such terms.[25]

His statement accurately reflected the state of mind of the Rumanians of the Banat. Led by Vincenţiu Babeş, a prominent lawyer, and Andrei Mocioni, a large landowner, they eagerly looked for ways to end their subordination to Carlovitz. They were the third generation to assert ecclesiastical independence of the Serbs. Their forefathers had initiated the movement at the beginning of the nineteenth century and had achieved their first successes in 1828 when the Rumanians of Arad had finally succeeded in electing one of their own as bishop to replace a long line of Serbs.[26] But Babeş's and Mocioni's intentions now were unabashedly national. In a strongly worded statement to the emperor's representative at Carlovitz explaining why they could not take part in the election of the new metropolitan of Carlovitz, they contended that a Serbian hierarchy could not possibly interest itself in the promotion of Rumanian culture and the strengthening of Rumanian national consciousness. Serbian treatment of the Rumanians, they alleged, had brought Orthodoxy, under continuous pressure from the Uniates, to the very brink of collapse in the Banat.[27] These sentiments were echoed by many Orthodox priests. Nicolae Tincu-Velea accused the Serbian clergy of sowing discord between the Rumanian Orthodox and their Uniate brothers in order to weaken their nationality and keep their Rumanian co-religionists in a state of subjugation. He saw Şaguna's metropolis as the salvation of the Rumanians of the Banat, for it would protect "nationality, [which] is the life of any nation, and language [which] is its soul."[28]

Babeş, Mocioni, and other Rumanian leaders in the Banat had strong political motives in seeking affiliation with the Transylvanian diocese. In 1864, at a time when the first hints of a rapprochement between the court of Vienna and the Magyars were discernible, they were eager to use the metropolis as a means of protecting their nationality in an area that would almost certainly remain an integral part of Hungary. Like many Rumanian intellectuals in Transylvania and Bukovina, they saw in a strong national church a means of attaining, at least partially, the unity which had eluded them in 1848.[29] So insistent had their demand for separation from Carlovitz become that only Şaguna's forceful and, in the end, successful campaign on behalf of a common metropolis for all the Rumanians of the monarchy and his stubborn defense of Orthodoxy in the Banat prevented the Banaters from seeking a metropolis of their own.[30] By making their cause his and by cultivating close relations with the Mocioni family and other influential persons, Şaguna succeeded in creating a solid front which impressed both the Serbs and the court and helped to lay the foundations for the united political action that occurred in subsequent decades.[31]

Maširević and the Serbian bishops finally acquiesced in the creation of an autonomous Rumanian church because it was Vienna's will, but the synod could come to no agreement on the details of separation. Instead, two commissions were established, one Serbian and one Rumanian, to draw up proposals for a division of church property and the delineation of parish and diocesan boundaries.[32] While they were at work, Francis Joseph notified Şaguna on December 24, 1864, that he had approved the establishment of the metropolis with suffragan bishoprics at Arad and Caransebeş, in the Banat. His action lent a new sense of urgency to the commissions' deliberations, but the Serbs, fearing that they would lose wealth and territory, were reluctant to resume negotiations with the Rumanians.[33]

Once again, the intervention of the court proved decisive in bringing the two sides to the conference table, but the imperial commissioner, Baron Joseph Philippovics, had no instructions to impose a settlement upon them. Consequently, there was considerable haggling and, in the end, no agreement. By way of compromise Şaguna proposed that the Rumanian share of joint funds of nearly 2,000,000 florins be 400,000 florins instead of the 550,000 recommended by his commission, and he promised that he would use these resources solely to enable the church to carry out its spiritual mission and not to further the interests of one nationality at the expense of another. He also proposed that four monasteries — Bezdin, Hodoş-Bodrog, Mesici, and Sîngeorz — be assigned to the new metropolis. He disclaimed any desire to people them exclusively with Rumanians and assured his Serbian colleagues that merit alone would determine admission to them and that both languages would be used in instruction and in the religious services. He appealed to the Serbs to compare the prosperity of their own church with the poverty of the Transylvanian diocese and then to ask themselves whether the cause of Orthodoxy would not be better served if his "modest requests" were granted.[34]

Although Şaguna tried to de-emphasize national rivalries by arguing that monasteries and religious endowments had been created to serve only spiritual ends, it was obvious to everyone present that Rumanian education and culture would benefit most of all from these new sources of income. He also found it necessary to resort to the idea of nationality to strengthen his canonical arguments, a procedure that merely confirmed the suspicions of the Serbs that the Rumanians' true motivation was secular rather than religious. Drawing upon his studies of Eastern European history, Şaguna contended that the Rumanians had precedence over the Serbs, since they were the oldest inhabitants of the Banat and, hence, the first in that area to receive the Eastern form of Christianity. He pointed out that the monasteries in dispute had been built in the midst of large Rumanian populations and had clearly been intended for them; moreover, three of them — Bezdin, Mesici, and Sîngeorz — had been founded in the sixteenth century, long before the metropolis of Carlovitz had come into existence (1690). The Serbs were unimpressed. They responded that whatever the origin of these endowments and monasteries, they had been the possessions of the Serbian nation for almost two centuries. Nonetheless, they expressed a willingness to make a "gift" of 200,000 florins to their sister metropolis, but absolutely refused even to discuss the disposition of the monasteries.[35] Neither side showed the slightest inclination to compromise, and on March 20 the Rumanian delegation departed Carlovitz for home.

Subsequent negotiations dragged on for a number of years, largely because of the court's preoccupation with a rapprochement with the Magyars and then, after 1867, because of the transfer from Vienna to Budapest of civil jurisdiction over both metropolises. Finally, on October 6, 1871, the Serbian hierarchy agreed to a division of church property. It granted the Rumanian metropolis endowments valued at 300,000 florins and the monastery of Hodoş-Bodrog in the new diocese of Arad.[36] As time passed, the bitterness caused by the separation of the two churches was largely assuaged, and, in spite of some lingering ill-will and suspicion, the religious settlement enabled the Rumanians and Serbs to draw closer politically at the end of the century.

Şaguna's success in the Banat was in some measure offset by his failure to gain the inclusion of Bukovina in the restored metropolis. The arguments he adduced in favor of such a union were drawn from the same ample sources of canon law that had served him so well in his polemics with the Serbian hierarchy. His controversy with Bishop Eugen Hacman evoked all his powers of analysis and rhetoric and led to the publication in 1861 of one of his most important works, *Anthorismos,* a refutation of Hacman's arguments in favor of an autonomous church organization for Bukovina. As with the Banat, Şaguna insisted that his concern for Bukovina was dictated by a desire to perfect the canonical organization of the church. No doubt it was, for he had made the establishment of a constitutional government for the church the foundation of all his other reforms, and he was adamant in his insistence that Hacman and his clergy give up their separatist pretensions, since these had no more basis in canon law than did the subordination of the diocese to Carlovitz in 1783.[37] When Hacman suggested reestablishing the old bonds that had existed between his church and the "mother church" of Moldavia before the Austrian annexation of Bukovina in 1774, Şaguna flatly declared that any hierarchical connection with a foreign state was contrary to canon law.[38]

In spite of his emphasis upon the constitutional nature of the conflict with Hacman and the Bukovinian clergy, Şaguna associated himself with the broad national aspirations of the majority of the lay intellectuals as he had done in the Banat. His cooperation with their leaders, the Hurmuzachi brothers, had begun in 1848, and he was, therefore, well informed about the political situation in Bukovina. It seemed to him that in this province, too, the interests of the nation and of Orthodoxy coincided and could best be served by the creation of a single metropolis.[39] Only a strong church, sheltering national schools and cultural organizations, could, he argued, provide the necessary continuity for national development in a region that had known frequent political crisis and was currently undergoing a far-reaching demographic change through the influx of large numbers of Slavs. In the final analysis, his attitude on the inclusion of Bukovina in the projected Rumanian metropolis owed less to national sympathies and formal arguments from canon law than to the evangelical sources of his religious and social thought: the unshakable conviction that the Christian faith was, or should be, the guiding force in the lives of individuals and nations, and that the church was the proper, though by no means the exclusive, instrument to achieve harmony between transcendental spiritual values and human institutions.

As in Transylvania and the Banat, Rumanian intellectuals in Bukovina enthusiastically supported the creation of a national Rumanian church organization. But their motives, unlike Şaguna's, were unequivocally political and social and reflected their own growing national consciousness.

The revolution of 1848 had produced the first important manifestations of Rumanian nationalism in Bukovina. Led by the Hurmuzachis, a small group of intellectuals and liberal landowners drew up a national program in June of that year. A characteristic statement of liberal and national ideas of the period, it demanded political autonomy for Bukovina, the free development of the Rumanian language and culture, and an equitable settlement of peasant grievances. It classified Bukovina as Rumanian and ignored its other inhabitants. In order to strengthen the Rumanian (and Orthodox) character of the province Rumanian leaders demanded that it be permanently separated from Galicia, to which it had been attached since 1817 and where Polish culture and Roman Catholicism predominated.[40] As the revolution progressed, the Hurmuzachis and their supporters adopted the idea of a union of all the Rumanians of the monarchy into an autonomous duchy, and in February 1849, as we have seen, they joined their colleagues from Transylvania and the Banat at Olmütz in presenting a general petition for political union to the emperor. This action was the high point of the revolution in Bukovina; it revealed a sense of ethnic unity which transcended political boundaries and which in the decades to come proved to be the chief sustenance of the national movement. The reaction which set in during the fall of 1849 dashed all hopes for unity, as in Transylvania, but a part of the national program was nonetheless fulfilled: Bukovina became a separate crownland; the peasant was freed from obligatory labor services and feudal dues; and measures were taken to expand the study of the Rumanian language in the schools.

The years that followed were filled with frustration, inasmuch as a strong, united national movement failed to develop. Rumanian intellectuals became increasingly anxious over the unceasing flow of Ruthenian emigrants from Galicia and the steady Germanization of the civil service and intellectual life — phenomena which, they feared, would drastically alter the "primordial" Rumanian character of the province. Under the circumstances, it was natural that they should turn to the one "native" institution which had so far resisted these encroachments — the church. They were eager to enlist the church and its clergy in the defense of nationality and were convinced that Şaguna's proposed metropolis would strengthen the Rumanian element in the Bukovinian church and protect it from threatened Ruthenization. Like their colleagues in Transylvania and the Banat, they were eager to make the church a more dynamic force in national affairs, and they heartily approved of Şaguna's social activism and his willingness to give laymen a strong voice in managing the church's schools and economic affairs.[41]

Their plans and Şaguna's were thwarted by Hacman. Ever since his installation as bishop in 1835 he had administered his diocese in an authoritarian manner, except for a short period during the revolution of 1848. In the spring of that year, a national church congress dominated by liberal landowners, lay intellectuals, and socially-minded clergy drastically reduced his powers. They transferred the management of church finances to the diocesan consistory and established an "Ecclesiastical Committee" to elaborate a general plan of church reform that would permit greater lay participation in cultural and social affairs. Hacman, who could no longer count upon the backing of Vienna, yielded on every point, and even went so far as to endorse the laity's demand for the inclusion of Bukovina in an autonomous Rumanian metropolis.[42] But with the installation of an absolutist regime in the 1850s, Hacman was able to return to his old ways.

From this time on Hacman stubbornly opposed Şaguna's plan for a single Rumanian metropolis and demanded instead the establishment of a separate metropolis for Bukovina. The contrast between the two men was striking: Şaguna thought in terms of universals — empire and nation; Hacman's horizons did not extend beyond his own province. He worried inordinately about his own career and the fate of his church's endowments (which were far more substantial than those of Transylvania) if his diocese became part of the new metropolis. He was also genuinely concerned about the possible repercussions of his allegiance to Sibiu on the Ruthenian minority.[43] He was afraid that they would abandon a purely Rumanian national church and join the Uniate Church of Bukovina, which was almost exclusively Ruthenian. Şaguna countered these arguments by pointing out that the presence of a small number of Orthodox Ruthenians did not alter the essential character of the church, which had always been and still was Rumanian, and he promised that the Ruthenians would have priests of their own and the right to use their own language in the holy liturgy. But Hacman could not be swayed. He turned a deaf ear to entreaties from the intellectuals to join the new metropolis for the sake of the national welfare and reminded them that the church was not a political party, that the "Kingdom of Christ was not of this world."[44]

Hacman left no device untried to mobilize his clergy in defense of an autonomous Bukovinian church. In February 1861 he convoked a church congress in Cernăuţi for the express purpose of endorsing his own project for a separate metropolis. In order to assure himself of a receptive audience he excluded laymen altogether — an act that was widely held to be uncanonical — and he included on the agenda a resolution raising the salaries of the clergy. The congress dutifully approved the contents of a brochure Hacman had had drawn up beforehand, entitled *Dorinţele dreptcredinciosului cler din Bucovina,* which summarized all his previous arguments in favor of a separate metropolis and criticized Şaguna's interpretation of canon law.[45] It drew a rejoinder from Şaguna in the form of his famous *Anthorismos,* but, as the Austrian government assumed a more indulgent attitude toward Hacman's aspirations than it had toward the Serbs', little more could be done to change his mind.

The matter was eventually decided in Hacman's favor. In his note of December 24, 1864, to Şaguna, Francis Joseph excluded Bukovina from the new metropolis. A final disposition of the maverick diocese was postponed until 1873 when the bishopric of Bukovina was raised to the rank of a metropolis. Its main function was to serve as the nucleus of the Orthodox Church in the Austrian half of the Dual Monarchy, just as the metropolises of Sibiu and Carlovitz were confined to the Hungarian half. In a sense, then, the Orthodox Church had also been divided territorially by the dualist pact; the joining of distant Dalmatia, which had remained under Austrian administration, to the metropolis of Bukovina is otherwise inexplicable. Although Hacman was nominated to be the first metropolitan, he failed to achieve his personal ambition, for he died before his formal installation could take place.

The conflicting demands of ecclesiastical and national-political leadership manifested themselves most strikingly in Şaguna's relations with the Rumanian Uniate Church. He never seriously questioned the patriotic sentiments of the Uniates, even during the most intense period of their rivalry in the 1850s, but he could not accept the Union, any more than he could the subordination of his diocese to Carlovitz, as canonical. Like Joseph II's action in the latter case, he regarded the various agreements, which had brought a large segment of the Orthodox clergy and faithful under the authority of Rome at the turn of the seventeenth century, as simple political acts with no foundation in church law. He contended that those who converted did so not out of religious conviction but rather in order to have a share of the political and economic advantages enjoyed by the privileged nations.[46] He branded Bishop Atanasie's action in signing the final Act of Union in 1700 as "perfidious," since it implied the renunciation of the oath he had taken at his consecration in Bucharest to defend Orthodoxy by all the means at his command, and he denied the bishop the power to transfer or take with him the office and prerogatives that the Orthodox Church had conferred upon him.[47] Şaguna insisted that the Orthodox Church had never ceased to exist, in spite of the claims of the new Uniate bishop and the court of Vienna that the Union with Rome had been total. He discerned in this general attitude the origins of both Uniate "arrogance" toward the Orthodox and the cavalier disregard of their rights by Austrian officials. The Instructions of 1810, which the court had forced upon the newly-elected bishop Vasile Moga as the precondition of his taking office, represented to Şaguna the final codification of Orthodox subjection to the Union, and they remained a source of humiliation to him until their annulment by revolution in 1848.

Declarations of religious equality in the constitution of 1849 and other state papers notwithstanding, Şaguna found during the absolutist regime that the spirit, if not the letter too, of the instructions still governed the relations between the Uniate Church and his own. Throughout the decade of the fifties he was constantly on the defensive against what seemed to him the Uniate hierarchy's drive to extend its dominance over the Orthodox. Especially galling were Şuluţiu's frequent public utterances in which he assumed the mantle of national leader and addressed himself to the Orthodox as well as the Uniates as though the former were simply persons who had not yet seen the light and "united." Şaguna protested that such behavior was simply proselytism at its worst and that Şuluţiu was violating both the principle of religious equality and the rules laid down by the military and civil government of Transylvania regulating the relations between the various churches.[48] The creation of the Uniate metropolis of Alba Iulia and Şuluţiu's elevation to the rank of metropolitan created a new source of conflict. Şaguna accused Şuluţiu of posing as the spiritual leader of all the Rumanians and of representing himself as the successor of Atanasie and the restorer of the old Rumanian metropolis of Alba Iulia. Şaguna interpreted his behavior as part of a plan to convert all the Rumanians to the Union by appealing to their deep sense of tradition and national feeling and by making the Orthodox despair of ever recovering their own metropolis.[49] He suspected that the main goal of the Uniates was to relegate the Orthodox once again to the status of "outcasts" which they had endured before 1848 and, in so doing, to assure themselves of dominance over the Rumanian nation.[50] Moreover, he was certain that the "ultramontanists" at court and the Roman Catholic hierarchy of Hungary in pursuit of their own centuries-old ambitions eagerly encouraged the Uniates in their endeavors; otherwise, Şuluţiu would not have acted so aggressively.[51]

Şaguna's protests to the Cultusministerium were ignored, treatment to which he had become accustomed and which now merely served to confirm his fears about its true intentions toward the Orthodox. Supported by Austrian officials from the ministry down to the local *Bezirksamt,* the Uniate hierarchy generally bested Şaguna in their major disputes over proselytism, mixed marriages, and the disposition of church property. Austrian indifference to the plight of his church was a cruel blow to him, for he believed that the sacrifices of his priests and faithful during the revolution had amply demonstrated their devotion and value to the Gesamtmonarchie.

The most serious issue to arise in the day-to-day relations of Orthodox and Uniates in the post-1848 period, and the one which contributed most to their division into two hostile camps was proselytism. Both sides engaged in the practice, but it is improbable that all the conversions and reconversions were made at the behest of Blaj and Sibiu or coordinated by them as part of some master plan. Frequently, the initiative was taken by the local priest or protopope without the prior knowledge of his superiors, who then found themselves confronted by a fait accompli and obliged to defend their priest and his new parishioners regardless of the legal merits of the case. Many of these incidents simply represented a continuation of disputes that went back three or four decades to the period of intense and highly successful proselytism under Bishop Ioan Bob. It is evident in most of these cases that the peasants took their religion far more seriously than did the intellectuals. Theirs was a fundamentalist faith in which outward symbols and popular traditions rather than theological subtleties dominated, and their piety was deep and abiding. The actual disputes between Orthodox and Uniate at the village level were often caused by such mundane matters as the control of the parish church or the expenses of maintaining the local school, rather than by crises of conscience.[52] The fact remains that religion, in whatever guise, preoccupied the great mass of the peasantry and influenced their daily lives far more intensely than the idea of nationality. Because for the most part they remained intellectually where they had been in the first half of the eighteenth century, they presented the intellectuals, who wished to raise the idea of nationality to full consciousness among all Rumanians, with a most formidable challenge.

Uniate proselytizing did not stop even with Şaguna himself. In the fall of 1850 Şuluţiu, who was then vicar of Sălaj in northwestern Transylvania and a leading candidate to fill the office of Uniate bishop left vacant by the forced retirement of Lemeni, urged Şaguna to put aside his religious scruples and accept the headship of the new Uniate metropolis. He argued that the welfare and progress of the Rumanian nation required such a personal sacrifice, since the court of Vienna was determined to press the Union with Rome with all possible vigor and would dispense its bounty only to those who cooperated with it. He further related that he had spoken to various ministers about this very problem and implied that they had encouraged him to approach Şaguna.[53] It is doubtful that Şuluţiu would have made such a proposal unless he had first consulted both the Roman Catholic hierarchy of Hungary and political leaders in Vienna. Both Bach and Thun, although irritated by Şaguna's persistence in pressing the cause of Orthodoxy, were impressed by his abilities, and had he been willing to accept Şuluţiu's offer, they would undoubtedly have welcomed his candidacy for the post of Uniate metropolitan. Moreover, conversion of a rival bishop as a quick and effective way of achieving their objectives rested on sound historical precedent. Şaguna was now presented with a most tempting opportunity to achieve national-political ambitions. But he was not primarily concerned with politics and political goals; rather, as he had made abundantly clear, the strengthening of Orthodox spirituality was the task to which he had dedicated himself. His reply to Şuluţiu was immediate and categorical: he would not "betray the religion of [his] forefathers."[54]

Şaguna's subsequent experiences with Uniate proselytism made him wary of any kind of contact between Orthodox and Uniates. He was particularly anxious to discourage mixed marriages, which seemed to him to offer the Uniates the very opportunity they had been seeking to win converts, since before 1848 the Uniate priest had customarily performed the ceremony and, not infrequently, had obliged the Orthodox spouse to bring up the children as Uniates. Since Şuluţiu refused to enter into an agreement with him regulating matters in dispute, Şaguna had frequent recourse to the provisions of the March 1849 constitution which guaranteed legal equality to all Christian religions and which he freely interpreted as covering such specific questions as mixed marriages. He proposed that the parish priest of the bride draw up the marriage contract as soon as he received an appropriate letter from the bridegroom's priest and that he also perform the ceremony.[55] Şuluţiu and the Gubernium and the Cultusministerium eventually accepted this formula as a guideline in settling disputes, and by the end of the 1850s a more or less strict enforcement of it had significantly reduced the tension between Orthodox and Uniates in the villages.

Şaguna also attempted to stop the reciprocal administering of the sacraments and the alternation of Orthodox and Uniate priests at church services. Such practices were frequent, especially in villages of mixed population that were served regularly by only one priest, but there were also many instances of Orthodox and Uniate priests aiding one another and their congregations in perfect harmony. For example, in Geoagiu-de-jos, a village near Sibiu, the Orthodox and Uniate priests took turns holding Sunday services, conducting funerals, giving communion, and visiting the sick. They also baptized each other's children.[56] Their cooperation had the full approval of their parishioners, who could discern no difference in the services they performed, and it constituted in the eyes of the intellectuals a welcome contrast to the religious strife that frequently characterized Orthodox-Uniate relations. But Şaguna strongly disapproved. Not only did he wish to restrict Uniate influences over his faithful, he also condemned such reciprocity as a blatant violation of canon law. He forbade his priests to give the sacraments to the members of another church or to allow them to be given to his own parishioners by the priest of another church even in the most extreme emergencies,[57] but he seems to have been only moderately successful in curtailing such practices.

The ill feeling between Şaguna and Şuluţiu and many of their clergy and faithful became so great during the 1850s that it seemed to many intellectuals of both churches that the Rumanians had actually become two nations instead of one.[58] A Uniate canon from Lugoj put matters more bluntly: "Our people are so divided that sometimes it is easier for Uniates and Non-Uniates [Orthodox] to make friends with foreigners than with one another. Why, they even refuse to call one another Rumanians. Instead the Non-Uniates call the Uniates 'papists', and the Uniates the Non-Uniates, 'Muscovites'."[59] The low point was probably reached in 1856, when, as we have seen, Şaguna forbade his priests and faithful to subscribe to *Gazeta de Transilvania* because of its alleged promotion of the Union and its irreverent attitude toward the Orthodox clergy.

The era of constitutionalism finally provided a favorable climate for an Orthodox-Uniate rapprochement.[60] The successes of the national movement, culminating in the legislation of the diet of Sibiu, demonstrated the value of cooperation, and the even-handed religious policy of the Schmerling government led Orthodox and Uniates to treat one another as members of the same nation. But the religious question still troubled Şaguna; he insisted that the Orthodox have absolute equality with the Uniates in all new appointments to the Transylvanian Chancellery in Vienna and the provisional government in Cluj.[61] To the dismay of the intellectuals, he appeared still to think in terms of Orthodox and Uniate rather than Rumanian.

8 / Secularism

The growth of secularism among the Rumanian educated classes generated for Şaguna a challenge far more serious in the long run than that represented by either his Serbian co-religionists or the Uniates; it threatened the position of the Orthodox Church in Rumanian society as well as his own role as bishop.

In the 1830s the rhythm of life in Transylvania had begun to quicken. The older intellectual heritage of East and West, represented by the Rumanian Enlightenment, was coupled with the beginnings of industrialization and the first serious attempts at agrarian reform. Rumanian society was deeply affected. The philosophy of the Enlightenment, Romanticism, and political and economic liberalism gave a small class of lay intellectuals a broader view of the world than earlier generations had had and inspired them to challenge not only the structure of society and politics generally, but also the traditional foundations of Rumanian society itself. They discovered that the Christian religion no longer provided them with an intelligible explanation of human existence or an adequate blueprint for social action, while the leadership that the Orthodox and Uniate bishops exercised in politics and cultural life, and even the government of the church, seemed to them hopelessly out of touch with the major issues of the day. Only the idea of nationality, as they conceived of it, seemed capable of satisfying their yearnings for change. The modern national movement which they created—a combination of Enlightenment, Romanticism, and liberalism—was all-encompassing, and with it as their instrument they sought to replace the theocratic organization of Rumanian society with a structure that was essentially secular.

On account of their opposing views on the nature of man and society, an open conflict between the traditionalists, led by the bishops and some of their clergy, on the one hand, and the lay intellectuals, on the other, was unavoidable. The period of decisive struggle had begun in the 1830s, when the educated classes first manifested a modern national consciousness, and it ended in 1869 at the Conference of Mercurea, where the intellectuals formally took over leadership of the nation from the bishops. Two outstanding personalities dominated this period and represented all that was best in the thought and actions of the contending parties: Simion Bărnuţiu—philosopher, teacher, and chief theorist of Rumanian nationalism, who provided the intellectuals with the ideology of the new secular society—and Andreiu Şaguna, who favored a more traditional approach to the solution of social and political problems. Their ideas about the individual and the nation and their roles in society reveal how complex the Rumanian national movement was and why it must be seen not merely as a struggle for political self-determination but also as a manifold process by which the very foundations of society were being transformed.

At the beginning of these four decades the church was indisputably the dominant social force. In politics the bishops were the nation's spokesmen. At the Transylvanian diet in 1834 Bishops Ioan Lemeni of the Rumanian Uniate Church and Vasile Moga of the Orthodox petitioned the privileged estates to grant the Rumanians constitutional rights equal to those of their Magyar, Szekler, and Saxon neighbors. The legislation and precedents they cited resembled in every significant detail the arguments that their predecessors had used in the Supplex Libellus Valachorum, that imposing declaration of nationhood submitted to the diet forty-three years before.[1] Then, as now, the clergy stood forth as the representatives of the nation and, in so doing, they symbolized the preeminence of the church in its political life. Lemeni and Moga maintained the political initiative during most of the Vormärz. Moga petitioned the diet twice, first in 1837 to obtain economic benefits and relief from taxes and tithes for his clergy and faithful on the Saxon-dominated Fundus regius, and again in 1842 to obtain a reaffirmation of the principle of freedom of worship for the Orthodox, enunciated in 1791.[2] Moga, whom the historical literature has usually pictured as pusillanimous and lacking in political skill, on these occasions, at least, made good use of the strained relations between the court and the Transylvanian nobility and the endemic rivalry between the Magyar and Saxon nations to press the Rumanian cause with vigor.[3] In 1842 he and Lemeni joined forces again to seek the support of the diet against alleged discrimination toward the Rumanian inhabitants of the Fundus regius. In 1847 Lemeni renewed their appeal. None of these efforts was successful; the bishops' petitions were either filed away in the diet's archives or referred to a study committee and quietly forgotten.[4]

Lemeni and Moga represented large constituencies. The Uniate and

Orthodox consistories and teaching faculties at Blaj and Sibiu, respectively, the district protopopes, a few parish priests, and individual laymen applied constant pressure on them to act and helped to formulate the grievances contained in their petitions. The failure of the bishops to move the diet gradually aroused serious doubts about the efficacy of their leadership. But their role had been well established since the episcopate of Ion Inochentie Micu-Clain in the first half of the eighteenth century, and the majority of the population, intellectuals and peasants, continued to turn to them whenever they sought a redress of grievances. Sometimes their appeals dealt with matters of broad national interest, but usually they concerned purely local disputes, as in 1846, when the municipality of Braşov refused to allow three Rumanian lawyers to practice on the grounds that their Orthodox faith had automatically disqualified them.[5]

The church's dominance of Rumanian society in the 1830s extended well beyond the realm of politics to include education, literature, and philosophy, not to mention the spiritual and moral upbringing of the vast majority of the population. The only Rumanian institutions of higher learning in Transylvania were the gymnasium at Blaj and the Orthodox seminary at Sibiu; the village elementary schools throughout the country were in the hands of the two churches as was the training of their teachers, and, consequently, the curricula and textbooks emphasized traditional religious teachings; the only Rumanian publishing house in Transylvania was operated by the Uniate Church at Blaj; the district protopopes and the parish priests were the spiritual and, usually, the political leaders of their people; and the majority of Rumanian intellectuals were either priests or the sons of priests. The main focus of all these human and material resources was the formation of good Christians and law-abiding subjects.

Dominant though the church may have been in Rumanian society, it was, in its turn, subordinate to the state. Neither the court of Vienna nor the Transylvanian Gubernium treated the two Rumanian churches with trust and respect. Instead, they established an elaborate system of controls over the bishops and their clergies. The subordination of the Uniate diocese to the Roman Catholic (and Magyar) archdiocese of Esztergom and the appointment of a Jesuit "theologian" early in the eighteenth century to oversee the bishops' activities, and the subjection of the Orthodox diocese to the Serbian Orthodox metropolis of Carlovitz in 1783 are among the more striking manifestations of official policy. Joseph II, as part of his program of centralization, required both bishops to put the welfare of the state ahead of all other considerations, and he himself issued numerous decrees and instructions regulating every aspect of church affairs. He seems to have been especially wary of the Orthodox, reserving for himself the final choice of their bishop. Francis II formalized the subjection of the Orthodox Church to the state in 1810, when he forced Vasile Moga to accept a set of nineteen conditions which severely restricted his freedom of action. In the following three decades Moga and even his Uniate counterpart, whose position was far more bearable than his, were expected to represent official policy to their clergy and faithful and were held responsible for their political conduct, a position which eventually proved to be inconsistent with their roles as national leaders.

The church's dominance of Rumanian political and cultural life began to be seriously challenged in the late 1830s and early 1840s by a restless and increasingly vocal class of lay intellectuals. These men, whose liberal social thought was to have such a profound effect upon all aspects of Rumanian life, were relatively few in number. On the eve of the revolution of 1848 there were approximately 10,000 Rumanians in Transylvania and the adjoining areas of Hungary who could read and write. Of these, 4,250 were priests (2,550 in Transylvania) and over 1,000 were teachers (300 in Transylvania). The number of persons with some form of higher education (excluding normal-school and theological training) probably did not exceed several hundred.[6] More precise statistics are lacking, but some idea of the number and occupations of intellectuals may be had from the lists of subscribers to Rumanian books and newspapers in the 1830s and 1840s. In 1838 there were approximately 500 subscribers to *Gazeta de Transilvania,* and in 1842, over 600 to both *Gazeta* and its literary supplement, *Foaia pentru minte, inimă şi literatură,* the only Rumanian newspapers then published in Transylvania. In 1847 there were 296 subscribers to *Organul Luminării* of Blaj, a weekly published by Timotei Cipariu and devoted primarily to cultural affairs.[7] Most of these subscribers were priests and teachers; there were in addition a few lawyers, civil servants, doctors, merchants, gymnasia students, and small landowners or farmers (*economi*). A list drawn up in October 1849 by Rumanian leaders in Transylvania to show Austrian authorities how many Rumanians were qualified to hold public office contained some

300 names, including thirty lawyers, ten notaries, ten physicians, ten professors, four publicists, and over one hundred persons with degrees in liberal arts or legal studies.[8] Fragmentary though these figures are, they indicate that the number of lay intellectuals who were shortly to assume the burdens of national leadership was exceedingly small in a total Rumanian population in Hungary and Transylvania of some two million. Their numbers had not increased greatly by 1860, when *Gazeta de Transilvania* and *Telegraful Român* had about 400 subscribers each, and there were approximately 200 Rumanians holding public office in Transylvania.[9] The absence of a numerous class of intellectuals was to be one of the major weaknesses of the national movement during the whole of the nineteenth century.

Paucity of numbers in no way dampened the intellectuals' enthusiasm, for they were believers (before 1848) in the swift and splendid transformation of society. In many ways they were the heirs of the Transylvanian School, that coterie of historians and philologists who flourished in the final decades of the eighteenth and the beginning of the nineteenth century and gave the Rumanian Enlightenment its special character. Like their predecessors they advocated the use of reason and knowledge as the only certain means of achieving intellectual and material progress and of emancipating their people from political bondage. Like them also, they urged their countrymen to study and polish their language in order to make it a proper instrument for modern thought and to build schools and train teachers in order to spread the benefits of the new learning among the peasant masses. They also shared with the Transylvanian School an enthusiasm for history, a remarkable freedom from narrow class prejudices, and a strong commitment to promote the "general welfare."[10]

All these characteristics demonstrate the continuity of thought from the late eighteenth century to the 1830s. But after that there were significant changes in mood and a radical movement toward new forms of social thought and organization. The new generation of intellectuals, for example, displayed a different attitude toward history. They accepted the theory of the Roman origins of the Rumanians and of their continuous sojourn in Dacia since the Roman conquest of the second century, as propounded by the Transylvanian School, but they no longer based their demands for national equality upon historical right. Natural law and the concept of inalienable human rights seemed to them to be more compelling arguments. They were also more aggressive in their political and economic thought, and more impatient to transform theory into productive programs and visible institutions than their forebears had been. Moreover, armed with the dogma of progress, they possessed unlimited confidence in their ability to direct the destinies of their people. Underlying their thought was a single principle: the idea of nationality; and they concentrated their political activity and mobilized literature and philosophy to achieve its fruition. This new spirit can best be characterized as secular, and it manifested itself most profoundly in the attitude of the lay intellectuals toward the role of the two churches in society.

Unlike the members of the Transylvanian School, the intellectuals of the 1830s and 1840s showed little interest in theology. They produced no works on the subject; their writings — belles-lettres, pedagogy, philosophy, and politics — were concerned with contemporary man and his happiness in this world. They also shunned the priesthood as a career; the atmosphere of the monastery and the bishop's court, where learning and religious observances were conducted with great attention to form but with little concern for the actual needs or desires of the faithful, repelled them. Original inquiry into ethical and theological questions had long since been abandoned. One of the residents of Blaj summed up the feelings of many: "Blaj is just as you knew it; we fast as at Mount Athos; we go to church and to school and we learn in the same mechanical way. We take great pains with the building of a church, but care little about true religion; we busy ourselves with plans for building a seminary, but care little about those who will study in it or about what they will learn."[11] To the author of this letter and to many intellectuals it seemed that the church had lost touch with the vital issues of the day and the deepest aspirations of men. The mood of impatience was particularly strong among the younger generation. Increasing numbers of students at Blaj turned away from the prescribed curriculum to liberal, and largely forbidden, writings, like the works of Baron Miklós Wesselényi, the leader of the Magyar noble opposition in Transylvania, and of Sándor Farkas of Bölön, whose account of travels in the United States in the early 1830s went through two editions in just two years.[12] Rumanian students at the Piarist lyceum in Cluj were also preoccupied with secular matters; they filled their weekly newspaper, Zorile (The Dawn), with news of scientific progress and with affirmations of patriotism.[13]

For the generation of 1848 it was mainly the rationalism and empiricism which the intellectuals had absorbed from the philosophy of the Enlightenment, in part directly and in part through the intermediary of the Transylvanian School, that had undermined the authority of the church and attenuated faith itself.[14] This philosophy found its most eloquent expression in the writings of Simion Bărnuțiu. A teacher of philosophy in the lyceum at Blaj in the 1830s and early 1840s, he was the only Rumanian of his generation to devise his own philosophic system and to merit the epithet "philosopher." Both as a teacher and as the chief exponent of the idea of nationality in the decade preceding 1848 and during the revolution itself, he exerted a compelling influence over his contemporaries, especially the younger generation who were to give the revolution its élan.

The philosophy of Kant provided the general framework for Bărnuțiu's own thought on the course of human development and the major issues of the day. It is especially evident in his assumptions about the nature of God and the significance of religious faith. He did not deny the existence of God or the possibility of eternal salvation, but he argued, as Kant had done, that His existence could not be rationally demonstrated. God was a superior being whose nature could not be apprehended by man, and hence He could be only an object of faith. Bărnuțiu seems to have accepted religious belief as a natural attribute of man and a matter of individual conscience subject to neither the control of the state nor the scrutiny of other individuals. But he was critical of the forms which organized religion had imposed upon these "natural" religious feelings and, dismissing them as irrational, he condemned them as inimical to progress.[15]

Bărnuțiu saw in philosophy an instrument which, if properly used, could bring about beneficial changes in society. The tasks of philosophy, as he conceived of them, were the cultivation of reason and the investigation of human nature in order to reveal to man what he was or should be — a rational, free being possessing inalienable rights. Accordingly, philosophy by its very nature needed to concern itself with the aspirations of contemporary man and therefore required unlimited freedom to develop its capabilities and to examine all aspects of individual and social behavior. He was especially eager to divorce philosophy from theology, which he regarded as sterile and ill-attuned to the realities of modern life. For these reasons also he was convinced that theology could not adequately serve modern man as the basis of his ethical system. Instead, he equated the moral responsibility of the individual with the promotion of the "general welfare."

Bărnuţiu did not intend for the individual to be swallowed up in the mass. Rather, he recognized that the individual, as a conscious, rational being, possessed certain inherent rights which society as a whole could not violate: every person had the right to live and work, to acquire material possessions to sustain life, and to develop his intellect and his moral sense, by which means he might gain knowledge of the world and increase his happiness and prosperity. Ideas such as these provided Bărnuţiu with the theoretical basis for his condemnation of serfdom as an "unnatural constraint on human development."[16] He contended that these rights could not be reserved in greater degree to any particular individual because all human beings were by their very nature equal.[17] The same was true of aggregates of human beings, or nations, since individuals lived in groups, not in isolation from one another. Philosophy, then, in Bărnuţiu's view, provided an explanation for and a justification of the burgeoning national movements, something which theology could not hope to do. He was satisfied that he had brought the struggle of the Rumanians for self-determination into harmony with the natural order of things.

These ideas formed the basis of a new moral code which large numbers of lay intellectuals enthusiastically embraced. Their new morality had a general human character and was independent of any specific religious doctrine. It was based upon the supposedly natural attributes of man — reason and good sense — and the belief in his innate goodness and his unlimited perfectibility. Among the virtues it extolled were honesty, tolerance, a belief in the need for social change, and a commitment to improve the condition of the masses; but however they might be formulated, traditional religious teachings were seldom mentioned. The more militant intellectuals eagerly applied the new code. At the schools of Blaj the lay teachers ceased to attend religious services with their students and turned instead to plans for social reform. They claimed that fathers had not sent their sons to school merely to pass their time in church, and they denied that religious services could have any appeal for enlightened minds, since these ceremonies were the product of an earlier, "dark age."[18] This was a more extreme position than most intellectuals were willing to take. They continued to attend church and to observe age-old religious practices. Even "radicals" like

George Barițiu and August T. Laurian drew back from the agnosti-
cism of the revered Kant.[19] Nonetheless, it is significant that a moral
system separate from traditional Christianity steadily gained converts
and tended increasingly to guide the public and private behavior of
leading intellectuals. To these men with their broad humanistic outlook the conflicts between Orthodox and Uniates, which divided the
nation and dissipated its energies, seemed both irrational and unpa-
triotic. Everywhere they made a strenuous effort to reduce tensions by
bringing Orthodox and Uniates together for joint church services and
other religious ceremonies and by disseminating a spirit of toleration
in education and cultural affairs generally.[20]

Although most intellectuals found the teachings of the church
largely irrelevant to the modern world, they did not seek to abolish the
church, nor did they embrace atheism. Their attitude cannot accurately be described as anti-clerical either, for they had no desire to exclude the clergy from the new society they intended to build. On the
contrary, they readily acknowledged the vital role the priest played in
the moral, intellectual, and even political life of his parish or district.
Here he served not only as an intermediary between this world and the
hereafter; he was also usually the village schoolmaster and the most
important molder of public opinion. His position rested mainly upon
his formal schooling, which was often elementary but more substantial
than anyone else's in the village, and upon the sympathy which existed
between him and his parishioners because of the economic hardships
and civil disabilities they had long shared. For the majority of peasants'
sons the priesthood also represented, as it had for centuries, the first
step in intellectual and social advancement. If, then, in these circumstances the intellectuals had taken an anti-religious stand or had
chosen to ignore the clergy, they would have risked isolating themselves from the great mass of the people. Such a turn of events would
have thwarted their whole purpose, which was to raise the moral, intellectual, and material existence of the peasantry to such a level that
they, too, might share the benefits of modern learning and technology.

Both Orthodox and Uniate intellectuals considered the church primarily a social institution. While ignoring dogma and condemning
sectarianism, they intended to make full use of the church and its
clergy to attain their ends. In the first place, they were anxious to preserve the church as an institution, for they recognized the important
services it had rendered the nation in the past, particularly as a defense

against wholesale assimilation in the centuries before their people had awakened to national consciousness. As a distinctive sign of Rumanian nationality and as a preserver of language and culture the church, then, had served well. But, they argued, if it were to continue to promote the national interest, its activities would have to be greatly expanded. Because of the peculiar historical circumstances which had developed between the church and the nation, the intellectuals saw it primarily as a national institution which must be at least as responsive to the worldly as to the spiritual needs of its people. They intended, therefore, to transform the church and its ministers into instruments of social change and to bring them into harmony with the ideas and aspirations of the modern age.

Beginning in the early 1840s both Uniate and Orthodox intellectuals attempted to gain a greater voice for themselves in the affairs of their respective churches as a necessary prelude to a general reform of its administration and institutions. The Uniates, led by Bărnuţiu and Bariţiu, demanded restoration of the diocesan synod, which was composed of laymen as well as clergy, as the chief governing body of the church.[21] In a newspaper article written in December 1842 and inspired by Bishop Lemeni's lack of vigor in opposing the Magyar Language Law of 1842, Bărnuţiu demanded an end to "one-man rule" of the church and the recognition of the principles of government by synod and lay representation in all its bodies.[22] Orthodox intellectuals voiced a similar dissatisfaction during the election of a successor to Bishop Moga in 1847. They objected to the fact that participation in this important "national event" was restricted, contrary to canon law, to the protopopes and that the sentiments of the people, as expressed through the parish clergy or themselves, would not be heard.[23]

The intellectuals of both churches were convinced that church government and the leadership of national affairs had become "aristocratic" and subject to the will of but a few individuals—the bishops and their bureaucracies—with results wholly detrimental to the welfare of the nation. They blamed the failure of the national movement of 1791-1792 and the rejection of the petitions of 1834 and 1842 on the unwillingness of the bishops to mobilize the entire nation behind them; as a result, the court and the Transylvanian diet had simply dismissed them as private petitioners.[24] There were other reasons, too, why they were reluctant to entrust the national cause to the bishops any longer. They were convinced that both Lemeni and Moga were too closely associated with the civil authorities and too subject to outside pressures to be able to provide independent, forceful leadership. Moreover, past sectarian struggles demonstrated to them that the bishops could not serve the nation and their respective churches equally well at the same time, since their ecclesiastical interests did not always coincide with the national welfare.

For the time being, the intellectuals nourished little hope of displacing the bishops. Instead, they decided to make what use they could of the incumbents. As we have seen, they were impressed by Şaguna, who as the newly appointed vicar of the Orthodox Church had within a short time demonstrated his commitment to education and church reform and had won the confidence of the Transylvanian government. Although they disapproved of his policy of separateness from all that was Uniate, they believed that his eagerness for reform and his growing influence with the bureaucracy might prove useful to them in building a strong national movement.[25] But their relations with Bishop Lemeni had long been strained because of his refusal to relinquish any of his power or to make concessions to national feeling. A complete break finally occurred in the mid-1840s as the result of a celebrated clash between him and Bărnuţiu and a number of teachers and students at Blaj over the whole range of issues to which the intellectuals had committed themselves.[26] Although Lemeni won this particular battle by causing the expulsion of Bărnuţiu and his followers from their posts, in the process he destroyed forever his influence over the national movement.

The intellectuals were unsuccessful before 1848 in accomplishing their ambitious program: the Vormärz in Transylvania was hardly conducive to political and social reform. Subsequently, their most strenuous efforts were directed toward the improvement of education, which they considered the precondition for any serious national progress. Bărnuţiu and others criticized the churches' reluctance to reduce the amount of time given to religion and related subjects in the curricula of their schools and their slowness in introducing courses in science, modern languages, and philosophy and in establishing special vocational schools, where practical instruction could be offered in all aspects of agriculture and business. Bărnuţiu railed at the "monkish spirit" which dominated education and demanded that the training of young people be taken out of the hands of those who were isolated from the real world.[27] He was primarily concerned about the curricu-

lum in the schools of Blaj, but he and his colleagues also thought that
the time had come for radical changes in the village elementary
schools, where most Rumanians still received their only formal education. They wanted to apply the principles of modern pedagogy to the
training of teachers and the writing of textbooks. They were especially
anxious to replace the *Bucoavna,* a reader widely used in both Uniate
and Orthodox elementary schools for almost a century which had been
designed to make the pupil a god-fearing Christian and a loyal subject.
The *Bucoavna* was objectionable to them because it made no reference
to Rumanian history or literature or to all the other things they
thought necessary for a young man who wished to make his way in the
world.[28]

Although the intellectuals wanted a more secular upbringing for
their children, they did not intend to remove religious training entirely
from the curriculum or to replace all priests with lay teachers. They
acknowledged the fact that many of the nearly 2,500 Uniate and Orthodox priests in Transylvania were well qualified to teach, and they
urged their compatriots to make full use of their talents, since the burdens of instruction would have to be borne by them until modern
pedagogical institutes could be established and a large professional
corps of teachers trained.[29] The intellectuals also recognized the need
for systematic moral training, particularly for the very young, and they
did not wish to interfere with the church's vital role in this matter.
They believed that for the time being traditional religious teachings
offered the unsophisticated masses more suitable moral guidance than
their own worldly philosophy. Their ideal seems to have been the combination of evangelical Christianity and social consciousness preached
by the French priest, Hugues Félicité Robert de Lamennais, whose
Paroles d'un croyant made a deep impression upon the Rumanian
generation of 1848, clergy and laymen alike.[30]

The intellectuals regarded the preservation of Rumanian nationality as one of the foremost tasks of education; here, too, the clergy
had an important role to play. Since the number of Uniate and Orthodox village schools was small and the only secondary schools were at
Blaj, many Rumanian children attended state schools or those operated by the Roman Catholic, Calvinist, and Lutheran churches, where
instruction was in German or Magyar and where no attention was paid
to Rumanian language or history. The intellectuals, deeply concerned
about the danger of denationalization, heartily approved the practice

of having Rumanian priests give Rumanian pupils in "foreign" schools systematic religious instruction, and they urged both churches to see to it that these children attended religious services regularly. They hoped that Rumanian pupils would thereby maintain contact with their own culture and avoid assimilation with the Magyars or Germans, which had happened centuries before to the Rumanian nobility when it had abandoned Orthodoxy.[31]

The revolution of 1848 at last gave the intellectuals an opportunity, albeit short-lived, to realize their plans for a just and rational organization of society. Their blueprint was the Sixteen Points adopted on the Field of Liberty, in which, as we have seen, they concerned themselves primarily with secular matters—the achievement of fundamental human freedoms and the political and economic development of the Rumanian nation. Nonetheless, they had to concern themselves with an ecclesiastical problem that had aroused great emotion on all sides: the possibility of a reunion of the Orthodox and Uniate churches. The laity strongly favored ending all sectarian differences between Rumanians on the grounds that they had kept the nation divided for a century and a half and had obstructed its progress. In the spring of 1848, at public and private meetings, the clamor for reunion became overwhelming. Its advocates ignored dogma and canon law. Instead, they pointed to the need for national unity and, at the same time, demanded that both Rumanian churches be freed at long last from "foreign domination." Many intellectuals, Bărnuţiu and Alexandru Papiu-Ilarian among them, regarded the Uniate movement as an attempt by Hungarian Catholics to extend their control over the Rumanians and so check their national development,[32] and many Orthodox, as we have seen, had come to regard the connection with Carlovitz as oppressive.

In May, on the eve of the national assembly at Blaj, the pressure to heal once and for all the religious divisions of the past reached its height, as the younger intellectuals tried to insert in the Sixteen Points a blunt declaration in favor of a reunion of the two churches.[33] So uncompromising did they become that, far from strengthening national solidarity, they threatened instead to disrupt it by upsetting the delicate balance between Orthodox and Uniates. Both bishops and most of the clergy adamantly opposed a reunion of the churches in the form demanded by the laymen. Şaguna, who had just been consecrated bishop, was eager to reestablish the Orthodox metropolis of

Alba Iulia and insisted that this be done in strict conformity with canon law, while Lemeni flatly refused even to discuss the matter and urged his clergy to do everything in their power to preserve the status quo.[34]

Bărnuțiu perceived the dangers to the national movement inherent in the burgeoning religious controversy, and in his address to the intellectuals on the eve of the great assembly he recounted the pernicious effects of past religious strife and pleaded with his listeners never again to allow "either Jesuits or Serbian monks or the missionaries of Esztergom or the agents of foreign nations or even the devils of hell" to destroy the "brotherly love" that had united all Rumanians long before there were separate churches. Bărnuțiu was afraid that vain, irrational controversy would impede the rebuilding of Rumanian society in accordance with the principles of liberty, equality, and fraternity. Moreover, he was simply not interested in religious questions. "My purpose," he declared, "is not to summon the Rumanians to religious unity but to national unity."[35] He wished to bring about a separation of church and state as the most efficient way of removing sectarian rivalries from the national consciousness. He tried to persuade his colleagues that the nation had its own spheres of activity (political organization and economic development) quite distinct from those of the church, and he proposed that each be allowed to pursue its goals without interference from the other.

The sentiment for religious unity was too strong for Bărnuțiu to overcome, and a general declaration to this effect was included in the Sixteen Points. Article II proclaimed the immediate independence of the "Rumanian church" and its legal equality with the other churches of the land. At Șaguna's insistence, it also provided for the eventual reestablishment of the "Rumanian metropolis," to which all Rumanian bishops would be subordinate. But the intellectuals omitted any mention of how these things were to be accomplished and made no reference to either Orthodox or Uniate, for they were preoccupied with *national* unity and had no interest in the details of ecclesiastical organization. Besides Article II, only Article XII, which requested state support of the Rumanian clergy, dealt with the church. But religious fervor was by no means foreign to the intellectuals; it harmonized with the almost biblical atmosphere of the times: the religious ceremonies on the Field of Liberty were for them symbols of the deep, spiritual unity of the nation.

The main objective of the intellectuals in the Sixteen Points was to lay the foundations of an autonomous Rumanian nation. They placed special emphasis upon the immediate abolition of serfdom and all out-moded restraints upon commerce and industry and on the drawing up of a new constitution for Transylvania that would assure every citizen freedom of speech, the press, and assembly, public trials with a jury, protection from arbitrary arrest, and a just allocation of taxes and other public responsibilities. To justify such sweeping demands they appealed not to God or even to history but to the principles of liberty, equality, and fraternity and the inalienable rights of man.[36]

With the onset of absolutism following the collapse of their revolution, Rumanian intellectuals were forced to abandon, at least temporarily, their plans for the reorganization of Rumanian society. It is symbolic that Simion Bărnuţiu, who best typified their thought and aspirations in the preceding decade, left Transylvania for self-imposed exile first in Italy and then in Moldavia. Yet in spite of the obstacles that absolutism put in the way of national fulfillment, the Rumanians made some progress in education and general cultural development. Since these were matters which had traditionally been the preserve of the church and since the church had been the sole national institution to survive the revolution, the Orthodox and Uniate bishops resumed their roles as national leaders. The absolutist system itself encouraged the restoration of the old relationship between the state and the bishops.

Şaguna became the dominant figure of the decade and was generally recognized as such by both Orthodox and Uniates and by the court of Vienna. It was he who set the tone for the fifties just as Bărnuţiu had done for the forties and it was his conception of society and his views on the proper relationship between the spiritual and the temporal, the church and the state, and religion and nationality that guided the development of the Rumanian nation. Şaguna and the lay intellectuals found themselves in agreement on many issues. They approved his emphasis upon education and moral training, his insistence upon separating the transcendental functions of the church from its social role, and his willingness to allow broad lay participation in church affairs. But fundamental differences remained. The intellectuals demanded that the Orthodox and Uniate bishops be guided by the will of the nation as expressed on the Field of Liberty.[37] Şaguna, however, was primarily concerned with the welfare of his church and the strengthening of religious faith. His whole orientation, unlike that of the lay intellectuals, was religious; he believed that eternal salvation must be man's ultimate quest and that the Christian faith, because it offered man his only hope of achieving that goal, was the most decisive force in the life of every person.[38] Nations, too, he was convinced, had to be guided by the eternal moral values taught by the church if they genuinely aspired to political freedom and social justice.[39]

This commitment to a higher morality and spirituality represented for Şaguna the indissoluble link between the church and the national aspirations of his people. He also recognized a special, deeper relationship between Orthodoxy and nationality. He believed that the church had been the chief instrument of the Rumanians' survival as a separate people during the preceding four hundred years and that the fate of the one was joined to that of the other as the "soul to the body." As a historian of the church he knew that the Rumanians had suffered discrimination in the past because they were Orthodox and that the decline of the church could be dated from the denial of political rights to the Rumanian nation.[40] He went even further and implied that the ritual and practices of Rumanian Orthodoxy were peculiar expressions of the Rumanian soul and that, consequently, it was upon their strength and vitality that the spiritual and intellectual progress of the Rumanian nation would ultimately depend.[41]

Şaguna's belief in the transcendental mission of the church and his determination to fulfil his responsibilities as its head go far toward explaining why he thought religion in education and the preservation of church schools were important and why he was reluctant to commit the church and its resources unconditionally to the national movement as the lay intellectuals conceived of it. He insisted that elementary and secondary schools remain under the control of the church, for he regarded the educational process not simply as the acquisition of knowledge or the preparation for a career, but as a moral and spiritual awakening as well. In his opinion, therefore, it was incumbent upon each church to maintain its own separate school system and to include religious subjects in the curriculum. He opposed the establishment of so-called mixed or national schools, so ardently desired by leading laymen of both churches, branding such institutions as "illegal and abnormal."[42] He feared that the Orthodox, lacking the support of the state and the material resources enjoyed by the Uniates, would be exposed to proselytism, or, worse, that in the interests of national harmony religious training would be neglected or abolished altogether. He raised similar objections to the establishment of public or state schools in place of church schools; he found them inadequate not only on religious but also on national grounds, since he was certain that they would devote little time to Rumanian language and culture and would thereby defeat one of the main purposes of education, which, in his opinion, was to strengthen a child's awareness of his origins and national identity.[43] In spite of these strong reservations, he permitted the members of his church to join with their Uniate neighbors in establishing a common school whenever the true interests of learning would be served.[44]

Şaguna was far from indifferent to national feeling. He acknowledged the special link between Eastern Orthodoxy and all its peoples and showed how the church itself had encouraged national feeling by employing the national languages in the church service and by allowing native priests to officiate.[45] He had also had numerous opportunities to observe how strong a force national feeling had become among his own people and the peoples of the Habsburg monarchy generally. He recognized that they were all striving to further their own political and cultural development and he warmly defended their right to do so.[46] The idea of nationality, he admitted, was so powerful a force among his contemporaries that it determined in large measure the spirit of the times in which they were living, and he acknowledged it to be his own duty as bishop to protect the welfare of his people in worldly as well as in spiritual matters.[47]

His estimate of the vitality of nationalism and his appreciation of the important role the church had played in the political and social development of the Rumanian people notwithstanding, Şaguna refused to allow the church to become merely an instrument in the hands of laymen for promoting the cause of nationality. He abhorred the idea of the church's becoming entangled in secular affairs and, as a result, dependent for its very existence upon the vicissitudes of domestic and foreign policy, as determined in Vienna or Budapest by persons who had little knowledge of the Rumanian Orthodox and even less sympathy for their fate. Whether at the highest levels of government or simply in his daily contacts with his parish clergy he insisted that church affairs be kept separate from purely political matters.[48] For this reason, to the surprise of many, he urged the diet of Sibiu to enact one law recognizing the constitutional status of the Rumanian nation and another granting rights and privileges to the Orthodox church, rather than combine both matters in a single piece of legislation.

In order to maintain the independence of his church he also tried to prevent his clergy from jeopardizing their religious office by overly zealous political activity. He sharply rebuked those priests who used the pulpit to criticize public officials or insist too vehemently upon the use of Rumanian in local affairs, matters he considered inappropriate for a religious ceremony.[49] But he did not object to the clergy's participation in politics; he encouraged them to do so as one of their rights and duties as citizens in a constitutional state. In the summer of 1861, when Franz Salmen, the Saxon count, accused the Orthodox clergy of "agitating against public order," Şaguna energetically defended his priests.[50] He did not, however, miss the opportunity to remind them that the welfare of the church must be their chief concern, and he required them to obey the law and refrain from all acts that might adversely affect the church.[51] The church, he maintained, must be independent of governments and even of national politics because it had its own special, transcendental mission to fulfil — the salvation of man — which knew no boundaries of time or place. Furthermore, the church, as he conceived of it, had special obligations to the state, the most important of which were the support of the dynasty, the constitution, and all duly appointed officials. He could not, therefore, allow the church or its clergy to be used for purposes that might jeopardize the success of its spiritual mission or upset what he considered the proper relationship between church and state. Such support did not imply, in his mind, the submission of the church to the state. On the contrary, he believed that the civil authority was obliged to respect the right of the church to manage its affairs in accordance with its own canon law and he saw in the maintenance of this autonomy the unassailable refuge of Rumanian nationality.

Although Şaguna thought that the lay intellectuals erred in seeking to involve the church too deeply in their own worldly enterprises, he had no desire to exclude them from the government of the church. Rather, he believed that the vitality of its institutions and its ability to reach the broad masses of the people effectively would largely depend upon how successful it was in enlisting lay participation in all its social activities. His guide, as in all other matters affecting the church, was canon law, and from the beginning of his episcopate he sought to revive the synod, composed of both laymen and clergy, as the basic unit of church government from the parish to the diocese. Not only did he consider the synod necessary for the success of his plan to restore representative government to the church; he also intended to use it to bring the church's activities into harmony with the liberal political and social ideas of 1848. Every institution, he believed — even one like the church, which was founded upon eternal principles — had continually to adapt itself to the changing material and spiritual needs of its people.[52] In determining the extent to which laymen might participate in the various organs of church government, he adhered strictly to canon law, which allowed them an important voice in economic and educational affairs, but reserved questions of dogma and ritual to the clergy and granted the bishop special powers as general superintendent of the church.[53]

In the early 1860s relations between the lay intellectuals and Şaguna became increasingly strained, as fundamental differences, suppressed during the preceding decade, finally came to the surface. The intellectuals grew more vocal in their opposition to ecclesiastical leadership in politics and even in the affairs of the church, and they demanded that the nation itself assume full responsibility for its welfare. They rejected Şaguna's view that the church should be the focus and inspiration of their national existence and deplored his sectarianism in religious matters and what seemed to be his willingness to follow the lead of the court in political questions. They considered religion a personal matter, and their own religiosity, as we have seen, was largely a matter of tradition rather than of deep conviction.

What is especially striking about the growth of secularism is the strong influence it had even among the clergy. Increasing numbers of priests began to take part regularly in national politics in the 1860s and to be permanently concerned with broad social problems. Paradoxically, Şaguna himself was largely responsible for this important change in the preoccupations of the priest, since he had made the success of his broad program of church reform dependent upon a well-educated and socially conscious clergy. A typical representative of the new clergy was one of Şaguna's protégés, Nicolae Cristea, a priest whom Şaguna had sent to the University of Leipzig to finish his studies and whom he had later appointed editor of *Telegraful Român*. Although Cristea remained a devout Christian and never doubted God's influence over the lives of men, he nonetheless devoted most of his time to the national movement. Like many of his contemporaries, he advo-

cated the creation of a middle class, which he considered the most pro-
gressive force in modern society, and he demanded a thorough agrarian reform to ensure a decent living for the peasantry. He also recognized that the era of priestly dominance over the affairs of the Rumanian nation was coming to an end and he looked to the lay intellectuals
to provide leadership.[54]

Even in those areas where Şaguna and the intellectuals found it possible to cooperate, their respective goals were quite different. For example, the intellectuals, as we have seen, wholeheartedly supported
Şaguna's efforts to free his church from the jurisdiction of the Serbian
metropolitan of Carlovitz and to assert its autonomy vis-à-vis the state
through the establishment of a separate metropolis for all the Rumanian Orthodox of the Habsburg monarchy. But their concern was not
with canon law. Rather, their objective was to make the church a more
effective instrument of their own national policy by freeing it from foreign control and, in the long run, by substituting themselves for the
clergy as the managers of its affairs.[55] Şaguna, on the other hand, desired to bring the institutions of the church into conformity with the
canons and to reassert its ancient rights and privileges. He recognized
the material benefits and the political advantages that the new metropolis was certain to bring to his people, but he was utterly opposed to
those who would use the church simply as a tool to achieve national
political goals. He condemned such tactics as "emanations of a blind
and barren national pride," and when his foes persisted, he began to
doubt the efficacy of nationalism and referred to it disdainfully as the
"unfortunate idea of nationality."[56]

The decisive struggle between Şaguna and the intellectuals for national leadership occurred in the late sixties. An open confrontation
was avoided so long as the policies advocated by Şaguna were successful. But even during the diet of Sibiu the intellectuals chafed at the
subordinate role assigned to them.[57] They were convinced that their
own theories of social development provided the most comprehensive
plan for national progress and, with the expanded opportunities for
political action offered by the constitutional era, were more eager than
ever to apply them. Especially odious to them was Şaguna's alleged
unwillingness to challenge Austrian political leadership, as well as his
failure (so it seemed to them) to initiate a policy based solely upon the
national interest or to establish a permanent political organization
separate from his own episcopal chancellery. Ioan Raţiu, as we have

seen, took the lead in demanding vigorous and independent national policy and the participation of all groups in formulating it.[58] Pavel Vasici, Şaguna's own councillor for Orthodox school affairs, objected strenuously to his bishop's disregard of the "intelligentsia's" wishes in his choice of candidates for the diet of Sibiu; Şaguna seemed to be acting more like a church head than a national leader.[59] From abroad the forty-eighters — Simion Bărnuţiu in Iaşi and Alexandru Papiu-Ilarian in Bucharest — offered encouragement and urged their former colleagues to make no agreements with Austria until she had guaranteed the autonomy of the Rumanian nation.[60]

The political changes inaugurated in 1865, which led to the Austro-Hungarian Compromise, largely discredited Şaguna's leadership in the eyes of the intellectuals and led to such manifestations of independence on their part as the Raţiu mission to Vienna in the winter of 1866 and Şaguna's own virtual dismissal from the presidency of ASTRA in the summer of 1867. The intellectuals at last took it upon themselves to direct the political development of the Rumanian nation. The almost evangelical fervor with which they set about their work owed little to traditional religious enthusiasm, but they had, nonetheless, found themselves a new religion. Although they were pragmatists and did little formal philosophizing about society or their own role in it, they possessed an ideology with all the power of a religion and, in its own way, just as all-encompassing — the idea of nationality. Like a religion, it offered them an explanation of society and provided them with a purpose that justified their own existence. Many priests served it as eagerly as laymen. It had become, in the words of the inhabitants of a small village near Turda, a "sacred cult," whose principal dogma taught that every people possessed the right to develop as it wished free from all outside constraints.[61] Şaguna himself recognized its enormous power of attraction and the competition it offered organized religion; he complained that the "immoderate spirit of nationality" had completely obsessed the minds of the young, and he blamed it for their growing indifference to the church and religion.[62] Indeed, the idea of nationality represented to many something loftier than denominationalism, and like-minded Uniates and Orthodox discovered in it the source of their brotherhood and the dogma of progress.

The intellectuals were not satisfied with their domination of political life; they intensified their efforts to gain a greater voice in the governance of both the Orthodox and Uniate churches. Here, too, they achieved some success. At the first national church congress of the restored Orthodox metropolis held in Sibiu from September 16 to October 7, 1868, they succeeded in making substantial changes in Şaguna's project for church government. Şaguna had, indeed, recommended the extensive participation of laymen at all levels, but he intended to reserve final authority in all church affairs to the clergy. The laymen, who showed little understanding of the principles or spirit of canon law and were mainly inspired by the theories of liberal democracy, transformed the synods and other governing bodies of the church into more representative institutions than Şaguna had thought desirable. Although he considered these changes a dangerous intrusion of the laity into church government, he nonetheless accepted most of them lest any delay play into the hands of Magyar nationalists, who were hostile to any measure that would strengthen Rumanian national institutions.[63]

Uniate intellectuals, resuming the work begun by Bărnuţiu in the 1840s, also attempted to gain a greater voice for themselves in church government. They were worried by evidence of internal decay and by indications that the Hungarian Catholic hierarchy intended to strengthen the bonds of union between the two churches as a prelude to Magyarization. They were convinced that if their church were to continue to play a significant role in national affairs, the general synod, which Bishop Ioan Bob had allowed to fall into disuse, must be restored to full vigor as the main legislative body of the church and laymen, particularly, be encouraged to participate in its work.[64]

These matters came to a head with the death of Archbishop Şuluţiu at the beginning of September 1867 and the search for a successor. Strong support developed among political passivists for the candidacy of Grigore Silaşi, the vice-rector of the Central Greek Catholic Seminary in Vienna and an ardent supporter of their cause. They did, in fact, make an offer to Silaşi, which he readily accepted.[65] Some priests and laymen toyed with an even more imaginative plan to involve their church in national political affairs. They proposed the election of Lucien Bonaparte, a cousin of Napoleon III and a cardinal in Rome, as Archbishop of the Uniate Church, as a means of gaining the support of France for their cause. Ioan Raţiu was enthusiastic and was even willing to risk curtailment of the church's autonomy, which the election of a Roman Catholic cardinal might entail, if that would contribute to the restoration of Transylvania's autonomy, full political rights for the Rumanians, and Western European guarantees for both. In Pest he spoke about the project with Mihail Kogălniceanu, a liberal statesman from Moldavia who had played an important role in the union of the Rumanian principalities in 1859. Though he expressed great surprise at the idea, Kogălniceanu agreed to sound out opinion in Paris.[66] The whole affair does not seem to have gone any further. When informed of it, Barițiu warned that the election of a foreigner would cause too many political complications and urged support for a native candidate instead. The electoral synod, which met on August 11, 1868, chose as archbishop Ioan Vancea, Bishop of Gherla, who had vigorously supported Rațiu's mission to Vienna in 1866. Even though he sympathized with their cause, Vancea was determined to uphold canon law and maintain his own prerogatives. As a result, Uniate intellectuals gained much less at their national church congress in 1868 than they had expected.[67]

Nonetheless, they maintained their vigilance over church affairs and did not hesitate to intervene whenever its position as a national institution seemed threatened. They were especially sensitive to any effort by the Roman Catholic hierarchy of Hungary to strengthen its control over the Uniate Church. From Pest in March 1871 Vasile L. Pop sounded the alarm, warning that a conference of Roman Catholic bishops had decided to draw up a new statute governing church administration and planned to include in it the Uniate churches in both Hungary and Transylvania. Since the protests of Rumanian Uniate bishops had been ignored, Pop urged his fellow laymen to take the initiative and organize a general conference to let both the court and the Hungarian government know their true feelings.[68] At a spirited meeting of some 135 delegates in Alba Iulia on April 13 and 14, the intellectuals voiced their deep misgivings about the intentions of the Roman Catholic hierarchy, to which they unfailingly attached the epithet "Magyar." In a strongly worded address to Metropolitan Vancea they emphasized their devotion to both church and nationality and warned that the one could not exist without the other. It was evident that they regarded the promotion of nationality as the chief end of all their endeavors and the church as the means, for they cited at length all the material benefits the Union with Rome had brought the Rumanian nation, but they passed over in silence the spiritual heritage it had bequeathed them.[69]

The intellectuals also took the occasion to blame their own church hierarchy for its failure to hold regular church synods, at which the laity might be heard and the welfare of the church fostered accordingly. Regarding themselves as more effective opponents of Magyarization than the clergy, and having little faith in the willingness of Vancea or his bishops to risk government displeasure by too forceful a protest, the conference entrusted Pop and a delegation of its own choosing with a petition to the emperor objecting to any attempt by the Roman Catholic Church of Hungary to assert its jurisdiction over Rumanian Uniates.[70] They stressed the vital role of the church in national life:

For us Rumanians, whose entire social, moral, and intellectual and even our political life has been so closely linked to the church, a separation of the nation from the church in today's circumstances would cause immense harm. . . . Yet, precisely because of this unity of church and people, we Rumanians must make our moral, intellectual, and spiritual progress with the aid of the church.[71]

And they demanded that the church be completely reorganized on a "constitutional basis" to enable it to fulfil its "heavy responsibilities." As it turned out, their fears were, at least for the time being, unwarranted, but their suspicions of the Roman Catholic Church as an instrument of Magyarization were never completely allayed.

The attention which the intellectuals accorded economic development was a significant innovation in the movement for national self-determination. They recognized the fact that cultural and political struggle alone was no longer sufficient to protect their national interests. George Barițiu, who had been in the vanguard of the movement to obtain equal economic opportunities for the Rumanians, had placed his journalistic talents in the service of liberal economic doctrines, slightly tinged with notions about the survival of the fittest, for thirty years.[72] He and his colleagues were convinced that, to attain their goals, they must have a prosperous peasantry and middle class, which they looked to as the indispensable sources of material support and leadership. Their immediate task was to defend the "national patrimony," that is, the land worked by Rumanian peasants. The poverty and lack of education of the peasants had made them easy prey for rapacious landlords, most of whom were Magyar, and Rațiu and his colleagues, who had labored unceasingly at the diet of Sibiu to free Rumanian peasants from the remnants of manorialism that had survived the emancipation of 1848, feared that in time most of the land they presently held would be taken over by "foreigners."[73] Consequently, they established a standing committee to which Rumanian peasants might turn for aid if they became involved in legal disputes with their landlords or with the state. Their view of the agrarian question was broader than that of most of the forty-eighters. They found the cause of peasant misery to be more complex than simply the lack of land, and they observed with growing anxiety the steady increase of population in the villages and the reduction of many peasants to the level of a rural proletariat. They proposed to relieve the pressure of overpopulation, as we have seen, by encouraging the peasant to learn a trade and move to the city. In order to finance their ambitious plans and to protect the nation from economic subservience and the peasant masses from social degradation, they decided to establish their own credit institutions. Visarion Roman founded the first Rumanian savings and loan association in Răşinari in 1868. It was not the success he had hoped for, but in 1871, he, Bariţiu, and other political leaders, the majority of whom were activists, founded the Albina Bank of Sibiu, which in time became the strongest Rumanian credit institution in pre-World War I Hungary.[74] Their efforts to found a Rumanian bank at the very time Şaguna was trying to ensure the autonomy of the new Orthodox metropolis symbolized their sharply divergent views about the nature of the national movement and its future course.

The intellectuals were convinced that they had taken an important step toward the attainment of their social and political goals by convoking the Conference of Mercurea in March of 1869. They viewed the very fact of the conference itself as a declaration of independence from the long tutelage of the two church hierarchies. They believed that the nation's business was their special province, a job for professionals, not a side-interest of churchmen, and they rejoiced that they would soon have an instrument in the form of a modern political party with which to carry out their will.

The Conference of Mercurea has a deeper meaning as well. It signalled the end of an era in the Rumanian national movement. Bărnuţiu, who had died in 1864, and now Şaguna, whose leadership had been repudiated, passed from the scene. Gone with them were those characteristic figures who had dominated the national movement since the eighteenth century—the scholar, who could lead by virtue of his erudition and the lofty ideals he conceived, and the churchman, who preached morality as the essence of a nation's life. A new generation of pragmatists had taken their places.

9 / Church and State

The supreme end to which Șaguna devoted his episcopate was the establishment of an autonomous national church. He was certain that such an institution would go far towards eliminating all the evils that afflicted Orthodoxy in the Austrian empire and prevented it from carrying out its sacred and worldly missions. The key to the problem, as he saw it, was the restoration of the Rumanian Orthodox metropolis of Alba Iulia; it would place the government of the church on a solid constitutional foundation, which, in turn, would render it largely immune from outside political interference and enable it to respond more effectively to the growing needs of an awakening nation. It seemed to him that of all the churches of Transylvania only the Orthodox lacked a charter or some other document sanctioned by the crown recognizing its legal existence and specifying its rights and privileges. The Roman Catholics, he pointed out in a long memorandum to the emperor in 1855, had their Concordat with Rome; the Lutherans a new statute of self-government; and the Uniates their own metropolis; but the Orthodox were still treated as a barely tolerated sect.[1]

Șaguna was determined to carry out the promise he had made at his consecration as bishop. Only by bringing the government of the church into full conformity with the canon law of the Eastern Church could he establish a beneficial working relationship with the state and avoid the dangers of sudden political changes. He pronounced the existing status of the Rumanian Orthodox of the empire "anti-canonical" and he judged the causes of this "unhealthy situation" to have been political acts rather than church legislation: the abolition of the old metropolis as a result of the Union with Rome and the subordination of the diocese of Transylvania to Carlovitz in the 1780s. In seeking the restoration of the metropolis, which he hoped would include Bukovina and the Banat, he appealed mainly to the apostolic canons, which he interpreted as meaning that a metropolitan must belong to the same nation as his bishops and the people to whom they ministered.[2]

A systematic campaign to restore the metropolis proved impossible during the first decade of Șaguna's episcopate. The intense nationalism of the revolutionary period overwhelmed sectarian ambitions, and the absolutism and Catholic resurgence of the 1850s permitted only piecemeal endeavors. Only with the advent of constitutionalism in 1860 did significant progress occur, culminating in the emperor's sanction of the metropolis in December 1864 and the adoption of a constitution for it in 1868.

During his long and often frustrating efforts on behalf of the metropolis Şaguna was careful to cultivate a "proper" relationship with the state. The principle of church autonomy was his constant guide in all his dealings with the civil authority, from the court in Vienna to the most isolated district official. According to his conception of church-state relations, each party had its own jurisdictions and spheres of activity into which the other might not intrude. Since the Orthodox Church in Transylvania had been subservient to the state ever since the appointment of its first bishop by Maria Theresa in 1761, the question of church autonomy had rarely been an issue until Şaguna's investiture, and the boundaries between civil and ecclesiastical administration had become so thoroughly blurred that they were nearly non-existent. Consequently, in his dealings with the civil authority Şaguna was always conscious of the need to assert his own prerogatives and redefine the limits of state power. Tradition, in the form of church law, imperial legislation, especially the constitution of March 1849, and even the principle of the natural rights of man, gave him his strongest weapons. He also recognized the importance of setting new precedents as the church continually assumed greater responsibilities and Rumanian society itself became more complex and gained in sophistication.

He conceived of the ideal relationship between church and state as one of harmony and cooperation in furthering the general welfare of the Christian community rather than one of hostility and rivalry, which had characterized Rumanian Orthodoxy's existence in Transylvania for centuries. To bring about the change he desired, he urged the state to recognize not only the principle of church autonomy but also that of national equality. Since Orthodoxy was so closely associated with the historical development of the Rumanian people, he could see no hope for his church's enjoying the same status as the historically dominant Protestant and Roman Catholic churches until the Rumanian nation itself had been raised to the same constitutional rank as the old privileged nations.[3] But his experiences during the revolution of 1848 and the decade of absolutism had taught him not to

rely upon the promises of politicians, however solemn, but rather to
establish the validity of ecclesiastical and national rights by asserting
them at every opportunity.[4] His conviction that a church or a nation
preserved its rights best by exercising them explains his tenacity in his
long struggle with the Cultusministerium in the 1850s and his refusal
in the following decade to accept passivism as an effective political
weapon.

In his campaign to reestablish the metropolis he kept before him two
principles: reliance upon the crown as the ultimate source of law, and
respect for the dynasty as a guarantor of social stability and legal continuity. Belief in the divine right of the Habsburgs to rule had nothing
to do with these feelings. Şaguna's approach was a pragmatic one
based upon a keen understanding of Rumanian historical development under Habsburg rule. Like every Rumanian leader of his day, he
recognized the fact that the modest cultural and economic gains of the
Rumanians—Orthodox and Uniate alike—had come as a result of the
court's intervention on their behalf against the privileged estates of
Transylvania. Like them, too, he had no illusions about the existence
of a special bond between the Rumanians and the "good Emperor," a
belief that seems to have been widespread among the peasant masses.
Rather, he recognized as the source of the court's beneficence its pursuit of self-interest. Unlike many intellectuals who wanted to lessen the
Rumanians' dependence upon the dynasty, he believed that their progress, perhaps even their very survival, necessitated a strengthening of
the bonds that had long existed between them. For this reason he drew
a careful distinction between the Austrian bureaucracy and the Transylvanian estates, on the one hand, and the dynasty, on the other; he
attacked the first without hesitation when he thought they were in the
wrong, but it never occurred to him to challenge the emperor or criticize the ruling house.

Şaguna recognized the fact that the origins and nature of church
and state were different. The church was founded by Christ, and its
purpose was to instill in the faithful a sense of morality and spirituality
in keeping with His teachings in order to prepare them to achieve their
eternal salvation. The means it used were preaching the Word of God
and administering the sacraments. The state, on the other hand, was
created by a union of families under a commonly accepted leader. Its
purpose was to maintain order among its citizens and protect their
lives, their honor, and their property, and its main instruments were

political and judicial. Although each had its own mission to fulfil—
the one divine, the other worldly—they had need of one another, for
neither could hope to accomplish its goals in isolation. The state gave
the church material support and respected the autonomy of its institutions and the liberty of conscience of its faithful. The church, in turn,
gave the state moral support regardless of its form—absolutist, constitutional, or republican. Şaguna looked beyond these services to what
he regarded as the essential importance of religion to the state. He was
convinced that the state could not achieve its goals without it—simply
through the use of its political and economic power, or the arts and
sciences, or on the basis of some "system of abstract morality." None of
these means would be effective, he argued, because its citizens could
not find in them the satisfaction of their spiritual needs. With its citizens deprived of "spiritual rest," he concluded, the state could not enforce order or assure material well-being, and hence its whole reason
for being would be jeopardized.[5]

Within this theoretical framework Şaguna looked for practical ways
to bring about a fruitful collaboration between church and state. He
reserved an important, though loosely defined, function for the head
of state in church government. In the preliminary draft of a constitution for the new metropolis, which he completed in 1864, he recognized the right of the emperor to exercise "supreme inspection" over
the church and to sanction the election of the new bishop or metropolitan. Although he did not specify what duties and powers supreme
inspection entailed, he stated unequivocally that it must conform to
the laws of the land, which guaranteed the Orthodox Church the right
to regulate and administer its affairs in accordance with its own canon
law, and free from the interference of state officials or any other
church.[6] On numerous occasions he tried to elicit some kind of statement from the Cultusministerium defining what it understood by the
term "church autonomy," but neither it nor any other ministry was
willing to commit itself. Consequently, he worked out his own definition: the legal foundations of church autonomy were Holy Scripture,
the canons, and "local church requirements"; in all matters relating to
the church the canons had the same force of law as secular legislation,
but whenever there was a conflict between the two, canon law took
precedence; when canonical sources offered no guidance, Roman-
Byzantine law, in so far as it corresponded to the principles of the Orthodox Church, was to be consulted.[7]

No Austrian ministry, either Bach's or Schmerling's, could accept such a sweeping definition of church autonomy. The impasse which developed between Şaguna and the Cultusministerium in the 1850s was undoubtedly in part the result of this fundamental disagreement over the respective roles of church and state in society. The official attitude toward Orthodoxy and the Rumanians in general, inherited in its essentials from the age of the Counter-Reformation, proved to be a strong influence on the relations between Vienna and Sibiu. Austrian ministers persisted in treating the Rumanians as an uncultivated *Bauernvolk* and dismissed their clergy as superstitious and ignorant and, hence, requiring the strictest possible control. This mistrust of the Orthodox and their bishop was hardly justified, for behind Şaguna's strivings for autonomy lay his urgent desire to bring the aspirations of his faithful into harmony with the interests of the Gesamtmonarchie.[8]

In his conception of church-state relations the state did not play the role of merely a remote superintendent; on the contrary, it had both a moral duty and a practical interest in furthering the work of the church, since the church was engaged in the formation of a devout and law-abiding citizenry. The idea of a separation of church and state, in the ordinary meaning of the term, was foreign to him; he saw nothing unusual in seeking state subsidies to pay the salaries of priests or to provide religious instruction in state schools.[9] Good Christians, he argued, made loyal subjects, who in turn laid the foundations of a stable and prosperous society. It was therefore incumbent upon the state to assist the church in this vital social mission by respecting its independence and by providing it with necessaries to carry on its work.

At the same time, Şaguna was wary of the state's embrace. He warned his clergy and faithful not to turn to the government for the solution of all their problems; in so doing they merely extended its powers into areas that were rightly the preserve of the church. One of his principal goals in seeking full autonomy for the Orthodox Church was to free it from its hitherto almost total dependence upon the state. He was anxious to dissociate it from any particular political system, for he recognized that too often the Christian churches had been sidetracked in the pursuit of their goals by entanglement in the secular affairs of state.

The *modus vivendi* between church and state that Şaguna envisaged was by no means one-sided. The church was not merely a receiver of

state beneficence; it, too, had something of value to offer. In return
for autonomy and material support Şaguna promised the state a devoted clergy capable of using its almost unlimited influence among the
peasant masses to enhance the position of the dynasty and ensure
obedience to its laws. The church's action would not, however, be contingent upon state support. He considered it the duty of the church, by
the very nature of its social mission, to assist the civil authority in carrying out its legal functions and, in general, to encourage all undertakings that promoted the public welfare. For this reason he instructed all
his priests to subscribe to the state loan of 1854 as an example to their
parishioners,[10] and he required them to cooperate fully with local officials in taking the census and keeping vital statistics.[11] As he pointed
out time and again to the various ministries in Vienna and the Transylvanian government, increased material assistance from the state
would enable the clergy to perform these and other public services
more effectively, and hence with greater benefit to the state.

Shortly after the cessation of hostilities in August 1849 and his return to Transylvania Şaguna resumed his campaign to restore the
metropolis and bring about a thorough reorganization of church government. On September 22 he assembled his consistory for its first
meeting since the previous December. He made clear his determination to proceed as rapidly as possible with a comprehensive reform of
church administration and the status of the clergy. In spite of the
desperate financial situation in which the church found itself, he expressed confidence that under the protection of the March constitution, which guaranteed them religious and political equality, they
would in the end achieve their goals. As a preliminary to any reform he
instructed his protopopes to make a thorough survey of the resources
and needs of all the parishes under their respective jurisdictions.[12]

The first order of business was the convocation of the diocesan
church synod. Şaguna considered it the key to systematic church reform, since it would allow him to consult with the representatives of
the clergy and laity from every part of Transylvania and to mobilize
men and resources for what he himself realized would be a long and
arduous task. He did not doubt that the synod would support him, and
promptly set about mobilizing the laity. Aware of the intellectuals'
own eagerness to foster cultural development, he planned to reintro-
duce full lay representation in the synod in the proportion of two delegates from the laity to one from the clergy. At first, Austrian authori-

ties flatly refused to consider his proposals. Governor Wohlgemuth
objected to the convocation on the grounds that electioneering and the
public discussion of controversial issues would rekindle nationalist passions and upset the orderly transition from war to peace. Eventually,
for political reasons, Wohlgemuth modified his stand. He was also
suspicious of the Saxons and Magyars, with whom he was particularly
annoyed at the beginning of 1850 because of their "exaggerated political ambitions." For example, the Saxons had prolonged the meeting of
their reconstituted *Universität* many weeks beyond the original time
limit and were acting with too much independence to suit him. Aware
of Wohlgemuth's feelings, Şaguna suggested a counter demonstration in the Fundus regius in the form of an Orthodox Church synod.
To his surprise, Wohlgemuth responded favorably to the idea, and
the synod was set for March 24.[13] But the limitations Wohlgemuth
imposed upon the selection of delegates and the topics to be discussed
dashed Şaguna's hopes for a truly representative assembly with the
power to legislate a new direction in church government. Instead of
letting parishes and districts hold elections—a procedure Şaguna
favored—Wohlgemuth ordered him to choose the delegates himself.
He complied, mainly to save the synod, but he allowed the three parishes in Braşov, where Orthodox intellectuals were particularly numerous, to elect their own representatives, a deviation that brought a
stern reprimand from Wohlgemuth that electoral meetings and the
discussions they occasioned could not be tolerated in a "well-ordered
state."[14] Wohlgemuth restricted the agenda of the synod to the immediate problems of church and school and he appointed his own representative to make certain that no political discussions took place. He
reminded Şaguna that the synod was not a national assembly and
warned him that any violation of his instructions would result in the
immediate dissolution of the synod.[15]

In the face of such intimidation the forty-four delegates displayed
remarkable courage. They reiterated the demands for full equality
for the Rumanian nation and its churches contained in the national
petition of February 25, 1849, and requested the immediate reestablishment of the Orthodox metropolis and the convocation of a church
congress to organize it. Church autonomy, expanded state aid to the
Orthodox clergy on the same basis as that given to other churches, and
the establishment of a special section in the Cultusministerium for
Orthodox church and school affairs were also debated at great length

and included in a petition sent to the emperor on April 10.[16] Although adhering to Wohlgemuth's injunctions against open political discussion, Şaguna permitted great freedom of debate. But he refused to bring before the synod the draft of a church constitution, in spite of the pleas of many intellectuals who were eager to use the occasion to establish a form of parliamentary self-government that had been denied them in 1848. He reasoned that under existing conditions any statutes dealing with church government that the Cultusministerium might approve would undoubtedly provide for strict state supervision of church affairs, a condition he did not want to make a permanent feature of church-state relations.[17]

Şaguna was proud of the courage displayed by the synod and pleased with its unequivocal stand on church reform and the restoration of the metropolis.[18] He felt his position towards both the civil authority and Rajačić immensely strengthened, and in October he went to Vienna to attend the conference of Orthodox bishops, confident that far-reaching changes in church government and an improvement in the status of Orthodoxy in Transylvania were about to occur. Yet, as the conference dragged on into the following year without significant accomplishment, and as neither the court nor Wohlgemuth showed much inclination to carry out the recommendations of the March synod, he was finally forced to admit that "ingrained prejudice" still colored the attitudes and behavior of the highest echelons of government toward Orthodoxy.

In its treatment of the Rumanian Orthodox the court seemed to have reverted to Maria Theresa's policies of a century before. The religious sentimentality of the empress may have been lacking, but her concern with the political consequences of religious policy was fully shared by Bach and his fellow ministers. They believed that the strengthening of the Roman Catholic Church would promote the centralization of the monarchy and help to discourage centrifugal tendencies such as those perennially manifested by the Magyars. Like Maria Theresa's ministers, they too regarded the Uniate movement in Transylvania as an important element of such a policy, since the Rumanians could serve as a useful makeweight to the Calvinist Magyars, who, in their eyes, constituted the most serious challenge to the reincorporation of Transylvania into the Gesamtmonarchie.

The most enthusiastic champion of this policy was Count Leo Thun, the minister of religions and education from 1849 to 1860. He was a staunch Roman Catholic who championed the autonomy of his church and its paramountcy over the other churches of the monarchy. He regarded the Orthodox as schismatics and their church as a danger to the security of the state. In his view, it could not provide adequate guarantees against the willful behavior of its priests because of their ignorance and its own lack of strong centralized authority. Furthermore, he wanted to preserve the so-called historico-political crown lands and was little inclined to experiment with new institutions that might lead to concessions to the "non-historical" nationalities. Consequently, he used his powers to the fullest to promote the Church Union with Rome among the Rumanians and, in so doing, to thwart Şaguna's reform of the Orthodox Church. He ignored Şaguna's frequent memoranda on the organization of the diocesan consistory, rejected an impartial solution of the problem of mixed marriages in favor of one that was clearly advantageous to the Uniates, and persisted in treating the Orthodox in accordance with the conditions imposed upon Vasile Moga in 1810, which Şaguna scorned as an instrument that had turned his church into a business regulated by the state and the bishop into a servant of government bureaucrats.[19]

Not surprisingly, Thun and Şaguna rarely agreed on anything. They generally carried on their long polemic by correspondence, but on at least two occasions they met face-to-face in order to clarify their respective positions. At their first meeting, which took place in 1855, Thun tried to justify the strict control his ministry exercised over Orthodox affairs. The gist of his argument was that, unlike the Roman Catholic Church, which possessed numerous councils to enforce canon law and archbishops to supervise the activities of bishops, the Orthodox Church in Transylvania had no means of dealing with a "capricious bishop." Şaguna, at once angry and amused, assured Thun that the Orthodox Church had a canon law of its own, which the bishop, who was ultimately responsible to God for his actions, was obliged to respect. He pointed out that his church offered the state a special guarantee of its loyalty, in that it could not, like the Roman Catholic Church, appeal to a higher authority outside the monarchy. He argued that any irregularities in the governance of his church were caused by centuries of subjugation rather than by defects in its constitution.[20] He dismissed Thun's misgivings about the Orthodox as completely unwarranted, since the Christian community, in spite of its division into numerous churches, was one in its adherence to the teachings of Christ. "That," rejoined Thun, "as a Catholic I cannot accept."[21] Their second meeting, in 1857, produced a similar impasse. Şaguna respected Thun as a man of considerable learning and ability, but he found him woefully ignorant of Orthodox history and institutions. He found solace in the conviction that Thun's successors would ultimately see the folly of trying to govern the Orthodox Church in accordance with the institutions and practices of Roman Catholicism.[22]

But Şaguna did not underestimate the danger to Orthodoxy inherent in Thun's deep-seated prejudices. As we have seen, he regarded the progress of the Uniate movement as a matter of life and death for his church, and there was no doubt in his mind that the creation of the Uniate metropolis of Alba Iulia and Făgăraş, in 1853, and especially of the new bishopric of Lugoj in the Banat, was a deliberate attempt by the Bach government to win over large numbers of Orthodox by appealing to their national sentiments.[23] He found additional evidence of such a policy in Thun's support of Serbian candidates for bishop in the vacant Orthodox see of Arad in 1852. Thun hoped that their success would persuade the Orthodox to abandon a "foreign" (Serbian) church in favor of the new "national" (Uniate) Rumanian metropolis.[24] Şaguna thought such proselytizing efforts inimical to the state's own best interest; they disturbed the conscience of the faithful and disrupted their religious practices and, eventually, made them indifferent to religion, since they had abandoned the old and could never fully accommodate themselves to the new.[25] He concluded that such a spiritual trauma was hardly conducive to the formation of law-abiding and loyal citizens, which he took to be the state's chief interest in religion.

Şaguna's struggle with Thun and what he often referred to as the "ultramontanist current" in Vienna encompassed every aspect of church affairs, even the proper designation of the Orthodox Church. Thun persisted in using the negative and, to Şaguna, deprecatory term "nicht uniert" (non-united).[26] Şaguna's protest against being addressed as "non-united Bishop of Hermannstadt" instead of "Greek Orthodox Bishop of Transylvania" went unanswered for many years, until finally, on August 9, 1856, the council of ministers agreed to consider the matter. After a lengthy but largely one-sided discussion it approved Thun's argument that the term "non-united" be retained because it tended to make the differences between the two Rumanian churches less obvious, thus reducing friction between them, and because it served to emphasize the "naked fact" that the union of the Eastern with the Western Church had been only partially completed.[27] On December 14, 1856, the Reichsrat reviewed the whole controversy —Șaguna's original petition, Thun's objections, the findings of the council of ministers, and a by now bulging file of supporting documents—and then adopted Thun's recommendation that a final decision be postponed until a complete study of all the petitions against the term "non-united" could be made.[28] There the matter rested until 1860.

Although Vienna was generally hostile or indifferent to the plight of his church, Șaguna found in Governor Karl Schwarzenberg (1851-1858), Wohlgemuth's successor, a man who shared his views on church-state relations and accepted the principle of national equality.[29] Schwarzenberg had no special sympathy for the Orthodox, although he and Șaguna became friends, nor was he a liberal. He was in fact a staunch Roman Catholic and was as devoted to centralization and dynastic right as his aristocratic friends in Vienna. Unlike most of them, he recognized the practical necessity of coming to terms with the nearly 650,000 Orthodox, if there was to be order and prosperity in Transylvania. He thoroughly disapproved of Thun's policy of supporting the Uniates at the expense of the Orthodox, which he thought displayed a total lack of understanding of the religious problem there.[30] Șaguna's strenuous efforts to improve elementary education, raise the moral and intellectual level of his clergy, and bring order into the affairs of his church deeply impressed Schwarzenberg; to his way of thinking, this was the kind of energy and leadership the empire needed, and he was appalled by the Cultusministerium's crude handling of Șaguna. He made his own influence felt mainly in Transylvanian local government, where he encouraged officials to adopt a similar approach to religious affairs. As a result, the treatment of the Orthodox improved, and Șaguna had far less to complain of than during Wohlgemuth's tenure.

Șaguna had no illusions about where the ultimate decisions concerning the future of his church would be made; it was Vienna, not Cluj. It was equally clear to him that as long as Thun determined official policy toward the Orthodox, he could not hope to proceed with his projects for the metropolis and a new church constitution. Consequently, Șaguna decided to test his church's legal rights in specific areas and gradually to build his case for autonomy on whatever favorable decisions might be forthcoming. He also felt compelled to act out of sheer necessity because of the poverty of his clergy and teachers, who in many parishes were nearly destitute and unable to perform their duties. Since his own treasury was empty, he had to establish their right to share in the material support the imperial government provided the other churches of Transylvania.

A legal problem that preoccupied him throughout his episcopate, largely because of its financial implications, was the administration of church endowments. During the 1850s he made repeated attempts to gain some measure of financial independence for his church by asserting its right to control its own funds. There were four main sources of income totalling almost 130,000 florins: the Sydoxial Fund, created by Joseph II for the purpose of paying the new Orthodox bishop's salary and maintained by an annual tax on every Orthodox household; the Seminary Fund, established from collections of money made throughout the diocese between 1816 and 1828 to support Bishop Moga's theological institute; the 30,000 Gulden Fund, a sum left over after indemnities had been paid to families displaced by the establishment of the Transylvanian military districts in 1764 and assigned to the Orthodox Church in 1837 to assist indigent priests; and the Bishop Moga Fund, consisting of debentures willed to the diocese by Moga in 1845 to cover general church and school expenses. Although the origins and purpose of these funds were clear, the Orthodox themselves had never been allowed to manage them. Instead, various Transylvanian financial offices and, after 1849, the Cultusministerium in Vienna had decided how the money should be allocated without prior consultation with the bishop. They had not even considered it necessary to make an annual report to him on the condition of the funds.

If he accomplished nothing else, Şaguna was determined to put an end to this "humiliating" state of affairs. In June 1849 he petitioned Bach to provide a full accounting of Orthodox endowments and made clear his intention to seek control of them as soon as hostilities ended.[31] He cited the provisions of the March constitution guaranteeing equality to all churches as justification for his request and he foresaw no difficulty in settling the matter quickly. But no action was taken for four years. During that time he complained repeatedly about irregularities in the government's handling of the endowments, and pointed out that he had been told nothing at all about the Bishop Moga Fund and had received no interest from the 30,000 Gulden Fund, in spite of

promises that a modest sum would be forthcoming to assist poor
priests.[32] All his protests were in vain; Thun was convinced that the
Orthodox were incapable of managing their own financial affairs and
avoided replying to Şaguna by continually requesting additional information.[33] Finally, in 1853, the council of ministers accepted Thun's
recommendation that the Cultusministerium continue as before to
administer the endowments, but it now required the ministry to make
an annual report to the bishop on income and disbursements. Francis
Joseph made a slight modification before the annual allocation of
funds was approved: he instructed the ministry to submit a budget to
the bishop for "suggestions."[34] But the Cultusministerium made a
habit of ignoring Şaguna's advice and in some years, 1859 for example,
did not bother to consult him at all.[35]

Şaguna was hard put to keep control of those few sources of income
he already possessed. In 1853 he strenuously objected to the Transylvanian government's plan to abolish the *singhelie* tax, a payment
made to the bishop by every newly installed priest in proportion to
the size of his parish. Şaguna's concern was both legal and financial.
He argued that by interposing itself between a bishop and his clergy
and by annulling an article of canon law, the state would not only be
depriving him of a sum essential for the operation of church government, but would also be violating the principle of church autonomy.[36]
Perhaps because of these protests, the government abandoned its
plans. At the village level Şaguna was constantly on guard against the
misappropriation of parish funds by local officials. The peasants could
easily be cowed by someone in authority, and such abuses as the pilfer-
ing of a small church treasury near Tîrgu-Mureş by the *Unterbezirks-
commissar* to defray the court expenses of the commune were not
infrequent. Şaguna condemned such episodes as blatant violations of
church autonomy.[37]

Unsuccessful in his efforts to gain control of church endowments or
to obtain a regular subvention from the state, Şaguna tried to assure
the financial stability of the church by investing in land. For several
years after the revolution he made small purchases with his own
money, but in 1856 he decided to carry out his plan all at once by
acquiring the estate of Drasso, near Sibiu, for the considerable sum of
120,000 gulden. He turned for help to Baron Simon Sina, a wealthy
Macedo-Rumanian banker in Vienna well known for his generosity to
Orthodox causes. Şaguna presented financial arguments—the estate

was worth 180,000 gulden and would therefore be an excellent invest-
ment — and appealed to Sina's religious sentiments. But Sina refused to
help on the grounds, apparently, that he had already committed himself to numerous projects in Greece and that the Orthodox Church in
Transylvania was neither so destitute nor so oppressed as Şaguna
claimed.[38] The project had perforce to be abandoned.

The main purpose of all Şaguna's financial strivings was to improve
the living standards and training of the parish priest, on whom, in the
last analysis, depended the general welfare of the church and the fate
of all the projected reforms. His condition had not improved significantly for decades; in many cases it had worsened as a result of the
revolution and the advent of absolutism. It was still common for the
priest to spend much of his time working in the fields of a local landlord in order to earn enough to support his family. Manual labor had
become even more imperative after the fall of 1849, when the military
government eliminated the priest's traditional immunities to the capitation and various communal taxes and obliged him to quarter soldiers
and provide transport services like the rest of the population.[39] The
priest generally had no regular salary unless he was fortunate enough
to serve a parish in a large town, for most Orthodox parishes were too
poor to offer more than modest fees (usually in kind) for weddings,
baptisms, and funerals. He received no other compensation, unlike the
Lutheran ministers and Roman Catholic priests, who had endowments
in land (canonical portions) or could draw money or supplies from the
village treasury or collect a tithe from their own faithful.[40]

The unfortunate consequences of abiding poverty were all too apparent to Şaguna. Adult education hardly existed, and the schoolhouse door in many villages remained closed because the priest could
not afford to take time from earning a living to perform his duties as
schoolmaster. Even more alarming to Şaguna was the general mood of
rebelliousness among the parish clergy, which expressed itself in acts of
defiance against government decrees and the officials sent to enforce
them. Orthodox priests had assumed that because of the provisions of
the March constitution, and in return for their loyalty to the emperor
during the revolution, they would enjoy the same living standards and
receive the same privileges as their Lutheran and Roman Catholic
counterparts. Many of them interpreted equality to mean that those
who bore the burdens of society should have a proportionate share of
the benefits.[41] Instead, especially during the decade of absolutism,

they found themselves burdened with new taxes and deprived of the
few immunities they had managed to preserve. Şaguna was particularly worried about the effects of poverty and discrimination on the
recruitment of new candidates for the priesthood. He warned both the
court and Governor Schwarzenberg that it would be impossible to attract bright young men to a profession that had little else to offer
except want and degradation and that the long-term result would be a
decline of public morality and a concomitant weakening of loyalty to
the throne.[42]

The heart of Şaguna's plan to improve the priest's standard of living
was to assure him a regular income through the grant of a canonical
portion. In many parts of Transylvania local government had long
taken care of the clergy by appropriating communal land and providing a fixed quantity of wood and food and sometimes even a house.
Şaguna argued that the principle of religious equality set forth in the
March constitution required all communes to make similar arrange-
ments for the Orthodox clergy. Moreover, he noted that Transylvanian authorities themselves had already recognized their responsibilities in this matter; the diet of 1846-1847 had passed a law requiring the
grant of a canonical portion for every priest or minister, and in the
spring of 1848 the Saxon Universität had agreed to create such endowments for every Orthodox parish church in the Fundus regius. In obtaining the implementation of these laws, Şaguna was less successful,
since neither the Cultusministerium nor the Transylvanian government recognized the validity of pre-revolutionary or revolutionary
legislation.[43] Only in 1861 did Francis Joseph approve a plan to provide Orthodox priests with regular state subsidies,[44] but the problem of
their poverty and its manifold consequences remained unresolved.

Şaguna was also deeply concerned about the training given candidates for the priesthood. He was dissatisfied with the level of instruction at the theological institute in Sibiu and immediately after the end
of hostilities in 1849 he introduced a thorough reform of its general
organization and curriculum.[45] In 1853 he purchased a new building
for the institute with funds obtained from a public collection. The
move to larger quarters enabled him to increase the course of study
from one to two years and to open a teacher-training institute which
every candidate for the priesthood was obliged to attend. In 1862 the
theology curriculum was extended to three years. Şaguna continually
introduced new courses to enable the parish priest to carry out success-

fully the varied duties of his spiritual and social mission. He studied Greek, church history, canon law, the Bible, ethics, pastoral care, pedagogy, church singing, agriculture, and practical medicine, among other subjects. Financing this ambitious program was a constant cause of anxiety to Şaguna, and not until the end of the era of absolutism did he succeed in assuring the institute an adequate income.

The era of constitutionalism brought fundamental changes in the relations between the court and the Rumanian Orthodox Church. Leo Thun's departure from the Cultusministerium on October 20, 1860, had more than symbolic significance. Coinciding with the convocation of the Verstärkter Reichsrat and the expanded role the Rumanians were to have in Transylvanian affairs was a new receptivity on the part of Austrian officials toward Şaguna's plans for the restoration of the metropolis and the improvement of his clergy's standard of living. There are numerous examples of their sympathy toward the Orthodox. In the fall of 1860 the council of ministers approved the establishment of a section on Orthodox church and school affairs in the Cultusministerium, ignoring Thun's long-standing objection that there were no educated trustworthy Rumanians or Serbs to man such a department.[46] In the following year the Cultusministerium published a booklet outlining the history and organization of the Orthodox Church in the Habsburg monarchy as a guide for its personnel in handling Orthodox affairs. State support of the Orthodox clergy was now at last put on a regular basis. In 1861 Şaguna received the first of what were to become annual grants of 24,000 florins and 1,000 florins for the support of the parish clergy and the Orthodox theological seminary in Sibiu, respectively;[47] in 1862 he obtained a commitment of 4,000 florins yearly for the Orthodox *Obergymnasium* in Braşov; and in 1863 he began to receive 25,000 florins yearly to pay the salaries of diocesan administrative personnel and provide scholarships for students at the seminary and at foreign universities.[48]

The new atmosphere of understanding brought fresh approaches to the problem of the metropolis. The dispatch with which the court handled the controversy between the Serbs and the Rumanians in the summer of 1860 augured well for favorable action. In June negotiations between Şaguna and Rajačić had broken down over the latter's pretensions to still greater concentration of authority in the hands of the Serbian hierarchy. On August 21, Andrei Mocioni and Nicolae

Petrino, representing the Rumanians of the Banat and Bukovina, respectively, accompanied Şaguna when he personally presented a long memorandum on the metropolis to the emperor. They urged immediate sanction of a metropolis encompassing all the Rumanians of the monarchy and requested the convocation of a congress of bishops and lay leaders to organize it.[49] Francis Joseph replied on September 27 that he was "not disinclined" to permit the establishment of a Rumanian Orthodox metropolis, but he made the "regulation of hierarchical relations" between the Rumanians and Serbs a matter for an episcopal synod, which he instructed Rajačić to convoke in the near future.[50] Although the stipulation about more direct negotiations with the Serbs was not a happy prospect, Şaguna took heart from the general tenor of the note; it was the first positive pronouncement that any Austrian government had made on his innumerable petitions and memoranda concerning the metropolis.

Taking advantage of this favorable moment, Şaguna convoked a diocesan synod, which met in Sibiu between October 24 and 26, 1860. The delegates unanimously approved all his actions on behalf of the metropolis and voted an address to the emperor calling attention to the anomaly of Serbian control over Rumanian dioceses and restating all the arguments, canonical and national, that Şaguna had already raised during the previous decade. While taking the usual exception to the administrative subordination of the Transylvanian diocese to Carlovitz in the 1780s, the synod also made the point that the Rumanians of Hungary, i.e., the Banat and Crişana, had never formally been linked to the Serbian metropolis by either an ecclesiastical or a political decision, and it urged that they be removed from limbo by the immediate establishment of the metropolis.[51]

A process which had begun so auspiciously was soon stalled by conflicts between the Rumanian Orthodox, on the one hand, and their Serbian co-religionists and the Uniates, on the other, and by uncertainty and indecision at the highest levels of government. Şaguna also had the separatist tendencies of Bishop Hacman of Bukovina to contend with. As we have seen, Rajačić had refused to consider even the possibility of a separate Rumanian metropolis. After his death in 1861 the nearly three-year delay in the election of his successor prevented serious negotiations between the Serbs and Şaguna, which the court had stipulated as a necessary preliminary to any final action of its own. Moreover, Şuluţiu, Şaguna's colleague in numerous joint political undertakings during the early sixties, mounted a determined campaign of his own against the erection of a rival metropolis—a move which again strained relations between the two national leaders.[52] On May 9, 1862, he submitted a strongly worded protest to the emperor against the violation of any rights and privileges enjoyed by the Uniate Church resulting from the establishment of an Orthodox metropolis.[53] The papal nuncio in Vienna was even more forceful; he expressed amazement that the court could contemplate the creation of a "schismatic" metropolitan see in Transylvania, which would cause "irreparable harm" to the Uniate movement, and he demanded that the whole idea be dropped at once.[54]

These controversies, together with the complications caused by the broader demands of imperial foreign and domestic policy and the ponderous ways of the Austrian bureaucracy, held up a final resolution of the problem until the end of 1864. The delay cannot be ascribed to lingering prejudice toward the Orthodox or to doubts about their loyalty. Şaguna's unwavering commitment to the dynasty and his support of its social and political goals had persuaded most Austrian leaders that the Rumanians could become a valuable asset. Consequently, at the highest levels of government there was little opposition in principle to the restoration of the Orthodox metropolis, although some matters of detail defied a quick and easy solution.

Political considerations were uppermost in the minds of Minister of State Schmerling and his colleagues. They were anxious to settle the dispute between the Rumanians and Serbs and somehow in the process to appease the national aspirations of both, so that they might take their places in the new constitutional system and devote their full energies to its efficient operation. They seemed especially eager to satisfy Şaguna, whose cooperation was judged essential for the successful political reorganization of Transylvania.[55] But they were also careful to safeguard the privileges of the Roman Catholic and Uniate churches, particularly the latter, since it had always served imperial interests well.

Schmerling and his fellow ministers seemed to be most deeply concerned about how far the boundaries of the new metropolis should extend. The inclusion of Bukovina, for example, presented numerous difficulties: national, because the province had a large Slav population, and administrative, because it was Austrian, while the other dioceses to be included in the metropolis were Hungarian. In the end, they decided to postpone the assignment of Bukovina until after the metropolis had come into being. Partly because of the nationality problem, some ministers would even have limited the metropolis, at least in its initial stage, to Transylvania alone. Chancellor Nadásdy strongly favored this course in order to avoid offending the Serbs by "precipitate action" and to allow sufficient time for the settlement of complex constitutional questions that were bound to arise in Hungary. He argued that only after the creation of the metropolis could the delicate business of drawing the boundaries between it and the Serbian metropolis and dividing up common church property be done efficiently. The council of ministers approved this procedure,[56] and had it not been for Şaguna's stubborn insistence upon the inclusion of the Banat and Crişana, it seems probable that the jurisdiction of the metropolis would not have extended beyond the old historical principality of Transylvania.

On June 25, 1863, Francis Joseph informed Şaguna that he had approved the recommendations of his ministers concerning the metropolis, but reminded him that an agreement with the Serbian hierarchy must precede the final act of restoration.[57] There now followed what seemed to Şaguna an interminable correspondence with the Transylvanian Chancellery focussing on matters of procedure and requests for additional information: where should the seat of the metropolis be?; how many suffragan bishops should be appointed and where?; how great an endowment did the metropolis need?; should the metropolis encompass the Rumanians of Hungary as well as of Transylvania? These were questions Şaguna had already answered, but in reply to Nadásdy's urgent request of June 29, 1863, he obliged once again. He was firm in his insistence that the metropolis should include all the Rumanians of the Habsburg monarchy and that it should be composed of the existing dioceses of Transylvania, Arad, and Bukovina and three new ones: Timişoara and Caransebeş in the Banat, and Cluj, to be formed by a division of the diocese of Transylvania. He also demanded cession by the Serbs of four monasteries and a proportionate share of common church funds in the Banat in order to provide the new bishoprics with a solid financial base. Finally, he asked that the metropolitan be chosen in accordance with canon law, that is, by a church congress composed of priests and laymen from the entire eparchy rather than appointed by the emperor.[58]

The response from the chancellery the following March was a new request for information. The court had obviously not yet settled on the boundaries of the metropolis, and now Şaguna was invited to provide two sets of answers to the same questions: one in the event the metropolis was limited to Transylvania, and another if it were to include Hungary as well.[59] Şaguna, thoroughly exasperated, did not reply personally, but allowed a church synod, which was then meeting, to transmit the opinions of his clergy and faithful. It did so with great vigor. Ignoring the idea of a reduced metropolis, the delegates unanimously called for the speedy restoration of a metropolis encompassing "all our co-religionists in Transylvania, the Banat, Crişana, and Bukovina."[60]

There now ensued the long-delayed negotiations with the Serbian hierarchy in August 1864, which, as we have seen, resulted in an agreement in principle to separate the two churches administratively. Now that the last formal obstacle had been removed, the state council in Vienna on November 12 drew up a final proposal for the emperor's signature. It confined the metropolis to Transylvania and to the Rumanian parishes of the Banat and the existing diocese of Arad, and it stipulated that the title of the new metropolitan be "Archbishop and Metropolitan of the Greek Orthodox Rumanians in Hungary and Transylvania." This specific territorial designation was thought necessary to prevent the metropolitan from making claims to the diocese of Bukovina, "which might interfere with the later imperial disposition of this case." The council of state also reserved to the emperor the right to select the first metropolitan himself, but allowed the metropolis to organize itself by means of synods, as Şaguna had requested.[61]

At last, on December 24, 1864, in a short, businesslike note, Francis Joseph—referring to his earlier statements of September 27, 1860, and June 25, 1863—informed Şaguna that he had approved establishment of an autonomous Rumanian Orthodox metropolis and was appointing him its first metropolitan.[62] On the same day he instructed Patriarch Maširević to convoke a Serbian national council to work out a division of common funds with the new Rumanian metropolis. A few days later in a letter of congratulation to Şaguna Schmerling sketched the boundaries of the new dioceses and described the procedures to be followed in settling disputes with the Serbs.[63]

Şaguna was sorely disappointed that he was to have only two suffragan bishops—Arad and Caransebeş—but he was generally satisfied with the latitude he would have in organizing the metropolis. Negotiations with the Serbian hierarchy at Carlovitz in February and March of

the following year were, as we have seen, inconclusive, but Şaguna and
Maširević were able to agree on Ioan Popasu, protopope of Braşov, as
the first bishop of Caransebeş. The final act which, in Şaguna's mind,
marked the official inauguration of the metropolis was the imperial
edict of July 6, 1865, declaring the separation of the Rumanian and
Serbian hierarchies valid as of July 15.[64]

Şaguna could find no peace in the thought that his great work was
over. The changing relationship between the court and Hungary that
would result in the Compromise of 1867 caused him great anxiety,
since the metropolis existed only by virtue of the emperor's note of
December 24, 1864, and had yet to be formally articulated in the law
of the land. Because of the lengthy negotiations that preceded the
dualist pact and the time it took to organize the new government of
Hungary, action on the metropolis was delayed several years. Eventually, in June 1868, the Hungarian diet, acting on proposals of Joseph
Eötvös, the liberal minister of religions and education, passed a law
recognizing the existence of the metropolis and granting it the right to
manage its affairs in accordance with its own laws and practices, subject only to the "supreme inspection" of the crown. Francis Joseph's
sanction followed quickly on June 24. Known as Article of Law IX of
1868, this legislation subsequently became one of the bulwarks of
Rumanian resistance to Magyarization in the half-century that followed. Later in the year the government took the first steps to assure
the metropolis an adequate endowment when it transferred control
over the four Orthodox funds from the civil authority to the church.

Şaguna now turned his full attention to the passage of a church constitution, which in his opinion would make autonomy a reality. All his
actions were characterized by a sense of urgency, for by the summer of
1868, as had been evident in the parliamentary debates on Article IX,
a mounting tide of Magyar nationalism threatened every piece of legislation having to do with the non-Magyar nationalities. Şaguna had
particular trouble with the imperial council of state. It raised serious
objections to the draft statutes he had prepared and the method of
ratification he proposed. Specifically, it objected to the broad representation accorded laymen in managing the church's financial and
educational affairs as being too great a concession to liberalism, and it
demanded a strengthening of the emperor's supervisory powers over
the church and a curtailment of the clergy's independence.[65] It did,
however, accept Şaguna's contention that the creation of the metrop-

olis had raised so many fundamental questions of church government that only a competent legislative body could resolve them, and it approved the convocation of a national church congress.[66]

At the opening session of the congress on September 16, 1868, Şaguna presented his draft of a constitution with a sense of relief that he could at last shift some of the burdens of administration onto the shoulders of others. But it was soon apparent that a majority of the delegates (sixty laymen and thirty priests) had not come simply to approve Şaguna's ideas and then go home, leaving the government of the church in the hands of the clergy. The ambitious and frustrated national leaders who were present had no intention of letting such an opportunity to achieve their goals slip by. Moreover, many of them were opponents of political activism and were eager to use the congress to demonstrate their dissatisfaction with ecclesiastical leadership of the nation's affairs. It quickly became evident from the debates that they had a very different conception of the nature of the church and the significance of its role in society than did Şaguna.

Şaguna believed that the clergy should stand at the head of all the constituent organs of the church, from the village parish to the synod of bishops, as a consequence of the powers conferred upon it by both ancient custom and canon law. He contended that certain matters such as the purity of dogma and of ritual and the dispensing of ecclesiastical justice were exclusive prerogatives of the clergy. At the diocesan level he reserved broad executive powers to the bishop as the head of the clergy and the body of the faithful, for he placed upon him the ultimate responsibility for the proper functioning of every unit of church government. The bishop exercised this immense authority in a variety of ways through his right to ordain priests and assign them to parishes regardless of the wishes of the laity and through his power to appoint members of the consistory and the protopopate council, a judicial body of first instance at the district level. At the metropolitan level supreme power was concentrated in the episcopal synod, which decided all questions of dogma, acted as a court of final appeal in disciplinary cases involving both clergy and laity, served as the church's chief legislative body, settled the most important administrative problems, and represented the church in its relations with the state.

In his draft constitution Şaguna made it clear that tradition was not sacrosanct and that the church did not exist merely for the hierarchy; he wanted to make the church responsive to changing social conditions and the needs of the faithful. He likened the church to a living organism which functioned and grew only by the continuous and harmonious action of all its constituent parts. Consequently, while reserving legislative and judicial powers primarily to the hierarchs, he allowed laymen extensive participation in various branches of church administration, notably education and finance. He did not regard such action as a concession to prevailing liberal political theories, but rather as a revivifying of the practices of primitive Christianity. Nonetheless, at all levels of church government he expected the clergy, not laymen, to take the lead.

The lay majority of the congress showed little knowledge of church history and even less appreciation of the subtleties of canon law. The motivation behind their actions sprang chiefly from liberal political ideas, as was evident from their eagerness to transplant the practices of Western European parliamentary democracy into Orthodox church government. Their aim was to use the church to carry out their ambitious social and political program.[67] Consequently they attempted and in some measure succeeded in altering the basis of Şaguna's draft by substituting lay for hierarchical initiative in certain key areas of church government.

The Committee of Twenty-Seven, which the congress charged with the task of studying Şaguna's *Proiect* and making recommendations, was dominated by laymen, who proceeded to rewrite a number of essential provisions. Generally, the changes they made had to do with language and arrangement, as they gave a precise, juridical form to Şaguna's draft.[68] The text that they finally presented to the congress considerably expanded the role of the laity. It transferred most of the powers Şaguna had originally reserved to the episcopal synod to the metropolitan synod, which he had intended primarily as a body to choose the metropolitan. The episcopal synod, now composed two-thirds of laymen and one-third of clergy, was given the name National Church Congress and became the chief legislative organ of the metropolis. Şaguna had conceived of the consistory as an advisory body composed exclusively of clergy appointed by the bishop (the metropolitan in the archdiocese) and responsible to him alone. But the committee made it the executive committee of the diocese, elected by the national church congress and composed two-thirds of laymen. They made its decisions generally binding upon the bishop, who was thus obligated to carry out the expressed will of the majority.

The debate which these proposals elicited nearly disrupted the congress. Şaguna, at first utterly opposed to any compromise on his original draft, finally agreed to a division of the consistory into three separate committees or senates—ecclesiastical, school, and administrative. The first would concern itself with matters of dogma, ritual, and the discipline of the clergy and would have as members only clergy approved by the bishop; on the other two committees, laymen would outnumber the clergy in a proportion of 2 to 1 and would consequently dominate them.[69] On the other major points in dispute Şaguna stood firm and, in general, prevailed over his critics.[70]

This settlement notwithstanding, Şaguna remained deeply chagrined that the congress misused the consistory, and during the remainder of his episcopate it never enjoyed his full confidence. In his will, he entrusted the administration of the two foundations he established—the "Şaguna Foundation" and the "Fund for the Archdiocesan Press"—to autonomous and self-perpetuating committees rather than to the consistory, as church statutes provided. Because of the veneration in which he was held, no synod or metropolitan ever modified these dispositions, in spite of their extra-legal nature.

The congress approved Şaguna's revised draft, which became known as the Organic Statutes, on October 19, 1868, and submitted it to the emperor for sanction. A committee of the Hungarian ministry of religions and education, under the chairmanship of Joseph Eötvös, examined it and approved it with only minor changes. The most important specified the rights of the emperor to "supreme inspection" of church affairs and stipulated that the paragraphs concerning the management of schools and the use of Rumanian as the official language of the church would have to conform to other legislation dealing specifically with these matters. The question was now raised in the committee whether these and other changes necessitated resubmission of the whole document to a special national church congress for approval before sanction by the emperor. The two Rumanian members of the committee—Ioan Cavaler de Puşcariu and George Ioanovici, both close advisers of Şaguna—argued against further delay. Like Şaguna, they were worried by the hostility displayed by many Hungarian politicians in parliament toward the non-Magyar nationalities and were eager to avoid "complications." They accepted the modifications proposed by the ministry conditional only upon approval by the next regular church congress.[71] On May 28, 1869, the Organic Statutes received the emperor's sanction. The goal Şaguna had set for himself in April 1848 had been achieved.

Şaguna's eagerness to restore the metropolis was not merely canonical. He considered a solid constitutional foundation an essential precondition for the success of the ambitious social mission he planned for the church. Convinced that the church had a decisive role to play in the worldly affairs of its own faithful and of the Rumanian nation at large, he warned his clergy repeatedly that they could not afford to ignore the economic needs and political aspirations of their people, for both duty and history had created an intimate, indissoluble bond between the church and the nation.

This bond, according to Şaguna, was something more than that which usually existed between a religious organization and its adherents. The Orthodox Church in Transylvania had performed no less a service than the preservation of the Rumanian nation as a distinct ethnic and cultural entity. As he looked back over the history of the Rumanians from the Magyar conquest of Transylvania in the tenth century to his own day, Şaguna had no doubt that their attachment to Orthodoxy had saved them from assimilation, and he was at some pains to point out that the disappearance of the Rumanian nobility was caused by their abandonment of their "ancestral church" for the Roman Catholicism of the Magyars. He sensed an acceptance of these bitter lessons by the great mass of believers: "Since the Rumanian cannot conceive of his religion as separate from his nation and nationality, in order to assure his national existence he has remained faithful to that religion in which he grew up as a Rumanian and which he is convinced offers his nationality the strongest protection against any storm."[1]

In the formation of nationality Orthodoxy had also had a positive role. Şaguna emphasized the Eastern origins of Christianity among the Rumanians of Transylvania and their hierarchical dependence upon Constantinople rather than Rome at least as early as the ninth century. There was no inconsistency between his praise of Trajan's Rome and his disavowal of ecclesiastical Rome. He found in the combination of Roman ethnic origins and Eastern Christian faith a unique blend that had endowed the Rumanians with their distinctive national character.

To it they had owed their survival as a nation, since Orthodoxy had differentiated them from the surrounding Roman Catholic and Protestant Magyars and Germans, and their Latin heritage had preserved their individuality amongst their Bulgarian and Serbian coreligionists.[2] But whatever the importance Şaguna ascribed to Roman cultural origins, he left no doubt that he considered religion the true yeast of Rumanian nationality.

For Şaguna the social role of the church was preeminently a spiritual and moral one. Its duty was to provide the faithful with ethical values based upon universal Christian truths to guide them in their day-to-day existence both as individuals and as members of a nation. He took pride in the fact that he was following in the footsteps of illustrious predecessors who had made themselves "immortal" through their moral teachings and their contributions to learning. He particularly admired Metropolitan Simion Ştefan, who in the middle of the seventeenth century had had the Bible translated into the "Rumanian national language,"[3] and Metropolitan Sava Brancovici, whom he considered one of those "rare" hierarchs who spared neither himself nor his goods to make the lives of his priests more bearable.[4] He had no doubts whatever that belief in God and submission to His commandments ennobled the spirit and endowed the nation with a sense of mission that would allow it to achieve its full capabilities. He envisioned the church's contribution to the worldly endeavors of its faithful chiefly in these terms. At the same time, he recognized the importance of adapting its role to contemporary forms of social organization and the prevailing intellectual climate; otherwise, he thought, the church could not hope to achieve its spiritual goals.

Şaguna recognized the power of national feeling and took it as a matter of course that the social unit within which the church would carry on its mission was the nation. Paradoxically, his own belief in the deep and abiding relationship between the church and the nation made his position within the national movement ambiguous and lay at the root of his difficulties with the intellectuals. On the one hand, he thought it his own and the church's "sacred duty" to further the cause of nationality; on the other hand, he was determined not to compromise the essentially transcendental nature of the church by involving it in purely political undertakings or by allowing laymen to use it for their own mundane purposes. Furthermore, his belief that the idea of nationality could come to fruition only if it were founded upon a strong religious basis set him at odds with those laymen within his own church who were eager to "free" politics, morality, and education from "ecclesiastical tutelage." His unwillingness to place the church fully at their disposal led many to doubt the sincerity of his commitment to the national cause and to scorn his national feeling as superficial.

It is true that Şaguna judged the idea of nationality with a detachment that was utterly foreign to men like Bărnuţiu and Raţiu. He could not share their faith in it as the key to human development, for that was the role he assigned to the Christian religion. It may be that as a priest he viewed the national movement from a broader perspective than most of the intellectuals and looked beyond momentary political success or failure to some ultimate but as yet ill-defined harmony. Nonetheless, in assessing the nature of his national feeling, it is important to remember that he had thoroughly assimilated the main historical interpretations and linguistic theories that had sustained Rumanian intellectuals in Transylvania since the middle of the eighteenth century; without them the direction he gave to the social mission of the church would be inexplicable.

He was perhaps better acquainted than many of his lay contemporaries with the chief published works of the Transylvanian School, particularly Petru Maior's *Istoria besericei Românilor,* which, moreover, he cited as evidence of the existence of a Rumanian Orthodox metropolis in Transylvania in the seventeenth century,[5] and he subscribed fully to interpretations by the Transylvanian School of the beginnings and subsequent history of the Rumanians. He accepted without qualification the Roman origins of the Rumanians, as expounded by Maior and as it had entered the national consciousness:

We, who are Rumanians, bear witness to the fact that the Rumanian nation of today is composed of Roman colonists, part of whom came to Dacia as Trajan's soldiers and part as settlers sent by him and who remained there, because Trajan, seeing that Dacia had been deserted after the war with Decebal, brought great numbers of men from all over the Roman world to cultivate the fields and build cities.[6]

Şaguna employed history to account for the close bonds that united church and nation. He dated the beginnings of Christianity among the "Rumanian nation" from Roman times, citing the fact that many of the Roman colonists who settled in Dacia after the conquest were already Christian. Their presence so early in the history of the province

explained why there was no mention of their conversion in any contemporary written sources: given the facts, such information would
have been "superfluous."[7] Thus, in Şaguna's view, the Rumanian nation and the Rumanian church began their existence simultaneously
and over the centuries created a nearly perfect fusion of folk tradition
and religious faith. He therefore concluded that the Rumanian national character had been preserved best in the Orthodox Church. He
denied that the use of Slavonic in the church for a number of centuries
had interfered in any way with this process, and, arguing that the
Rumanians had had their own ritual books, he concluded that they
had preserved their own language in the church from the "very remot-
est times."[8]

Şaguna's interest in the history of the Rumanian language and his
concern with style also suggest strong national feelings. Language was
important to him as a symbol of nationality, as an organic link to the
past, and, no less important, as a means of communication and an
instrument of popular enlightenment. He attributed to language, particularly through translations of the Bible and other religious books,
the preservation of a sense of unity among Rumanians everywhere, in
spite of their separation by political boundaries. He believed, moreover, that this community of language, which manifested itself in the
mechanical acts of speaking and writing, was an outward expression of
far deeper psychic affinities of feeling and modes of thought.[9]

The importance he ascribed to the role of language in society
brought him into conflict with the prevailing linguistic theories in
Transylvania. Perhaps because he thought of himself first of all as a
teacher, he was mainly concerned with language as a means of disseminating useful knowledge and the articles of Christian faith. In his
view, the chief quality that language should possess was intelligibility,
not just for the sophisticated few but for the broad masses of the peasantry, for whom it was the indispensable vehicle of spiritual and
material progress. His own vocabulary and style had been greatly
influenced by the language of the old church books—particularly the
Cazanii, collections of sermons—and were, therefore, traditional, and
his pastoral letters and sermons consequently struck contemporaries as
slightly archaic.[10] The reason probably lies in the fact that until his
early teens he did not know Rumanian; when he undertook formal
study of it the texts available to him both in Pest and later on in the
Serbian monasteries were mainly religious ones which had not been

affected by the innovations of the Transylvanian School. Nonetheless, as the grammar he composed at Vršac in the early 1840s shows, his preoccupation with language was serious, and by the time he became vicar-general in Transylvania he had acquired a thorough command of Rumanian. His style was clear and direct, and he avoided rhetorical devices. He favored the language of the Bible and the ritual books, which seemed to him closer to the language spoken by the people than the hybrid of neologisms and foreign borrowings which many intellectuals employed.

Şaguna's strong stand on language inevitably led to controversy with proponents of the so-called Latinist current, which dominated Rumanian linguistic scholarship in the 1850s and 1860s. Ably led by the erudite canon of Blaj, Timotei Cipariu, they advocated both etymological spellings to bring the appearance of Rumanian words closer to their ancient Latin roots and the introduction of many new words of Latin or Romance origin to replace Slavic, Magyar, and other "foreign impurities." Although Şaguna shared the view that Slavic influence had had a negative effect on the development of Rumanian culture,[11] he nonetheless considered the Latinists' own product equally detrimental to his efforts to eliminate illiteracy among the peasantry; it created an artificial barrier between them and the intellectuals, whose primary task was the education of the masses.

Şaguna and the Latinists did agree, however, on the replacement of the Cyrillic alphabet by the Latin. Şaguna's motivation seems to have been mainly practical rather than philological or historical. By the 1860s the Latin alphabet had clearly gained much wider currency than the Cyrillic among intellectuals in both Transylvania and the Rumanian principalities, and its use in publications, especially newspapers, was steadily increasing. When the delegates to the annual meeting of ASTRA in 1862 approved a uniform Latin orthography for Rumanian Şaguna readily concurred in their decision, welcoming the introduction of "our ancient Latin letters."[12] But he urged caution in eliminating the Cyrillic alphabet and recommended that it continue to be used as a pedagogical tool, since the great majority of peasants who could read knew no other alphabet.[13]

Şaguna also considered himself as belonging to a culture that extended beyond the boundaries of Transylvania and even the Habsburg monarchy to embrace the Rumanian principalities and Rumanian communities elsewhere in the Balkans. Among other evidence is his

deep interest in the literary movement inaugurated by the Junimea
(Youth) Society, founded in Iași in 1863. He watched its development
carefully from its beginnings[14] and had reprinted in *Telegraful Român*
works by some of its leading members — the poems of Vasile Alec-
sandri; the critical study, *Despre poezia română*, by Titu Maiorescu,
the guiding spirit of the society; and Alecu Russo's strictures on the
Latinist current in Rumanian philology.[15] The admiration was recip-
rocated. *Convorbiri Literare*, the chief organ of Junimea, and perhaps the most influential Rumanian literary review of the nineteenth
century, published a lengthy and flattering review of Șaguna's *Compendiu de drept canonic*, and the editor, Iacob Negruzzi, praised the
beauty of Șaguna's prose in the introduction to his translation of the
Bible for its resonances of Old Rumanian.[16]

Șaguna made no distinction between the Rumanians living north of
the Danube and the Macedo-Rumanians to the south. He considered
the Macedo-Rumanian communities of Hungary, where his own family had settled, and the Rumanians of Transylvania and the principalities to be part of the same greater Rumanian nation. Although he did
not arrange his thoughts on the subject systematically, it is evident
from all his writings and actions that he regarded religion as the chief
bond of union among them. He made no distinction between the
Orthodox of Transylvania and those of the principalities. He wrote his
history of the Orthodox Church for the Rumanians on both sides of the
Carpathians and recommended it to "all who are interested in Orthodoxy not only from a strictly religious point of view but also as Rumanians."[17] After the revolution of 1848 he repeatedly turned to the
clergy and faithful in Moldavia and Wallachia for aid for his impover-
ished church or for contributions to new projects such as the construction of a cathedral in Sibiu.[18] He saw nothing unusual in sending out
his priests on such missions, and once confided to an acquaintance
from Wallachia that his church could, in the final analysis, rely only
upon their "Orthodox brothers" in the principalities.[19]

Șaguna's commitment to the Rumanian nation can no more be
doubted than his Orthodox faith. But he saw the role of the church in
the national movement, and in temporal affairs generally, in a far different light than did the lay intellectuals. He imposed definite, if not
always precise, limits on the involvement of the church in non-church
undertakings. He distinguished two broad categories of activity: the
transcendental, that is, the propagation of Christian beliefs and the

salvation of souls, and the mundane — political struggle and economic
organization. The first was preeminently the concern of the church;
the second, that of the nation. Although they might complement each
other, they could not fuse or subordinate. Şaguna argued that the
church, composed of Rumanians, was a part of the nation, but it
could never be wholly within the nation, since the primary goals it
pursued had no limitations of time or place. He recognized that the
church had a duty to further the political and economic well-being of
its faithful (and the nation as a whole), but he pointed out that it could
not take a significant initiative in these endeavors or transform itself
into a national committee or parliament. Nor could the bishop become a political leader in the sense that he made temporal goals his
main concern and turned the church into a mere instrument of achieving them. Rather, Şaguna argued, the main criterion he himself had
always to observe when involving the church in temporal affairs was
the preservation of its autonomy, since it alone offered the church the
protection it required to carry out its transcendental mission.

This, then, was the nature of the delicate balance between temporal
and spiritual obligations that Şaguna strove to maintain. It is best
exemplified by his efforts to promote the welfare of the church and the
nation through political action during the revolution of 1848 and in
the 1860s and by his implacable defense of church autonomy vis-à-vis
both the state and the lay intellectuals.

His views on church autonomy and his strained relations with the
Uniates notwithstanding, Şaguna had no intention of limiting the
social role of the Orthodox Church to its own faithful. The Orthodox,
as an integral part of the Rumanian nation, must assume a full share
of responsibility for its happiness and progress, and the church itself
must use every available opportunity to bring its spiritual influence to
bear on secular affairs. Although he adamantly opposed cooperation
with the Uniates in education and other areas where he feared the
autonomy of his church might be compromised, Şaguna regarded
common undertakings of a more general or "national" kind as highly
desirable.

One of the first products of the Orthodox-Uniate rapprochement
that occurred at the end of the decade of absolutism was ASTRA. The
idea of a learned society to promote Rumanian culture went back to
the last decades of the eighteenth century when the short-lived "Socie-

tate literaților din Sibiu" (1789) and "Societate filosofească a neamului românesc în mare principatul Ardealului" (1795) were founded. The effort lay dormant until a half-century later, when, in 1852, Avram Iancu and some of his companions in revolution raised a modest sum to establish an "academy," but failed to obtain official approval for an organization with such patently national goals. At the end of 1859, at a general meeting of clergy and intellectuals at Şaguna's home in Sibiu, called to discuss the impending constitutional changes, the project was brought forward once again.

Şaguna took charge. On May 10, 1860, he submitted a petition to the governor of Transylvania on behalf of 170 priests and intellectuals, requesting permission to establish a cultural society. When informed that no action could be taken until the society's by-laws had been examined, he invited Barițiu, Cipariu, and Ioan Pușcariu to prepare separate drafts of them. He himself combined their proposals into a single text, which he then submitted to the Transylvanian government for approval. The response was favorable; the government made only a few minor changes in the proposed by-laws. At a meeting on March 21, 1861, chaired by Şaguna, all the signers of the original petition ratified the amended statutes, and on September 6 the emperor formally approved the creation of the society.[20] The founding meeting of ASTRA was held on November 4, 1861. A generous fund of 5,600 florins was collected to enable the association to begin its educational and cultural work immediately. After a futile attempt by a number of intellectuals led by Barițiu to elect Cipariu president,[21] Şaguna was chosen for a three-year term. Cipariu became vice-president and Barițiu secretary.

As president (he would serve two terms until 1867) Şaguna insisted that politics and religion form no part of ASTRA's concerns — the first because the government had specifically forbidden it under penalty of dissolution, and the second because neither church would tolerate any interference by clergy and laymen of the other in its affairs. Consequently, neither subject came up for discussion at the formal sessions of the monthly executive committee meetings or the annual general assembly.[22] Instead, Şaguna emphasized the association's cultural and moral responsibilities, since he was certain that success in these domains would determine the character of the Rumanian nation and ensure its survival:

The material monuments of a civilized period may be destroyed by barbarian hands, and a free nation may be deprived of liberty by draconian laws. But the spiritual monuments and moral behavior remain indestructible for all time because they are beyond any physical and arbitrary power; the hand of the barbarian cannot touch them, the thief cannot steal them, moths cannot waste them.[23]

During its first six years ASTRA carried on a broad, if somewhat modest, social and cultural program. It awarded numerous scholarships to needy students and prizes to the authors of works ranging from agronomy to poetry, and, largely owing to the devoted efforts of Cipariu, who took a special interest in obtaining new scholarly and literary works from Bucharest and Iaşi,[24] it laid the foundations of a library that eventually became a rich treasure of Rumanian history and culture in Transylvania. In 1868, under the editorship of Bariţiu, the association began to publish a monthly bulletin entitled *Transilvania,* which contained learned studies on various aspects of Rumanian culture, primarily language and history. In the main, ASTRA's activities were directed toward its own membership, which was for the most part middle-class and clerical. In the early years it showed a lively interest in the products of the peasant household and in 1862 it sponsored an exposition of Rumanian crafts in Braşov. A special committee spared no effort to make it a varied and rich display of peasant skills. Şaguna, who served as a member, instructed his parish priests to see that their villages sent as many representative pieces of their workmanship as possible.[25] The exposition was an immense success, but the enthusiasm it generated was allowed to wane, and ASTRA's subsequent support of crafts and agriculture was mainly literary.

ASTRA itself did not prosper. Its membership declined from 728 the first year to 451 in 1864, and attendance at the annual general assemblies fell from a high of over 800 in 1862 to just 44 in 1866. The sections (philology under Cipariu at Blaj; history under Gabriel Munteanu, director of the Orthodox gymnasium in Braşov; and natural sciences under Şaguna at Sibiu) and various special committees functioned fitfully or not at all, as their members became absorbed in other activities. The enthusiasm that had brought ASTRA into existence failed to sustain itself as the association became bogged down in routine paper work. This disappointing turn of events is attributable only in part to the divisions within the membership caused by Şaguna's strained relations with the intellectuals and the struggle between activists and passivists. The problem was of long duration. In the seven years following Şaguna's ouster as president the membership reached a low of 120, and accusations of "bureaucracy" could be heard until the turn of the century.[26]

Şaguna regarded the economic problems of the Rumanian nation as another area of legitimate church concern, and he himself took a lively interest in them. Although he did not subscribe to any of the prevailing theories of social change, he accepted the general view that human society was gradually improving, and he acknowledged the connection between economic development and the rate of progress. Consequently, he admonished his clergy not to ignore this vital aspect of their people's life. He showed a deep understanding of the problems that confronted Rumanian agriculture: the continued growth of the peasant population; the steady diminution in the size of peasant holdings because of the absence of a law of primogeniture; and chronic low productivity. He thought the solution lay in a diversification of economic activity, and he repeatedly urged his protopopes and parish priests to impress upon their congregations the desirability of seeking ways of earning a living outside of agriculture—in the artisan crafts and small-scale commerce.[27] But however much he sympathized with the peasantry, he made it clear that the task of the church was to educate and encourage rather than to create or operate economic institutions.

By temperament Şaguna was admirably suited to direct a dynamic social mission on the part of the church. He was by nature an activist, and his entire career had been devoted to putting things in order, to systematizing and codifying. His was not the life of contemplation. Rather, he sought involvement in life, and he found his greatest satisfaction in public service.

It is perhaps significant that in all his plans to promote the general welfare of the church and its faithful he never made provision for the establishment of a monastic community. Undoubtedly, his unpleasant experiences in the Serbian monasteries early in his career had led him to doubt their usefulness. The monks had seemed to him to have cut themselves off from the real world. They did not use their isolation to seek a more sublime communion with the Almighty, nor did they work to transform their communities into true centers of learning. Given the slender financial resources at his disposal, Şaguna considered a monastery, even one well run, a luxury and preferred to build more village schools. His ideal clergyman was the parish priest who felt himself to be an integral part of his community and had as his paramount concern service to the people. Such a view of the clergy reveals much about the historical character of Rumanian Orthodoxy in Transylvania and helps to account for the close links that existed between the priest and his parishioners.

The same ideal of service to the Christian community was the chief motivation behind Şaguna's extensive literary activity. His most important works were religious and fall into four main categories: treatises on canon law and church government, manuals of theology and pastoral care, church history, and a masterful translation of the Bible. All were explicitly didactic and intended to fulfil some specific need. Şaguna produced no learned treatises on theology primarily because there was but a small audience for such works. He had to concern himself with a society that was overwhelmingly peasant, whose needs were too simple and too immediate to be satisfied by grave disquisitions on dogma and ritual.

The purpose of Şaguna's writings is best illustrated by his *Elementele dreptului canonic* (1854) and his *Compendiu de drept canonic,* which appeared in Rumanian and German editions in 1868 and is generally considered his most significant scholarly work. Neither book exhibits the marks of an original, speculative religious philosophy. Indeed, their author made no pretense of adding to the accumulated wisdom of the Church Fathers and the Ecumenical Church Councils, but attempted rather to systematize and explain. This task was by no means a simple one, since the study of canon law in the Rumanian Orthodox Church before his time had been sorely neglected.[28] His *Elementele dreptului canonic,* for example, was the first manual of canon law in the Rumanian Orthodox Church,[29] and he composed it expressly for the students of the theological institute in Sibiu, who had no access to any other work of its kind.[30] His main purpose was to raise the intellectual level of the clergy and to provide them with a knowledge of the essentials of church law and government, which he thought indispensable if they were to know their duties and defend their rights and administer the church's affairs justly and efficiently. The *Compendiu* was intended for both laymen and clergy. Since the laity bore major responsibilities in church government, Şaguna was anxious for them to know precisely what their role was in the hope that encroachments upon the prerogatives of the clergy could be avoided.[31]

If canon law was Şaguna's métier, then just as surely church history was his avocation. His preoccupation with it was both scholarly and practical, and his initial research was motivated at least in part by the urgent need to muster historical evidence in support of his claims to church autonomy and equality of rights. Besides innumerable brochures and memoranda dealing with these questions, he also wrote a two-volume general history of the Eastern Orthodox Church.[32] A large portion of the second volume was devoted to the Rumanian Orthodox Church in Transylvania and, except for Petru Maior's *Istoria besericei Românilor* (Buda, 1813), it was the only scholarly survey of the subject available until the beginning of the twentieth century. Again, his primary aim was to instruct. The needs of his students at the theological institute were uppermost in his mind, and he chose his material carefully. The history often reads like a textbook, as Şaguna is at pains to present lengthy excerpts from official documents and detailed descriptions of the operations of church government. Because he rarely intrudes into the narrative with his own opinions, his work at times seems closer to the chronicles of the preceding century than to modern histories. Nonetheless, he recognized that the main purpose of historical study was self-knowledge, and he was persuaded that his "modest effort" would enable the Rumanians to know better who they were and what they could become.

Şaguna seems to have regarded his translation of the Bible as his crowning literary achievement. As the "foundation of the Christian religion" the Bible had always occupied a central place in his studies, and he urged his clergy to read it regularly and to employ its "useful and sublime" teachings to awaken true Christian piety in their congregations. Translations of the Bible into Rumanian had a special significance for him when he reflected upon the close bonds that existed between church and nation:

The awakening of the Rumanian people from the barbarism of centuries, their gradual reconciliation with God's law, their striving toward the soft light of civilization and culture, the unity of our Rumanian nation, which the hand of Providence has sown in so many different lands and among so many foreign nations, the preservation of our national language — for all these unparalleled blessings we must . . . thank those eternal monuments of language, morality, and, above all, our national and religious life.[33]

As Şaguna himself observed on his frequent tours of inspection, many parishes were without either the New Testament of Belgrad

(1648) or the Bible of Bucharest (1688). The most recent translation—
that of Samuil Clain published in Blaj in 1795—seemed to him unsuitable for Orthodox readers because of its Uniate origins. Such was the
degree to which sectarian rivalry had divided Orthodox and Uniates in
the 1850s that Şaguna never mentioned Clain's work and apparently
did not use it in preparing his own translation. His translation was
published in 1858 in a large, sober edition with reproductions of illus-
trations by Gustave Doré. The introduction, which he composed with
great care, has been called "one of the most brilliant pieces of Rumanian religious literary history ever written."[34] Nonetheless, his main
concern had been to put in the hands of as many priests and parishes
as possible an instrument of public worship and personal inspiration
both pleasing and intelligible to the great mass of the faithful.

Şaguna made education the main object of the church's social mission. It seemed to him that education, which he understood to encompass spiritual and moral training as well as the acquisition of useful
knowledge, best exemplified the church's traditional role in the everyday affairs of its people. He was convinced that he and his clergy could
perform no greater service for their people than to offer them this
opportunity to take their long-denied place among the cultured nations of Europe. He emphasized the point again and again that the
lack of education was largely to blame for the backwardness of the
Rumanians, and he likened them to hard-working bees, whose honey
and wax had been harvested by others (the Magyars and Saxons). Like
the lay intellectuals, he hoped through education to create a class that
would take charge of their nation's political and economic development.[35]

Şaguna dismissed as nonsense the fears expressed by some among his
own and the Uniate clergy that the further a nation—particularly one
composed of peasants like the Rumanian—departed from its "natural
simplicity" the more likely it was to be corrupted morally. He was too
well acquainted with the realities of village life to accept any such
romantic notions. But he was firmly convinced that as a society became more diversified and sophisticated it required a corresponding
strengthening of its moral and spiritual fiber. A people must not only
be learned and prosperous, he argued; it must also have within itself
humanity and an awakened moral sense to guide it in the use of its new
knowledge and possessions. It was precisely in these domains—the

human and the moral—that he discerned the special province of the church.

Şaguna believed that the church could carry out its educational tasks best through the formal structure of a school system. Moreover, he had definite ideas about the kinds of schools that would most benefit his people. Convinced of the intimate relationship between the church and education, he concluded that sectarianism or, as he called it, the "confessional principle," should govern the organization of schools in Transylvania. In the first place, he considered church schools to be the only legal ones, since the Military and Civil Government itself on April 19, 1850, had reiterated the long-established principle that each religious denomination should build and administer its own elementary schools.[36] He had other reasons as well. Since he regarded both the village elementary school and the town gymnasium as "training grounds" for Orthodox Christians, he thought it essential that pupils receive regular instruction in the doctrines and history of the church and, in addition to formal study, that they also learn by practicing their religion in a community of their fellows. He recommended the strict observance of religious holidays, since they enabled young people to relate lessons taught in the classroom to the actual experience of life.[37] Orthodox church schools would by their very nature be national schools and, consequently, they would promote the vital interests of the Rumanian people. Church schools seemed to Şaguna highly desirable for purely practical reasons, too. He was certain that the Rumanian peasant, because of his strong attachment to his religion, would be more inclined to tolerate the financial burdens of education, if he saw a close bond between the church and his village school.[38]

Şaguna set forth his policy on confessional elementary schools in a long circular letter addressed to his clergy on April 24, 1852. For twenty years it was to govern the educational relations of the Orthodox with both the state and the Uniate Church. Şaguna stipulated that every Orthodox parish should have its own school; that no parish, even the poorest, should join with the parish of another religion to establish a school until it had exhausted all other possibilities; that all teachers should be Orthodox; and that all textbooks should be publications of the recently established diocesan publishing house.[39] Later on, he extended these instructions to cover secondary schools in order to fore-

stall the creation of non-sectarian gymnasia. He was especially distressed by the inclination of many leading Orthodox lay intellectuals
and civil servants in Zarand County in the early 1860s to join with their
Uniate counterparts in establishing a "national" gymnasium. He admonished them to accept the fact once and for all that in educational
matters Rumanian Orthodox could not cooperate with Rumanian
Uniates, even though they spoke the same language and belonged to
the same nation. He reminded them that schools were by their nature
church institutions and, consequently, by law organized on a confessional basis—limitations that made it impossible for Uniates to be
founders or co-founders of Orthodox schools or to have any part in
their governance. He was equally emphatic in denying civil authorities
jurisdiction over confessional schools on the grounds that education
was not a political but a church matter, and he urged Orthodox laymen not to allow officials to interfere in the operation of their
schools.[40]

Strong pressures were brought to bear to make Şaguna change his
stand on confessional schools. The Cultusministerium in Vienna and
the Gubernium in Cluj reminded him of the extreme poverty of many
Rumanian villages where the only possibility of providing the inhabitants with adequate schooling lay in cooperation between Orthodox
and Uniates, and they urged him to seek the help of local officials in
establishing common school districts.[41] Even more insistent were the
demands of lay intellectuals of both churches that education be secu-
larized and that it strengthen national unity rather than perpetuate
divisions among the Rumanians.

Şaguna refused to budge. His firmness was conditioned by the long
period of Orthodox subservience to the state and to other churches,
notably the Uniate. After 1849 he was extraordinarily sensitive to what
he considered infringements upon his church's newly acquired constitutional equality and efforts to relegate it once again to second-class
status. From this standpoint he considered the school to be as much a
constitutional issue as a pedagogical one, as he tried in this domain
also to establish the principle of Orthodox Church autonomy. Consequently, he criticized the intellectuals for their "exaggerated national
zeal," which "so shortened their vision" that they could conceive of no
higher earthly goal than the strengthening of nationality, and he accused the Uniate clergy of supporting mixed schools for the express
purpose of winning converts among the Orthodox.[42]

He found the attitude of the Transylvanian government vague and inconsistent: in 1850 it recognized the confessional character of elementary education, but in 1853 it instructed local officials not to interfere with the establishment of common schools by two religious communities in the same political subdivision.[43] He suspected that the government's chief aim in encouraging mixed schools was not to advance education but to promote the Union with Rome at the expense of Orthodoxy and to create a centralized educational system. Mixed schools under the jurisdiction of local and county officials would be the prelude to state control of education and, concomitantly, the gradual erosion of both the religious and national character of education.

In support of his position Şaguna appealed to both history and law. He reminded his critics that since the time of Joseph II education had been primarily the concern of the church and that the establishment of schools under some other authority would violate both the law of the land and church autonomy, which he considered the strongest guarantees of the continued growth of the "religious and national spirit" among Rumanian youth.[44] He argued that by the nature of things no Orthodox commune could join with another church commune to establish and operate a school, however deeply their national sentiments impelled them to take such action. The rights of nationality seemed to him too fragile a base upon which to build permanent institutions, for he had seen these rights given and taken away with alacrity during and after the revolution of 1848. He did not doubt the essential unity of the Rumanians, nor did he deny the legitimate rights of nationality. On the contrary, he expressed himself on these two questions unequivocally in a circular letter to his clergy in 1862: "As for their nationality and language, all Rumanians, regardless of their religious beliefs, are one people and one political body, that is, they are a homogeneous element, and in this regard they have one and the same interest."[45] The rights of a nation were not, however, to be confused with church autonomy; the Rumanians as "a people" might establish institutions such as ASTRA, to promote the general good, but they might not usurp the prerogatives of either the Orthodox or Uniate church by creating schools. Church autonomy was too precious; solemnly inscribed in law, it was the foundation upon which they could all hope to progress toward a better future, whereas the national rights of small peoples were continually subject to the vagaries of policies and goals dictated by others. He therefore refused to permit the church and its "sublime mission" to be compromised by anything so ephemeral as political theories.

Şaguna could not remain oblivious to the cruel poverty that afflicted many of his faithful, and, in the end, he reluctantly modified his stand on confessional schools. Although he acknowledged the need for some sort of amalgamation, if his faithful in poorer regions were to enjoy the benefits of education, he was careful to protect the prerogatives of his church and to avoid binding commitments to the Uniates. For example, he proposed that in villages where parishes of both churches existed but only the Orthodox had the necessary resources to build a school, they should do so with their own funds. Consequently, they would control the school, but would open its doors to Uniate pupils, provided their parents were willing to bear a proportional share of the operating expenses. All pupils would follow the same course of instruction except for classes in religion, which would be taught separately by their respective parish priests. The same rules would apply when the Uniates built the common school. But Şaguna was unhappy with this solution. He much preferred to establish Orthodox central schools through a pooling of resources by small Orthodox parishes, a program that eventually achieved some success by 1860 in the protopopates of Hațeg, Hondol, and Zarand.[46] In some areas neither of these solutions was possible, and Şaguna with considerable misgivings agreed to the establishment of joint Orthodox-Uniate elementary schools. But he insisted that the financial and other obligations of both sides be clearly defined, that local officials take no initiative themselves but leave matters to the respective district protopopes, and, finally, that the decision on whether or not to establish the new school rest with the two bishops.[47]

In upholding the confessional principle in education, Şaguna placed himself squarely in opposition to the majority of lay intellectuals, who sought fulfillment of the national idea through secular schools. His argument that the national character of education could best be preserved by the church went unheeded. They ignored his warnings that secular schools would sooner or later come under the jurisdiction of the state, which, as in the past, would allow the Rumanians little say in their management and would give scant attention to the national language and history.

In his efforts to revitalize Orthodox elementary education and create a secondary school system Şaguna faced two immediate problems — legal and administrative, the kind in which he had acquired special expertise. First of all, he had to assert the bishop's undisputed authority in educational matters within the church itself, and then he had to clarify the relationship between the church and the state in education. He was determined to assure his church jurisdiction over its own schools and to reserve all important decisions concerning their operation to the bishop. Consequently, he had to overcome the skepticism of the Cultusministerium about the ability of the Orthodox to manage their own affairs and to persuade government officials at all levels that the interests of education and of state and church could best be served through trust and cooperation.

Şaguna set about accomplishing his first task by systematically eliminating all competition for control of Orthodox schools within the church. He justified his action on both canonical and practical grounds. On the one hand, he argued that, given the spiritual character of the confessional school, the bishop's jurisdiction in educational matters could not be limited by lay or some other church authority; on the other hand, he pointed out that if he were to deal effectively with the state, he could not afford to share power with other individuals or groups. He had long chafed under the right of inspection over Orthodox schools granted to the Roman Catholic bishop of Transylvania in 1837, even though it had been nominal. At his urging, the Orthodox diocesan synod of 1850 transferred these powers to him; the Cultusministerium acquiesced, since it had already recognized the confessional principle in education. Next, at the beginning of 1852, he abolished the post of director of Orthodox schools, which had been created in 1786, and assumed the supervisory powers of the office himself.[48] While he was thus concentrating administrative power in his own hands, he was busy establishing a regular chain of command between the diocesan office and the parish. He put the protopopes in charge of educational affairs in their respective districts and made them directly responsible to him. He instructed them to see to it that each parish had its own school inspector, either a layman or a priest, who was to be elected by the members of the parish and was to report regularly to the protopope. He tried to involve the lay parish leaders in school affairs because he considered their support essential if educational standards were to be raised (the financial burdens would fall largely upon them), but, at the same time, he firmly opposed lay control on the grounds that education was a function of the church.[49]

In his efforts to establish a satisfactory relationship with the state Şaguna tried to obtain agreement on a comprehensive educational statute setting forth the rights and obligations of each party. For twenty
years the Cultusministerium refused to make such a commitment, and
Şaguna therefore had to establish his position piecemeal — case by case
as they came before him, even the most trivial — by a rigid adherence
to the principles of church autonomy and religious equality.

Most of the battles were fought at the local level. Şaguna recognized
the importance of the state's role in education and eagerly sought to
increase its financial support of confessional schools and place it on a
regular basis. He was equally determined to set precise limits to the
state's powers of intervention in Orthodox school affairs. On two subjects he was adamant: that civil authorities take no initiative whatever
without the assent of the district protopope or, in serious questions, the
bishop; and that they not appoint or dismiss teachers or judge their
academic qualifications, since these functions were the sole prerogative of the church.[50] He was especially anxious to prevent the granting
of broad discretionary powers to Bezirk and Kreis officials, lest they
revert to the practices of an earlier epoch when the Orthodox were
simply tolerated and it was not thought necessary to consult them. As
it was, in the 1850s these officials were guilty of numerous arbitrary
acts which almost continually required Şaguna's intervention on
behalf of local school committees. Characteristic was the action of
authorities in Bistriţa who forced a nearby Rumanian village to retain
a teacher, in spite of his obvious incompetence, on the grounds that
the commanding general in Transylvania had made the appointment
seventeen years before.[51] Even if well intentioned, local officials were
capable of causing immense harm. One case in point, which deeply
distressed Şaguna, had to do with a zealous Saxon school inspector who
wanted to improve the educational facilities in a small Rumanian village in the Fundus regius. Without consulting the district protopope or
acquainting himself in some other way with local needs and resources,
he ordered expensive architect's drawings of a new schoolhouse, payment for which wiped out the small communal school fund.[52]

In only one area was Şaguna willing to grant government officials
some measure of control over school personnel. He recognized as legitimate the state's concern that the education of young people be placed
in the hands of persons whose moral conduct and political ideas cor-

responded to prevailing norms. But even here he insisted that its role
be limited to the act of providing information about alleged miscon-
duct of teachers to the respective school committee or the bishop, who
would then investigate and take whatever action they thought necessary.[53]

Şaguna won few victories during the decade of absolutism, since the
Cultusministerium and government officials in Transylvania handled
confessional school problems as though the Orthodox Church hardly
existed. In the fall of 1857 the Transylvanian government announced
that only its own immediate intervention could bring about any substantial improvement in the level of Orthodox village schools. It declared its intention of sending out local officials on tours of inspection
with authority to effect reforms they deemed necessary. Şaguna objected strenuously on the grounds that the government was violating
both its own edicts and the principle of religious equality, since the
Orthodox were being singled out for "special treatment."[54] Nothing
came of the government's plan, owing to the general constitutional
changes that occurred a year and a half later. But this experience
increased Şaguna's suspicions of government intentions and strengthened his resolve to erect strong legal barriers against its intrusion into
church affairs.

The kind of cooperation between church and state that Şaguna
thought most beneficial was exemplified in the work of the Orthodox
school inspectorate, which functioned in the late 1850s and early
1860s. Ever since his arrival in Transylvania he had sought some
means of maintaining regular communication with the Transylvanian
government on educational matters in order to acquaint it with the
plight of the Orthodox village school and so gain its moral and financial support. In July 1850 he nominated Pavel Vasici, a physician and
prominent intellectual from the Banat, as "counsellor" for Rumanian
Orthodox schools—a position paid for by the government, which
made him a sort of intermediary between the state and church. His
chief duties, as Şaguna saw them, were to make regular tours of
inspection of school districts in order to check on subject matter and
methodology, the physical condition of buildings, and class attendance
and to meet with school committees and teachers in order to learn at
first hand about their needs and grievances; he was then to report his
findings and make recommendations directly to the Transylvanian

government. In spite of the government's professed concern for the "backwardness" of Orthodox schools, it delayed approval of Şaguna's recommendation for five years.

Şaguna was generally pleased with Vasici's work and instructed his clergy and the parish school committees to cooperate with him fully.[55] When, in 1861, it appeared that the government would not reappoint him, Şaguna wrote a strong letter on Vasici's behalf emphasizing his constant help and encouragement to protopopes and priests, which had enabled them to accomplish far more than would otherwise have been possible. He attributed much of Vasici's success to the fact that he was Rumanian and had consequently found it easier than a "foreigner" to gain the confidence of the clergy and peasants. Şaguna also used the occasion to restate his views on the nature of the inspectorate. He made it clear that he regarded Vasici as a liaison between the bishop and the government, not a director of church schools. Consequently he insisted that he could hold office only at the pleasure of the bishop and could have no independent jurisdiction over Orthodox schools, but must be satisfied with a purely advisory role.[56]

At Şaguna's insistence, Vasici remained at his post, but relations between them soon became strained. Şaguna took exception to Vasici's reports to the government, which were highly critical of the clergy's role in education and, in his view, did not take into account the enormous financial and social disabilities with which they had to contend. He also objected to Vasici's associating himself with the intellectuals' social program and to his support of national, non-sectarian schools.[57] Vasici claimed that the clergy kept tight control of the schools, not to further Şaguna's program of reform but solely to maintain their own power in the villages. In his opinion the school was simply an object of local politics with the result that the educational process in Orthodox communities all over Transylvania had ground to a halt. He concluded that complete control of schools by the church was detrimental to education, and he urged the state to take upon itself the enforcement of uniform high standards. Schools, he wrote in a long report to the Gubernium in 1864, should be the concern of the civil authorities and the whole nation, not of separate churches.[58] Such ideas placed him squarely on the side of the lay intellectuals and in opposition to the confessional principle in education and Şaguna's cherished goal of church autonomy.

He failed to reach a satisfactory agreement with the state on church

schools. In 1859, on the eve of the constitutional era, he appeared to
have won official recognition of his exclusive jurisdiction over Orthodox schools. On February 23 the Cultusministerium informed him that
his church would be allowed to administer its schools in essentially the
same way as the Roman Catholic bishops managed theirs. But Şaguna
found this formula completely unacceptable. He was struck by the fact
that the Cultusministerium was still applying the standards of the old
regime in its dealings with the Orthodox by deciding things without
consulting them and by using the Roman Catholic Church as a criterion. It seemed to him that the efforts of a decade to impress upon the
ministry the uniqueness and maturity of the Orthodox had gone for
nought. In his official reply Şaguna suggested that the ministry, instead of issuing separate and often contradictory instructions, draw up
a comprehensive education law for Transylvania that would recognize
the principle of church autonomy and would define the powers of the
various churches over their respective schools in accordance with their
own canon law and traditions.[59] Here, too, his efforts were largely in
vain, for such a law did not come into being until 1868, after the
inauguration of the Austro-Hungarian dual monarchy, which was to
pose an even greater threat to the confessional school than Austrian
absolutism.

Şaguna did not wait for questions of principle to be resolved before
embarking upon his ambitious school reform. He concentrated his
meager resources on the creation of a network of primary schools
throughout the diocese. Regarding them as the foundation of the
whole educational system and as the type of institution most needed by
the great majority of Rumanians, he made it his goal to establish a primary school in every church commune. There were to be two kinds:
the elementary, consisting of a single class to serve the smaller parishes,
and the *Hauptschule,* composed of three classes to serve cities and
larger towns and all other places where a church commune numbered
at least 2,000 persons. The task Şaguna had set for himself was monumental; most of the Hauptschulen, which prepared pupils to enter
either the gymnasium or specialized trade schools, had yet to be built,
and many communes did not even have an elementary school.

He himself devised the new curricula for the schools. It emphasized
Christian religious instruction and church singing and employed as
basic textbooks in reading classes the *Ceaslov* (a breviary) and *Psaltire*
(a psalter). Şaguna's emphasis upon religious texts reflected his con-

cern about the superstitions and illiteracy of the peasant masses and their dire need of moral and spiritual instruction. Other subjects to be taught included writing, arithmetic, and what might be called civics or, as Şaguna defined it, the duties of a loyal subject toward his monarch.[60] Şaguna insisted that all instruction be in Rumanian, since this was the language of the people, but he also advocated the intensive study of German as a necessary tool for those Rumanians who aspired to successful careers in business and public administration.[61] He regarded a knowledge of German as affording an entree into the higher economic and bureaucratic structure of the monarchy, and hence of immense importance for the long-term development of the Rumanian nation. He himself financed the publication of a German-Rumanian conversation guide and dictionary in 1852 and encouraged the introduction of German dictation and translation exercises in the better Hauptschulen like the one in Răşinari.[62]

Although Şaguna's main preoccupation was the primary school, he also drew up a comprehensive plan for Orthodox secondary education, which provided for six *Obergymnasien,* six *Untergymnasien,* and six *Realschulen.* He thought the Orthodox were entitled to at least this number because their 650,000 faithful made up the largest single denomination in Transylvania.[63] His request betrayed the sense of urgency he felt at the growing numbers of Orthodox who were attending state and Roman Catholic high schools.[64] In his view, these students were being exposed to proselytism or were running the risk of becoming indifferent to religion. He was only partially successful in carrying out his project. Gymnasia were opened in Braşov in 1853 and later on in Brad. He had received government permission to build a Realschule in Abrud in 1853 and, convinced that this was the type of school that would most benefit his people, he set about the task of mobilizing men and resources with characteristic determination. He encouraged close cooperation between the Orthodox parish committee and town officials, which resulted in full agreement on the site for the school (to be provided by the town) and on the expenses of materials and labor (to be shared by the two parties). Swift agreement was possible because the majority on the town council was Orthodox, but it is significant that members of other churches supported the school with equal enthusiasm because Şaguna had promised them that it would be open to all children, regardless of religious belief and nationality.

In the fall of 1853 Şaguna came to Abrud to see personally what progress was being made. He wanted to assure the financial independence of the new school and began to solicit donations for an endowment fund.[65] Although he continued to seek state support for the building of schools and the payment of teachers' salaries,[66] he wanted to avoid complete dependence upon the state, for he knew that in time it would mean complete subordination to the state. Accordingly, in Abrud he formed a committee of three priests and three laymen to supervise a public subscription. He intended to use any surplus they might collect to provide supplemental classes in mining and forestry, which he thought would help greatly to improve living standards in the region. But throughout the 1850s he received no encouragement from the Cultusministerium. It was only during the sessions of the Verstärkter Reichsrat in 1860 that he succeeded in obtaining final approval for the project.

On the whole, Şaguna showed little enthusiasm for the establishment of institutions of higher learning. His attitude was conditioned by priorities he had set for the Orthodox, his coolness toward the Uniates, and his estimate of needs and resources. He opposed a Rumanian university with a full complement of faculties because he considered the nation too poor to support it. A university struck him as a luxury, given the desperate state of primary and secondary education. He repeatedly chided the intellectuals for encouraging the people to spend their meager resources on a project that had little chance of realization and was of dubious value to them, and he warned them not to expect any sympathy from the Cultusministerium. His prognosis proved to be accurate, for in 1853 Thun rejected a request for aid on the grounds that the imperial treasury was short of funds and the "low level" of development of the Rumanian language made it unsuitable for advanced studies.[67]

Şaguna took a more flexible position on the establishment of a Rumanian law school. In 1850, while he still entertained hopes that the imperial government would honor its pledges about national equality, he petitioned the Cultusministerium to establish a "philosophical-juridical faculty" for the Rumanians of Transylvania as one of the ways they themselves could accelerate their own intellectual and material development and thereby achieve equality in fact with the former privileged nations.[68] Although he generally supported the intellectuals in this undertaking, which meant so much to them, he rejected their assumption that the operation of a law school was a responsibility of the church or of both churches working together. He contended that it was, rather, a good example of a national institution. As the decade of absolutism wore on, Şaguna lost most of his interest in a law faculty. In 1852 he rejected an invitation from Constantin Alutan, vicar-general of the Uniate Church, to join forces to establish a Rumanian law school.[69] He thought that the time for such a venture was "inappropriate" and suggested that, for the moment, qualified persons seek admission to Saxon and Magyar academies. He acknowledged that training in the law in Rumanian would undoubtedly stimulate national development, but he pointed out that there were as yet few good Rumanian elementary schools and gymnasia where students could be trained in the humanities and natural sciences and the use of the literary language and thereby obtain the preparation he thought essential if they were to profit from a legal education.[70]

Şaguna did not restrict his activities on behalf of education to the classroom. He considered it the church's responsibility to use as many instruments as it could to disseminate its spiritual and moral teachings. In order to provide the church with modern means of bringing its message regularly to large numbers of people he made plans after 1849 to establish a diocesan publishing house. His immediate concern was to replace the thousands of liturgical works that had been destroyed in the revolution. As the project matured in his mind, he came to see the printing press as the means of providing low-cost textbooks for Orthodox primary and secondary schools. Such books had generally been obtained in small quantities and at irregular intervals from the University of Buda Press or the metropolitan press in Carlovitz. The few items printed by local Saxon houses were too expensive for most parish school committees, and the importation of Rumanian books from outside the monarchy, especially from Moldavia and Wallachia, required special government permission and involved long delays.

Official approval for an Orthodox press came far more quickly than Şaguna had dared to hope. In announcing the government's decision, Governor Wohlgemuth professed full confidence in Şaguna's loyalty and "wisdom" in using the printing privilege. On August 27, 1850, Şaguna formally dedicated the press, and it began operations immediately with two cast-iron presses and Cyrillic letters that he had found in Pest and had paid for personally.[71] At first the press experienced lean years, and Şaguna was obliged to make up the deficits out of general church revenues. But his difficulties were not only financial. Throughout the period of absolutism, because of the government's suspicion of the printed word generally, there was uncertainty about the duration of the operating privilege of the press. Then, in 1855, the Uniate consistory formally protested against the establishment of an Orthodox press on the grounds that it infringed upon the privileges granted the seminary press at Blaj to print Rumanian books. Although the protest did not affect the operations of the Orthodox press, it succeeded in opening up a new area of conflict between the two churches.[72] The survival of the diocesan press, both politically and financially, was largely owing to Şaguna's careful management of it. In order to avoid provoking the regime, he allowed no book to be printed until he had approved its contents.[73] He was also an astute businessman, who knew how to market his product. Beginning in 1852 in Braşov he set up a number of sales agencies throughout Transylvania to distribute all the publications of the diocesan press.[74] During the first decade these amounted to thirty-five religious works, including *Catechismul cel mic* (1851), the first book to be published by the press, Şaguna's translation of the Bible, and innumerable schoolbooks. With the advent of the constitutional era, the legal existence of the press was finally assured. An imperial decree of December 14, 1860, granted it the definitive right to print church schoolbooks for Transylvania and the Orthodox dioceses of Arad, Timişoara, Vršac, and Bukovina, even though they were still under the jurisdiction of Carlovitz.

One of the most successful publications of the diocesan press was the newspaper *Telegraful Român*. It finally enabled the press to achieve some measure of financial independence, but its cultural and political services to the cause of Orthodoxy and the Rumanians generally in Transylvania far exceeded its monetary value. During Şaguna's lifetime and for a decade after his death it was one of the most influential molders of Rumanian public opinion.

Early in his career Şaguna had recognized the social significance of newspapers. In 1846, as we have seen, he had supported those intellectuals who wanted a second Rumanian newspaper in Transylvania alongside *Gazeta de Transilvania,* and in 1849 and 1850 he worked hard to establish a Rumanian- and German-language newspaper in Vienna in order to influence Austrian policy-makers. Although none of these efforts was successful, the idea remained with him, and in December 1852 he petitioned the Transylvanian government to allow him to publish a weekly newspaper for his diocese. The welfare of his church was uppermost in his mind. He suspected *Gazeta de Transilvania* of promoting the Uniate movement at the expense of Orthodoxy[75] and wanted a weapon with which to defend his church. He also thought a newspaper would be an effective means of bringing Christian teachings to bear upon the economic and social development of the Rumanian people as a whole;[76] he wanted "to enlighten [them] with practical ideas and information suitable to the times and commensurate with their needs in the domains of politics, industry, commerce, and literature; to direct their minds toward all that will contribute to their . . . progress; and to teach them to know their rights in the state."[77] The government once again responded favorably to his petition to publish. By this time his management of the diocesan press had convinced Transylvanian officials that he would work within the system. They also welcomed the opportunity to provide *Gazeta* with a little competition and to have an additional means of reaching the Rumanian masses with official announcements and a point of view favorable to the Gesamtmonarchie.

The first issue of *Telegraful Român* appeared on January 3, 1853. It was published twice a week until 1878, and then three times. Its management was Şaguna's favorite occupation during the decade of absolutism, even though it added greatly to an exhausting work load. He often corrected proofs himself, and no important piece was printed without his approval.[78] On the major issues of the day, therefore, *Telegraful* represented his views. By and large the fare it offered was sober. Considerable coverage was given to political events at home and abroad—the Crimean War and the political evolution of the Rumanian principalities were treated in great detail—but never did *Telegraful* call into question the policies of the court or the general principles upon which the monarchy was founded. There were numerous articles on religious and moral, as well as political, themes, and many pieces about education. Şaguna also saw to it that *Telegraful* gave special attention to economic problems. He was eager to bring some relief to the peasantry and published learned and popular articles on a variety of subjects ranging from better farming methods to the advantages of economic diversification. Within a few years *Telegraful* became the authoritative organ of the majority of the Orthodox clergy and faithful. It reached large numbers. Priests were obliged to subscribe to it as the official diocesan organ, and they were encouraged to read appropriate articles from it to their congregations on Sunday. It reached the height of its influence under the editorship of Nicolae Cristea (1865-1883), when it led the opposition to both political passivism and Magyarization and brought together a talented young staff who were to play a major role in literature and politics as well as journalism down to the outbreak of the First World War.

Şaguna's accomplishments in the field of education are difficult to measure precisely. One can, of course, cite the increase in the number of Orthodox village schools from a few hundred in 1846 to six hundred in 1858, the inauguration of a secondary school system, the introduction of new textbooks embodying recent advances in pedagogy like the ABCs of 1852 and 1862,[79] the better-trained teachers from the theological-pedagogical institute who entered primary education, the annual teachers' conferences, which he inaugurated in 1863,[80] and the introduction of an orderly system of controls and responsibilities in school administration. These were substantial achievements, especially in the light of what Şaguna had found when he arrived in Transylvania. Yet in spite of sanguine reports to the government and encouraging circular letters to the clergy, he was deeply dissatisfied with the rate of progress. During his long episcopate he was acutely aware of the discrepancies between the statistics of progress and the actual state of things.

He acknowledged his own inability to overcome the two major obstacles to a general and sustained improvement of education: the endemic poverty of his diocese and the persistent indifference to the value of formal education exhibited by the majority of his faithful and not a few of his priests. Although he obtained modest grants from the imperial treasury, mostly in the form of scholarships,[81] this aid was mainly *ad hoc* and fell far short of the permanent endowments he had envisioned. He frequently had to make up deficits in school budgets out of general church funds or from his own pocket.[82] Particularly discouraging to him was the utter incomprehension with which numerous village school committees, priests, and lay teachers went about their tasks. School buildings were allowed to fall into disrepair or were sometimes abandoned entirely,[83] and teachers often did not meet their classes and made no effort to improve their own skills.[84] He was also disappointed by the attitude of those who should have been most receptive to the new opportunities offered them. Many peasant families would not send their children to school. They could see no connection between learning how to read and write and earning a living, since the only career open to their sons was what their fathers and grandfathers had done—till the land and tend the flocks. Consequently, they thought it wiser to keep their children home, especially at planting and harvest time, to contribute their share to the meager family income.[85]

In spite of his inability to overcome all the physical and mental obstacles to the advancement of education, Şaguna must be recognized as the founder of the modern Orthodox school system. He introduced new men and new ideas into an institution that had been turned towards the past rather than the future.

Although the social mission that Şaguna had undertaken failed to produce immediately the tangible results he had hoped for, it had reaffirmed the role of the church in society at a time when the political power of the hierarchy was ebbing. Through the expanded educational activities which he had conceived and directed, he had assured the church a permanent place in the new national movement that developed after the Austro-Hungarian Compromise of 1867. Of even greater historical significance was the impetus he gave to that harmonizing of the Orthodox and Western traditions which his own career symbolized. Through all the instruments at his command—the school, the pulpit, the publishing house, and the newspaper—he broadened the intellectual horizons of both clergy and laity and helped to prepare the Orthodox for the transition from the essentially patriarchal society of the first half of the nineteenth century to the modern age.

Epilogue

Şaguna considered the reestablishment of the Orthodox metropolis and the subsequent legislation ensuring the autonomous administration of its affairs by the clergy and laity together as the crowning achievements of his episcopate. The years that followed seemed to him anti-climactic, and he complained on numerous occasions to his intimates, Nicolae Popea and Ioan Puşcariu, that he was being ignored by all and sundry. These feelings were perhaps natural for one who had directed the affairs of a large diocese for nearly a quarter of a century. Although he continued to enjoy immense prestige among his clergy and faithful—reverence and even awe would be more accurate terms, since the beginnings of a Şaguna cult were already discernible—he could not adjust to the letdown that followed the achievement of his life's ambition. In a sense he was the cause of his own "neglect," in that he was the chief author of that legislation—primarily the Organic Statutes—which had shifted many of his responsibilities onto the shoulders of others and had provided them with the machinery to carry on without his direct supervision.

In the final years of his life his work on behalf of the church followed a familiar pattern. He was anxious, first of all, to bring the Organic Statutes fully to life and to give a broad scope to what he considered their "latent creative powers." With these ideas in mind and in spite of ill health, he presided over the first national church congress and eparchal synod held under the provisions of the statutes in October 1870. As we have seen, the aggressive behavior which the intellectuals displayed was highly disagreeable to him and even alarmed him, as they attempted to turn the congress into a national parliament. He had to intervene forcefully to prevent a group of them from pushing through a remonstrance to the Hungarian government criticizing various changes it had introduced into the original draft of the statutes.[1]

Education continued to occupy much of his time, but he gradually turned over the day-to-day administration to Nicolae Popea, who had become the general vicar of the archdiocese. He now had more leisure for writing and study than ever before, preoccupations which at times seemed to serve almost as a refuge from a world that had become increasingly alien to him. He pursued his work on Orthodox canon law in *Enchiridion de canoane* (1871) and published a revised version of his essay on pastoral theology, *Manual de studiul pastoral* (1872). At the same time, he took up the study of Hebrew and French, primarily, it seems, to have access to original religious texts and works of criticism.

Even in these final years, in spite of the repudiation of his policies by the most vocal leaders of the lay intellectuals, he could not extricate himself from the turbulence of national politics. He had always shown great zest for politics, probably because it satisfied his active and creative nature. Yet, in spite of the opinions of many of his contemporaries and the subsequent judgments of scholars, who regarded him first and foremost as the consummate politician, he engaged in the art not to fulfil political ambitions but primarily to assure the welfare of the Orthodox Church and its faithful.

Political developments in Hungary since the inauguration of the Austro-Hungarian dual monarchy in 1867 had caused him considerable misgivings. He was especially worried by the provisions of proposed new school laws, which would allow the government to substitute state schools for church schools that failed to meet proper standards. Aware of the pitiable condition of many village primary schools, he was afraid that a strict application of these laws would deprive large numbers of parishes of their schools and thereby cripple the ambitious social mission of the church.

He had to rely upon the liberalism of men like Ferenc Deák and his old friend, Joseph Eötvös, whose tour of Transylvanian schools in the fall of 1869 proved reassuring. While Şaguna's guest in Sibiu, Eötvös emphasized that his main objective was to extend educational opportunities to all citizens without regard to nationality or the language they spoke, and he admitted that the state could assure itself of the loyalty of its citizens only if it demonstrated a genuine concern for their needs and aspirations. In a public address he went out of his way to praise Şaguna's contributions to both state and Christian institutions — a comment that was widely interpreted to mean that the Hungarian government intended to respect the confessional principle in education and the autonomy of the Orthodox Church.[2] Nonetheless, its disposition to interfere was manifest in new school laws. Government policy caused Şaguna much anxiety, for if the church's right to manage its own schools could be successfully challenged, then the very principle of church autonomy would be destroyed. Anxiety turned into alarm in

1870, when the Hungarian government began to carry out its plan to establish a network of state-operated village schools in competition with the parochial schools, particularly those of the non-Magyar nationalities. Articles reflecting the position Şaguna had long held on the essentially moral-religious nature of education began to appear regularly in *Telegraful Român*. Warnings against indolence and division in the face of danger were sounded, and the denationalization of the Rumanians in the Szekler district of Háromszék, "who had been lost because of the lack of national-confessional instruction," was held up as an example of what could happen in other places as well, if state (that is, Magyar) schools replaced those of the church.[3]

Şaguna saw little hope of successful resistance to these encroachments among those who had so recently arrogated national leadership to themselves. The consequences of political passivity seemed to him to have been entirely negative. As he surveyed the situation in 1870 and 1871, the best words he could find to describe the prevailing mood were "lassitude" and "confusion." He roundly criticized the lay intellectuals for abandoning the people in the interests of attaining sophisticated goals of their own that had little to do with the day-to-day national struggle at the village and district level. He argued that in attempting to promote a boycott of the elections to the Hungarian parliament, they had merely made easier the election of Magyars and Saxons in predominantly Rumanian electoral districts. Although he recognized that they had not intended to abandon local political struggle, neither, in his opinion, had they made any significant effort to strengthen their ties with the people and provide them with proper leadership.[4] He repeatedly emphasized the fact that the best way for a nation to ensure its rights was to exercise them. If, for example, the Orthodox wished to have the same status as the Calvinists and Roman Catholics, then, he argued, they could not wait for someone else to make them a gift, but had rather to plunge into the thick of political struggle to win it.[5]

Although Şaguna's watchword remained "activity," he had little sympathy for the sort that operated in the shadows and attempted to combat a constitutional regime by illegal means. For example, he dismissed the circulation of so-called "Epistole volante" in the spring of 1868 as "foolishness." The authors of these circulars, which purported to represent the views of all the Rumanians of Transylvania, warned that if they failed to obtain satisfaction of their "just demands" by legal means, they would resort to other methods. Şaguna considered the leaflets the work of Transylvanians living in Bucharest "who had nothing better to do than concoct senseless *Brandbriefe*."[6] He was certain that such actions could have no beneficial effect because they were utterly divorced from reality; the achievement of a nation's goals, he argued, began not with appeals to the emotions but with a program rooted firmly in constitutional law.

Şaguna's misgivings about the direction national politics had taken since the diet of Cluj in 1865 were shared by many laymen and clergy of both churches. Even George Bariţiu and Ioan Raţiu, the chief architects of passivity, had serious doubts about the efficacy of their tactics. They recognized that a complete boycott of parliamentary elections would be impossible partly because local authorities would know how to attract Rumanian voters to the polling places, and partly because many Rumanians would be active in village and county affairs and would find it inconsistent and confusing to stand idly by while the most important political event of the year unfolded around them. Like the activists, they saw the greatest danger resulting from passivity to be a mood of indifference toward great national issues and the intellectuals' loss of influence over the people.[7] In the fall of 1871 and the spring of 1872 similar concerns were voiced in meetings of clergy and intellectuals all over Transylvania, in Sibiu, Braşov, Făgăraş, Blaj, Cluj, Sebeş, and Turda. Both passivists and activists agreed on the need for a new national conference before the 1872 parliamentary elections in order to reevaluate the decisions taken at Mercurea.[8] Even more important to both sides than agreement on temporary electoral tactics was the opportunity such a conference presented for restoring national unity as it had existed during the diet of Sibiu. But the prospects for unity were dim, as activists and passivists continued to pursue their own separate goals.

The activists, with the full support of Şaguna and *Telegraful Român*, engaged in a vigorous organizing campaign in the counties between the autumn of 1871 and the following spring. Many groups appealed directly to Şaguna, as the only surviving president of the permanent committee established in 1861, to call his colleagues out of retirement and together convoke a national congress.[9] With Şaguna's blessing a "national conference" of activists was held in Sibiu on May 5 and 6, 1872, at which a general coordinating committee was established and a formal declaration of intent to participate in the forthcoming parliamentary elections was adopted.[10] The delegates publicly lamented the disintegration of that earlier solid front of intellectuals which had existed when the bishops led the nation, and they urged Şaguna and his Uniate colleague, Ioan Vancea, to bring them together once again.[11]

Şaguna saw in the projected congress the opportunity for a wide-ranging, open discussion of national policies and goals, which he had eagerly awaited. He thought periodic consultations of this sort were healthy for the body politic just as synods helped to infuse new life into the church. Controversy did not worry him, so long as it was constructive and did not become an end in itself. He therefore plunged into the work of organizing the congress with something of his old zest for politics. On May 17 he wrote to Vancea urging him to join in convoking a congress at a time and place suitable to Vancea. He stressed his desire for a genuinely representative assembly and suggested that their respective protopopes meet at once with intellectuals in every district and municipality to plan for the election of delegates.[12] In spite of his evident enthusiasm, he had grave doubts concerning his own physical ability to carry out the heavy responsibilities he was about to assume, and on the day after writing to Vancea he gave up plans to travel to Arad to meet the emperor out of fear that the journey would be too strenuous.[13]

While Şaguna was thus preparing to resume large-scale political activity, Vancea displayed considerable reserve. Citing their responsibility as metropolitans to be absolutely "correct" in all their actions, he urged a limited gathering of intellectuals without an electoral campaign and made it plain that he would proceed with the congress only on the condition that the government gave permission beforehand.[14] Şaguna thought such permission unnecessary. In a constitutional state —and he assumed that Hungary was one—citizens had the right to meet at all times to discuss political questions. The only obligation the metropolitans had, as far as he could see, was to inform the civil authorities that a political meeting was to take place on a particular date. He informed Vancea that he intended to follow the same principles as those that had guided him for the past twenty-five years: respect for the law, concern for the welfare of the nation, and the maintenance of national solidarity. But he preferred not to make an issue of the matter; if Vancea wished to seek prior government approval of the congress and thought it best to restrict the number of delegates, he would not object.[15]

At last, the date of the conference—June 18—and the place—Alba Iulia—were decided upon. Preliminary meetings of laymen and clergy were held in most cities and large towns at the beginning of June amidst general satisfaction that the national interest had been well served. But on June 13, Minister-President Menyhért Lonyay, who was then in Cluj, rejected Vancea's and Şaguna's request to convoke the conference; it could be held, he said, only *after* the parliamentary elections. Şaguna appears to have taken no further action. A few days later Vancea discussed the matter with Lonyay, who seemed eager to reach a settlement with the Rumanians. Lonyay proposed an early meeting with Bariţiu, Raţiu, Elie Măcelariu, and the two metropolitans, and Vancea wrote to Şaguna to inquire if he could come to Alba Iulia on July 1. Şaguna thought the idea a good one, but expressed his regret that "failing health" would prevent him from attending.[16]

The lay intellectuals once again stepped into the breach. Bariţiu, Raţiu, Măcelariu, and a few others, had followed the efforts of the metropolitans to convoke a conference with little enthusiasm. They gave both their due as churchmen, but in political matters they could accord them no greater consideration than "other citizens"; as Raţiu put it: "The Metropolitans must never again be in a position to lead the nation by its nose; on the contrary, they must go forward *with* the nation, if they wish to be respected." With Lonyay's tacit approval they held a conference of some two hundred persons at Alba Iulia on June 27. A week earlier Raţiu had sent Şaguna a curt note to the effect that a conference was being planned and that his presence was desired,[17] but Şaguna had not deigned to reply. Raţiu was elected chairman by acclamation, and once he had assured his colleagues that the government had no objection to an ad hoc meeting, and after the singing of the imperial hymn, they proceeded to business. An overwhelming majority concluded that nothing had changed since 1869 and voted to continue the policy of complete passivity.[18]

The action of the conference signalled the final defeat of Şaguna's efforts to unite the nation behind a program of vigorous participation in the new political system. In July, when the Sibiu committee again urged him to convoke a national congress, he indicated a willingness to do so, but Vancea, citing the fact that national politics had taken "a different course," refused to join him.[19] This seems to have been Şaguna's last important political effort. Still the disunity of the nation, which showed no signs of healing, continued to trouble him, and shortly before his death he contemplated making an "appeal to the nation" to end the deadlock between activists and passivists. Severe illness denied him the opportunity.[20]

In the last year of his life he experienced a marked physical decline, which forced him to curtail even those activities he considered most essential such as the ordination of priests and deacons.[21] He died on June 28, 1873, at the age of sixty-five, of a combination of heart trouble, hardening of the arteries, and overwork. His entire estate, valued at some 600,000 Austrian crowns, was willed to the church in the form of a charitable and philanthropic foundation. As he had requested, he was buried in the cemetery of the parish church of Răşinari in a simple ceremony.[22]

An assessment of Şaguna's place in the historical development of the Rumanians of Transylvania must be sought in the two main areas in which he worked: the church and politics. Many of his contemporaries, especially the lay intellectuals, tended to see him primarily as a political being, a master strategist whose chief goal was to dominate the national movement. This view seems to have been the prevailing one among Austrian officials in both Vienna and Transylvania. Such an appraisal, however, merely reveals their own absorption with politics and betrays their lack of perspective.

Şaguna was, in fact, not primarily interested in politics as a career or in achieving purely political goals. Nor, it must be said, was he a particularly creative political leader. Although he was certainly the major figure in Rumanian political life of his time, he conducted the affairs of the nation in accordance with the traditional ways of his Orthodox and Uniate predecessors. He did not, for example, try to organize a regular political party, and he seems even to have shunned the practice of politics as divisive and inefficacious—a view conditioned perhaps by his belief that the Rumanians could not by their own efforts become an effective, independent, political force. He preferred to think in terms of spiritual and moral values rather than political parties and ideologies. There is abundant evidence to suggest that he did not appreciate the all-embracing nature of either the idea of nationality or the modern state. In a sense, he was opposed to both, for he persisted in thinking in terms of separate categories like church and state and nation, each with rights and a mission all its own which set it apart from the others. It is little wonder that the subordination of church to nation struck him as unnatural.

Şaguna's major successes and his most enduring contributions to Rumanian historical development lay in his ecclesiastical activities. He made the Orthodox Church a more active social force than it had ever been before, by endowing it with strong institutions and by regularizing the participation of the laity in its affairs at all levels and in this way rendering it more responsive to the needs and desires of the mass of the faithful. He based these accomplishments upon what he discerned as the underlying pattern of human development or, as he put it, the eternal sources of human vitality and progress, namely, the Christian spiritual tradition and the primacy of law. These he strove to adapt to the specific needs and aspirations of his own people in their own time. In so doing, he gave the lie to the old cliché about the other-worldliness of Orthodoxy. His method was to reconcile his people's centuries-old Eastern Orthodox heritage with the new learning coming from the West; the first, he thought, would put the second in proper perspective and enable his people to derive full benefit from secular learning rather than be dominated by it. In a sense, all his major works — the restoration of the Orthodox metropolis, the drafting of the Organic Statutes, and the revival of the church's social mission — were directed toward the attainment of harmony between the inner spirituality of Orthodoxy, which transformed the life of man from within by changing his heart and mind, and the outward forms of social organization, which were intended to satisfy a nation's immediate strivings for political and economic progress. In an age of nationalism he was not a nationalist. Rather, he was the last of the great bishop-national leaders.

Notes, Selected Bibliography, Index

Abbreviations

ABM	Arhiva Bibliotecii Mitropoliei, Sibiu
AIIC	*Anuarul Institutului de Istorie din Cluj*
AIIN	*Anuarul Institutului de Istorie Naţională*
AV	Allgemeines Verwaltungsarchiv, Vienna
BARSR	Biblioteca Academiei Republicii Socialiste România (Bucharest, unless Cluj is specified)
CA	Consistory Archive, Sremski Karlovci
EK	Erdélyi Kancellária
FM	*Foaia pentru minte, inimă şi literatură*
GT	Gubernium Transylvanicum
GTr	*Gazeta de Transilvania*
HHStA	Haus-, Hof- und Staatsarchiv, Vienna
MCS	Militär und Civilgouvernement in Siebenbürgen
OL	Magyar Országos Levéltár, Budapest
PA	Patriarchal Archive, Sremski Karlovci
TR	*Telegraful Român*

Notes

Chapter 1: Apprenticeship

1. Valeriu Papahagi, "Les Roumains d'Albanie et le commerce vénétien aux XVIIe et XVIIIe siècles," *Mélanges de l'École Roumaine en France,* 9 (1939), 48, 112, 114, 116; Valeriu Papahagi, "Familia Şaguna în documente veneţiene din secolul al XVIII-lea," *Revista Istorică,* 18 (1932), 1-5.

2. The expansion of Macedo-Rumanian merchants into the Habsburg monarchy is described in detail in Anastase N. Hâciu, *Aromânii* (Focşani, 1936), 299-368. The most extensive history of Moscopole and its merchants is by Ioakim Martinianou, *E Moskhopolis 1330-1930* (Thessalonike, 1957).

3. OL, Magyar Helytartótanács, Departamentum Religionis Graeci Ritus non-Unitorum: Archbishop of Eger to the Royal Lieutenancy, October 7, 1814.

4. *Ibid.:* Ioannes Boráros, senator of Pest, to the magistrate of Pest, April 17, 1816.

5. *Ibid.:* declaraţion of Anastasiu Şaguna in Hungarian, September 12, 1816; Ioan Lupaş and Eugen Todoran, "Documente istorice: I. Acte privitoare la lupta Anastasiei Şaguna pentru apărarea copiilor săi şi a credinţei strămoşeşti," *Transilvania,* 41, no. 4 (1910), 185, 193-194; Ioan Lupaş, "Anastasia Şaguna," *Convorbiri Literare,* 42, no. 12 (1908), 595-603.

6. Eugen Todoran, "Documente istorice. Acte privitoare la reîntoarcerea lui Atanasiu Şaguna în sînul bisericii strămoşeşti," *Transilvania,* 41, no. 6 (1910), 455.

7. *Ibid.,* 456-460.

8. Nicolae Popea, *Archiepiscopul şi Metropolitul Andreiu Baron de Şaguna* (Sibiu, 1879), 22.

9. A useful survey of intellectual and cultural currents among the Macedo-Rumanians of the Austrian Empire in the last half of the eighteenth century and the early nineteenth is Max Demeter Peyfuss, "Rom oder Byzanz," *Österreichische Osthefte,* 12, no. 6 (1970), 337-351.

10. Petru Maior, *Istoria pentru începutul Românilor în Dacia,* 2nd ed. (Buda, 1834), 147-148.

11. Theodor Capidan, "Petru Maior şi Aromânii," *Junimea Literară,* 12, no. 4-5 (1923), 63-69, and *Aromânii. Dialectul aromân,* in Academia Română, *Studii şi Cercetări,* no. 20 (Bucharest, 1932), 85-87.

12. Pericle Papahagi, *Scriitori aromâni în secolul al XVIII (Cavalioti, Ucuta, Daniil)* (Bucharest, 1909), 22. The most detailed study of Greek-Wallachian relations in Pest is Ödön Füves, *Görögök Pesten (1686-1931)* (3 vols., Budapest, Kandidaturi értekezés, 1972), particularly vol. I.

13. Ioan Bianu, Nerva Hodoş, and Dan Simonescu, *Bibliografia românească veche,* 1508-1830 (4 vols., Bucharest, 1903-1944), II, 398-403.

14. Capidan, *Aromânii,* 71-76.

15. Arno Dunker, "Der Grammatiker Bojadži," *Zweiter Jahresbericht des Instituts für rumänische Sprache zu Leipzig* (Leipzig, 1895), 1-146.

16. OL, EK, Acta generalia, 1813/3553: Grabovszky to Bishop Moga, June 24, 1813.

17. Pest Városa Levéltára, Budapest, Intimata a.m., Numerus 4294/I, f. 351 (1808); *ibid.*, Numerus 4294/II, ff. 19-23 (1820), and f. 560 (1835).

18. Popea, *Archiepiscopul,* 20.

19. Ştefan Pascu and Iosif Pervain, eds., *George Bariţ şi contemporanii săi* (2 vols., Bucharest, 1973-1975), II, 184: Vasici to Bariţiu, June 29, 1873.

20. The most complete description of the institute is by Radu Flora, *Relaţiile sîrbo-române. Noi contribuţii* (Panciova, 1968), 107-134.

21. PA, Sremski Karlovci, 1833/303: 1. Karlovci, October 2, 1833; 2. Hopovo, October 13, 1833.

22. *Ibid.*, 1837/247: 1. Vršac, July 10, 1837; 2. Karlovci, July 19, 1837.

23. Djoko Slijepčević, *Istorija srpske pravoslavne crkve* (2 vols., Munich, 1966), II, 108-129.

24. Émile Picot, *Les Serbes de Hongrie* (Prague, 1873), 406: cites Metropolitan Stanković's report of January 7/19, 1837.

25. CA, Sremski Karlovci, 1841/43: 8. Karlovci, January 1, 1841; PA, 1843/2758: 5. Bešenova, March 15, 1841.

26. *Ibid.:* 2. Minutes of the meeting of the archdiocesan consistory in Carlovitz on January 23, 1841; 6. Bešenova, October 6, 1841; 9. Bešenova, December 9, 1841; 10. December 21, 1842; CA, 1843/151: Ofen, March 21, 1843.

27. Slijepčević, *Istorija,* II, 182: Stratimirović to the Rumanians of Timişoara, 1822.

28. Gheorghe Ciuhandu, *Episcopii Samuil Vulcan şi Gherasim Raţ; pagini mai ales din istoria Românilor crişeni (1830-40)* (Arad, 1935), 365: petition of the Rumanians of Timişoara to Stanković, 1838.

29. Slijepčević, *Istorija,* II, 183.

30. *Istoria bisericii romîne. Manual pentru institutele teologice* (2 vols., Bucharest, 1957-1958), II, 452-461. For a detailed account of the early phases of this campaign, see Cornelia C. Bodea, *Moise Nicoara (1784-1861) şi rolul său în lupta pentru emanciparea naţional-religioasă a Românilor din Banat şi Crişana* (Arad, 1943), 41-127.

31. Ciuhandu, *Episcopii Vulcan şi Raţ,* 305-322. Vulcan has also been portrayed as a vigorous supporter of Orthodox efforts to elect a Rumanian as bishop of Arad: Iacob Radu, *Samuil Vulcan, Episcopul Român-Unit al Orăzii-Mari (1806-1839) şi Biserica Ortodoxă-Română* (Oradea-Mare, 1925), 12-26; Octavianus Bârlea, *Ex historia romena: Ioannes Bob, Episcopus Fagarasiensis (1783-1830)* (Freiburg, 1951), 267-280; Slijepčević, *Istorija,* II, 142-155.

32. Ştefan Pop, "Gramatica română a lui Şaguna: Vârşat, 1843," *Foaia Diecezană* (Caransebeş), 38, no. 27 (1923), 2-3; Iacob Mârza, "Gramatica lui Andrei Şaguna," *Limba Română,* 20, no. 1 (1971), 21-32.

33. OL, EK, Praesidialia, 1847/163; HHStA, Staatsratsakten, 2173/2078, 1846.

34. OL, EK, Acta generalia, 1846/3531: Transylvanian Chancellery to the emperor, June 27, 1846; HHStA, Staatsratsakten, 2173/2078, 1846.

35. BARSR, Ms. rom., vol. 1000: Puşcariu to Bariţiu, August 22/September 3, 1846.

36. PA, 1846/977: Şaguna to Rajačić, November 14, 1846: Silviu Dragomir, "André Şaguna et Joseph Rajačić," *Balcania,* 6 (1943), 271-272: Şaguna to Rajačić, February 2/14, 1847.

37. PA, 1846/747: Şaguna to Rajačić, September 6, 1846; ABM, Şaguna Collection, no. 201: Şaguna to Eduard Bach, November 10, 1849.

38. OL, EK, Acta generalia, 1847/1046: report on Orthodox schools in Transylvania for the 1845-46 school year.

39. The status of the Rumanians and their church is succinctly described by David Prodan, *Supplex Libellus Valachorum* (Bucharest, 1971), 62-72, 98-112.

40. The evolution of the Transylvanian diet and related institutions in the sixteenth and seventeenth centuries is described in Zsolt Trócsányi, *Az erdélyi fejedelemség korának országgyűlései* (Budapest, 1976), especially pp. 141-179.

41. General accounts of the church union may be found in: Zoltán Tóth, *Az erdélyi román nacionalizmus első százada, 1697-1792* (Budapest, 1946), 18-44, and Prodan, *Supplex,* 113-133.

42. Nicolae Popea, *Vechia metropolia ortodosa romana a Transilvaniei, suprimirea si restaurarea ei* (Sibiu, 1870), 149-152.

43. OL, GT (in Politicis), 1847/5904; 1847/10,431.

44. GTr, October 14 and 24, 1846.

45. OL, EK, Acta generalia, 1847/8190.

46. *Ibid.,* 1847/2373; *ibid.,* GT (in Politicis), 1847/5012.

47. Gheorghe Tulbure, *Mitropolitul Şaguna. Opera literară. Scrisori pastorale. Circulari şcolare. Diverse* (Sibiu, 1938), 137-139.

48. BARSR, Ms. rom., vol. 1000: Puşcariu to Bariţiu, August 29, 1847; GTr, August 18, 1847.

49. PA, 1846/977: Şaguna to Rajačić, November 14, 1846; OL, EK, Acta generalia, 1847/8190: Şaguna to the Gubernium, July 1, 1847.

50. GTr, August 4, 1847.

51. Dragomir, "André Şaguna et Joseph Rajačić," 275-277: Şaguna to Rajačić, June 3, 1847.

52. The contest between the peasants and the treasury in the 1820s and 1830s is described in Zoltán Tóth, *Mişcările ţărăneşti din Munţii Apuseni pînă la 1848* (Bucharest, 1955), 172-253.

53. Simeone Balinth, "Scurta descriere a unoru evenimente intemplate in muntii apuseni ai Transilvaniei," *Transilvania,* 7, no. 2 (1876), 14-15.

54. Catharine Varga's efforts on behalf of the peasants is described sympathetically in Zoltán Tóth, *Mişcările ţărăneşti,* 259-306. One may also consult Keith Hitchins, "Andreiu Şaguna and Catharine Varga; a New Document," *Revue des Études Roumaines,* 11-12 (1969), 183-187. Catharine Varga's own sketch of her life up to February 1847 was published by András Kiss, "Varga Katalinnak tulajdon kézivel tett életleírása," *Korunk,* n.s. 1, no. 12 (1957), 1634-1642.

55. Allgemeines Verwaltungsarchiv, Vienna, Ministerium des Innern, Pras. Z. 140.852: kurze Lebensskizze des Bischofs Schaguna.

56. George Bariţiu, *Părţi alese din istoria Transilvaniei,* 3 vols. (Sibiu, 1889-1891), I, 661-662; Zsolt Trócsányi, *Az erdélyi parasztság története, 1790-1849* (Budapest, 1956), 202-206.

57. OL, MCS, 1850/9322: report of the prefect of Zlatna, October 4, 1846; Nicolae Popea, *Memorialul Archiepiscopului şi Mitropolitului Andreiu baron de Şaguna sau luptele naţionale-politice ale Românilor, 1846-1873,* I (Sibiu, 1889), 14-15: Şaguna's report to Transylvanian Chancellor Samuel Jósika, October 7, 1846.

58. *Ibid.,* 9-10, 12-13.

59. *Ibid.,* 10-12, 13-17.

60. *Ibid.,* 24.

61. GTr, January 16, 1847.

62. Popea, *Memorialul,* 31-32: Şaguna's report to Teleki, January 20, 1847.

63. OL, EK, Acta generalia, 1848/2539.

64. OL, GT (in Politicis), 1847/290: Şaguna to the Gubernium, February 18, 1847.

65. PA, 1846/747: Şaguna to Rajačić, September 6, 1846.

66. Dragomir, "André Şaguna et Joseph Rajačić," 269 and 276: Şaguna to Rajačić, February 2/14 and June 3, 1847.

67. BARSR, Ms. rom., vol. 993: Nifon Bălăşescu to Bariţiu, November 9/21, 1847.

68. OL, EK, Acta generalia, 1845/7303: petition of Popasu, summarized in a report of the Gubernium to the chancellery, November 20, 1845; OL, GT (in Politicis), 1846/2710: Gubernium to the chancellery, February 24, 1846; [George Bariţiu], "Epistole de ale repausatilor," *Transilvania*, 8 (1877), 198: Georgie Pantazi to Bariţiu, January 3/15, 1848.

69. BARSR, Ms. rom., vol. 1000: Puşcariu to Bariţiu, December 11/23, 1847.

70. Pascu and Pervain, *Bariţ şi contemporanii săi*, II, 14: Vasici to Bariţiu, end of December 1847.

71. Dragomir, "André Şaguna et Joseph Rajačić," 277-278: Şaguna to Rajačić, October 5/17, 1847.

72. HHStA, Staatsratsakten, 3063/2920, 1847: proposal of the Transylvanian chancellor, June 9, 1847.

73. OL, EK, Acta generalia, 1847/3658.

74. Ioan Lupaş, "Vieaţa şi faptele Mitropolitului Andreiu Şaguna," in *Mitropolitul Andreiu baron de Şaguna: Scriere comemorativă la serbarea centenară a naşterii lui* (Sibiu, 1909), 61.

75. OL, EK, Acta generalia, 1846/6407: Transylvanian Chancellery to the Gubernium, December 10, 1846.

76. BARSR, Ms. rom., vol. 1000: Puşcariu to Bariţiu, August 29, 1847; *ibid.*, vol. 993: Bălăşescu to Bariţiu, January 18/30, 1847; Pascu and Pervain, *Barit si contemporanii săi*, II, 11: Vasici to Bariţiu, November 22, 1847.

77. *Ibid.*, II, 14: Vasici to Bariţiu, end of December 1847.

78. Şaguna himself describes the synod in his *Istoria bisericei ortodocse răsăritene universale* (2 vols., Sibiu, 1860), II, 203-209.

79. OL, EK, Acta generalia, 1848/725: HHStA, Staatsratsakten, 175/168, 1848; *ibid.*, 246/239, 1848: proposal of the Transylvanian chancellor, January 7, 1848.

80. Dragomir, "André Şaguna et Joseph Rajačić," 280: Şaguna to Rajačić, February 18, 1848.

81. Popea, *Archiepiscopul,* 40.

Chapter 2: Revolution

1. There is an abundant literature on the subject. Among the general works are: Dumitru Popovici, *La littérature roumaine à l'époque des lumières* (Sibiu, 1945), 185-263; Werner Bahner, *Das Sprach- und Geschichtsbewusstsein in der rumänischen Literatur von 1780-1880* (Berlin, Akademie Verlag, 1967), 14-48; Keith Hitchins, *The Rumanian National Movement in Transylvania, 1780-1849* (Cambridge, Mass., Harvard University Press, 1969), 58-111; and Dumitru Ghişe and Pompiliu Teodor, *Fragmentarium Iluminist* (Cluj, 1972), 5-212. Each contains extensive bibliographical references.

2. *Organul Luminării,* March 24, 1848; Alexandru Papiu-Ilarian, *Istoria Românilor din Dacia superioară* (2 vols., Vienna, 1852), II, 76-85.

3. GTr, March 15, 1848.

4. FM, April 12, 1848.

5. *Ibid.,* March 22, 1848.

6. The ideas of Alexandru Papiu-Ilarian, a lawyer at the High Court of Transyl-

vania in Tîrgu-Mureş, as he expressed them in an open letter, were typical: *ibid.,* March 29, 1848.

7. *Ibid.,* September 16 and 30, 1853. My translation.

8. Gheorghe Bogdan-Duică, "Viaţa şi ideile lui Simion Bărnuţiu," in Academia Română, *Studii şi Cercetări,* no. 8 (Bucharest, 1924), annex VI, 211; Papiu-Ilarian, *Istoria,* I, 245-246.

9. FM, March 2, 1842.

10. Victor Chereşteşiu, *Adunarea naţională de la Blaj* (Bucharest, 1966), 211-214.

11. Papiu-Ilarian, *Istoria,* II, 107-108.

12. Győző Ember, *Iratok az 1848-i magyarországi parasztmozgalmak történetéhez* (Budapest, 1951), 162, 210; Bariţiu, *Părţi alese,* II, 76; Trócsányi, *Az erdélyi parasztság,* 276-300.

13. Papiu-Ilarian, *Istoria,* II, 274-277; Elek Jakab, *Szabadságharczunk történetéhez visszaemlékezések 1848-1849-re* (Budapest, 1880), 110-111.

14. Papiu-Ilarian, *Istoria,* II, 145. Papiu-Ilarian was an eyewitness.

15. Allgemeines Verwaltungsarchiv, Ministerium des Innern, Pras. Z. 140.852: kurze Lebensskizze des Bischofs Schaguna; OL, GT (in Politicis), Praesidialia, 1848/693 and 838: Şaguna to Teleki, April 3 and 12, 1848.

16. *Ibid.,* 1848/1070: Şaguna to Teleki, April 26, 1848.

17. Popea, *Archiepiscopul,* 204.

18. *Memoriile Arhiepiscopului şi Mitropolitului Andrei Şaguna din anii 1846-1871* (Sibiu, 1923), 14.

19. Silviu Dragomir, *Studii şi documente privitoare la revoluţia Românilor din Transilvania în anii 1848-1849* (vols. 1-3, 5, Sibiu and Cluj, 1944-1946), V, 166.

20. GTr, May 6, 1848.

21. Simion Bărnuţiu, *Românii şi Ungurii: Discurs rostit în catedrala Blajului 2/14 maiu 1848,* ed. Gheorghe Bogdan-Duică (Cluj, 1924), 9, 31.

22. Chereşteşiu, *Adunarea,* 459-465. My translation.

23. Popea, *Archiepiscopul,* 210; Stephan Ludwig Roth, *Gesammelte Schriften und Briefe* (6 vols., Hermannstadt, 1927-1939), V, 301-307.

24. Tulbure, *Mitropolitul Şaguna,* 139-140.

25. Papiu-Ilarian, *Istoria,* II, 252.

26. Dragomir, *Studii,* II, 7-8.

27. Tulbure, *Mitropolitul Şaguna,* 393-394: letter dated May 29, 1848.

28. OL, EK, Acta generalia, 1848/7038: Şaguna to the Gubernium, May 31, 1848.

29. OL, GT (in Politicis), Praesidialia, 1848/1395: Georg Lázár to Teleki, May 23, 1848.

30. *Ibid.,* 1848/1847: Şaguna to Teleki, July 2, 1848.

31. Emilian Cioran, "Corespondenţa unui preot din anii 1848 şi 1856 şi fost duhovnic militar," *Revista Teologică,* 33 (1939), 6; Dragomir, *Studii,* III, 10-12: petition dated June 16, 1848.

32. *Ibid.,* 13; OL, GT (in Politicis), Praesidialia, 1848/1847: Şaguna to Teleki, July 2, 1848: Sterie Stinghe, *Documente privitoare la trecutul Românilor din Şchei* (4 vols., Braşov, 1901-1903), IV, 13-15: Ioan Bran to the church council of Şchei, May [June] 24, 1848.

33. Árpád Károlyi, *Az 1848-iki pozsonyi törvenycikkek az udvar előtt* (Budapest, 1936), 344, 345.

34. GTr, June 23, 1848.

35. ABM, Şaguna Collection: Şaguna to the Orthodox consistory, July 5, 1848; *ibid.:* two notes from Széchenyi to Şaguna, both dated July 11, 1848.

36. *Ibid.*: minutes of a conference held in Şaguna's residence in Pest, July 27, 1848.

37. *Ibid.*: Şaguna to the Protopope of Haţeg, August 15, 1848.

38. OL, Vallás és Közoktatásügyi Ministerium, Görög nem egyesült osztály: VKM to Şaguna, July 29, 1848.

39. Tulbure, *Mitropolitul Şaguna,* 145-146 and 147-148: pastoral letters of July 18 and August 16/28, 1848.

40. ABM, Şaguna Collection: Şaguna to the Rumanians of Sălişte, [1848], and to the Orthodox consistory, July 22, 1848.

41. GTr, August 2, 1848. My translation.

42. Silviu Dragomir, "Din corespondenţa dascălilor ardeleni în anul 1848," in *Omagiu lui I. Bianu* (Bucharest, 1927), 166-169; *Anul 1848 în principatele române* (6 vols., Bucharest, 1902-1910), III, 731; IV, 224, 229; [George Bariţiu], "Epistole de ale repausatiloru," *Transilvania,* 8 (1877), 173.

43. Ion Breazu, "Alecu Russo în Ardealul revoluţionar la 1848," *ibid.,* 72 (1941), 126. A strong case that the political union of all Rumanians was a serious goal of the forty-eighters is made by Cornelia C. Bodea, *The Romanians' Struggle for Unification 1834-1849* (Bucharest, 1970), 169-201.

44. Trócsányi, *Az erdélyi parasztság,* 346-347, 364-384.

45. ABM, Şaguna Collection: petition of the Rumanians of Sighişoara to Şaguna, July 1, 1848.

46. *Ibid.*: Orthodox consistory to Şaguna, August 10, 1848.

47. Ion Breazu, *Michelet şi Românii* (Cluj, 1935), 123.

48. ABM, Şaguna Collection: Orthodox consistory to Şaguna, July 17, 1848.

49. Popea, *Archiepiscopul,* 219-221.

50. János Beér, *Az 1848-49 évi népképviseleti Országgyűlés* (Budapest, 1954), 491, 501.

51. ABM, Şaguna Collection: Orthodox and Uniate protopopes of Mediaş to Şaguna, August (?) 1848; *ibid.,* Şaguna to Deák, August 8, 1848; Deák to Şaguna, August 11, 1848; Dragomir, *Studii,* II, 166-168: Şaguna to minister of justice, August 11, 1848.

52. Sándor Márki, "Az erdélyi unió-bizottság," *Budapesti Szemle,* 95 (1898), 335-336.

53. BARSR, Ms. rom., vol. 999: Dimitrie Moldovan to Bariţiu, February 14, 1861.

54. Jenő Horváth, "A magyar kormány nemzetiségi politikája 1848-49-ben," in *A Háborús Felelősség,* 2, no. 1-2 (1930), 24.

55. Beér, *Országgyűlés,* 583-585; Stinghe, *Documente,* IV, 28-29: Ioan Bran to the Rumanians of Braşov, September 26, 1848.

56. Dragomir, *Studii,* II, 432, 491; Sebestyén Szőcs, *A kormánybiztosi intézmény kialakulása 1848-ban* (Budapest, 1972), 167-168. Vay's mission to Transylvania and the worsening of relations between Hungarian authorities and the Rumanians is described by Szőcs, 144-169.

57. Márki, "Az erdélyi unió-bizottság," 353.

58. FM, September 27, 1848.

59. "The generals promise us everything": August Treboniu Laurian to Bariţiu, September 22/October 4, 1848, in Pascu and Pervain, *Bariţ şi contemporanii săi,* I, 150; BARSR, Ms. rom., vol. 993: Bălăşescu to Bariţiu, September 24/October 6, 1848; Stinghe, *Documente,* IV, 30-31: Laurian to Bran, October 14/26, 1848.

60. FM, October 18, 1848.

61. Dragomir, *Studii,* II, 191-192; Popea, *Memorialul,* 196-197.

62. *Ibid.,* 227-228.

63. *Ibid.,* 221.

64. *Ibid.,* 230-232.

65. FM, January 24, 1849.

66. Paul Müller, *Feldmarschall Fürst Windischgrätz. Revolution und Gegenrevolution in Österreich* (Vienna-Leipzig, 1934), 221, 223, 224; Erzsébet Andics, *A Habsburgok és Romanovok szövetsége* (Budapest, 1961), 102-106; Kenneth Rock, "Schwarzenberg versus Nicholas I, Round One: The Negotiation of the Habsburg-Romanov Alliance against Hungary in 1849," *Austrian History Yearbook,* 6-7 (1970-1971), 109-122.

67. Roza A. Averbukh, *Tsarskaia interventsiia v bor'be s vengerskoi revoliutsiei 1848-1849 gg.* (Moscow, 1935), 86; Popea, *Memorialul,* 235-236.

68. Bogdan-Duică, *Bărnuţiu,* 240-241.

69. Bariţiu, *Părţi alese,* II, 400-405.

70. Popea, *Memorialul,* 238-239: Şaguna's report to the Rumanian national committee, January 10, 1849; Imre Deák, *1848; ahogyan a kortársak látták* (Budapest, 1943), 294-295: Austrian consul in Bucharest to Schwarzenberg, January 9, 1849.

71. Teodor Balan, *Eudoxiu Hurmuzachi* (Cernăuţi, 1924), 20-21; József Thim, *A magyarországi 1848-49-i szerb fölkelés története* (3 vols., Budapest, 1935), III, 295-296.

72. Popea, *Memorialul,* 248-249.

73. Mihail Popescu, *Documente inedite privitoare la istoria Transilvaniei între 1848-1859* (Bucharest, 1929), 32-36.

74. *Ibid.,* 38-40, 42.

75. *Ibid.,* 44-45, 47.

76. Popea, *Memorialul,* 270-272, 276-278.

77. Popescu, *Documente,* 61-62.

78. HHStA, Kabinettsarchiv, Geheime Akten, Nachlass Schwarzenberg, box II, fasc. 5, no. 279: Şaguna to Schwarzenberg, April 23, 1849.

79. Lajos Steier, *A tót nemzetiségi kérdés 1848-49-ben* (2 vols., Budapest, 1937), II, 394-403.

80. Popescu, *Documente,* 66-68. Kossuth's policy toward the non-Magyar nationalities in the spring of 1849 is described by Zoltán Tóth, "Kossuth és a nemzetiségi kérdés 1848-1849-ben," in *Emlékkönyv Kossuth Lajos* (2 vols., Budapest, 1952), II, 325-339.

81. Silviu Dragomir, "Bălcescu în Ardeal," AIIN, 5 (1928-1930), 33-34.

Chapter 3: Absolutism

1. Popea, *Archiepiscopul,* 43.

2. Nicolae Bănescu, *Stareţul Neonil. Corespondenţa sa cu C. Hurmuzachi şi Andreiu Şaguna* (Vălenii-de-Munte, 1910), 93: Şaguna to Neonil, November 27, 1851.

3. Dragomir, *Studii,* I, 334.

4. The character of the absolutist period is discussed in Josef Redlich, *Das österreichische Staats- und Reichsproblem* (2 vols., Leipzig, 1920-1926), I, 382-459; Robert A. Kann, *Das Nationalitätenproblem der Habsburgermonarchie,* II (Graz-Köln, 1964), 70-95; and Eduard Winter, *Revolution, Neoabsolutismus und Liberalismus in der Donaumonarchie* (Vienna, 1969), 77-128.

5. Wohlgemuth's tenure as governor is discussed in Helmut Klima, "Guvernatorii Transilvaniei 1774-1867," AIIN, 9 (1943-1944), 284-294.

6. Ioan cavaler de Puşcariu, *Notiţe despre întâmplările contemporane* (Sibiu, 1913), 42.

7. Albert Berzeviczy, *Az abszolutizmus kora Magyarországon, 1849-1865* (2 vols., Budapest, 1922), I, 218-219; BARSR, Ms. rom., vol. 998: Grigore Mihali to Bariţiu, December 19, 1849.

8. Puşcariu, *Notiţe,* 40-42.

9. Gheorghe Bogdan-Duică, "1848/9 în Ţara Bârsei," *Ţara Bârsei,* 1 (1929), 195-196; Popescu, *Documente,* 228-229.

10. FM, February 1, 1851; Berzeviczy, *Az abszolutizmus kora,* I, 151-152; Dragomir, *Studii,* II, 131-132; BARSR, Ms. rom., vol. 993: Bălăşescu to Bariţiu, April 30/May 12, 1850.

11. Popescu, *Documente,* 86: letter to the emperor, July 27, 1849; Popea, *Memorialul,* 347: letter to Bach, July 30, 1849.

12. Ioan Bianu and G. Nicolaiasa, *Catalogul manuscriptelor româneşti,* III (Craiova, 1931), 461-463, 465, 466, 467; Bogdan-Duică, "1848/9 în Ţara Bârsei," 195-197; Henry Miller Madden, "The Diary of John Paget, 1849," *Slavonic and East European Review,* 19 (1939-1940), 261; P.P. Panaitescu, *Emigraţia polonă şi revoluţia română dela 1848* (Bucharest, 1929), 124: report of Polish agent Lenoir, December 7, 1849.

13. Pascu and Pervain, *Bariţ şi contemporanii săi,* I, 70-71: Aaron Florian to Bariţiu, December 29, 1849/January 10, 1850; FM, January 16 and 30, 1850.

14. *Ibid.,* December 26, 1849; Dragomir, *Studii,* I, xviii; Pascu and Pervain, *Bariţ şi contemporanii săi,* I, 161: A.T. Laurian to Bariţiu, January 4/16, 1850.

15. HHStA, Kabinettsarchiv, Geheime Akten, Nachlass Schwarzenberg, box 9, fasc. 2, no. 85: Wohlgemuth to Schwartzenberg, November 26, 1849; Popea, *Memorialul,,* 364; *Memoriile Şaguna 1846-1871,* 33.

16. Ştefan Manciulea, "Atestate de purificaţiune," *Cultura Creştină,* 18 (1938), 473-483.

17. GTr, December 8, 1849.

18. Popescu, *Documente,* 245, 255-259.

19. *Ibid.,* 176, 275-276; Dragomir, *Studii,* II, 137; Madden, "Diary of John Paget," 261; Nicolae Bălcescu, *Scrieri istorice,* notes and introduction by P.P. Panaitescu (Craiova, n.d.), 214: Bălcescu to Ion Ghica, October 22, 1849.

20. Pascu and Pervain, *Bariţ şi contemporanii săi,* I, 81: Florian to Bariţiu, September 14/26, 1850.

21. Gheorghe Bogdan-Duică, "Notes-ul de însemnări al lui Simeon Bărnuţiu, 1849-1863," AIIN, 2 (1923), 213-215; George Fotino, *Din vremea renaşterii naţionale a României. Boierii Goleşti* (4 vols., Bucharest, 1939), III, 37-38; Enea Hodoş, *Din corespondenţa lui Simion Bărnuţiu şi a contemporanilor săi* (Sibiu, 1944), 6. *Gazeta* reappeared on September 9, 1850, with Iacob Mureşanu as editor.

22. BARSR, Ms. rom., vol. 996, fall of 1850. My translation.

23. Simion Bărnuţiu, *Reporturile Romaniloru cu ungurii si principiele libertatei natiunali,* 2nd ed. (Vienna, 1852); Alexandru Papiu-Ilarian, *Istoria Românilor din Dacia superioară* (2 vols., Vienna, 1852).

24. Nicolae Albu, "Problema facultăţii juridice pentru români din Transilvania după revoluţia din 1848/49," *Studia Universitatis Babeş-Bolyai,* Series Historia, 1 (1968), 59-71; Vasile Curticăpeanu, *Mişcarea culturală românească pentru unirea din 1918* (Bucharest, 1968), 60-62; FM, August 2, 1851, and April 15, 1853.

25. Hodoş, *Din corespondenţa lui Simion Bărnuţiu,* 35: Papiu-Ilarian to Iosif Hodoş, November 10, 1852, quoting from a letter from Bărnuţiu.

26. FM, November 20, 1850.

27. Popea, *Memorialul,* 364; Barițiu, *Părți alese,* III, 556-557: Șaguna to Barițiu, January 4, 1850.

28. Andreiu Șaguna, *Compendium des kanonischen Rechtes der einen, heiligen, allgemeinen und apostolischen Kirche* (Hermannstadt, 1868), 284-285; Andreiu Șaguna, *Anthorismos, sau deslușire comparativă asupra broșurei "Dorințele dreptcredinciosului cler din Bucovina . . ."* (Sibiu, 1861), 6.

29. Șaguna, *Compendium,* 280-283.

30. Popea, *Memorialul,* 374-377: Șaguna's Christmas message, December 6, 1849; Popea, *Archiepiscopul,* 262.

31. ABM, Șaguna Collection: Șaguna to School Commissioner Heufler, July 1, 1850.

32. Popea, *Memorialul,* 364, 369-370; Lupas, "Vieața și faptele . . . Șaguna," 97-98 n. 1: Șaguna to Ioan Maiorescu, May 21, 1850; OL, MCS, 1850/21,162: Șaguna to Wohlgemuth, September 16, 1850.

33. *Ibid.,* 1850/17,759: Șaguna to Wohlgemuth, August 9, 1850; ABM, Șaguna Collection: Șaguna to Wohlgemuth, July 27, 1850.

34. Popea, *Memorialul,* 364-367.

35. ABM, Șaguna Collection, no. 180: Wohlgemuth to Șaguna, December 29, 1849.

36. Barițiu, *Părți alese,* II, 184-190.

37. ABM, Șaguna Collection.

38. *Ibid.,* Șaguna to Wohlgemuth, December 1/13, 1849; Wohlgemuth to Șaguna, December 22, 1849.

39. Pușcariu, *Notițe,* 48. The work was written by Pușcariu: *Comentariu la preinalta patenta din 21 iunie 1854,* vol. I (Sibiu, 1858).

40. ABM, Șaguna Collection: Șaguna to Mureșanu, no date [August 1850].

41. See chapters 9 and 10, below.

42. Pușcariu, *Notițe,* 42, 45-46.

43. Iosif Kovács, *Desființarea relațiilor feudale în Transilvania* (Cluj, 1973), 61-74.

44. Ludovic Vajda, "Cu privire la pătrunderea capitalului austriac în industria minieră și siderurgică a Transilvaniei între 1848 și 1867," *Studia Universitatis Babeș-Bolyai,* Series Historia, 2 (1965), 63-78, and "Începuturile revoluției industriale în mineritul și metalurgia din Transilvania," AIIC, 10 (1967), 173-195.

45. Tulbure, *Mitropolitul Șaguna,* 218-220: Șaguna's pastoral letter, April 20, 1859.

46. Popescu, *Documente,* 275-276, 281-284, 296, 304-309.

47. *Ibid.,* 181, 244-245, 248, 294.

48. Ștefan Pascu, "Ecoul unirii Țării Românești și Moldovei în Transilvania," in *Studii privind unirea principatelor,* ed. Andrei Oțetea (Bucharest, 1960), 455-459.

Chapter 4: A Change of System

1. *Verhandlungen des verstärkten Reichsrats* (Vienna, 1860), 42-43: Șaguna's speech, June 21, 1860.

2. *Ibid.,* 125 and 432: Șaguna's speeches of September 14 and 26, 1860.

3. *Ibid.,* 431.

4. "Din corespondența Baronului Vasile L. Pop," *Răvașul,* 8, no. 1-2 (1910), 1: Saguna to Pop, November 3/15, 1860. My translation.

5. *Verhandlugen des verstärkten Reichsrats,* 432.

6. See chapter 9, below.

7. Coriolan Suciu, *Corespondenţa lui Ioan Maniu cu Simeon Bărnuţiu* (*1851-1864*) (Blaj, 1929), 263: Maniu to Bărnuţiu, July 9, 1860: BARSR, Cluj, Arhiva Istorică, Blaj Collection, Fodor Archive: inhabitants of Haţeg to Şaguna, July 23, 1860; inhabitants of Hunedoara to Şaguna, August 5, 1860; *ibid.*, Miscellaneous papers: Rumanians of Sibiu to Şaguna, June 22, 1860.

8. Louis Eisenmann, *Le compromis austro-hongrois* (Paris, 1904), 207-259; Kann, *Nationalitätenproblem*, II, 107-114.

9. Redlich, *Das österreichische Staats- und Reichsproblem*, II, 233-238.

10. GTr, November 6, 1860.

11. *Ibid.*, November 1, 1860.

12. FM, January 4 and 11, 1861.

13. "Din corespondenţa Baronului Vasile L. Pop," pp. 1-2; Ilarion Puşcariu, *Documente pentru limbă şi istoriă* (2 vols., Sibiu, 1889-1897), I, 347-348.

14. BARSR, Ms. rom., vol. 992: Ioan Axente to Bariţiu, December 11, 1860.

15. Puşcariu, *Documente*, I, 349: Şuluţiu to Şaguna, December 11, 1860.

16. BARSR, Ms. rom., vol. 992: Axente to Bariţiu, December 23 and 27, 1860.

17. *Ibid.:* Axente to Bariţiu, December 11, 1860.

18. Puşcariu, *Documente*, I, 352-353.

19. OL, EK, Praesidialia, 1861/19: Eder to Governor Lichtenstein of Transylvania, January 9, 1861; 1861/54: Lichtenstein to Kemény, January 16, 1861.

20. Teodor V. Păcăţian, *Cartea de aur, sau luptele politice-naţionale ale Românilor de sub coroana ungară* (8 vols., Sibiu, 1904-1915), II, 193-217.

21. Popea, *Archiepiscopul*, 277-278.

22. FM, January 11, 1861.

23. Puşcariu, *Notiţe*, 52.

24. BARSR, Ms. rom., vol. 992: Axente to Bariţiu, January 26, 1861.

25. HHStA, Kabinettsarchiv, Kabinettskanzlei, 14c., 2184 and 2185, 1861.

26. GTr, January 11 and 14, 1861.

27. *Ibid.*, January 7, 1861.

28. Păcăţian, *Cartea de aur*, II, 225-260.

29. Miklós Mester, *Az autonom Erdély és a román nemzetiségi követelések az 1863-64-évi nagyszebeni országgyűlésen* (Budapest, 1936), 82-106; Lajos Ürmössy, *Tizenhét év Erdély történetéből* (2 vols., Temesvár, 1894), I, 256-265.

30. BARSR, Ms. rom., vol. 992: Axente to Bariţiu, February 15, 1861; Pascu and Pervain, *Bariţ şi contemporanii săi*, I, 57: Vasici to Bariţiu, February 7/19, 1861.

31. Popea, *Archiepiscopul*, 279.

32. Redlich, *Das österreichische Staats- und Reichsproblem*, II, 241-243 n.

Chapter 5: National Fulfillment

1. Bariţiu's activity between 1861 and 1864 is summarized in Vasile Netea, *George Bariţiu. Viaţa şi activitatea sa* (Bucharest, 1966), 247-260.

2. ABM, Şaguna Collection, no. 1683: Şaguna's notes on a petition drawn up at his home in Sibiu on March 22, 1861.

3. *Ibid.*, no. 1601: Şuluţiu to Şaguna, December 11, 1861; no. 1602: Şaguna to Şuluţiu, December 6, 1861 (old style).

4. *Ibid.*, no. 1580: Şaguna to Şuluţiu, November 4/16, 1861.

5. BARSR, Cluj, Arhiva Istorică: Fondul Blaj, Şuluţiu Archive: Moldovan to Şuluţiu, October 6, 1861.

6. ABM, Şaguna Collection, no. 1568: Şaguna to Ioan Alduleanu, October 16/28, 1861.

7. BARSR, Ms. rom., vol. 999: Moldovan to Barițiu, February 27, 1861; vol. 992: Axente to Barițiu, July 28, 1861; Suciu, *Corespondența Maniu-Bărnuțiu:* Ioan Maniu to Bărnuțiu, November 24, 1861.

8. BARSR, Cluj, Arhiva Istorică: Fondul Blaj, Șuluțiu Archive: Șuluțiu to Moldovan, January 12/24, 1862; FM, September 6, 1861: Șuluțiu to the governor of Transylvania, June 29, 1861; BARSR, Ms. rom., vol. 999: Moldovan to Barițiu, March 23, 1861.

9. Redlich, *Das österreichische Staats- und Reichsproblem*, II, 256-258.

10. Keith Hitchins and Liviu Maior, *Corespondența lui Ioan Rațiu cu George Barițiu 1861-1892* (Cluj, 1970), 45-46; Rațiu to Barițiu, June 25, 1861; HHStA, Kabinettskanzlei, K.Z. 2508.61 and K.Z. 3098.61: petitions of the Rumanians of Zarand County; Suciu, *Corespondența Maniu-Bărnuțiu*, 347-351, 357-360, 364-366: Maniu to Bărnuțiu, August 17, September 21, and October 23, 1861.

11. Hitchins and Maior, *Corespondența Rațiu-Barițiu*, 47-48: Rațiu to Barițiu, June 25, 1861; on the attitude of Magyar leaders, see: György Szabad, *Forradalom és kiegyezés válaszútján (1860-61)* (Budapest, 1967), 508-513, 547-555.

12. Hitchins and Maior, *Corespondența Rațiu-Barițiu*, 53: Rațiu to Barițiu, July 1, 1861.

13. *Ibid.*, 51.

14. *Ibid.*, 62-63, 69-70: Rațiu to Barițiu, July 15 and 30, 1861.

15. *Ibid.*, 61: Rațiu to Barițiu, July 12, 1861.

16. BARSR, Cluj, Arhiva Istorică, Fondul Blaj, Rațiu Correspondence: Rațiu, Măcelariu, and Bologa to Șaguna, July 15, 1861.

17. BARSR, Ms. rom., vol. 992: Axente to Barițiu, May 18 and June 11, 1861; FM, September 6 and 13, 1861.

18. BARSR, Cluj, Arhiva Istorică, Fondul Blaj, Fodor Archive: Georgiu Carean (?) to Fodor, June 24, 1861; HHStA, Kabinettskanzlei, K.Z. 1796.61: Kemény's proposal, June 4, 1861.

19. ABM, Șaguna Collection, no. 1539: Șaguna to Salmen, August 15/27, 1861.

20. *Aemtliche Actenstücke betreffend die Verhandlungen über die Union Siebenbürgens mit dem Königreiche Ungarn* (Hermannstadt, 1865), 143-145.

21. ABM, Șaguna Collection, no. 1559: Șuluțiu to Șaguna, October 12, 1861.

22. Pușcariu, *Notițe*, 60.

23. ABM, Șaguna Collection, no. 1571: the Rumanian community of Szász Reghin to Șaguna, November 1/13, 1861; no. 1577: Șuluțiu to Șaguna, November 12/24, 1861.

24. Barițiu, *Părți alese*, III, 518-519: Șuluțiu to Barițiu, November 13, 1861.

25. ABM, Șaguna Collection, no. 1569: Șuluțiu to Șaguna, October 29, 1861.

26. BARSR, Cluj, Arhiva Istorică, Fondul Blaj, Șuluțiu Archive: Șuluțiu to Moldovan, September 8/20, 1861.

27. ABM, Șaguna Collection, nos. 1577 and 1579: Șuluțiu to Șaguna, November 11 and 12/24, 1861; Arhivele Statului, Sibiu, Fondul Brukenthal, BB no. 19: "Denkschrift der zum nächsten siebenbürger Landtag einzuberufenden Regalisten."

28. ABM, Șaguna Collection, no. 1601: Șuluțiu to Șaguna, December 11, 1861.

29. *Ibid.*, no. 1602: Șaguna to Șuluțiu, December 6, 1861 (old style).

30. BARSR, Cluj, Arhiva Istorică, Fondul Blaj, Șuluțiu Archive: Moldovan to Șuluțiu, October 6, 1861.

31. *Ibid.:* Șuluțiu to Moldovan, January 12/24, 1862.

32. Suciu, *Corespondența Maniu-Bărnuțiu*, 383: Maniu to Bărnuțiu, December 7, 1861.

33. BARSR, Ms. rom., vol. 992: Barițiu to Axente, June 26, 1861. Vasile L. Pop,

vice-president of the Gubernium supported Barițiu. See ABM, Șaguna Collection, no. 2652: Pop to Șaguna, December 19/31, 1861.

34. Barițiu, *Părți alese*, III, 578-579: Șaguna to Barițiu, December 21, 1861; ABM, Șaguna Collection, no. 1675: Șuluțiu to Șaguna, December 15/27, 1861.

35. HHStA, Kabinettskanzlei, K.Z. 587/1863, M.R.Z. 1120.

36. BARSR, Cluj, Arhiva Istorică, Fondul Blaj, Moldovan Archive: Moldovan to Nadásdy, April 25, 1863.

37. HHStA, Kabinettsarchiv, Nachlass Reichenstein, box I: Barițiu to Franz Reichenstein, April 4, 1863.

38. BARSR, Cluj, Arhiva Istorică, Fondul Blaj, Moldovan Archive: Moldovan to Nadásdy, April 25, 1863.

39. *Protocolul Congresului natiunei romane din Ardeal* (Sibiu, 1863), 67-68, 72: Șaguna's speech on the opening day of the congress.

40. *Ibid.,* 93-94: Șaguna's speech at the second session of the congress, April 21.

41. Barițiu, *Părți alese,* III, 160; Hitchins and Maior, *Corespondența Rațiu-Barițiu,* 71-73: Rațiu to Barițiu, March 15 and 27, 1863.

42. *Protocolul Congresului,* 176.

43. *Wiener Zeitung,* May 6 and 7, 1863.

44. Simion Retegan, "Pregătirea dietei de la Sibiu din 1863-1864," AIIC, 12 (1969), 63-64.

45. *Ibid.,* 71-79; BARSR, Cluj, Arhiva Istorică, Fondul Blaj, Moldovan Archive: Ioan Papiu, protopope of Deva, to Moldovan, June 9, 1863; *ibid.,* Axente Archive: Axente to Moldovan, June 1, 1863.

46. ABM, Șaguna Collection, no. 1856: Șaguna to Nadásdy, June 2/14, 1863.

47. Barițiu, *Părți alese,* III, 181. For Șaguna's connection with *Telegraful Român,* see below, ch. 10.

48. ABM, Șaguna Collection, no. 1853: Ladai to Șaguna, June 8, 1863, and Șaguna to Ladai, June 12, 1863.

49. *Ibid.,* no. 1872: Șaguna to Nadásdy, July 5, 1863.

50. There are two general works on the diet: Valeriu Moldovan, *Dieta Ardealului din 1863-1864* (Cluj, 1932), and Mester, *Az autonom Erdély.*

51. Pușcariu, *Notițe,* 70-71.

52. Mester, *Az autonom Erdély,* 152-160.

53. Arhivele Statului, Sibiu, Fondul Brukenthal: BB no. 19.

54. BARSR, Cluj, Arhiva Istorică, Fondul Blaj, Moldovan Archive: Nadásdy to Moldovan, August 25 and September 7, 1863.

55. HHStA, Kabinettsarchiv, Nachlass Reichenstein, box I: Șaguna to Reichenstein, June 13, 1863.

56. *Ibid.:* Vasile L. Pop to Reichenstein, June 20, 1864.

57. *Ibid.,* box III: minutes of the Diet of Sibiu: Șaguna's speech at the seventh session (July 27, 1863), and at the 29th session (September 16, 1863).

58. Teodor V. Păcățian, *Cartea de aur, sau luptele politice-naționale ale Românilor de sub coroana ungară* (8 vols., Sibiu, 1904-1915), III, 632-633.

59. GTr, May 16/28, 1864; HHStA, Kabinettsarchiv, Nachlass Reichenstein: Gustav Groisz to Reichenstein, May 3, 1864.

60. Popea, *Archiepiscopul,* 295-296; HHStA, Kabinettsarchiv, Nachlass Reichenstein: Vasile L. Pop to Reichenstein, June 20, 1864; Barițiu, *Părți alese,* III, 260-261.

61. Simion Retegan, "Problema agrară în desbaterile dietei de la Sibiu," AIIC, 11 (1968), 286-289.

Chapter 6: The Great Compromise

1. GTr, June 26/July 8 and June 30/July 12, 1865; HHStA, Kabinettsarchiv, Nachlass Reichenstein, box I: Şaguna to Franz Reichenstein, July 10, 1865.

2. Redlich, *Das österreichische Staats- und Reichsproblem*, II, 410-411.

3. Barițiu, *Părți alese*, III, 314-315; Pușcariu, *Notițe*, 85-86.

4. Hitchins and Maior, *Corespondența Rațiu-Barițiu*, 79: Rațiu to Barițiu, September 15, 1865.

5. *Ibid.*, 79-80 and 84-85: Rațiu to Barițiu, September 15 and 27, 1865; GTr, September 18/30, 1865.

6. Hitchins and Maior, *Corespondența Rațiu-Barițiu*, 79-80: Rațiu to Barițiu, September 15, 1865; BARSR, Ms. rom., vol. 994: Cipariu to Barițiu. October 3/15, 1865; GTr, October 20/November 1, October 30/November 11, November 10/22, and November 13/25, 1865.

7. BARSR, Cluj, Arhiva Istorică, Şuluțiu Archive: Barițiu to Şuluțiu, October 14, 1865. At the end of Barițiu's letter, in another handwriting, is a list entitled: "The Grounds for a General Abstention from the Elections in 1865"; Hitchins and Maior, *Corespondența Rațiu-Barițiu*, 84: Rațiu to Barițiu, September 27, 1865.

8. *Ibid.*, 88-89 and 91: Rațiu to Barițiu, November 1 and 16, 1865.

9. OL, EK, Praesidialia, 1865/7255 and 884: Crenneville to Haller, October 30 and November 8, 1865; 1865/1182: Transylvanian Gubernium to Transylvanian Chancellery, October 18, 1865; 1865/846: Gustav Groisz, vice-president of the Gubernium, to Haller, October 21, 1865, enclosing a German translation of the Rumanian proclamation; 1865/799: Crenneville to Şuluțiu, n.d. [October 1865]; GTr, October 2/14, 1865.

10. BARSR, Cluj, Arhiva Istorică, Pamfilie Archive: Simeon _____ (?) to Pamfilie, September 24, 1865; Andreiu Şaguna, *Scrisori apologetice* (Sibiu, 1867), 2: Şaguna to Şuluțiu, September 11/23, 1865.

11. See chapter 8, below.

12. Hitchins and Maior, *Corespondența Rațiu-Barițiu*, 86-87 and 90: Rațiu to Barițiu, October 11 and November 10, 1865.

13. BARSR, Cluj, Arhiva Istorică, Şuluțiu Archive: Barițiu to Şuluțiu, October 14, 1865: "The Grounds for a General Abstention from the Elections in 1865."

14. Hitchins and Maior, *Corespondența Rațiu-Barițiu*, 86 and 88: Rațiu to Barițiu, September 30 and November 1, 1865.

15. *Ibid.*, 89-93: Rațiu to Barițiu, November 10 and 16, 1865.

16. *Ibid.*, 93-94 and 95-96: Rațiu to Barițiu, November 21 and 26, 1865.

17. Păcățian, *Cartea de aur*, III, 790-792. The final text of the Rumanian memorandum, dated December 9, 1865, is published in *Aemtliche Actenstücke, Fortsetzung*, 214-219.

18. *Ibid.*, 240-242; Barițiu, *Părți alese*, III, 347-348.

19. Păcățian, *Cartea de aur*, IV, 5, 6-7, 9; GTr, March 2/14 and March 5/17, 1866.

20. TR, February 10/22, 1866.

21. *Ibid.*, January 16/28 and January 20/February 1, 1866.

22. *Ibid.*, January 16/28 and February 24/March 8, 1866.

23. *Ibid.*, January 27/February 8, 1866.

24. GTr, January 12/24, 1866.

25. Păcățian, *Cartea de aur*, IV, 17-18.

26. Barițiu, *Părți alese,* III, 383-388; GTr, July 13/25 and July 16/28, 1866.

27. BARSR, Cluj, Arhiva Istorică, Barițiu Archive: President of the Transylvanian Gubernium to Barițiu, August 14, 1866; OL, EK, Praesidialia, 1866/657: Crenneville to Haller, July 22, 1866.

28. *Ibid.,* 1866/867: report of Haller to the emperor, August 4, 1866. Francis Joseph approved the recommendation on August 7.

29. *Ibid.,* 1866/1609: György Pogány, prefect of Alsófehér County to the Transylvanian Gubernium, August 29, 1866.

30. *Ibid.,* 1866/789: Gustav Groisz to Haller, undated [beginning of September 1866]; Hitchins and Maior, *Corespondența Rațiu-Barițiu,* 107-109: Rațiu to Barițiu, August 31, 1866.

31. *Ibid.,* 109.

32. Șaguna, *Scrisori apologetice,* 6 and 45-46: Șaguna to Șuluțiu, October 20/November 1, 1866, and February 1, 1867; Teodor Scorobeț, "Mitropolitul Ioan Mețianu, 1828-1916," *Revista Teologică,* 31, no. 3-4 (1941), 184-185: Șaguna to Mețianu, October 28, 1866.

33. Hitchins and Maior, *Corespondența Rațiu-Barițiu,* 110: Rațiu to Barițiu, September 2, 1866.

34. *Ibid.,* 117: Rațiu to Barițiu, October 7, 1866; BARSR, Cluj, Arhiva Istorică, Suluțiu Archive: Barițiu to Șuluțiu, October 16, 1866.

35. ABM, Șaguna Collection, no. 2256: Șaguna to Crenneville, November 6, 1866; OL, EK, Praesidialia, 1866/909: Crenneville to Haller, November 21, 1866.

36. Hitchins and Maior, *Corespondența Rațiu-Barițiu,* 121-122: Rațiu to Barițiu, October 25, 1866.

37. Șaguna, *Scrisori apologetice,* 51-52: Șaguna to Șuluțiu, February 1, 1867; Scorobeț, "Mitropolitul Ioan Mețianu," 183: Șaguna to Mețianu, October 11, 1866.

38. BARSR, Cluj, Arhiva Istorică, Șuluțiu Archive: Șuluțiu to Șaguna, October 11/23, 1866.

39. Șaguna, *Scrisori apologetice,* 6-10: Șaguna to Șuluțiu, October 20/November 1, 1866.

40. Hitchins and Maior, *Corespondența Rațiu-Barițiu,* 125-126: Rațiu to Barițiu, December 9, 1866.

41. Ilarion Pușcariu, "Câteva epistole dintre celece se păstrează dela arhiepiscopul-mitropolit Andreiu baron de Șaguna," in *Mitropolitul Andreiu baron de Șaguna. Scriere comemorativă la serbarea centenară a nașterii lui* (Sibiu, 1909), 506: Șaguna to Jacob Rannicher, December 22, 1866.

42. TR, December 4/16, 1866, and January 26/February 7, 1867.

43. OL, EK, Praesidialia, 1866/1168: Crenneville to Haller, November 13, 1866; 1866/3562: Austrian Foreign Ministry (?) to Haller, September 11, 1866; 1866/1040: Polizei Ministerium to Haller, September 16, 1866.

44. *Ibid.,* 1866/896 and 1168: Crenneville to Șuluțiu, and Haller to Crenneville, November 15, 1866.

45. Hitchins and Maior, *Corespondența Rațiu-Barițiu,* 134-135: Rațiu to Barițiu, December 31, 1866.

46. *Ibid.,* 136-138: Rațiu to Barițiu, January 2, 1867.

47. HHStA, Kabinettskanzlei, 593/1867: Vortrag des siebenbürgischen Hofkanzlei, February 9, 1867.

48. BARSR, Cluj, Arhiva Istorică, Rațiu Archive: telegram from the "Rumanian intelligentsia" of Turda to Barițiu, May 22, 1867; Barițiu, *Părți alese,* III, 408.

49. Hitchins and Maior, *Corespondența Rațiu-Barițiu,* 149: Rațiu to Barițiu, May 18, 1867.

50. BARSR, Ms. rom., vol. 993: Bologa to Barițiu, March 19, 1867.

51. Pușcariu, *Notițe,* 111-113.

52. Hitchins and Maior, *Corespondența Rațiu-Barițiu,* 165: Rațiu to Barițiu, December 22, 1867.

53. "Protocolu Adunarei generale a Asociatiunei transilvane . . . in Clusiu la 26-28 Aug. 1867," in *Transilvania,* 1 (1868), 1-2.

54. Hitchins and Maior, *Corespondența Rațiu-Barițiu,* 171-172: Rațiu to Barițiu, January 29, 1868.

55. The best account is Simion Retegan, "Pronunciamentul de la Blaj (1868)," AIIC, 9 (1966), 127-142.

56. Hitchins and Maior, *Corespondența Rațiu-Barițiu,* 179-180: Rațiu to Barițiu, May 7, 1868.

57. Păcățian, *Cartea de aur,* IV, 354-356.

58. Hitchins and Maior, *Corespondența Rațiu-Barițiu,* 183-184, 188, 192: Rațiu to Barițiu, July 14, July 20, and November 4, 1868.

59. Gábor G. Kemény, *Iratok a nemzetiségi kérdés történetéhez Magyarországon a dualizmus korában,* I (1867-1892) (Budapest, 1952), 129-162.

60. Hitchins and Maior, *Corespondența Rațiu-Barițiu,* 198: Rațiu to Barițiu, January 24, 1869; Vasile Netea, *Noi contribuții la cunoașterea vieții și activitătii lui Visarion Roman* (Sibiu, 1942), 15 and 17: Roman to Barițiu, February 15/28 and March 2, 1869.

61. Păcățian, *Cartea de aur,* V, 6-7, 8-11, 16-25; Netea, *Noi contributii,* 9: Roman to Barițiu, February 17, 1869.

62. BARSR, Cluj, Arhiva Istorică, Antonelli Archive: Mețianu to Antonelli, February 4/16 and 15/27, 1869.

63. The most recent account is Bujor Surdu, "Conferința națională de la Mercurea (1869)," AICC, 8 (1965), 173-211.

64. TR, February 27/March 11, 1869.

65. Păcățian, *Cartea de aur,* V, 83-85, 87, 91.

66. TR, January 23/February 4 and January 30/February 11, 1869. See also *ibid.,* December 29, 1868/January 10, 1869, and February 6/18, 1869.

67. Netea, *Noi Contribuții,* 24: Roman to Barițiu, n.d.

68. BARSR, Cluj, Arhiva Istorică, Antonelli Archive: Mețianu to Antonelli, March 24 and 28, 1869.

Chapter 7: Orthodoxy, Serbs, and Uniates

1. See chapter 8, below.

2. Popea, *Archiepiscopul,* 38.

3. Ilarion Pușcariu, *Metropolia Românilor ortodocsi din Ungaria si Transilvania* (Sibiu, 1900), Annex, 12, 17-18, 38-39; Popea, *Memorialul,* 356-357.

4. Andreiu Șaguna, *Promemoria über das historische Recht der nationalen Kirchen-Autonomie der Romanen morgenländ. Kirche in den k.k. Kronländern der österreich. Monarchie* (Vienna, 1849).

5. Șaguna's efforts to restore the metropolis are described in: Mircea Păcurariu, "100 de ani de la reînființarea Mitropoliei Ardealului," *Mitropolia Ardealului,* 9, no. 11-12 (1964), 814-840; and Keith Hitchins, "Andreiu Șaguna and the Restoration of the Rumanian Orthodox Metropolis in Transylvania, 1846-1868," *Balkan Studies,* 6 (1965), 1-20.

6. Pușcariu, *Metropolia,* Annex, 70-71: Șaguna to Rajačić, July 27, 1850.

7. *Actele soboarelor bisericei greco-răsăritene din Ardeal din anii 1850 și 1860*

(Sibiu, 1860), 38-41. Popea, *Memorialul,* 385-389: Puşcariu, *Metropolia,* 114.

8. Andreiu Şaguna, "Tagebuch über die bischöflichen Berathungen in Wien," in Puşcariu, *Documente,* I, 292-294.

9. Puşcariu, *Metropolia,* Annex, 88-97.

10. *Antwort auf die Angriffe einiger Romanen und der Presse gegen die Einheit der Hierarchie der morgenländischen catholischen orthodoxen Kirche* (Vienna, 1851). The author was Nikanor Gruić, but Rajačić paid for the publication. See Ioan Lupaş, *Mitropolitul Andreiu Şaguna,* 2nd ed. (Sibiu, 1911), 101-103; Popea, *Archiepiscopul,* 129-132; Dragomir, "André Şaguna et Joseph Rajačić," 264.

11. *Memoriile Şaguna 1846-1871,* 56.

12. ABM, Şaguna Collection, no. 2544: Şaguna to Rajačić, November 24, 1851.

13. *Ibid.,* no. 2532: consistory of Timişoara to consistory of Sibiu, January 17, 1852; no. 2533: Şaguna to consistory of Timişoara, February 7, 1852.

14. Puşcariu, *Metropolia,* Annex, 102-107.

15. ABM, Şaguna Collection, nos. 2573, 2578, 2591: Şaguna to Rajačić, December 30, 1856, March 26 and November 13, 1857.

16. *Ibid.,* no. 2579: Rajačić to Şaguna, April 16, 1857; no. 2591: Şaguna to Rajačić, November 13, 1857.

17. *Ibid.,* nos. 955 and 2547: Şaguna to Rajačić, January 12 and May 18, 1854; Popea, *Archiepiscopul,* 103-109.

18. ABM, Şaguna Collection, nos. 2573 and 2569: Şaguna to Rajačić, October 17, 1856, and undated (probably the end of 1855 or the beginning of 1856).

19. *Ibid.,* no 2550: Şaguna to Rajačić, March 1, 1854; no. 2554: Şaguna to the bishop of Vršac, January 8, 1855; no. 2555: Şaguna to the bishop of Timişoara, January 9, 1855.

20. Tulbure, *Mitropolitul Şaguna,* 195-201.

21. A recent study of Serbian support for the Orthodox of Transylvania is Aurel Jivi, "Relaţiile Mitropoliei din Carloviţ cu Biserica Ortodoxă Română din Transilvania în secolul al XVIII-lea," *Biserica Ortodoxă Română,* 88, no. 5-6 (1970), 587-596. See also Silviu Dragomir, *Istoria desrobirei religioase a Românilor din Ardeal în secolul XVIII* (2 vols., Sibiu, 1920-1930), I, 207-217; II, 15-31.

22. ABM, Şaguna Collection, no. 2578: Şaguna to Rajačić, March 26, 1857; *ibid.,* no. 2570: Şaguna to Samuil Maširević, March 6, 1856.

23. Şaguna, "Tagebuch," 331.

24. HHStA, Kabinettskanzlei, Minister Conferenz Kanzlei, K.Z. 2800.60, M.C.Z. 578.

25. *Ibid.,* Unterrichtsministerium, Prot. 6067: telegram from Joseph Philippovics, the emperor's representative at the synod of bishops, to Francis Joseph's adjutant, August 26, 1864.

26. *Istoria bisericii romîne,* II, 452-461.

27. Puşcariu, *Metropolia,* Annex, 225. The declaration was dated August 1, 1864.

28. Nicolae Tincu-Velia, *Istorioara bisericească politico-naţională a Românilor peste tot, mai ales a celor ortodocşi orientale din Austria* (Sibiu, 1865), x, xiii.

29. Puşcariu, *Metropolia,* Annex, 247: Babeş to Şaguna, no date, but clearly during or immediately after the synod of bishops.

30. Ion Mateiu, *Contribuţiuni la istoria dreptului bisericesc. Vol. I: Epoca de la 1848-1868* (Bucharest, 1922), 106.

31. Şaguna's relations with the Banaters in 1862, which appear to have been deci-

sive, are described in Teodor Botiș, *Monografia Familiei Mocioni* (Bucharest, 1939), 62, 67-71.

32. These questions are dealt with in I.D. Suciu, *Nicolae Tincu Velia (1816-1867). Viața și opera lui* (Bucharest, 1945), 146-162, 331-396.

33. Pușcariu, "Câteva epistole," 489: Șaguna to Jacob Rannicher, March 2, 1865.

34. Patriarchal-Metropolitan Archive "B", Sremski Karlovci, no. 16: petition of the Rumanian delegation to Philippovics, March 6, 1865.

35. Pușcariu, *Metropolia,* Annex, 342: Șaguna's statement to the Rumanian delegation at Carlovitz, March 17, 1865; Patriarchal-Metropolitan Archive "B", Sremski Karlovci, no. 34 (1864), no. 10 (1865); Pușcariu, *Metropolia,* Annex, 332: protocol of conferences of the Rumanian delegation in Carlovitz, March 17-20, 1865.

36. Patriarchal-Metropolitan Archive "A", Sremski Karlovci, no. 486, September 8, 1871; no. 542, October 6, 1871.

37. ABM, Șaguna Collection, no. 2648: Șaguna to George Hurmuzachi, January 4, 1862; Șaguna, *Anthorismos,* 6-7, 22-32.

38. HHStA, Unterrichtsministerium, Prot. No. 6615/1864: Philippovics to Schmerling, September 19, 1864, on the conversations between Șaguna and Hacman at the synod of bishops in Carlovitz.

39. ABM, Șaguna Collection, no. 1453: Șaguna to Hacman, October 6, 1860.

40. Erich Prokopowitsch, *Die rumänische Nationalbewegung in der Bukowina und der Dako-Romanismus* (Graz-Köln, 1965), 39-45.

41. Ion Nistor, *Istoria bisericii din Bucovina* (Bucharest, 1916), 83.

42. Pușcariu, *Metropolia,* Annex, 42: Hacman to Rajačić, July 6, 1849.

43. *Ibid.,* 187-188: Hacman to Șaguna, June 22, 1861; 252: Hacman's statement to the synod of bishops at Carlovitz, September 14, 1864.

44. Eugen Hacman, *Nationale und kirchliche Bestrebungen der Rumänen in der Bukowina 1848-1865,* 199, cited by Ion Nistor, *Românii și rutenii în Bucovina* (Bucharest, 1915), 152.

45. Nistor, *Istoria bisericii,* 79-80.

46. ABM, Șaguna Collection, no. 309: Șaguna to the Cultusministerium, August 3, 1850.

47. *Ibid.,* no. 2641: Șaguna to Professor Karl Kuzmany of the Evangelical Theological Faculty in Vienna, April 17, 1858.

48. *Ibid.,* no. 767: Governor Karl Schwarzenberg to Șaguna, June 4, 1852; Allgemeines Verwaltungsarchiv, Oberste Polizeibehörde, Präsidium II, 1018/1856: Governor Schwarzenberg to the Oberste Polizeibehörde in Vienna, January 29, 1856.

49. Pușcariu, *Metropolia,* Annex, 148-149: Șaguna to Emperor Francis Joseph, December 1, 1855; Popea, *Vechia Metropolia,* 167-169.

50. ABM, Șaguna Collection, no. 356: Șaguna to Eduard Bach, October 21, 1850.

51. *Memoriile Șaguna 1846-1871,* 53-54.

52. ABM, Șaguna Collection, no. 406: Șaguna to Leo Thun, January 25, 1851; OL, MCS, fasc. 32/173-20, 288/1852, 31/84-19,590/1852, 32/191-22,913/1852: Șaguna to the Transylvanian Gubernium, September 4 and 16, 1852, and October 15, 1852.

53. Pușcariu, *Metropolia,* 75.

54. *Memoriile Șaguna 1846-1871,* 53.

55. Tulbure, *Mitropolitul Șaguna,* 427-428: Șaguna's circular letter to his clergy, June 13, 1857; Arhiva Mitropoliei, Sibiu: Șaguna to Wohlgemuth, June 12, 1850; Șa-

guna to his protopopes, December 22, 1849.

56. *Ibid.:* Şaguna to Orthodox protopope Petru Pipoş, December 18, 1853.

57. Tulbure, *Mitropolitul Şaguna,* 410-411, 434-435: Şaguna's circular letters to his clergy, December 4, 1852, and October 16, 1858: OL, MCS, fasc. 32/182-21,019/ 1852.

58. Lupaş, "Vieaţa şi faptele Şaguna," 136 n.3: Aaron Florian to Ioan Maiorescu, July 3, 1852.

59. Hodoş, *Din corespondenţa lui Simion Bărnuţiu,* 52-53: Liviu Andrei Pop to Iosif Hodoş, February 24, 1855; Allgemeines Verwaltungsarchiv, Oberste Polizeibehörde, Präsidium II, 4282/1856, July 13, 1856.

60. ABM, Şaguna Collection, no. 1506: Şaguna to Şuluţiu, May 20, 1861.

61. *Ibid.,* no. 1578: Şaguna to Şuluţiu, November 16, 1861.

Chapter 8: Secularism

1. The text of the petition has been published and analyzed by Ladislau Gyémánt, "Memoriul Românilor ardeleni din anul 1834," *Anuarul Institutului de Istorie şi Arheologie Cluj-Napoca,* 17 (1974), 98-117.

2. Prodan, *Supplex,* 421-424; *Organul Luminării,* December 6 and 13, 1847; FM, October 27 and November 3, 1840.

3. Ladislau Gyémánt, "Acţiuni petiţionare ale Românilor din Transilvania în perioada 1834-1838," *Studia Universitatis Babeş-Bolyai,* Series Historia, fasc. 2 (1971), 30-51.

4. Zoltán Tóth, *Az erdélyi és magyarországi román nemzeti mozgalom (1790-1848)* (Budapest, 1959), 69.

5. "Petitiunea din 1846," *Transilvania,* 9 (1878), 278.

6. Bariţiu, *Părţi alese,* II, 70-71.

7. GTr, November 12, 1838, and December 7, 14, and 21, 1842; Tóth, *Az erdélyi és magyarországi,* 57.

8. Dragomir, *Studii,* II, 144-160.

9. Bariţiu, *Părţi alese,* III, 27, 60.

10. Pompiliu Teodor, "Ideologia revoluţiei din 1848 şi opera istorică a lui Samuil Micu," *Studia Universitatis Babeş-Bolyai,* Series Historia, fasc. 2 (1965), 57-62.

11. BARSR, Ms. rom., vol. 1001: Ioan V. Rusu to Bariţiu, June 26, 1839.

12. Bariţiu, *Părţi alese,* I, 632.

13. George E. Marica et al., *Ideologia generaţiei române de la 1848 din Transilvania* (Bucharest, 1968), 233-235.

14. For a lucid discussion of the influence of Western philosophy on the thought of the intellectuals, see *ibid.,* 50-77.

15. Dumitru Ghişe and Pompiliu Teodor, "Contribuţii la cunoaşterea activităţii filozofice a lui Simion Bărnuţiu," *Revistă de Filozofie,* 11, no. 3 (1964), 362-363.

16. Avram Andea, *"Libertate şi proprietate* în concepţia lui Simeon Bărnuţiu," *Studia Universitatis Babeş-Bolyai,* Series Historia, 1 (1973), 33-51.

17. Radu Pantazi, *Simion Bărnuţiu. Opera şi gîndirea* (Bucharest, 1967), 161-162.

18. Coriolan Suciu, "Preambule la procesul Lemenian," *Cultura Creştină,* 27 (1938), 640-643, 646-647.

19. FM, October 1, 8, and 15, 1839, and July 30 and August 6, 1845.

20. BARSR, Ms. rom., vol. 992: C. Alpini to Bariţiu, June 17, 1844; GTr, January 24, 1846.

21. *Ibid.,* April 3, 1844; FM, April 1, 1846.

22. *Ibid.*, January 25 and February 1, 1843.

23. BARSR, Ms. rom., vol. 933: Nifon Bălășescu to Barițiu, November 3/15, 1847; vol. 1000: Ioan Pușcariu to Barițiu, December 11/23, 1847.

24. Papiu-Ilarian, *Istoria,* I, 97-98; Aurel A. Mureșanu, *Simion Bărnuțiu în preajma marei adunări naționale a Românilor din Ardeal și Ungaria din 3/15 Mai 1848* (Sibiu, 1921), 14-15: Bărnuțiu to Mureșanu, April 7, 1848.

25. BARSR, Ms. rom., vol. 993: Bălășescu to Barițiu, January 3/15, 1847.

26. The most complete account is in Coriolan Suciu, *Crâmpeie din procesul dintre profesorii dela Blaj și episcopul Lemeni (1843-1846)* (Blaj, 1938).

27. Bogdan-Duică, *Bărnuțiu,* 191-195: an article entitled "The Condition of the Schools of Blaj," published in *Vasárnapi Újság* (Kolozsvár), December 4, 1842.

28. Onisifor Ghibu, *Din istoria literaturii didactice românești* (Bucharest, 1975), 51-87, 106-109; FM, December 4 and 11, 1844.

29. G. Baricz [Barițiu], *Cuvântare scolasticească la ecsamenul de vară în școala românească din Brașov în cetate* (Brașov, 1837), 26-27; see also GTr, August 4, 1847.

30. Ion Breazu, "Lamennais la Românii din Transilvania în 1848," *Studii Literare,* 4 (1948), 183-190.

31. GTr, October 14 and 24, 1846.

32. August T. Laurian demanded "religious independence" and an end to the "union with the Hungarian Catholics": Pascu and Pervain, *Barit și contemporanii săi,* I, 145: Laurian to Barițiu, April 8, 1848; see also Dragomir, "Din corespondența," 156-157: Laurian to Bălășescu, April 5, 1848; Bărnuțiu, *Românii și Ungurii,* 20-21.

33. Papiu-Ilarian, *Istoria,* II, 193-194, 210; Bărnuțiu, *Românii și Ungurii,* 43.

34. Popea, *Memorialul,* 77-79.

35. Bărnuțiu, *Românii și Ungurii,* 23, 43.

36. Papiu-Ilarian, *Istoria,* II, 246-249; Cherestesiu, *Adunarea,* 459-469.

37. Vasile Pârvan, "Anul 1850 și studenții români din Viena," *Luceafărul,* 2, no. 5 (1903), 91; BARSR, Ms. rom. 2242: Ioan Rațiu to Papiu-Ilarian, January 9, 1853.

38. ABM, Șaguna Collection, no. 135: Șaguna to a young priest, Saint Dumitru's Day, 1850.

39. Pușcariu, *Documente,* I, 369-370: Șaguna to Emanuil Gojdu, May 11, 1861.

40. ABM, Șaguna Collection: Șaguna to the Austrian ministry of the interior, November 16, 1850.

41. Șaguna, *Compendium,* xii; Popea, *Archiepiscopul,* 262.

42. Tulbure, *Mitropolitul Șaguna,* 325-328: Șaguna's circular letter, August 26, 1862; ABM, Șaguna Collection, no. 533: Șaguna to Thun, April 9, 1851.

43. Tulbure, *Mitropolitul Șaguna,* 263: Șaguna's circular letter, September 7, 1853; Popea, *Archiepiscopul,* 316; *Memoriile Șaguna 1846-1871,* 67.

44. Tulbure, *Mitropolitul Șaguna,* 254 and 265-266: circular letters, April 24, 1852, and September 7, 1853.

45. Șaguna, *Compendium,* x-xi.

46. *Verhandlungen des verstärkten Reichsrats,* 42: Șaguna's speech, September 21, 1860.

47. Pușcariu, *Documente,* I, 369.

48. *Ibid.*, 378; Andreiu Șaguna, *Manual de studiul pastoral* (Sibiu, 1872), 16-17.

49. ABM, Șaguna Collection, no. 1776: Șaguna to Protopope Nicolae Crainic, October 27, 1862.

50. Păcățian, *Cartea de aur,* II, 624-627, 629-631.

51. ABM, Șaguna Collection, no. 1500: Șaguna to Mikó, May 21, 1861.

52. Mateiu, *Contribuțiuni,* 257-258.

53. *Ibid.*, 207-235; Şaguna, *Anthorismos*, 101-104, 122-123.

54. Cristea's career is described in Keith Hitchins, *Studii privind istoria modernă a Transilvaniei* (Cluj, 1970), 117-166.

55. ABM, Şaguna Collection: petition of Rumanian leaders to the emperor, December 30, 1850; GTr, November 8, 1860: the national program of twenty-five points advocated by the Rumanians of Braşov; Pascu and Pervain, *Bariţ şi contemporanii săi*, II, 103: Vasici to Bariţiu, April 25, 1864.

56. ABM, Şaguna Collection, no. 844: Şaguna to another Orthodox bishop, January 12, 1853.

57. BARSR, Ms. rom., vol. 992: Axente to Bariţiu, October 12 and 25, 1861.

58. GTr, November 1 and 22, 1860; Hitchins and Maior, *Corespondenţa Raţiu-Bariţiu*, 73 and 74-75: Raţiu to Bariţiu, March 27 and June 17, 1863.

59. Pascu and Pervain, *Bariţ şi contemporanii săi*, II, 85.

60. FM, November 18 and 25, 1861; Ioan Colan, "O scrisoare a lui Papiu-Ilarian," *Ţara Bârsei*, 3, no. 4 (1931), 375.

61. BARSR, Cluj, Arhiva Istorică, Bariţiu Archive: petition of the inhabitants of Silvaş de cîmpie, May 15, 1867.

62. ABM, Şaguna Collection, no. 1120: Şaguna to Metropolitan Nifon of Wallachia, February 23, 1856.

63. Mateiu, *Contribuţiuni*, 246-263.

64. BARSR, Cluj, Arhiva Istorică, Moldovan Archive, Correspondence: Demetrie Dosanie (?) to Moldovan, April 11, 1869; Cipariu Archive, no. 11, f. 229: Alexandru Roman to Cipariu, October 29, 1867.

65. Hitchins and Maior, *Corespondenţa Raţiu-Bariţiu*, 187 and 189: Raţiu to Bariţiu, July 20 and August 1, 1868.

66. *Ibid.*, 185: Raţiu to Bariţiu, July 14, 1868.

67. *Actele sinodului archidiecesei greco-catolice de Alba Iulia-Făgăraş ţinut în 10-11 August 1868* (Blaj, 1869), 31-42, 52-55.

68. *Actele conferenţei ţienute de românii gr.-catolici dein provincia metropolitană de Alba Iulia la Alba Iulia în 13-14 Aprile 1871* (Blaj, 1871), 18-21.

69. *Ibid.*, 30, 33-34.

70. GTr, March 27/April 8 and April 21/May 3, 1871.

71. *Ibid.*, May 12/24, 1873. My translation.

72. Dumitru Ghise, I. Kecskés, and Pompiliu Teodor, "Idei economice în opera lui George Bariţ privind promovarea industriei la românii din Transilvania," AIIC, 6 (1963), 41-76.

73. BARSR, Cluj, Arhiva Istorică, Dimitrie Moldovan Archive: Matei Nicola to Moldovan, January 18, 1865; Hitchins and Maior, *Corespondenţa Raţiu-Bariţiu*, 103 and 155: Raţiu to Bariţiu, April 25, 1866, and November 6, 1867; Simion Retegan, "Problema agrară în dezbaterile dietei de la Sibiu," AIIC, 11 (1968), 284-287.

74. Nicola P. Petrescu, *Monografia institutului de credit şi economii 'Albina' 1872-1897* (Sibiu, 1897), 12-22; Vasile Netea, *Noi contribuţii*, 32 and 51-53: Roman to Bariţiu, July 5, 1869, and March 20, 1870.

Chapter 9: Church and State

1. Puşcariu, *Metropolia*, Annex, 150: Şaguna to Francis Joseph, December 1, 1855.

2. ABM, Şaguna Collection, no. 1447: Şaguna to Hacman, September 26, 1860.

3. Şaguna, "Tagebuch," 312.

4. Puşcariu, "Câteva epistole," 521: Şaguna to Jacob Rannicher, February 20, 1868.

5. Şaguna, *Compendium*, 280.

6. Andreiu Şaguna, *Proiectu de unu Regulamentu pentru organisarea trebiloru bisericesci, scolare, si fundationale romane de Relegea greco-orientale in Statele austriace* (Sibiu, 1864), 83-84.

7. ABM, Şaguna Collection, no. 1927: Şaguna to Eudoxiu Hurmuzaki, January 17, 1864.

8. *Ibid.*, no. 1060: Şaguna to Governor Karl Schwarzenberg, July 8, 1855.

9. OL, MCS, 9232/585/1851: Şaguna to Thun, April 9 and September 9, 1851.

10. ABM, Şaguna Collection, no. 975: Şaguna to Protopope Moise Fulea, July 29, 1854; no. 988: Şaguna to Military and Civil Government in Transylvania, August 1854.

11. *Ibid.:* Şaguna to all protopopes, March 30, 1850; OL, MSC, fasc. 12/17,655/ 1851: Şaguna to government, July 21, 1851.

12. ABM, Şaguna Collection, no. 100: session of the Orthodox consistory, September 10/22, 1849.

13. *Memoriile Şaguna 1846-1871*, 42.

14. Puşcariu, *Metropolia*, Annex, 62: Wohlgemuth to Şaguna, March 15, 1850; 62-64: Şaguna to Wohlgemuth, March 16, 1850.

15. *Ibid.*, 64-65: Wohlgemuth to Şaguna, March 21, 1850.

16. *Ibid.*, 66-67.

17. Mateiu, *Contribuţiuni*, 209.

18. Lupaş, *Şaguna* (1909), 116: cites letter from Şaguna to Ioan Maiorescu, March 17, 1850.

19. ABM, Şaguna Collection, no. 1064: Şaguna to Karl Schwarzenberg, August 27, 1855.

20. Puşcariu, *Documente*, I, 314-316.

21. *Ibid.*, 318.

22. ABM, Şaguna Collection, no. 1257: Şaguna to the Orthodox consistory, September 8, 1857.

23. *Memoriile Şaguna 1846-1871*, 52.

24. HHStA, Kabinettsarchiv, Minister Conferenz Kanzlei, K.Z. 3839.852, M.C.Z. 3062/852: Hodoş, *Din corespondenţa lui Simion Bărnuţiu*, 21: Alexandru Roman to Papiu-Ilarian, December 1, 1852.

25. Şaguna, *Compendium*, 304.

26. Allgemeines Verwaltungsarchiv, Oberste Polizeibehörde, No. 1018, Präsidium II, 1856.

27. HHStA, Kabinettsarchiv, Minister Conferenz Kanzlei, K.Z. 3141.856, M.C.Z. 2870.856.

28. *Ibid.*, Reichsrat, 1419/R, 1856.

29. ABM, Şaguna Collection, no. 1062: Schwarzenberg to Şaguna, August 15, 1855.

30. Puşcariu, *Metropolia*, Annex, 155-156: Schwarzenberg to the Cultusministerium, [1856].

31. OL, MCS, fasc. 17/25,537/1851: Alexander Bach to Eduard Bach, July 30, 1849.

32. *Ibid.*, fasc. 38/125-28,188/1852, and fasc. 38/98-22,352/1852: Şaguna to

Transylvanian government, December 21, 1852, and October 6, 1852.

33. *Ibid.,* fasc. 14/8184/1851: Thun to Transylvanian government, March 9, 1851.

34. HHStA, Kabinettsarchiv, Minister Conferenz Kanzlei, K.Z. 4091.853, M.C.Z. 3304.853.

35. Puşcariu, *Metropolia,* Annex, 147-148: Şaguna to Francis Joseph, December 1, 1855; ABM, Şaguna Collection: Şaguna to Transylvanian government, May 14, 1859.

36. *Ibid.,* no. 909: Şaguna to Transylvanian government, July 25, 1853.

37. OL, MCS, fasc. 115/146-5068/1852: Şaguna to Transylvanian government, February 28, 1852.

38. ABM, Şaguna Collection, no. 1183: Şaguna to Zenobie Hagi Constantin Pop, October 6, 1856; no. 1184: Pop to Şaguna, October 24, 1856; no. 1185: Şaguna to Pop, October 19/31, 1856.

39. *Ibid.:* Şaguna to Francis Joseph, April 1854; no. 397: Şaguna to Alexander Bach, January 9, 1851.

40. *Ibid.,* no. 201: Şaguna to Eduard Bach, undated, in reply to Bach's letter of November 10, 1849; OL, MCS, fasc. 12/17,655/1851, and fasc. 14/27,172/1851: Şaguna to Transylvanian government, July 21 and November 20, 1851.

41. ABM, Şaguna Collection, no. 100: minutes of Orthodox consistory meeting, November 24/December 6, 1849.

42. OL, MCS, fasc. 38/49-10,492/1852: Şaguna to Schwarzenberg, April 26, 1852.

43. *Ibid.,* Abt. 5/19/10 and 21: Şaguna to Transylvanian government, August 6, 1857, and December 30, 1859.

44. ABM, Şaguna Collection: Şaguna to Orthodox consistory, March 29, 1862.

45. Eusebiu R. Roşca, *Monografia institutului seminarial teologic-pedagogic "Andreian"* (Sibiu, 1911), 19-21.

46. HHStA, Kabinettsarchiv, Minister Conferenz Kanzlei, K.Z. 3184/1860, M.C.Z. 595: minutes of the meeting of the council of ministers, September 20, 1860.

47. *Ibid.,* Kabinettskanzlei, K.Z. 1703/1861, M.P. 239: proposal of Archduke Rainer, May 28, 1861.

48. *Ibid.,* Nachlass Reichenstein, Box I: Vasile L. Pop to Şaguna, April 19, 1864.

49. Puşcariu, *Metropolia,* Annex, 166-167.

50. *Ibid.,* 167-168.

51. *Ibid.,* 168-173: petition of the synod to the emperor, October 26, 1860.

52. *Ibid.,* 207: Şaguna to Mocioni, March 25/April 6, 1863.

53. HHStA, Kabinettsarchiv, Kabinettskanzlei, K.Z. 4072/1862, M.R.Z. 1093: minutes of the meeting of the council of ministers, November 25, 1862.

54. *Ibid.,* K.Z. 1895/1862: proposal of the Minister of Foreign Affairs Count Rechberg, June 24, 1862.

55. *Ibid.,* K.Z. 4072/1862, M.R.Z. 1093.

56. *Ibid.*

57. *Ibid.,* K.Z. 4073/1862, M.R.Z. 1437, ad. 4073/1862.

58. Puşcariu, *Metropolia,* Annex, 212-215: Şaguna to Nadásdy, July 26, 1863.

59. *Ibid.,* 217-218: Vice-Chancellor Reichenstein to Şaguna, March 28, 1864.

60. *Ibid.,* 218-221: petition of the synod to the emperor, April 3, 1864.

61. HHStA, Kabinettsarchiv, Jüngerer Staatsrat, Z. 972, November 12, 1864.

62. Puşcariu, *Metropolia,* Annex, 305.

63. *Ibid.,* 307-310: Schmerling to Şaguna, December 29, 1864.

64. *Ibid.,* 388-389: Schmerling to Şaguna, July 8, 1865; 391-393: Şaguna to Schmerling, July 15, 1865.

65. HHStA, Kabinettsarchiv, Jüngerer Staatsrat, Z. 81, February 3, 1867.

66. *Ibid.*, Kabinettskanzlei, K.Z. 436/1867.

67. Mateiu, *Contribuţiuni,* 258-259.

68. Dumitru Stăniloae, *În zadar: Statutul Organic e şagunian* (Sibiu, 1933), 11-12.

69. Parteniu Cosma, "Statutul Organic", in *Enciclopedia Română,* ed. C. Diaconovich, vol. 3 (Sibiu, 1904), 1009-1012. Cosma was a delegate to the national church congress and a member of the Committee of twenty-seven. His article is the only detailed account of the confrontation between Şaguna and the lay intellectuals.

70. One commentator argues persuasively that the changes introduced into Şaguna's original draft did not affect its essential character and concludes that the Organic Statutes deserve to be called Şaguna's work. See Stăniloae, *În zadar,* 5-32.

71. Puşcariu, *Notiţe,* 135.

Chapter 10: Social Activism

1. Şaguna, *Istoria,* II, 124.

2. *Ibid.,* 61-62, 67, 96.

3. Şaguna was referring to the New Testament translation of Belgrad (1648).

4. Şaguna, *Istoria,* II, 103-104.

5. Şaguna, *Promemoria,* 9-10.

6. Şaguna, *Istoria,* II, 55.

7. *Ibid.,* 59-61.

8. *Ibid.,* 63-64.

9. Şaguna's introduction to his translation of the Bible (Sibiu, 1858), vi-vii.

10. Tulbure, *Mitropolitul Şaguna,* 71-72.

11. Şaguna, *Istoria,* II, 72.

12. Tulbure, *Mitropolitul Şaguna,* 330: circular letter of October 6, 1862.

13. ABM, Şaguna Collection, no. 1734: Şaguna to Nadásdy, August 20, 1862. Some years before, he had expressed concern about the ability of his own theological students to use the Latin alphabet: *ibid.,* no. 142: Şaguna to Ioan Hannia, December 23, 1850.

14. Ioan Slavici, *Lumea prin care am trecut* (Bucharest, 1930), 81.

15. Ion Breazu, "Literatura Tribunei," *Dacoromania,* 8 (1934-1935), 13.

16. N. Mandrea in *Convorbiri Literare,* 2 (1869), no. 23, 375-377; no. 24, 389-395; I.E. Torouţiu, *Studii şi documente literare,* V (Bucharest, 1934), 151: Iacob Negruzzi to Ilarion Puşcariu, August 11/23, 1874.

17. Ioan Lupaş, "Din corespondenţa lui Şaguna cu Filaret Scriban," AIIN, 1 (1921-1922), 341: Şaguna to Scriban, March 19, 1860.

18. ABM, Şaguna Collection, no. 1542: Şaguna to two priests, September 15, 1861.

19. *Ibid.,* no. 1058: the letter is dated July 1, 1855.

20. Şaguna received the first news of the emperor's action from Ilarion Puşcariu who was in Vienna at the time: ABM, Şaguna Collection, no. 1545: Puşcariu to Şaguna, September 10, 1861.

21. BARSR, Cluj, Arhiva Istorică, Cipariu Archive, no. 3405: Bariţiu to Cipariu, October 16, 1861.

22. Allgemeines Verwaltungsarchiv, 1862/1308: police commissariat in Braşov to Polizei Obercommissar in Sibiu, August 1, 1862.

23. *Actele privitoare la urzirea şi înfiinţarea asociatiunei transilvane pentru literatura română şi cultura poporului român* (Sibiu, 1862), 46-47.

24. Muzeul Astrei, Sibiu, Manuscript Collection, mapa VII, no. 2: Cipariu to the Gubernium, April 8, 1862.

25. ABM, Şaguna Collection: Şaguna to his protopopes, May 3, 1862.

26. ASTRA's accomplishments, which were many, are discussed in Curticăpeanu, *Miscarea culturală,* 69-139.

27. Tulbure, *Mitropolitul Şaguna,* 285-286: Şaguna's circular letter, May 17, 1855.

28. Nicolae Popea, *Andreiu baron de Şaguna.* Academia Română. *Discurs de recepţiune,* no. 21 (Bucharest, 1900), 30.

29. Constantin Secelea, "Dreptul canonic în literatura românească: I. Opera lui Andrei baron de Şaguna," *Cercetări Istorice* (Iaşi), II-III (1926-1927), 9.

30. ABM, Şaguna Collection, no. 954: Şaguna to Leo Thun, May 9, 1854. Şaguna presented Thun with a manuscript copy and asked him to transmit it to the emperor.

31. Şaguna, *Compendium,* xvii.

32. *Istoria bisericei ortodocse răsăritene universale* (Sibiu, 1860).

33. Şaguna's introduction to his translation of the Bible, vi-vii.

34. Grigore Marcu, "Sfînta Scriptură 'în pom românesc' (100 de ani de la apariţia Bibliei lui Şaguna)," *Mitropolia Ardealului,* 3, no. 11-12 (1958), 797.

35. ABM, Şaguna Collection: Şaguna to Thun, December 8/21 [sic], 1850.

36. OL, MCS, Abt. 6/5/2: Şaguna to Schwarzenberg, July 4, 1853.

37. *Ibid.,* 6/5/2: Şaguna to the Transylvanian government, February 14, 1856.

38. *Ibid.:* Şaguna to the Transylvanian government, December 24, 1851.

39. Tulbure, *Mitropolitul Şaguna,* 253-255.

40. ABM, Şaguna Collection, no. 1810: Şaguna to the protopope of Zarand County, March 9, 1863; no. 1839: Şaguna to the supreme count of Zarand, March 9, 1863.

41. *Ibid.,* no. 906: Militär und Civilgouvernement in Siebenbürgen to Şaguna, undated [probably summer, 1853].

42. OL, MCS, Abt. 6/5/2: Şaguna to Schwarzenberg, July 4, 1853.

43. *Ibid.,* fasc. 40/269, 1853: Şaguna to the Transylvanian government, February 20, 1853. Şaguna continued to protest government support of common schools in the 1860s; see Puşcariu, "Câteva epistole," 502: Şaguna to Jacob Rannicher, September 26, 1866.

44. Tulbure, *Mitropolitul Şaguna,* 327: Şaguna's circular letter to his clergy, August 26, 1862.

45. *Ibid.,* 325-326.

46. *Ibid.,* 314-315: Şaguna's circular letter to his clergy, April 25, 1860.

47. OL, MCS, Abt. 6/5/2: Şaguna to Schwarzenberg, July 4, 1853: *ibid.,* Acta generalia, 1853, fasc. 40/432: Şaguna to the Transylvanian government, July 15, 1853.

48. ABM, Şaguna Collection, no. 580: Şaguna to Militär und Civilgouvernement in Siebenbürgen, undated [end of 1851].

49. OL, MCS, Abt. 6/5/53: Şaguna to the Transylvanian government, August 1, 1859.

50. *Ibid.,* Acta generalia, 1853, fasc. 40/156: Şaguna to the Transylvanian government, March 10, 1853; Tulbure, *Mitropolitul Şaguna,* 257-258: Şaguna's circular letter to his clergy, April 8, 1853.

51. OL, MCS, Acta generalia, 1854, fasc. 40/608: Şaguna to the Transylvanian government, November 5, 1854.

52. *Ibid.:* Şaguna to the Transylvanian government, December 24, 1851.

53. *Ibid.,* Acta generalia, 1854, fasc. 40/608: Şaguna to the Transylvanian government, November 5, 1854.

54. *Ibid.,* Abt. 5/43/1: Şaguna to the Transylvanian government, November 30, 1857.

55. Tulbure, *Mitropolitul Şaguna,* 291-294: Şaguna's circular letter to his clergy, February 9, 1856.

56. OL, EK, Acta generalia, 4021/1862: Şaguna to the Transylvanian government, June 4/16, 1861.

57. Puşcariu, "Câteva epistole," 487: Şaguna to Jacob Rannicher, March 14, 1863.

58. BARSR, Ms. rom., vol. 1003: Vasici to Bariţiu, May 3, 1860, and April 8, 1864: "Raport în cauza şcolilor."

59. OL, MCS, Abt. 6/5/53: Şaguna to the Transylvanian government, August 1, 1859.

60. Puşcariu, Metropolia, Annex, 84-85: Şaguna to the Austrian ministry of the interior, November 16, 1850.

61. ABM, Şaguna Collection: Şaguna to the Transylvanian government (?), probably at the beginning of 1851.

62. Ibid., no. 805: Şaguna to Alexander Bach, October 10, 1852; no. 896: Ioan Brote, school director in Răşinari; to Şaguna, May 1, 1853.

63. Ibid.: Şaguna to Heufler, Transylvanian educational commissioner, July 1, 1850.

64. OL, MCS: Şaguna to Leo Thun, April 9, 1851. In 1850 there were 99 Orthodox pupils in state Normalschulen and 39 in Roman Catholic gymnasia in Sibiu; in 1851 these figures were 168 and 60, respectively. The Orthodox were the largest group in the Normalschulen, followed by 127 Roman Catholics, 44 Uniates, and 22 Lutherans. See ABM, Şaguna Collection, no. 532: Moise Fulea to Şaguna, March 15, 1851.

65. OL, MCS, Acta generalia, 1853, fasc. 40/660: Şaguna to the Transylvanian government, November 2, 1853.

66. Ibid.: Şaguna to Thun, November 19, 1850.

67. HHStA, Kabinettsarchiv, Reichsrat, 484/R, 1853: protocol of the meeting of December 22, 1853.

68. ABM, Şaguna Collection: Şaguna to Thun, December 9/21, 1850.

69. Ibid., no. 708: the letter is dated March 8/20, 1852.

70. Ibid., no. 709: Şaguna to the consistory of Blaj, undated [undoubtedly late March or early April 1852].

71. Bănescu, Stareţul Neonil, 90-91: Şaguna to Neonil, September 7, 1850; Lupaş, "Vieaţa şi faptele Şaguna," 178.

72. Bariţiu, Părţi alese, III, 560-561.

73. ABM, Şaguna Collection, no. 142: Şaguna to Protopope Ioan Hannia, December 23, 1850.

74. Ibid.: Şaguna to the Transylvanian government, September 29, 1852.

75. Tulbure, Mitropolitul Şaguna, 195-201: Şaguna's pastoral letter, December 5, 1855. On December 22, 1855, Şaguna made a full report of the matter to Governor Schwarzenberg, giving his reasons for forbidding his clergy to subscribe to Gazeta: Allgemeines Verwaltungsarchiv, Militär und Civilgouvernement in Siebenbürgen, Pras. no. 11940.855.

76. ABM, Şaguna Collection, no. 977: Şaguna to the bishop of Buzău, August 8, 1854.

77. TR, "Prenumeraţiune," December 8, 1852. The article was signed by the editor, Aaron Florian, but it accurately expressed Şaguna's own ideas.

78. Ioan cavaler de Puşcariu, Reminiscentie din anul 1860 de un contemporan (Sibiu, 1897), 22-23.

79. OL, MCS, fasc. 43/29-3905, 1852: Şaguna to the Transylvanian government, November 26, 1851; Tulbure, Mitropolitul Şaguna, 319-320: Şaguna's circular letter to his clergy, August 2, 1862.

80. Adunarea cuvântărilor comisarilor şcolari din anii 1863 şi 1864 (Sibiu, 1864), 3-4, 21-27.

81. In 1851, for example, he received a grant of sixty stipends of five florins each for poor students: ABM, Şaguna Collection, no. 581: Şaguna to Alexander Bach, November 1, 1851. In 1864, he received a sum to support fifty needy students enrolled at Orthodox schools in Transylvania: HHStA, Kabinettsarchiv, 1015/1864: Vortrag des Erzherzogs Rainer, April 8, 1864.

82. HHStA, Kabinettskanzlei, 3493/1865: Vortrag des Leiters der k. siebenbürgischen Hofkanzlei Grafen Haller, November 12, 1865. Haller noted the "generally known fact" that in the 1850s Şaguna had spent all that his own personal resources would allow in support of the clergy and the theological institute, and recommended that he be compensated at least in part by a grant of 12,000 florins.

83. Tulbure, *Mitropolitul Şaguna,* 339: Şaguna's circular letter to his clergy, October 14/26, 1864.

84. *Ibid.,* 300, 315-316, 316-317: circular letters of July 14, 1857, December 29, 1860, and September 7, 1861.

85. ABM, Şaguna Collection, no. 896: Ioan Brote, school director in Răşinari, reported to Şaguna on May 1, 1853, that the main reason for poor attendance at his school was the inability of parents to see any benefits in education. Şaguna issued numerous pastoral letters on the subject. One, dated October 14/26, 1864, contains the following appeal: "In the interest of educating our Christians, I instruct all the parents of boys and girls not to keep their children from enjoying a great spiritual benefit simply for some small material gain and not to take greater care of their flocks and herds than of their children's souls, but to send them to school and catechization when the time comes." (Tulbure, *Mitropolitul Şaguna,* 340.)

Chapter 11: Epilogue

1. Ilarion Puşcariu, "Din anii ultimi ai vieţii mitropolitului Andreiu baron de Şaguna, despre boala şi moartea lui," in *Mitropolitul Andreiu baron de Şaguna. Scriere comemorativă la serbarea centenară a naşterii lui* (Sibiu, 1909), 410, n.1.

2. TR, September 21/October 3 and September 25/October 7, 1869.

3. *Ibid.,* January 11/23, February 5/17, and September 6/18, 1870.

4. Şaguna's attitude on passivity was faithfully represented in numerous editorials in *Telegraful Român,* many of which were written by his editor, Nicolae Cristea. Characteristic were those which appeared in issues for January 11/23 and January 29/February 10, 1870.

5. HHStA, Ministerium des Aeussern, Politisches Archiv, Informationsbüro, box 22: a police report about Şaguna, Hermannstadt, January 23, 1869.

6. *Ibid.:* police reports about Şaguna from Hermannstadt, March 30 and 31, 1868.

7. Hitchins and Maior, *Corespondenţa Raţiu-Bariţiu,* 212-213: Raţiu to Bariţiu, March 24, 1872. Iosif Hossu, a deputy in the Hungarian parliament, wrote to the Uniate vicar of Făgăraş, Ioan Antonelli, on December 13, 1871, that if passivity continued much longer, the people would cease to follow the intellectuals and the Rumanian nation would regress to the year 1437, when the union of the three nations, which marked the beginning of their political decline, was concluded without their participation: BARSR, Cluj, Arhiva Istorică, Antonelli Archive.

8. TR, December 16/28, 1871.

9. ABM, Şaguna Collection, no. 2405: a group of Rumanian intellectuals of Braşov to Şaguna, December 23, 1871; no. 2416: Meţianu, protopope of Zârneşti, to Şaguna, December 13/25, 1871.

10. *Ibid.*, no. 2455: address of the committee to all national clubs, May 7, 1872.

11. *Ibid.*, no. 2458: committee of the national conference in Sibiu to Şaguna, April 28/May 10, 1872.

12. *Ibid.*, no. 2462: Şaguna to Vancea, May 5/17, 1872.

13. Puşcariu, *Câteva epistole,* 537: Şaguna to Puşcariu, May 6/18, 1872.

14. ABM, Şaguna Collection, nos. 2465 and 2468: Vancea to Şaguna, May 19 and 29, 1872.

15. *Ibid.*, nos. 2466/1 and 2469: Şaguna to Vancea, May 12/24 and May 20/June 2, 1872.

16. *Ibid.*, no. 2476: Şaguna to the committee of the national conference in Sibiu, June 1/13, 1872; no. 2479: Vancea to Şaguna, June 5/17, 1872; no. 2480: Şaguna to Vancea, June 7/19, 1872.

17. Hitchins and Maior, *Corespondenţa Raţiu-Bariţiu,* 215: Raţiu to Bariţiu, June 21, 1872; ABM, Şaguna Collection, no. 2481: Raţiu to Şaguna, June 19, 1872.

18. GTr, June 24/July 6, 1872.

19. ABM, Şaguna Collection, no. 2488: Vancea to Şaguna, July 15/27, 1872; GTr, October 21/November 2, 1872.

20. Popea, *Archiepiscopul,* 307.

21. ABM, Şaguna Collection, no. 2466: Şaguna to all protopopes, May 15, 1872. He informs them that because of his illness ordinations will take place only in the summer months.

22. The funeral is movingly described by Popea, *Archiepiscopul,* 373-377.

Selected Bibliography

The major biographies of Şaguna are those of Nicolae Popea and Ioan Lupaş, published in 1879 and 1909, respectively. They are comprehensive and laudatory. In the interval between the two World Wars a number of articles were written about selected aspects of Şaguna's life and career, but there was no attempt to undertake a full-scale examination of his place in the history of the Transylvanian Rumanians. Perhaps the most important work published during the period was Gheorghe Tulbure's volume of sources (1938).

After the Second World War Şaguna suffered the same fate as many prominent Rumanian figures of the past who did not fit in with the prevailing political and social theories. Until about 1960 his activities were generally passed over in silence, or if he was mentioned, he was usually the subject of one-sided criticism as a reactionary and a mere instrument of Habsburg policy. An important exception are the chapters devoted to him in the second volume of *Istoria bisericii romîne* (Bucharest, 1958), which provide a brief, factual account of his ecclesiastical career, but say little about his political activities beyond mention of his role at the Blaj assembly in 1848. In the past three decades the few articles about him that have appeared in church periodicals, including those published in *Mitropolia Ardealului* and *Mitropolia Banatului* in 1973 to commemorate the hundredth anniversary of his death, have limited themselves to his pastoral and cultural activities.

In general works on Rumanian history published in the past fifteen years, Şaguna's career has been dealt with in a highly selective manner, a method doubtless responding to prevailing ideological considerations. There has been no major research by Rumanian scholars on either his ecclesiastical or his secular activities. In the 1960s two larger works on Transylvanian history appeared, which provided an opportunity for a reevaluation of Şaguna's career. The collective work published by the Rumanian Academy, *Din istoria Transilvaniei* (volume 2, Bucharest, 1961), however, did little more than repeat the prevailing notions about Şaguna's "retrograde" policies and his eagerness to serve the imperial cause in the Vormärz and during the revolution of 1848. His mission to Olmütz in 1849 is dealt with at some length and, on the whole, is seen in a favorable light. For the decade of absolutism he is not mentioned at all, except as one of the founders of ASTRA. His political role during the constitutional era of the 1860s is referred to only once, as again serving the interests of the court. His activist policy after 1865 is characterized as "collaboration" with the newly created Dual Monarchy, while the significance of the restoration of the Orthodox metropolis is dismissed as merely a "reward" to Şaguna for services rendered the monarchy. On the whole the same attitude is present in Victor Cheresteşiu, *Adunarea Naţională de la Blaj* (Bucharest, 1966). There is more detail about Şaguna in 1847 and the spring of 1848, but no attempt is made to explore the deeper motives of his actions. For example, his dealings with the peasantry — first the Catharine Varga episode, then the mission to Hunedoara in April 1848, and finally his admonitions to the peasants at Blaj that they remain obedient to the emperor — are viewed as "deceptive" and motivated by a desire to keep the peasants from having a part in their own emancipation. In this work, as in all the others mentioned below, the lay intellectuals — Bărnuţiu, Bariţiu, Iancu, Papiu-Ilarian, and others — are recognized as the leaders of the nation and the formulators of policy.

The general works on the history of Rumania published in the last decade give a good indication of Şaguna's place in contemporary Rumanian historiography. In the collective work sponsored by the Rumanian Academy, *Istoria Rominiei* (volume 4, Bucharest, 1964), Şaguna's relations with the peasantry and the court in the Vormärz are condemned as "Reactionary" and he himself is described as "young, ambitious, and clever," the implication being that he was trying to win the favor of both Vienna and the Magyar aristocracy in Transylvania. For the rest of his career only fleeting mention is made of his role at Blaj in 1848, the petitions to the court in 1849, his summons to the Verstärkter Reichsrat in 1860, his advocacy of activism after 1865 (dismissed as collaboration with the Austro-Hungarian ruling classes), and his brief return to national leadership in 1872. No mention is made of his church and cultural activities, except to note that he was named Metropolitan in 1865.

In *Istoria Romăniei,* edited by Miron Constantinescu, Constantin Daicoviciu, and Ştefan Pascu (Bucharest, 1969), Şaguna is mentioned only once — in a discussion of events that preceded the outbreak of the revolution of 1848 where he is described as the representative of moderate views. He is accorded far more attention in *Istoria poporului român,* edited by Andrei Oţetea (Bucharest, 1970). The main facts of his public life, ecclesiastical as well as political and cultural, are noted briefly but in generally positive terms. Finally, a favorable, though succinct appreciation of his cultural activities is to be found in Constantin C. Giurescu and Dinu C. Giurescu, *Istoria Românilor* (Bucharest, 1971). The authors stress his attempts to provide the Rumanian Orthodox with the kind of church organization that would reinforce their struggle for political and cultural rights, and they view the *Statut Organic* as a means of strengthening the links between the mass of the faithful and their cultural leaders.

The sympathetic treatment given Şaguna by Oţetea and the Giurescus reflects the growing recognition in contemporary Rumanian historiography of the significant role played by the church in the Rumanians' struggle for national rights in the Habsburg Monarchy and its contribution to the creation of the modern Rumanian state. It also suggests that the dogmatism of the 1950s and early 1960s has moderated sufficiently to allow judgments of historical figures to be made within the context of their own times.

Archival Sources

1. Vienna
   A. Allgemeines Verwaltungsarchiv
      a. Militär und Civilgouvernement in Siebenbürgen
      b. Ministerium des Innern
      c. Oberste Polizeibehörde
   B. Haus-, Hof- und Staatsarchiv
      a. Kabinettsarchiv
         - Geheime Akten, Nachlass Schwarzenberg
         - Jüngerer Staatsrat
         - Kabinettskanzlei Akten
         - Minister Conferenz Kanzlei
         - Nachlass Reichenstein
         - Reichsrat
         - Staatsratsakten
      b. Ministerium des Aeussern
         - Politisches Archiv, Informationsbüro
      c. Ministerium für Kultus und Unterricht (Unterrichtsministerium)
2. Budapest
   A. Magyar Országos Levéltár
      a. Erdélyi Kancellária, Acta Generalia
      b. Erdélyi Kancellária, Praesidialia
      c. Gubernium Transylvanicum, Praesidialia
      d. Gubernium Transylvanicum (in Politicis)

e. Magyar Helytartótanács
   - Departamentum Religionis Graeci Ritus non-Unitorum
f. Militär und Civilgouvernement in Siebenbürgen
g. Vallás és Közoktatásügyi Ministerium
   - Görög nem egyesült osztály
B. Pest Városa Levéltára
3. Sremski Karlovci
   A. Patriarchal Archive
   B. Consistory Archive
   C. Patriarchal-Metropolitan Archive "A" and "B"
4. Bucharest
   Biblioteca Academiei Republicii Socialiste România, Manuscrise românești, vols.
   992-993, 996, 998-999, 1000-1001, 1003
5. Cluj
   Biblioteca Academiei Republicii Socialiste România, Arhiva Istorică: Personal
   archives of Ioan Antonelli, George Barițiu, Timotei Cipariu, Ioan Fodor, Dimi-
   trie Moldovan, Ioan Micu Moldovan, Ioan Pamfilie, Ioan Rațiu, and Alexandru
   Sterca Șuluțiu
6. Sibiu
   A. Arhiva Bibliotecii Mitropoliei Ortodoxe, Șaguna Collection
   B. Arhiva Mitropoliei Ortodoxe
   C. Arhivele Statului
      a. ASTRA Collection
      b. Brukenthal Collection
   D. Muzeul Astrei

Newspapers

Foaia pentru minte, inimă și literatură (Brașov), 1838-1865.
Gazeta de Transilvania (Brașov), 1838-1873.
Organul Luminării (Blaj), 1847-1848.
Telegraful Român (Sibiu), 1853-1873.

Works by Șaguna

*Adaos la Promemoria despre dreptul istoric al autonomiei bisericești naționale a Ro-
mânilor de relegea răsăriteană în ces. reg. provinții ale Monarhiei Austriace.* Sibiu,
1850.
*Anhang zu der Promemoria über das histor. Recht der nationalen Kirchen-Authono-
mie der Romanen morgenländ. Kirche in den k. k. Kronländern der österreich.
Monarchie.* Hermannstadt, 1850.
*Anrede . . . an die Geistlichkeit und National-Versammlung am 28 December 1848 zu
Hermannstadt.* Olmütz, no date.
*Anthorismos, sau deslușire comparativă asupra broșurei "Dorințele dreptcredincio-
sului cler din Bucovina în privința organisarei canonice a diecezei, și a ierarhicei
sale referințe in organismul bisericei ortodocse din Austria."* Sibiu, 1861.
*Bibliia, adeca dumnezeiasca Scriptură a legii cei vechi și a cei noao, după originalul
celor Șeptezeci și doi de Tălcuitori din Alecsandria. Tipărită . . . supt priveghiarea
. . . Prea Sfințitului Domn Andreiu Baron de Șaguna.* Sibiu, 1858.

Compendiu de dreptul canonic alu unei sântei sobornicesci şi apostolesci biserici.
Sibiu, 1868.

*Compendium des kanonischen Rechtes der einen, heiligen, allgemeinen und aposto-
lischen Kirche. Aus dem romanischen übersetzt von Alois Sentz.* Hermannstadt,
1868.

*Cunoştiinţe folositóre despre trebile căsătoriilor, spre folosul preoţimei şi al scaunelor
protopopeşti.* Sibiu, 1854.

*Denkschrift, wodurch die Bitte der Romanen des orientalischen Glaubens in Oester-
reich um Herstellung ihrer Metropolie aus dem Gesichtspunkte der Kirchensatzung-
en beleuchtet wird. Dem k. k. Ministerium für Cultus . . . überreicht, 1851.* Hermannstadt, 1860.

*Elementele dreptului canonic al bisericii drept-credincióse răsăritene spre întrebuinţ-
area preoţimei, a clerului tînăr, şi a Creştinilor.* Sibiu, 1854.

*Enchiridion adeca arte manuale de canone ale unei, sântei, sobornicesci, si apostolesci
Biserici cu comentare.* Sibiu, 1871.

*Geschichte der griechisch-orientalischen Kirche in Oesterreich. Bruchstücke aus der
allgemeinen Kirchengeschichte . . . wortgetreu übersetzt von Z. Boiu und Y.
Popescu.* Hermannstadt, 1862.

Istoria bisericei ortodocse răsăritene universale. 2 vols. Sibiu, 1860.

*Memorial, prin care se lămureşte cererea Românilor de religiunea resariteană în Aus-
tria pentru restaurarea Mitropoliei lor din punct de vedere a Ss. Canoane. Aşternut
c.r. Ministeriu pentru Cult şi Instrucţiune 1851.* Sibiu, 1860.

Memoriile Arhiepiscopului şi Mitropolitului Andrei Şaguna din anii 1846-1871. Sibiu,
1923.

Predici. With an introductory study by Florea Mureşanu. Cluj, 1945.

*Proiect de un Regulament pentru organisarea trebilor bisericeşti, şcolare, şi funda-
ţionale române de relegea greco-orientale în Statele austriace.* Sibiu, 1864.

"Proiectul original de constituţie bisericească," in Mateiu, *Contribuţiuni la istoria
dreptului bisericesc,* vol. I, Bucharest, 1922, 321-369.

*Promemoria über das historische Recht der nationalen Kirchen-Autonomie der Ro-
manen morgenländ. Kirche in den k.k. Kronländern der Österreich. Monarchie.*
Vienna, 1849.

*Promemorie despre dreptul istoric al autonomiei bisericeşti naţionale a Românilor de
relegea răsăriteană în ces. reg. provinţii ale monarhiei austriace şi adaos.* Sibiu,
1849.

*Rânduiala hirotonirei noului episcop de relegea ortodocsă răsăriteană, din manuscrise
compusă şi tipărită . . . prin Andreiu baron de Şaguna.* Sibiu, 1864.

Respingere a unor atacuri în treaba unei traduceri nouă a Bibliei. Sibiu, 1858.

Scrisori apologetice. Sibiu, 1867.

"Tagebuch über die bischöflichen Berathungen in Wien," in Puşcariu, *Documente
pentru limbă şi istoriă,* I, 269-313.

"Ziar despre consiliul imperial înmulţit," in Puşcariu, *Documente pentru limbă şi
istoriă,* I, 321-339.

Printed Works

*Actele conferentiei tienute de romanii greco-catolici dein provincia metropolitana de
Alba Iulia la Alba Iulia în 13-14 Aprile 1871.* Blaj, 1871.

Actele privitoare la urzirea şi înfiinţarea asociaţiunei transilvane pentru literatura

română şi cultura poporului român. Sibiu, 1862.
Actele sinodului archidiecesei greco-catolice de Alba Iulia-Făgăraş ţinut în 10-11 august 1868. Blaj, 1869.
Actele soboarelor bisericii greco-răsăritene din Ardeal din anii 1850 şi 1860. Sibiu, 1860.
Adunarea cuvântărilor comisarilor şcolari din anii 1863 şi 1864. Sibiu, 1864.
Aemtliche Actenstücke betreffend die Verhandlungen über die Union Siebenbürgens mit dem Königreiche Ungarn. Hermannstadt, 1865.
Albu, Nicolae. "Problema facultăţii juridice pentru români din Transilvania după revoluţia din 1848/49," *Studia Universitatis Babeş-Bolyai,* Series Historia, Fasc. 1 (1968) 59-71.
Andea, Avram. "*Libertate* şi *proprietate* în concepţia lui Simeon Bărnuţiu," *Studia Universitatis Babeş-Bolyai,* Series Historia, Fasc. 1 (1973), 33-51.
Anul 1848 în principatele romîne. Acte şi documente. 6 vols. Bucharest, 1902-1910.
Bălcescu, Nicolae. *Scrieri istorice.* With notes and introduction by P.P. Panaitescu. Craiova, n.d.
Balinth, Simeone. "Scurta descriere a unoru evenimente intemplate in muntii apuseni ai Transilvaniei," *Transilvania* 7, no. 2 (1876), 13-16.
Bănescu, Nicolae. *Stareţul Neonil. Corespondenţa sa cu C. Hurmuzachi şi Andreiu Şaguna.* Vălenii-de-Munte, 1910.
Bariţiu, George. *Părţi alese din istoria Transilvaniei.* 3 vols. Sibiu, 1889-1891.
Bârlea, Octavianus. *Ex historia romena: Ioannes Bob, Episcopus Fagarasiensis (1783-1830).* Freiburg: Herder, 1951.
Bărnuţiu, Simion. *Românii şi Ungurii. Discurs rostit în catedrala Blajului 2/14 maiu 1848.* Edited by Gheorghe Bogdan-Duică. Cluj, 1924.
Beér, János. *Az 1848-49 évi népképviseleti Országgyűlés.* Budapest, 1954.
Berzeviczy, Albert. *Az abszolutizmus kora Magyarországon, 1849-1865.* 2 vols. Budapest, 1922.
Bianu, Ioan; Hodoş, Nerva; and Simonescu, Dan. *Bibliografia românească veche, 1508-1830.* 4 vols. Bucharest, 1903-1944.
Bianu, Ioan, and Nicolaiasa, G. *Catalogul manuscriptelor româneşti,* vol. 3. Craiova, 1931.
Bodea, Cornelia C. *Moise Nicoara (1784-1861) şi rolul său în lupta pentru emanciparea naţional-religioasă a Românilor din Banat şi Crişana.* Arad, 1943.
————. *The Romanians' Struggle for Unification, 1834-1849.* Bucharest, 1970.
Bogdan-Duică, Gheorghe. "Notes-ul de însemnări al lui Simeon Bărnuţiu, 1849-1863," *AIIN,* 2 (1923), 205-232.
————. "1848/9 în Ţara Bârsei," *Ţara Bârsei,* 1, no. 3 (1929), 195-201.
————. "Viaţa şi ideile lui Simion Bărnuţiu," in Academia Română, *Studii şi Cercetări,* no. 8, Bucharest, 1924.
Botiş, Teodor. *Monografia Familiei Mocioni.* Bucharest, 1939.
Breazu, Ion. "Alecu Russo în Ardealul revoluţionar la 1848," *Transilvania,* 72, no. 2 (1941), 122-132.
————. "Lamennais la Românii din Transilvania în 1848," *Studii Literare,* 4 (1948), 176-197.
————. "Literatura Tribunei," *Dacoromania,* 8 (1934-1935), 2-111.
————. *Michelet şi Românii.* Cluj, 1935.
Capidan, Theodor. "Aromânii. Dialectul aromân," in Academia Română, *Studii şi Cercetări,* no. 20. Bucharest, 1932.
Cheresteşiu, Victor. *Adunarea naţională de la Blaj.* Bucharest, 1966.

Cheresteşiu, Victor; Mureşan, Camil; and Marica, George, eds. *George Bariţiu. Scrieri social-politice*. Bucharest, 1962.

Cioran, Emilian. "Corespondenţa unui preot din anii 1848 şi 1856 şi fost duhovnic militar," *Revista Teologică*, 33 (1939), 3-9.

Ciuhandu, Gheorghe. *Episcopii Samuil Vulcan şi Gherasim Raţ; pagini mai ales din istoria Românilor crişeni (1830-40)*. Arad, 1935.

Curticăpeanu, Vasile. *Mişcarea culturală românească pentru unirea din 1918*. Bucharest, 1968.

"Din corespondenţa Baronului Vasile L. Pop. O scrisoare a Mitropolitului Şaguna," *Răvasul*, 8, no. 1-2 (1910), 1-2.

Dragomir, Silviu. "André Şaguna et Joseph Rajačić," *Balcania*, 6 (1943), 242-282.

———. *Avram Iancu*. Bucharest, 1965.

———. "Bălcescu în Ardeal," AIIN, 5 (1928-1930), 1-34.

———. "Din corespondenţa dascălilor ardeleni în anul 1848," in *Omagiu lui I. Bianu*. Bucharest, 1927, 155-170.

———. *Istoria desrobirei religioase a românilor din Ardeal în secolul XVIII*. 2 vols. Sibiu, 1920-1930.

———. *Studii şi documente privitoare la revoluţia Românilor din Transilvania în anii 1848-1849*. 4 vols. (1-3, 5). Sibiu and Cluj, 1944-1946.

Eisenmann, Louis. *Le compromis austro-hongrois*. Paris, 1904.

Ember, Győző. *Iratok az 1848-i magyarországi parasztmozgalmak történetéhez*. Budapest, 1951.

Flora, Radu. *Relaţiile sîrbo-române. Noi contribuţii*. Panciova, 1968.

Fotino, George. *Din vremea renaşterii naţionale a României. Boierii Goleşti*. 4 vols. Bucharest, 1939.

Füves, Ödön. *Görögök Pesten (1686-1931)*. 3 vols. Budapest, Kandidaturi értekezés, 1972.

Ghibu, Onisifor. *Din istoria literaturii didactice româneşti*. Bucharest, 1975.

Ghişe, Dumitru, and Teodor, Pompiliu. "Contribuţii la cunoaşterea activităţii filozofice a lui Simion Bărnuţiu," *Revista de Filozofie*, 9, no. 3 (1964), 357-369.

Ghişe, Dumitru, and Teodor, Pompiliu. *Fragmentarium Iluminist*. Cluj, 1972.

Ghişe, Dumitru; Kecskés, I.; and Teodor, Pompiliu. "Idei economice în opera lui George Bariţ privind promovarea industriei la românii din Transilvania," AIIC, 6 (1963), 41-76.

Gyémánt, Ladislau. "Acţiuni petiţionare ale Românilor din Transilvania în perioada 1834-1838," *Studia Universitatis Babeş-Bolyai,* Series Historia, Fasc. 2 (1971), 30-51.

———. "Memoriul românilor ardeleni din anul 1834," *Anuarul Institutului de Istorie şi Arheologie Cluj-Napoca,* 17 (1974), 98-117.

Hâciu, Anastase N. *Aromânii*. Focşani, 1936.

Hitchins, Keith. "Andreiu Şaguna and Catharine Varga; a New Document," *Revue des Études Roumaines,* 11-12 (1969), 183-187.

———. "Andreiu Şaguna and the Restoration of the Rumanian Orthodox Metropolis in Transylvania, 1846-1868," *Balkan Studies,* 6 (1965), 1-20.

———. "The Early Career of Andreiu Şaguna (1808-1849)," *Revue des Études Roumaines,* 9-10 (1965), 47-76.

———. "Laic şi ecleziastic în mişcarea naţională românească din Transilvania (1830-1869)," in K. Hitchins, *Cultura şi naţionalitate în Transilvania*. Cluj, 1972, 30-72. English translation: "The Sacred Cult of Nationality," in *Intellectual and Social Developments in the Habsburg Empire from Maria Theresa to World War I*. Edited by Stanley B. Winters and Joseph Held. Boulder: East European Quarterly, 1975, 131-160.

————. *The Rumanian National Movement in Transylvania, 1780-1849.* Cambridge, Mass.: Harvard University Press, 1969.

————. "Rumanian Opposition to the Austro-Hungarian Compromise of 1867," *Studia et Acta Musei Nicolae Bălcescu,* 1 (1969), 133-137.

————. "The Rumanians of Transylvania and Constitutional Experiment in the Habsburg Monarchy, 1860-1865," *Balkan Studies,* 5 (1964), 89-108.

————. *Studii privind istoria modernă a Transilvaniei.* Cluj, 1970.

————— and Maior, Liviu. *Corespondenţa lui Ioan Raţiu cu George Bariţiu 1861-1892.* Cluj, 1970.

Hodoş, Enea. *Din corespondenţa lui Simion Bărnuţiu şi a contemporanilor săi.* Sibiu, 1944.

Istoria bisericii romîne. Manual pentru institutele teologice. 2 vols. Bucharest, 1957-1958.

Jakab, Elek. *Szabadságharczunk történetéhez visszaemlékezések 1848-1849-re.* Budapest, 1880.

Jivi, Aurel. "Relaţiile Mitropoliei din Carloviţ cu Biserica Ortodoxă Română din Transilvania în secolul al XVIII-lea," *Biserica Ortodoxă Română,* 88, no. 5-6 (1970), 587-596.

Kann, Robert A. *Das Nationalitätenproblem der Habsburgermonarchie.* 2 vols. Graz-Köln: Böhlau, 1964.

Károlyi, Árpád. *Az 1848-iki pozsonyi törvénycikkek az udvar előtt.* Budapest, 1936.

Kemény, Gábor G. *Iratok a nemzetiségi kérdés történetéhez Magyarországon a dualizmus korában.* Vol. I (1867-1892). Budapest, 1952.

Kiss, András. "Varga Katalinnak tulajdon kézivel tett életleírása," *Korunk,* n.s. 1, no. 12 (December 1957), 1634-1642.

Klima, Helmut. "Guvernatorii Transilvaniei 1774-1867," AIIN, 9 (1943-1944), 225-328.

Kovács, Iosif. *Desfiinţarea relaţiilor feudale în Transilvania.* Cluj, 1973.

Lipăneanu, M. "Şaguna Mitropolitul," *Dacoromania,* 4, part 2 (1924-1926), 1487-1490.

Ludu, Octavian. *Rolul lui Visarion Roman în vieaţa economică a Ardealului.* Sibiu, 1940.

Lupaş, Ioan. "Anastasia Şaguna," *Convorbiri Literare,* 42, no. 12 (1908), 595-603.

————. *Anastasia Şaguna. Viaţa unei mamei credincioase.* Sibiu, 1943.

————. "Din corespondenta lui Şaguna cu Filaret Scriban," AIIN, 1 (1921-1922), 337-342.

————. "Vieaţa şi faptele Mitropolitului Andreiu Şaguna," in *Mitropolitul Andreiu baron de Şaguna. Scriere comemorativă la serbarea centenară a naşterii lui.* Sibiù, 1909, 1-400.

————. *Şaguna şi Eötvös.* Arad, 1913.

————, and Todoran, Eugen. "Documente istorice: I. Acte privitoare la lupta Anastasiei Şaguna pentru apărarea copiilor săi şi a credinţei strămoşeşti," *Transilvania,* 41, no. 4 (1910), 184-195.

Madden, Henry Miller. "The Diary of John Paget, 1849," *Slavonic and East European Review,* 19 (1939-1940), 237-264.

Manciulea, Ştefan. "Atestate de purificaţiune," *Cultura Creştină,* 18 (1938), 473-483.

Marcu, Grigore. "Sfînta Scriptură 'în pom românesc' (100 de ani de la apariţia Bibliei lui Şaguna)," *Mitropolia Ardealului,* 3, no. 11-12 (1958), 782-812.

Marica, George E. *Foaie pentru minte, inimă şi literatură*. Bucharest, 1969.

———, et al. *Ideologia generaţiei române de la 1848 din Transilvania*. Bucharest, 1968.

Márki, Sándor. "Az erdélyi unió-bizottság," *Budapesti Szemle*, 95 (1898), 321-358.

Martinianou, Ioakim. *E Moskhopolis 1330-1930*. Thessalonike, 1957.

Mârza, Iacob. "Gramatica lui Andrei Şaguna," *Limba Română*, 20, no. 1 (1971), 21-32.

Mateiu, Ion. *Contribuţiuni la istoria dreptului bisericesc*. Vol. I: *Epoca de la 1848-1868*. Bucharest, 1922.

———. "Problema unităţii religioase în revoluţia din 1848," in *Omagiu Fraţilor Alexandru şi Ion Lăpedatu*. Bucharest, 1936, 469-490.

Mester, Miklós. *Az autonom Erdély és a román nemzetiségi követelések az 1863-64-évi nagyszebeni országgyűlésen*. Budapest, 1936.

Meteş, Ştefan. *Relaţiile Mitropolitului Andrei Şaguna cu românii din principate române*. Arad, 1925.

Moldovan, Valeriu. *Dieta Ardealului din 1863-1864*. Cluj, 1932.

Netea, Vasile. *George Bariţiu. Viaţa şi activitaţea sa*. Bucharest, 1966.

———. *Noi contribuţii la cunoaşterea vieţii şi activităţii lui Visarion Roman*. Sibiu, 1942.

Nistor, Ion. *Istoria bisericii din Bucovina*. Bucharest, 1916.

———. *Românii şi rutenii în Bucovina*. Bucharest, 1915.

Păcăţian, Teodor V. *Cartea de aur, sau luptele politice-naţionale ale Românilor de sub coroana ungară*. 8 vols. Sibiu, 1904-1915.

Păcurariu, Mircea. "100 de ani de la reînfiinţarea Mitropoliei Ardealului," *Mitropolia Ardealului*, 9, no. 11-12 (1964), 814-840.

Panaitescu, P.P. *Emigraţia polonă şi revoluţia română dela 1848*. Bucharest, 1929.

Pandrea, Petre. *Filosofia politico-juridică a lui Simion Bărnuţiu*. Bucharest, 1935.

Pantazi, Radu. *Simion Bărnuţiu. Opera şi gîndirea*. Bucharest, 1967.

Papahagi, Valeriu. "Familia Şaguna în documente veneţiene din secolul al XVIII-lea," *Revista Istorică*, 18 (1932), 1-5.

Papiu-Ilarian, Alexandru. *Istoria Românilor din Dacia superioară*. 2 vols. Vienna, 1852.

Pârvan, Vasile. "Anul 1850 şi studenţii români ardeleni din Viena," *Luceafărul*, 2, no. 5 (1903), 89-92.

Pascu, Ştefan. "Ecoul unirii Ţării Romîneşti şi Moldovei în Transilvania," in *Studii privind unirea principatelor*. Edited by Andrei Oţetea. Bucharest, 1960.

——— and Pervain, Iosif, eds. *George Bariţ şi contemporanii săi*. 2 vols. Bucharest, 1973-1975.

Petra, Nicolae N. *Băncile româneşti din Ardeal şi Banat*. Sibiu, 1936.

Petrescu, Nicola P. *Monografia institutului de credit şi economii 'Albina', 1872-1897*. Sibiu, 1897.

Peyfuss, Max Demeter. "Rom oder Byzanz," *Österreichische Osthefte*, 12, no. 6 (1970), 337-351.

Pop, Ştefan. "Gramatica română a lui Şaguna: Vârşaţ, 1843," *Foaia Diecezană* (Caransebeş), 38, no. 27 (1923), 2-3.

Popea, Nicolae. *Andreiu baron de Şaguna*. Academia Română, *Discurs de recepţiune*, no. 21. Bucharest, 1900.

———. *Archiepiscopul şi Mitropolitul Andreiu Baron de Şaguna*. Sibiu, 1879.

———. *Escelentia Sea Archiepiscopul şi Mitropolitul Andreiu baron de Şiaguna*. Sibiu, 1873.

————. *Memorialul Archiepiscopului şi Mitropolitului Andreiu baron de Şaguna sau luptele naţionale-politice ale Românilor, 1846-1873.* Vol. I. Sibiu, 1889.

————. *Vechia metropolia ortodosa romana a Transilvaniei, suprimirea si restaurarea ei.* Sibiu, 1870.

Popescu, Mihail. *Documente inedite privitoare la istoria Transilvaniei între 1848-1859.* Bucharest, 1929.

Popovici, Dumitru. *La littérature roumaine à l'époque des lumières.* Sibiu, 1945.

Prodan, David. *Supplex Libellus Valachorum.* Bucharest, 1971.

Prokopowitsch, Erich. *Die rumänische Nationalbewegung in der Bukowina und der Dako-Romanismus.* Graz-Köln: Böhlau, 1965.

Protocolul Congressului natiunei romane din Ardeal. Sibiu, 1863.

Puşcariu, Ilarion. "Câteva epistole dintre celece se păstreăza dela arhiepiscopul-mitropolit Andreiu baron de Şaguna," in *Mitropolitul Andreiu baron de Şaguna. Scriere comemorativă la serbarea centenară a naşterii lui.* Sibiu, 1909, 467-539.

————. "Din anii ultimi ai vieţii Mitropolitului Andreiu baron de Şaguna, despre boala şi moartea lui," in *Mitropolitul Andreiu baron de Şaguna. Scriere comemorativă la serbarea centenară a naşterii lui.* Sibiu, 1909, 405-433.

————. *Documente pentru limbă şi istorie.* 2 vols. Sibiu, 1889-1897.

————. *Metropolia Românilor ortodocşi din Ungaria şi Transilvania.* Sibiu, 1900.

Puşcariu, Ion cavaler de. *Notiţe despre întâmplările contemporane.* Sibiu, 1913.

————. *Reminiscenţie din anul 1860 de un contemporan.* Sibiu, 1897.

Radu, Iacob. *Samuil Vulcan, Episcopul Român-Unit al Orăzii-Mari (1806-1839) şi Biserica Ortodoxă Română.* Oradea Mare, 1925.

Redlich, Josef. *Das österreichische Staats- und Reichsproblem.* 2 vols. Leipzig, 1920-1926.

Retegan, Simion. Pregătirea dietei de la Sibiu din 1863-1864," AIIC, 12 (1969), 53-82.

————. "Problema agrară în dezbaterile dietei de la Sibiu," AIIC, 11 (1968), 279-290.

————. "Pronunciamentul de la Blaj (1868)," AIIC, 9 (1966), 127-142.

Rock, Kenneth W. "Schwarzenberg versus Nicholas I, Round One: The Negotiation of the Habsburg-Romanov Alliance against Hungary in 1849," *Austrian History Yearbook,* 6-7 (1970-1971), 109-122.

Roşca, Eusebiu R. *Monografia institutului seminarial teologic-pedagogic "Andreian."* Sibiu, 1911.

Scorobeţ, Teodor. "Mitropolitul Ioan Meţianu, 1828-1916," *Revista Teologică,* 31, no. 3-4 (1941), 176-189.

Secelea, Constantin. "Dreptul canonic în literatura românească: I. Opera lui Andrei baron de Şaguna," *Cercetări Istorice* (Iaşi), 2-3 (1926-1927), 3-43.

Slavici, Ioan. "Arhiepiscopul şi Mitropolitul Andrei de Şaguna," *Convorbiri Literare,* 14, no. 1 (1880), 5-21.

Slijepčević, Djoko. *Istorija srpske pravoslavne crkve.* 2 vols. Munich, 1966.

Stăniloae, Dumitru. *În zadar: Statutul Organic e şagunian.* Sibiu, 1933.

Stinghe, Sterie. *Documente privitoare la trecutul Românilor din Şchei.* 4 vols. Braşov, 1901-1903.

Suciu, Coriolan. *Corespondenţa lui Ioan Maniu cu Simeon Bărnuţiu (1851-1864).* Blaj, 1929.

————. *Crâmpeie din procesul dintre profesorii dela Blaj şi episcopul Lemeni (1843-1846).* Blaj, 1938.

_____. "Preambule la procesul Lemenian," *Cultura Creştină*, 27 (1938), no. 8-9, 501-520; no. 10-11, 640-663.

Suciu, Ioan D. *Nicolae Tincu Velia (1816-1867). Viaţa şi opera lui.* Bucharest, 1945.

Surdu, Bujor, "Conferinţa naţională de la Mercurea (1869)," AIIC, 8 (1965), 173-211.

Szabad, György. *Forradalom és kiegyezés válaszútján (1860-61)*. Budapest, 1967.

Szőcs, Sebestyén. *A kormánybiztosi intézmény kialakulása 1848-ban.* Budapest, 1972.

Teodor, Pompiliu. "Ideologia revoluţiei din 1848 şi opera istorică a lui Samuil Micu," *Studia Universitatis Babeş-Bolyai*, Series Historia, Fasc. 2 (1965), 57-62.

Todoran, Eugen. "Documente istorice. Acte privitoare la reîntoarcerea lui Anastasiu Şaguna în sînul bisericii strămoşeşti," *Transilvania*, 41, no. 6 (1910), 455-461.

Tóth, Zoltán. *Az erdélyi és magyarországi román nemzeti mozgalom, 1790-1848.* Budapest, 1959.

_____. *Az erdélyi román nacionalizmus első százada, 1697-1792.* Budapest, 1946.

_____. "Kossuth és a nemzétisegi kérdés 1848-1849-ben," in *Emlékkönyv Kossuth Lajos*, vol. 2. Budapest, 1952, 249-340.

_____. *Mişcările ţărăneşti din Munţii Apuseni pînă la 1848.* Bucharest, 1955.

Trócsányi, Zsolt. *Az erdélyi fejedelemség korának országgyűlés.* Budapest, 1976.

_____. *Az erdélyi parasztság története, 1790-1849.* Budapest, 1956.

Tulbure, Gheorghe. *Activitatea literară a mitropolitului Şaguna.* Sibiu, 1909.

_____. *Mitropolitul Şaguna. Opera literară. Scrisori pastorale. Circulări şcolare. Diverse.* Sibiu, 1938.

_____. *Şcoala sătească din Ardeal în epoca lui Şaguna.* Cluj, 1937.

Ürmössy, Lajos. *Tizenhét év Erdély történetéböl.* 2 vols. Temesvár, 1894.

Vajda, Ludovic. "Cu privire la pătrunderea capitalului austriac în industria minieră şi siderurgică a Transilvaniei între 1848 şi 1867," *Studia Universitatis Babeş-Bolyai*, Series Historia, Fasc. 2 (1965), 63-78.

_____. "Începuturile revoluţiei industriale în mineritul şi metalurgia din Transilvania," AIIC, 10 (1967), 173-195.

Verhandlungen des verstärkten Reichsrates. Vienna, 1860.

Winter, Eduard. *Revolution, Neoabsolutismus und Liberalismus der Donaumonarchie.* Vienna: Europe, 1969.

Index

Harvard Historical Studies

84. *Marvin Arthur Breslow*. A Mirror of England: English Puritan Views of Foreign Nations, 1618-1640. 1970.
85. *Patrice L. R. Higonnet*. Pont-de-Montvert: Social Structure and Politics in a French Village, 1700-1914. 1971.
86. *Paul G. Halpern*. The Mediterranean Naval Situation, 1908-1914. 1971.
87. *Robert E. Ruigh*. The Parliament of 1624: Politics and Foreign Policy. 1971.
88. *Angeliki E. Laiou*. Constantinople and the Latins: The Foreign Policy of Andronicus, 1282-1328. 1972.
89. *Donald Nugent*. Ecumenism in the Age of the Reformation: The Colloquy of Poissy. 1974.
90. *Robert A. McCaughey*. Josiah Quincy, 1772-1864: The Last Federalist. 1974.
91. *Sherman Kent*. The Election of 1827 in France. 1975.
92. *A. N. Galpern*. The Religions of the People in Sixteenth-Century Champagne. 1976.
93. *Robert G. Keith*. Conquest and Agrarian Change: The Emergence of the Hacienda System on the Peruvian Coast. 1976.
94. *Keith Hitchins,* Orthodoxy and Nationality: Andreiu Şaguna and the Rumanians of Transylvania, 1846-1873. 1977.